GAELIC NEIGH

This book is dedicated in tribute to the sterling lives and work of these distinguished Gaels of Scotland and Ireland.

1. <u>Scotland</u>: Messers' Donald John Mackay, Donald John Macivor, Simon Mackenzie, Professor Kenneth Mackinnon (all sadly deceased), and Mr John Angus Mackay.

2. <u>Northern Ireland</u>: Mr Aidon MacPolin (sadly deceased), Mr Gearoid O'Caireallain and Dr Gordon McCoy.

May God bless their noble hearts, and in his time, welcome each to the eternal reward of Heaven promised by the Gospels. – Beannacht De lena gcroi uasal, agus go gcuire se a luach saothair ar fail doibh ina am agus ina uair fein, mara gealladh sna Soisceil.

CONTENTS

PREFACE

I must commence this book with the frank admission that notwithstanding a personal zest for Gaelic culture, the language and sports, I am certainly no Celtic scholar. Nor does this book make pretensions to anything of the kind. Actually, my interests lie in British and Irish Contemporary History, as well as Church History, underpinned by a modest background in Political Science. My previous published writings are concentrated in those areas, and only by accident, some years ago, did I develop a desire to re-educate the Anglophile UK establishment of misunderstandings, indeed plain ignorance, about Gaelic culture, identities and groups in both Scotland and my native North of Ireland.

What particularly grated with me was the ***poignant arrogance*** of so many Anglophile academics, publishers, journalists and media people, even teachers, who presumed to know better than culture-conscious Celts about ***our*** language and identity, and indeed ***our*** history. That Anglophile reluctance to accept corrections added insult to injury, and left me feeling that something positive was required if only for setting the records straight and accurate. Yet the gaps went much further than cross-channel piques, as I was to discover.

Initially, three pointers fired me up. First, was the penchant by several English and Anglo-Scottish academics – among them the mercurial Samuel E. Finer - for deploying a spurious title called "Erse" to denote Gaelic medium in Scotland. Aside from innate anti-Gaelic prejudices, this trait highlights sheer ignorance, but is made worse by the unwillingness of those 'ignoramuses' to amend their vocabulary. There have even been instances where so-called "reliable" companion guides have produced blatantly misleading accounts of Gaelic organisations that speak volumes about their authors ignorance. Take for example, the 'Encyclopedia of British and Irish political organisations of the Twentieth Century' – composed by Peter Barberis, John McHugh and Mike Tyldesley (2000, Continuum Publishers, London)! Page 387 contains a curious entry, No 1378, with its sole comment on An Comunn Gaidhealach, Scotland:

" – *Dates of Activity, 1930s. An Comunn Gaidhealach was an anti-nationalist culture group, largely dominated by Unionist gentry."*

Surely that nonsense must be challenged, especially where its authors fashion images among foreigners of the United Kingdom? I hope that on balance folks will be guided by my account of An Comunn rather than that trio!!

Second, the extent to which Gaelic culture – inclusive of language, sports and arts – has long thrived in Northern Ireland, appears scarcely understood, not just in England, but, regrettably, in the South too. The narrow-minded imagery of so many Southern Irish people was and remains to me, a proud Ulster Gael, utterly depressing. From where did Southerners imagine those many top Ulster Gaelic football and hurling sides that over the past 63 years have taken Croke Park by storm, originated? Had they not heard of Feis na nGleann or Feis an Dun, both popular festivals of Ulster Gaeldom, or indeed Belfast's thriving Gaelic Culturlann and Gaeltacht Quarter, or the North's growing Gaelic medium schools sector? Seemingly not, and more is the pity!

Third, while a nominal awareness of fellow Gaels has long existed in Scotland and Northern Ireland of each other, in fact I noted the prevalence of glass walls that discouraged exchanges and contacts beyond the formal. Only occasional academics and curious travellers ventured in either direction across the Sea of Moyle. Otherwise, the two Gaelic nations resembled cool cousins who beyond Christmas cards and funeral attendances otherwise kept their distance. This lesson was even more true of Southern Ireland, which over a century showed little of the pan-Celtic solidarity that one might reasonably have expected. Truly, I was shocked to note just how many well-educated Gaels from either side of the North Channel who had never visited the other nation.

Religious tensions between Catholic Eireann and Presbyterian Alba may have played some part in earlier years, but aside from the fact that the Gaels whom I encountered on both sides were without exception models of tolerance and respect, there was no evidence of different religious affiliations having kept the Gaelic peoples of Scotland and the North of Ireland apart. Instead, there were other factors – such as distance, history, political alignments and perceptions, etc. I am not equipped to work through the linguistics or dialectical strains, far less cultural diversity, but the political historian in me here traces events from previous times, and most especially developments of the past century. After all, since the creation of Southern Ireland in 1922, Ulster and Scottish Gaeldom have been thrown upon the tender mercies of a temperamental, sometimes indifferent, sometimes hostile, occasionally beneficent British state. From that vantage point, and taking account of declining numbers of native speakers, the common goal for both Gaelic worlds has been one of survival.

This book seeks to identify and compare the different characters and struggles of the two Gaelic nations down the years. It looks at their specific journeys of development and diverse priorities, characteristics and strategies, as well as the degree of leadership offered by those groups championing their interests. So too does it acknowledge that through historical circumstances Gaeldom in Ireland was of necessity aligned to political nationalism, and remains as such. Conversely, Gaidheal na-h-Alba has offered a less fractious lobby, but also one where Gaeldom was regionalised to the West Highlands and Hebrides, from where it has struggled to emerge as a national force.

I can only offer what is in my chest. Drawing upon the rich tapestry of Gaelic academics like the eminent Professor Wilson McLeod and his Edinburgh University colleagues, plus Professor Micheal O'Mainnin at Queens University, Belfast, and the late Belfast Gaelgeoir, Aodan MacPoilan, not forgetting my dear, late and much-missed friend, Professor Ken MacKinnon (RIP), plus many others, I have composed a treatise here which hopefully offers a creditable perspective on Gaeldom's struggles over the past century? No arrogant claims are made to definitive status, or even that this material represents tablets of stone. Not at all! Indeed I am hoping and trusting that in the fullness of time other informed theses may emerge on this very same subject, where perhaps future authors may choose to take a different approach to mine. Plurality is part and parcel of the character of intellectual freedom, and long may the day be away when any author feels he/she has the right to the last word or some kind of elevated status to their commentaries on this or any other subject.

Meanwhile, as I am not aware of any other book to have emerged on this subject at the time of writing, regrettably readers, both Gaels and non-Gaels alike, are saddled with my modest offering herewith, inclusive of all its faults and weaknesses. For those faults, I alone take responsibility.

Before concluding, I felt it necessary to clarify certain key points to the reader, so as to aid his/her interpretation of the script.

First, the general term *Gaelic* is preferred to Irish Gaeilge or Scottish Gaidhlig, and is equally applicable to the language in both countries. Apart from being grammatically correct, it is also my view that too much focus is placed on Gaelic dialectical differences, which risks giving non-Gaelic speakers the misleading impression of different languages. In fact there is one common Gaelic tongue, and the dialects are no greater than those characterising other European languages, including the diversity of British and American English. For the sake of varied vocabulary, I have sometimes used alternative terms for describing the language, but only to achieve a reader-friendly narrative.

Second, for logistical reasons of available computer technology, it has not been easy, or indeed feasible to include 'fadas' to Gaelic spellings. Hence I plead for the reader's tolerance in this matter. That said, where appropriate, I have used the Ulster dialect for spelling words in Ireland, while Scottish Gaelic has utilised the Lewis dialect. Differences are minor and should not be exaggerated.

Third, most importantly, it needs to be clarified that in using the term, *Ireland, unless otherwise specified, Ireland means the whole island of Ireland, and nothing less*. This author utterly repudiates the current BBC practice, and indeed that of many Southern Irish broadcasters (who really should know better), of referring to "*Ireland*" – as meaning the 26 Counties Republic only, and "*Northern Ireland*", as meaning the Six Counties. While of course Northern Ireland, however disputatious its status, is an accomplished reality of the past century, it is not the thriving Anglophile cultural zone so beloved of certain Unionist and British politicians. Nor is it culturally divorced from the Republic of Ireland in such a way as to lend credence to the distinctions of the Unionist mind-set. Indeed a prime aim of this book has been to highlight the roots and current wares of Gaelic Ulster, and in so doing counterpoising the mythical imagery of cultural Unionism and its British-based Anglophile sponsors.

Fourth, the term "*Ulster*" is taken to mean ***the nine counties of Gaelic Ulster***, with the distinctive red hand and amber back ground (see front cover of this book) as its historic flag. It is not the mixed contraption of red hand, St George's cross and crown, symbolising the post-1921 Northern Ireland state, which has long been so popular at Unionist political rallies. Indeed this issue of political jargon covering place names and pigeon-holing of people – encouraged by the BBC in Belfast and London, but also supported by elements of the former cultural establishment - has been no small factor in fashioning tensions over political identity among Gaels in Northern Ireland. It is less of an issue in Scotland, but only because until recently Gaidhlig was widely viewed by establishment elements in Edinburgh as a language in terminal decline. My hope that this book will disabuse impressionable people of that grave wrong?

Finally, before concluding, may I draw readers attention to my short book of 1997 titled *Gaelic Nations*. This was a brief summary of political developments in Northern Ireland and Scotland over the course of the 20th century, and in a compressed script of no more than 125 pages covered all that I felt to be relevant. Yet it was the late Ken MacKinnon who urged me, some years ago, to re-write the entire project, and this time from a more expansive perspective embracing a wider front including history, political developments, education, media growth, Gaelic arts, Gaelic economy and Gaelic initiatives, along with comparative assessments of the evolving state of Gaeldom in Scotland

and Northern Ireland. Ken particularly felt an evaluation of Gaelic fortunes under devolved administrations in Belfast and Edinburgh to be overdue. Moreover, being the encouraging mentor that he was, Ken felt I should expand on that little acorn from over a quarter century ago to embark upon a major expansion. In his own straight, yet kindly way, Ken was Scotland's 'wise old owl' seeking and demanding the best from this humble Irish 'grass hopper'!

Actually, Ken was the original figure designated to write the Foreword. Alas, however, the trumpet of Almighty God sounded first, calling away a most precious Christian friend, not to mention prodigious Gaelic scholar, to what I am certain is his eternal reward. In thanking my other friend, Robert Dunbar, for his kindness in stepping into the role, I only hope this work will do justice to the memory of Ken to whom so much is owed, not just by his fellow Gaels of Scotland, but indeed by Gaels everywhere. Being his friend was a great honour and privilege bestowed on me by a loving God whose ways remain a mystery.

In the final analysis, I leave it to you as readers to make your own judgements.

Meanwhile, may our blessed Lord in Heaven be as close to each of you in the reading as he has been to me in the preparation of this book. In the spirit of the Parable of the Talents, and on the strength of my own Christian faith, plus the goodness of those gone before me, I can only hope to have delivered a product that matches their expectations of worthiness if nothing less?

Dr Vincent McKee

St Patrick's Day, 17th March, 2022 – Coventry.

FOREWORD

I remember well my first trip to Belfast, in March 1998. I came to participate in a conference, Aithne na nGael, organised by the ULTACH Trust. The Trust had been set up in about 1990 jointly by the Northern Ireland Office and the Government of the Republic of Ireland to promote the Irish language throughout the entire community of Northern Ireland. A key objective was to encourage cross-community involvement in the Irish language. As someone who was reasonably familiar with the history of Ireland and in particular of the North, the idea that the Irish language could help to build bridges between communities in North struck me as being a hopeful one that would not necessarily produce too many short- to mid-term results. As is often the case in relation to the future of the Gaelic languages, I, like many others, was a little too pessimistic.

The Belfast I came to in March 1998 was a city that was deeply divided on political and religious grounds, as it remains to a considerable extent today. The ways in which the Irish language was and is still implicated in these divisions is traced in considerable detail in the present volume. A significant number of people like me, active in different ways in the Gaelic movement in Scotland, had been invited to speak at the conference. My recollection was that one of the aims of the conference was to illustrate that a language movement need not be associated with a particular political or religious tradition. Whatever the weaknesses of the Gaelic movement in Scotland, it is not, as Dr McKee illustrates, riven by differences of faith or political conviction, and it has long drawn on support from people of various faiths and none, and from each of the major political parties in Scotland.

At the same time, these were optimistic days, both in Northern Ireland and in Scotland. First, a ceasefire was in place. Although I had recently arrived in the UK from my native Canada, like virtually everyone in those days, I was well aware of the terrible violence of recent years. The divisions were certainly obvious to any visitor, but there was also a sense of calm. Much against my expectations, I felt quite relaxed, a feeling that was enhanced by the conference itself, and by the remarkable friendliness and good humour I found everywhere in the city, qualities that, after many more trips to Belfast, I know to be deeply characteristic of the place. We were only days away from the conclusion of the Belfast Agreement, or Good Friday Agreement as it is sometimes called, a treaty which, as Dr McKee notes in this volume, has had important implications for the Irish language in the North. In Scotland, people had voted overwhelmingly in favour of a devolved parliament, and on the Gaelic front, the lead Gaelic organisation at the time, Comunn na Gàidhlig (CNAG), had just a few months earlier produced serious and detailed proposals for a Gaelic language act, and these had already led to useful meetings with senior politicians and government officials.

As Dr McKee's detailed and informative historical account makes clear, there are very significant differences between Irish in Northern Ireland and Gaelic in Scotland. However, a key theme of his book is that Scottish Gaels and Irish Gaels, and particularly those in the North, are, indeed, neighbours. With that fact comes an awareness of similarities and commonalities as well as of differences, of shared identities and endeavours, and of the possibility to learn from each other. All of this accords with my own experience. In about 2003, POBAL, the umbrella organisation which then represented a variety of Irish language organisations in the North began developing proposals for an Irish Language Act for Northern Ireland. I and other Gaelic-speakers from Scotland were happy to lend our support to that process. The Columba Initiative, another product of those heady days of the late 1990s, has helped to foster and deepen a wide variety Gaelic ties across the Sea of Moyle. More recently, the remarkable work in East Belfast of Turas – itself, a word shared by the Irish and Scottish Gaelic languages – has, like the earlier efforts of the ULTACH Trust drawn on the example of Gaelic Scotland to show that our sister languages belong to people of different religious and political traditions, and can be a means of reconciliation. And as we in Scotland seek to develop spaces, particularly in urban areas, in which Gaelic can be used for a greater range of social purposes, we draw inspiration and guidance from institutions such as Cultúrlann McAdam Ó Fiaich.

As Dr McKee notes, we cannot be certain what the future will hold for the Gaelic languages. With the stresses which continue to afflict both Irish and Scottish Gaelic in their traditional rural heartlands, there is certainly cause for pessimism. However, as Dr McKee traces in this book, there have over the last number of years been very significant institutional developments to support Gaelic in Scotland and, to a lesser but still important extent, Irish in Northern Ireland.

If anything, the energy of the language movement in the North has grown – in May 2022, an estimated 17,000 people took to the streets of Belfast to demand an Irish Language Act. And, sixteen years after the British Government promised, in the Agreement at St Andrews, to introduce such an act, the Identity and Language (Northern Ireland) Bill is finally been put before the Westminster Parliament. In its manifesto for the 2021 Scottish Parliamentary elections, the SNP has also committed itself to introducing a languages bill that can be expected to build previous legislation such as the Gaelic Language (Scotland) Act 2005, legislation which, as Dr McKee rightly recognises, is a cornerstone of contemporary policy for Gaelic. It is hoped that volumes such as this one will help to inform future debates on these two linguistic neighbours.

Professor Robert Dunbar

June 2022

Professor of Scottish and Celtic Studies, University of Edinburgh.

Chapter One

HISTORIC DECLINE OF GAELDOM IN BOTH COUNTRIES

Aims: This introductory chapter seeks to establish the historic foundations for an assessment of the state of the Gaelic language in Scotland and Ireland by the end of World War 1. Relevant events in previous centuries such as the conquest and colonisation of Ireland by successive English administrations and the impact of its 'planter' population on Ulster life, along with compulsory de-Gaelicisation in Scotland by both Edinburgh and London governments are highlighted. So also was the legacy of famine in Ireland and crofter clearances in Highland Scotland a major factor in the marginalisation of Gaelic in both countries. Those issues, along with attempts at staging Gaelic revivals in Scotland and Ireland, are examined and evaluated, while further tracing the differences governing each country and its relationship with England. From the latter, it is possible to offer an acknowledgement of the diverse character of Scottish and Irish Gaelic revivalism, such as led each movement in different directions with different priorities and strategies over the ensuing century.

---

1. **_Overview_**: In a book with such a broad, all-embracing title, there is a clear need to apply specific parameters to the scope covered. As has already been discussed in the Introduction, this investigation is primarily concerned with political factors guiding the historic decline and near-collapse of the Gaelic language and culture in the North of Ireland and Scotland in the 300 years since the 17th century Ulster Plantation and suppression of the Scottish clans, along with tentative efforts at Gaelic revivalism manifesting in different forms throughout the 100 years since the end of World War 1.

That the revised Gaelic movements in both countries have assumed different characters, with apparently little in common and even less interaction, says much about varying political conditions within the British state over the same

1

period. Gaeldom's fortunes proved something of a hostage to the events and evolving character of both countries, and their respective accommodations with the British Crown over three centuries or more. Also, given their common minority positions, it is more than a mere coincidence that the revivalist movements experienced contrasting fortunes with the mainstream populations of Ireland and Scotland. This lesson applied particularly to the synthesis between cultural and political nationalism where the contrast was and remains most stark. Whereas Irish Gaelgeoiri claimed the historic affinity of the greater population of Ireland, with the exception of Ulster Unionists, conversely Scottish Gaels could only accurately appeal to ... at most ... historical sections of their society. Indeed Gaidheal na h-Alba had been excluded from power and control of the Scottish kingdom centuries before the country fell under English domination. The latter fact complicated the Scottish Gaelic position both for speakers and revivalists alike in the 20th century. Equally, Gaeil Uladh was cut off from the tentative achievements of its Southern colleagues by the partition of Ireland in 1922 and subsequent emergence of two Irelands. The Irish Free State was essentially Gaelic-friendly and resolved to revive the language, whereas in Northern Ireland Gaelic was viewed by its Unionist establishment as a subversive adjunct to Sinn Fein's programme for forcible incorporation within ... as they saw it ... a Catholic and priest-dominated all-Ireland.

Accordingly, assessments of the Gaelic language and culture must take account of relevant political factors in those three jurisdictions throughout most of the 20th century and since the millennium, namely the Irish Republic, Northern Ireland and Scotland. As will be demonstrated, approaches to the language and its cultural corollaries by the respective political authorities differed markedly. It remains to cast a general eye on the historic circumstances of each jurisdiction.*(1)

> **2.** *Ireland:* De-gaelicisation of Ireland was a straightforward act of English oppression, conducted over three centuries in order to secure Irish subordination to the English Crown. Simultaneously, successive English administrations caused dismemberment of the Gaelic social order, based on clans and territory, and repudiation of its Brehon legal system.

Until around 1645, Gaelic was the language of the entire country, save for the small area around Dublin, Wicklow and Meath, called the Pale, where

English law, customs and the language were spoken and practised. As noted by the distinguished Oxford historian, Roy Foster, the Gaelic system had managed to absorb challenges from previous invaders such as the Danes and Norman English in the Dark Ages and Middle Ages respectively.*(2) So also did Foster and Belfast historian, Jonathan Bardon, acknowledge that until the defeat of Ulster Chieftain, Hugh O'Neill, and his forces at the Battle of Kinsale (1601), Ulster was the strongest and most Gaelic province of all-Ireland. However, with the 17th century Anglo-Scottish Plantation, and subsequent English Cromwellian and Williamite re-settlements causing disintegration of the old Gaelic order, Irish-Gaelic became an inevitable victim of Crown-enforced Anglicisation and Protestantisation.*(3) The two went hand in hand.

As is a matter of historic record, Ireland did not align with either English Episcopalians or Scottish Calvinists in the Reformation, instead preferring the old Roman faith. Consequently, Crown repression was as much directed at the Irish Catholic Church with its strong monastic character as the Gaelic chieftains ... all in a combined campaign aimed at achieving full subjugation of Gaelic Ireland.*(4) The latter was particularly marked by the savage Cromwellian assault in the aftermath of the mid-17th century English Civil War, and subsequent victory of William of Orange at the Battle of the Boyne in 1690. A combination of the anti-Catholic Penal Laws, that followed William's seizure of power and the Boyne conquest, was followed by imposition of an English legal and administrative system, along with English domination of the Irish economy and nascent educational system. All of those factors sufficed to hasten the demise of the Gaelic order and language – primarily the medium of the Irish peasant – and its upstaging by the ascendant English tongue. Foster, along with D. Figgis and Kevin Nicholls, each provide reliable, graphic accounts of this process of conquest, colonisation and cultural Anglicisation, while Bardon's scholarly treatise focuses on its effects upon Ulster.*(5)

An additional cause of Gaelic demise was the devastating Irish potato famine of 1844-49, which cost over a million lost lives, plus a further 2.5 million Irish people emigrating to Britain, North America and Australasia. Foster highlights the dilemma across the whole country, while Bardon's account pays special attention to the effects of famine in Donegal, Tyrone, Armagh and Monaghan where its consequences proved ruinous both for local humanity and agriculture.*(6) It effectively spelt the final death knell for most of the Ulster Gaeltacht through general depopulation in favour of mass migration and emigration, rendering remaining Gaeltachtai language communities impoverished and restricted to a few strips of Donegal coastline and Sperrin villages in Tyrone and Derry.*(7)

Elsewhere, in North East Ulster throughout the 17th and 18th centuries, there existed among descendant communities of Lowlands Scots planters a Scots-English medium called Lallans. It was especially prevalent among Presbyterians, and amounted to an assortment of North Briton English intermingled with elements of Dornish, Gaelic and even Welsh. Studies by P.S. Robinson and Michael Montgomery offer a credible and documented account of that linguistic strain, along with its client communities.*(8) However, as a language, Lallans was never wholly detached from mainstream English and lacked definite roots.*(9) This reality holds true, notwithstanding a recent proliferation of Ulster-Scots cultural, historic and populist movements such as the Orange Schomberg Society. While offering an alternative Planter identity, the frank truth is that in Scotland the language came to be regarded as a Lowlands dialect of North Britain English, while in Northern Ireland Lallans offered a platform for modern Ulster Protestants to reconnect with the culture of their forefathers. Besides, among certain Presbyterian groups in rural Ulster, there was a penchant towards Gaelic, at least until the early 19th century, which explains why a Gaelic Psalms book and the Bible were published by Presbyterian missionaries. As a language, Lallans never really achieved definitive status, and despite its use by the celebrated Scottish national bard, Robert Burns, and publication of a Scots dictionary in 1985*(10), it could not credibly be promoted as a separate tongue.*(11)

As for reliable figures of Gaelic speakers, these are difficult to calculate, especially in the pre-census era prior to 1841. Accordingly, one is left with estimates based on whatever factual information is available for particular areas of the country. All the period surveys undertaken prior to 1841 point to a consistent trend towards Anglicisation that accentuated throughout the 19th century. According to Wakefield's survey, the predominantly monoglot Gaelic speaking population of Ireland in 1812 numbered around 3,000,000 from a total population of 5,937,856; a figure that by 1832 had increased in line with population growth to 4,100,000 out of a total population of 8,175,124.*(12) By contrast, the 1851 government census – the first to follow the potato famine – showed a sharp population decline with concomitant consequences for the Gaelic language. The Irish population had been decimated by a mixture of deaths from starvation and emigration; down by 1.7 million to 6,552,356, with registered native speakers reduced to 1,524,286

(23%), of whom 319,602 were listed as monoglot Gaels.*(13) Against the figures, it needs recalling that in the extreme conditions of economic privation, as many as 50% of Gaels are reliably estimated to have not declared their true mother tongue, as well as Anglicising their names. Such was the fear of losing out on famine relief and whatever little work was available from a hostile Crown and its various agencies, something to which the cartographer, Reg Hindley, drew poignant attention.*(14)

Self-evidently, even among native speakers, bilingualism had taken a firm hold, which in view of the socio-economic advantages accruing to English medium speakers, left Gaels at a grave disadvantage. From the Famine era onwards, the decline in Gaelic speakers accelerated with catastrophic consequences for the language. The 1861 Census put native speakers at 1,105,536 (19%) from a total Irish population of 5,798,564 *(15); by 1891 these numbers had dropped further to 680,174 (14.5%) from an overall population covering all-Ireland of 4,704750. Such trends were confirmed in separate published papers by the ecclesiastical Gaelic scholar, then based at Maynooth University, Tomas – later Cardinal – O'Fiaich, himself destined for the See of Armagh, 1977-90.*(16)

3. **_Gaelic Revivalism_**: Significantly, there followed in 1893 the formation of Conradh na Gaeilge (Gaelic League), under the joint leadership of Antrim Glens native and Dublin-based historian, Professor Eoin MacNeill, and its founding secretary, the dedicated Gaelgeoir, Douglas Hyde, a Church of Ireland rector's son from Roscommon, and who in 1938 was to become first President of the Irish Free State. Its initial aim was to stem the further decline of the Gaelic language. There had been previous initiatives aimed at stemming linguistic and cultural Anglicisation, such as the Society for the Preservation of the Irish Language (SPIL), founded in 1876 but largely focused among the educated 'literati' class of British Ireland. Though well intentioned, most SPIL patrons were disconnected by location and social conditions from the Gaeltachtai, and thus in no effective position to halt decline. Interestingly, at the same time, much concern at the dwindling Gaeltachtai came from Anglo-Irish professionals, gentry, clerics and anthropologists, many of whom were of

Unionist leanings, but feared the cultural decimation of indigenous Ireland so as to feed an onward roll of the Empire. Others were liberals, sympathetic to repeal of the Act of Union and some social and land reforms, but were a far way removed from supporting an alliance with political nationalism that later came to define the League.

The League drew active allegiances from nationally-minded Gaelic activists, many of whom, like co-founder Eoin MacNeill, played a significant role in the independence struggle of Ireland in the early 20th century. Other key figures included a youthful Eamon De Valera (future Taoiseach and President), Padraig Pearse (Gaelgeoir educationalist and lead figure in the 1916 rising) along with his brother Willie (also executed following the rising), Joseph Plunkett, Sean MacDiarmuid and Roger Casement (all republicans executed in 1916), plus Michael Collins, a Cork-born civil servant who was to achieve distinction as commander of the independence volunteers 1919-21, before meeting his own death by ambush in August 1922 at age 31 years. All those figures, plus others of the same persuasion, made a major nationalist input to the League, thereby ensuring that the League's programme reflected a symmetry of cultural and political nationalism from the start.

Whatever may have been the principal goals of the League, in practice its *raison d'être* was directed towards Gaelic revivalism among non-Gaelic speakers in schools, community groups, literary world and the public sector. It was also focused on winning support from the nationalist movement, both the Irish Parliamentary Party and independent republican groups drawing their impetus from the Fenian Brotherhood of earlier times, and who were later to align with Sinn Fein and the Irish Republican Brotherhood in the early 20th century. Significantly, the League did not devote so much energy towards defending the dwindling Gaeltachtai, which was widely seen as something of a lost cause. Instead, 'militants' were more concerned with re-gaelicising English speaking sympathisers as a way of radicalising the wider population in the direction of reclaiming a national identity. As a consequence, native speaking Gaels continued to decline; with the 1911 Census putting their numbers at 582,446, from an overall reducing population of 4,390,319. Moreover, the bulk of native speakers were concentrated in West coast Gaeltachtai in counties Donegal, Galway and Kerry, with additional small Gaeltacht communities in rural Cork, Waterford, Mayo, Omeath (Louth), Down, Tyrone, Sperrin mountains (Derry), Rathlin Island and the Antrim Glens.*(17)

Very significantly, with the exception of Galway, no other Gaeltacht covered a large town, and even Galway City was itself considerably anglicised by the time of the 1911 Census. Additionally, by the time of partition and the creation of separate jurisdictions in Ireland in 1922, Gaelic monoglotism had all but disappeared. By then, bilingualism was well established, which in the long term proved detrimental to the survival of spoken Gaelic within the Gaeltachtaí.*(18) Gaelic revivalist efforts were fundamentally impaired by three factors: first, English was the language of economic and social advancement at home; second, English was the essential language of emigration; third, Gaelic had low status, even at home. All three factors proved crucial in an Ireland whose agrarian economy rendered her subordinate to the economic power of British masters and their cultural acolytes. Any revivalist campaigns thus faced an uphill struggle, even under a pro-Gaelgeoir independent government in Dublin, not to mention a hostile administration in Belfast.

Interestingly, there was a diversity of views prevalent from within about the role of the League and its Irish revivalism campaigns. The place of education and specific role of the Catholic Church in a future independent Ireland generated some debate, as recalled by Oliver Rafferty and Joseph Crehan (both Jesuits) in separate studies.*(19) However welcome was the support of enlightened Protestant Gaelgeoiri, like Hyde himself, there was no way that in those Ultramontane times the League or other bodies could afford to alienate the Irish Catholic hierarchy, whose bishops and priests had – with some exceptions – proved invaluable allies.*(20) Additionally, there was another problem in defining the essential character of the League; either cultural or political? For Hyde, the League was a cultural vehicle to secure the Gaelic transformation of Irish society; it was not an adjunct to the Young Ireland League, Sinn Fein, IRB or other independence campaigners, or even the Home Rule Irish Party of pre-1914 Ireland. As recalled by his biographer, Brian Murphy, Hyde took this line to the point of resignation in 1915, when he felt the League's take-over by Irish Republican Brotherhood activists whom he believed would stifle its appeal, effectively discouraging non-nationalist interest and the outright opposition of political Unionists.*(21)

Conversely, for political nationalists like MacNeill, Plunkett, MacDiarmuid, Pearse and the recently converted British diplomat and humanitarian campaigner with roots in North Antrim, Sir Roger Casement, the League represented an opportunity to reach the wider Irish public through an alliance between the independence politics and new Gaelic forces in the language, literature, drama and Gaelic sports. Interestingly, historian and biographer, Owen McGee, in the course of a scholarly treatise on Arthur Griffith, noted the prevalence of a widespread view in the 1880s among political nationalists that however desirable might be Gaelic transformation, it would serve the cause of Irish political nationhood only marginally.*(22) The change of view was gradual and in no small way connected to the Irish clergy's gradual embracement of the League. Clerical support was initially grudging, as the suspicion prevailed that Gaelic revivalism – meaning the Gaelic League and GAA – were being driven by anti-clerical forces. For that reason, many leading Catholic grammar schools of the time like the Holy Ghost Fathers' Blackrock College, Dublin, opted for Rugby rather than Gaelic sports. That reticence slowly gave way towards positive embracement in the last years of the 19th century, but it was a very gradual process. Clerical approval, when it came, meant two key advantages for Gaelic revivalism. First, Gaelic values were transmitted to the wider Catholic population at parish level, with the result that GAA clubs and League branches were rapidly established in most rural and many urban parishes across the whole island in the early decades of the 20th century. Second, in the growing network of Irish Catholic grammar schools that had previously marginalised Gaelicism, a prominent place was found after 1900 for the Irish Language in the curriculum, while Gaelic football and Hurling were adopted as principal sports.*(23)

Even the Irish Protestant churches were not wholly immune to accommodating Gaelic revival tides. Presbyterianism had long facilitated multiple Gaelic authors and preachers like late 18/19th century scholar, Dr/Rev William Neilson, from Rademon, Co. Down, who wrote several church tracts and wider texts encouraging the Irish language. Another Gaelic preacher was Rev. Andrew Bryson from North Down, while his kinsman, Dr Samuel Bryson, produced several manuscripts in Gaelic. James McKnight, from Rathfriland, Co Down was a lead figure in the Presbyterian-led Ulster Tenants Rights Movement, and later edited the *Belfast Newsletter*,1830-45, where he openly embraced Irish content and editorials. That list is both explained and elaborated, along with the 19th century Ulster Gaelic Society, by Roger Blaney.*(24) As for the Church of Ireland, its propensity for retaining an Irish dimension was reaffirmed by a number of prominent Gaelic-speaking clergy like Rev. James Hannay and Rev Dr James Goodman (appointed Professor of Irish at Trinity College in 1879) during the years prior to the Gaelic League launch. Dr Douglas Hyde, a Rector's son from Frenchpark, Roscommon, as Gaelic League founder, was perhaps the most distinguished Protestant champion of the language of his time. In 1914 followed the launch of An

Cruinniu bunaidh agus Cuspoiri an Chunainn – The Irish Guild of the Church of Ireland, with a commitment to facilitating Gaelic services and prayerful publications – a story recounted by Risteard Giltrap.*(25) It also acted as a pressure group on the Church of Ireland leadership, and in the years after World War 1, through its journal, _Gaelic Churchman_, helped foster a sense of Irishness among a Protestant population, especially in the South, whose orientation was adjusting to the inevitability of independence and partition.

Taking the wider view, it is significant that by the turn of the 19/20th century, the strategies of Irish Gaelgeoiri working through Conradh na Gaeilge and their Scottish counterparts, operating through An Comunn Gaidhealach, diverged sharply. Whereas Scottish Gaels were primarily concerned with defending the shrinking Hebridean and Highlands Gaidhealtachd, along with securing language rights in education and literature, conversely for Irish Gaels there seemed no alternative to a political struggle with a hostile Anglo-Unionist cultural and political establishment whom they sought to displace from centuries-long control of Ireland. Scottish Gaels were not connected in any way to nascent Home Rulers or independence campaigners (both very marginal causes in late Victorian Scotland), whereas for Irish Gaels the alliance was one of political necessity.*(26) Even in the question of land redistribution, where Scottish crofters and Irish peasants had a common cause, beyond a few isolated seizures in the Outer Hebrides, there was nothing of the radicalism of Michael Davitt's Irish Land League to be found in in the Highlands or Western Isles. The reasons for this divergence are historical and need closer attention elsewhere in this book. That said, James Hunter's historical treatise on Hebridean crofters offers a good starting point for the enquirer.*(27)

Whether or not the Gaelic League was a success depends on how one interprets the legacy of its campaigns? In the short term, it did little to halt the Gaeltachtai decline, and further failed to generate a popular following for language revival. Yet the League was not without some influence. It became an effective proselytiser for Gaelgeoir ideals among the growing ranks of Irish intelligentsia, and, most importantly, to the rising independence movement. As is shown in separate studies by A. Hepburn and Tomas O'Fiaich, and propagating a view widely held by nearly all reputable historians, reviving the language, along with Gaelic sports, music, drama and literature were deemed to be essential foundations for cultivating a sense of political nationhood among the population.*(28) However, the essence of language and cultural revival only became a vital ingredient of political nationalism after 1900. It was for the latter reason that from 1900s onwards many independence campaigners like De Valera, Pearse and MacDiarmuid, and even the young Michael Collins, got drawn to the League. The same people – or at least the more able-bodied among them – had also been drawn to the ranks of Cumann Lutchleas Gael (Gaelic Athletic Association), founded in 1884, in a bid to modernise and popularise the ancient Gaelic field sports of Hurling, Gaelic Football and Camogie among Irish youth. The GAA's rapid growth may be partly explained by the natural appeal of sport to young men, but also there was the early backing of Catholic clergy. Indeed the decision by Archbishop Thomas Croke of Cashel and Emily (Tipperary) and Archbishop McHale of Tuam (Galway) to become early GAA patrons had far-reaching effects in terms of Church/Gaelgeoir relations over the next century in both the Irish Free State/Republic and Northern Ireland.

Archbishop Croke's acceptance letter to the GAA Secretary, Michael Cusack, vented very poignantly his concern about the encroaching forces of anglicisation:

"One of the most painful ..and.. frequently recurring reflections that, as an Irishman, I am compelled to make.. is derived from the ugly fact that we are daily importing from England not only her manufactured goods, which we cannot help doing since she has practically strangled our own manufacturing appliances, but together with her fashions, .. accents, .. vicious literature,.. music, .. dances and .. manifold mannerisms, her games also and.. pass-times, to the utter discredit of our grand national sports, and to the sore humiliation, as I believe, of every genuine son and daughter of the old land." *(29)

The archbishop's sentiments were echoed by MacNeill in an appeal to the Irish Clergy in _Ecclesiastical Review_ as early as 1891.

"We Irish have resisted fusion for seven centuries with the result that we are still a living, energetic and self-reliant nation... Fusion was prevented, first, by the difference of language and physical resistance; afterwards by difference of language and religion; latterly by religion alone. Were this last difference removed, as it yet may be, most probably by our own influence, it is a mere illusion to hope that national character could, without some other defence, withstand the forces of assimilation. Politics will not form a defence, for politics is not to be dreamt of. Clearly, unless the national character remains to attract the national aspirations and leaven the national life, Ireland must become a mere geographical expression". *(30)

So much for the emerging Gaelic Athletic Association, headed by Cusack and his coterie of Land Leaguers and Fenian advocates; their dominance was prominent from the start. However, with the Gaelic League the process of politicisation was much less inevitable, especially for as long as Hyde and his cultural liberals remained the dominant force. Yet the League was not unaffected by the changing temperatures permeating Irish politics at the turn of the 19th/20th century. In a sign of the radical direction that Irish Gaelgeoirism was taking, a youthful Padraig Pearse, writing in the separatist organ, *United Irishman*, in 1905, put a succinct case for an alliance between the nascent independence movement and forces of Gaelic revivalism.

"The Irish language is an essential of Irish nationality. It is more; it is chief depository and safeguard. When the Irish language disappears, Irish nationality will ipso facto disappear, and for ever. Political autonomy can be lost and recovered again ... Now if Ireland were to lose her language – which is, remember, an essential of her nationality – there might conceivably be a free state in Ireland at some future date: but that state would not be the Irish nation, for it would have parted from the body of traditions which constitute Irish nationality."*(31)

4. *Gaelgeoir Public Policy in Ireland*: This growing consensus among political separatists for a Gaelgeoir agenda was to fashion the newly independent Irish Free State a quarter of a century later. Indeed a Gaelgeoir policy for education, arts, communications, public administration, the armed forces and the state's cultural ethos constituted the first real consensus between the pro-Treaty Cumann na nGael (later Fine Gael) of early leader, W.T. Cosgrave and his associates (including Eoin MacNeill), and the pro-Republican Fianna Fail of first Dail president and later Taoiseach, Eamon de Valera. This "consensus" also included the Catholic Church, who as Hindley and O'Cuiv – from their different positions – acknowledged, had proved to be a reliable sponsor of Gaelic interests in culture and education long before the time of Croke and McHale.*(32)

Policies adopted included a compulsory Gaelic-learning programme at all levels of education, with basic Gaelic being required for school-leavers, university entrants, police, teachers and public servants. There was also a bilingual public communications policy for official documents and notices, broadcasting and statutory bodies, which required Gaelic usage at least as an option. Significantly, a comprehensive programme of assistance to the Gaeltachtai followed by way of grants, provision of native-speaking school teachers, eventually a Gaeltacht radio station (founded in 1972) and, later, a Gaelic television channel, Teilifis na Gaeilge (1996), all emanating from creation of a Gaeltacht ministry (in 1956) to encourage economic investment so as to halt de-population. Additionally, the Irish state has consistently and generously sponsored a range of Gaelic sporting and cultural bodies, including Conradh na Gaeilge, Gael Linn (separate Gaelgeoir linguists), Glor na nGael (in Northern Ireland), the Gaelic Athletic Association, along with the traditional musicians of Comhaltas Ceolteoiri Eireann and drama writers and performers of An Comhairle Naisiumta Dramaiochta.

Gaelic promotion has rendered mixed results. The same socio-economic pressures from the years of British rule continued to undermine the Gaeltacht communities for long after 1922, causing their numbers to decline further. Indeed the twin factors of emigration and ever-increasing travel and tele-communications diminished the cultural isolation on which the Gaeltacht depended, thereby making their survival prospects look bleak. Bilingualism also undermined the native-speaking character of the Gaeltachtai. The 1971 and 1981 Censuses put Gaelic speakers in the Irish Republic at 789,429 (28.3%) and 1,018,413 (31.6%) respectively, with this figure covering first and second language speakers. Actual native speaking numbers are difficult to estimate accurately, but these could not exceed 60,000, a figure that appears to have subsequently slipped over the last 20 years. Inevitably, survival will depend on a mixture of continuing government aid, economic regeneration, effective educational programmes and a general climate within and beyond the Gaeltachtai.

On the positive side, there has been a substantial Gaelic cultural regeneration at all levels, leaving a particular mark on rural Irish life. Although Gaeltachtai dwellers have declined, the level of Gaelic literacy among the wider population has increased to a figure exceeding 1.1 million. Significantly, there is an established and popular Gaelic cultural scene in the arts, media, Gaelic sports, music and literature, while the launch of Teilifis na Gaeilge followed on from the earlier success of Radio na nGaeltacht. While the obligatory Gaelic-learning programme has not been universally popular with sections of leftist and non-nationalist opinion, nevertheless it is difficult to imagine how Ireland's Gaelic ethos could survive without its prominence in the educational curriculum. Additional to Conradh na Gaeilge and its sister organisations, the other two bodies openly embracing Gaelgeoiri objectives have been the Gaelic Athletic Association and Fianna Fail – both of whose activists while not always Gaelic-fluent nevertheless overtly endorsed Gaelic linguistic and cultural symbols. More recently in the 1990s, Sinn Fein also adopted an active Gaelgeoir linguistic and cultural policy applicable to both jurisdictions of Ireland. – More later!

Overall, Gaelicism has experienced an uneasy rapport with the Irish state. On one hand, it has been heavily sponsored by successive governments ever since the inception of independence, but has failed to stem the tide of anglicisation or even stamp its imprimatur indelibly on the national character. Yet it is fair to ask if any other strategy would have achieved more positive results given the manner of social change in the Irish state over its first hundred years of development, much of which has been dictated by outside forces? Ironically, for a model of passionate Gaelicism, it is to Ulster and the remaining British jurisdiction in Ireland that one must turn for salient observations.

The Plantation changed all that with the introduction of an Anglo-Scottish Ascendancy of mixed Presbyterian and Anglican religious character. There was also the suppression of the Brehon legal code and clan system, and its replacement by an English law frame enforced by the English Viceroy and his establishment operating from Dublin Castle. So too did there occur enforced anglicisation of the language and cultural environment. Those changes had far-reaching effects on the emergent socio-political culture of Ulster, which over the ensuing 150 years acquired a distinctive Scots-Irish character that caused it to resemble the Scottish Lowlands more than anything recognisably Irish. Such characteristics were of great consequence to the evolution of rival Unionist and Nationalist forces later in 19th and 20th century Ulster, as too was the politically beleaguered position of the Gaelic language and Gaelgeoir organisations and activists.

5. *Ulster Factor*: Significantly, among the four historic provinces of Ireland, until the early 17th century Anglo-Scottish Plantation, Ulster was the most gaelicised of all. This fact has long been agreed by such diverse and reputable figures as the late Queens University academic, Professor A.T.Q. Stewart, Ulster historian, Jonathan Bardon, and respected

Gaelic writer, Padraig O'Snodaigh.*(33) There, the language prevailed along with the old Gaelic order, inclusive of the clans, chieftains and Brehon laws. Equally significant was Ulster's historic links with Scotland, from where the North-East counties of Antrim and Down were separated by the narrow Sea of Moyle, and with whom there had long been close cultural, commercial and missionary links, underpinned by centuries of cross-migration. Actual Gaelic dialects bore a close resemblance to the ancient Gaelic kingdom of Dalriada, itself located partly on the North Antrim coast and partly in modern Argyll. There had also been a long history of trading and military alliances, not the least of those being the aid given to Ulster chieftains in earlier struggles with English invaders by Robert Bruce's Gallowglass warriors.

The process of linguistic anglicisation occurred at a variable pace for which different perspectives are held by the various experts. Stewart, analysing the evolution of modern Ulster, acknowledged the place of spoken Gaelic among the native Irish, but noted its gradual demise throughout the late 18th and 19th centuries under assorted pressures of semi-industrialisation and repressive legislation against the native Irish peasantry.*(34) There was also the economic and political dominance of the Anglo-Scottish planter population, whose numbers were heavily concentrated in Antrim, North Down and East Derry round Coleraine, but extended to the fertile plains of Mid-Ulster, East Tyrone, mid-Derry and North Armagh. Areas of Fermanagh were also planted, especially around the garrison town of Enniskillen and Cavan. Although predominantly Presbyterian by the early 18th century, with the majority speaking a dialect of Scots-English (Lallans), still Bardon noted that until the 1820s Scottish Gaelic also held a following among rural Presbyterian communities along the east Ulster coast.*(35) Maolcholaim Scott further noted a tendency among 18th century Presbyterian ministers in the south Ulster counties of Armagh and Monaghan to preach in the Gaelic tongue, culminating in 1719 in the publication of a Gaelic (Irish) Presbyterian catechism.*(36)

Among the native Irish population, the anti-Catholic Penal Laws proved a major barrier.*(37) Literacy was largely limited to a tiny elite of merchants, clerics and occasional professionals, of which the Kerry-born liberator, Daniel O'Connell – continental-educated and well resourced – was an example. For the mainstream Catholic population from all parts of Ireland, there was almost no access to education or any catechetical literature, while as Macaulay observed, they were served by a fugitive priesthood many of whom were barely educated themselves.*(38) Ulster Catholics shared in the same grim experience as their co-religionists throughout Ireland. Additionally, there was the Catholic practice of celebrating Mass and the liturgy in Latin, which proved unhelpful for matching the medium of its Gaelic-speaking followers. However, in so far as Catholic priests were able to operate in the repressive Penal climate of 17th and 18th century Ulster, they used Gaelic for conducting their pastoral ministry. A typical example would be Drumnaquoile, near the market town of Castlewellan, Co. Down, where the rural population was served by a group of Franciscan Friars, all Gaelic-speaking, and who in the absence of churches conducted Masses and pastoral support at Mass rocks and other secret locations, perpetually at grave risk from the local militia.*(39)

Accordingly, those fugitive priests and friars provided the only educated Gaelic leadership for guiding their dispossessed lay brethren through a long era of repression and cultural mutation. That being the case, such few Gaelic publications as did appear were noteworthy on account of their rarity. Of the latter, Seamas MacGiolla Fhinnein's thesis on the 17th century Down 'hedge school' (fugitive) master, Eoin O'Ghripin, who translated the Catholic catechism from Latin into Gaelic, provides a valuable insight to a scarce, and it must be added, courageous, breed of Ulster Gaelic scribes, driven by an unremitting loyalty to Faith and Fatherland from that dark era.*(40)

Elsewhere, among the enduring Ulster Gaeltachtai, both numbers and communities dwindled throughout the course of the 19th and early 20th centuries. According to Seamas O'Casaide's authoritative study, spoken Gaelic had disappeared from Down – save for a few stalwarts cast around rural villages – by the onset of the Great War in 1914.*(41) Thereafter, the minor Gaeltachtai of Tyrone, Sperrins (Derry), Antrim Glens and Rathlin Island followed suit by the 1940s, leaving Donegal as the sole modern Ulster county with traditional Gaeltacht communities in present times. It also needs to be acknowledged that Omeath in North Louth, itself a part of modern Leinster, was in fact rooted in the Ulster Gaeilge dialect, and in earlier centuries had been part of ancient Ulster. The dwindling Omeath Gaeltacht, as will be later shown when acknowledging the work of leading Gaelgeoir priest, An Athair Lorcan O'Murrui, had struggled to preserve both Gaeilge and specifically its Ulster dialect against slow death and assimilation within the Dublin establishment's cultural directives that favoured the Galway dialect. More generally, Ulster Gaels embraced a Gaelic revival, figuring the Gaelic League and Gaelic Athletic Association with a redoubtable energy that quickly manifested in multiple clubs, campaigns and Feiseann across its nine counties.*(42) Also, the emergence of a modern Ulster Gaeltacht in 1980s West Belfast occurred in different circumstances, and was driven by political dynamics which are examined in separate chapters.

What is significant about the Ulster experience is that at different times since the mid-17th century the Gaelic language has been subject to cross-communal influences. While predominantly rooted in the Irish nationalist tradition, nevertheless there was also an accommodation of Plantation Scottish culture, complete with Scottish-Gaelic antecedents. The latter preceded the 1798 Presbyterian-led United Irishmen's insurrection in Ulster, but throughout the 19th century there followed the socio-economic and ultimate political assimilation of mainstream Ulster Presbyterians into the vanguard of Irish Unionism. Thereafter, Presbyterian cultural alignments reflected the Anglophile, non-Celtic course so beloved of the Unionist political establishment. Moreover, the increasing dichotomy between Gaelgeoir lobbyists in Conradh na nGael and the GAA and nationalist politics reinforced Unionist antipathy towards both language and culture. The fact that the North Antrim Gaelic League also boasted a small number of Presbyterian Gaelic activists like Ada McNeill, Margaret Dobbs, the Belfast antiquarian and philanthropist, Francis Joseph Biggar, and British Civil Servant – soon to be converted to Irish Nationalism, Sir Roger Casement – recalled by Phoenix et al – had by 1914 become exceptions to a trend.*(43) By the time of Ireland's partition in 1922, Gaelicism was viewed by Unionists as an appendix to Sinn Feinism, and thus there existed no desire for either supporting the language or its cultural/sporting ancillaries in the autonomous statelet of Northern Ireland.

Hence faced with entrenched and consistent political hostility from a Stormont Unionist authority and its cultural acolytes – who included broadcasters, unionist press, civil service and educational establishment – it was inevitable that Gaelic interests became inextricably linked to the politics and culture of Northern Ireland's Nationalist community. In that way did the Gaelic language and culture get drawn into the political divisions and communal identity of a polarised society.

6. **_Scotland_**: The historical experience of Scottish Gaeldom has much in common with that of its Irish brethren, but diverged with the distinctive course of Scottish history. Specifically, Scottish Gaeldom, like the wider civic entity of Scotland, was affected by the country's proximity to and political relations down the centuries with its powerful southern neighbour, England. So also was Scottish Gaeldom subject to limitations of its regional concentration on the West Coast, and latterly the Highlands and Hebrides. All those features impacted on the character of Scottish Gaeldom in a manner that defined its raison d'être and purpose over the past hundred years. That Scottish Gaeldom emerged with different characteristics and priorities to its Irish counterpart is a reflection of the manner in which the British Crown and its devolved political and administrative institutions, not to mention political establishment, have addressed the Gaelic question within the borders of both nations.

Unlike Ireland, where the Gaelic language remains central to the national cultural heritage, Gaelic was never the exclusive tongue of all Scots, although until the Middle Ages it was the language of a majority of Scotland's population. Significantly, as late Edinburgh University historian, Professor William Croft Dickinson, recounts, save for a period in the early Middle Ages, Gaelic has not commanded principal place in Scotland's modern political development nor cultural evolution.*(44) Its high point was around 1100, but thereafter went into slow decline. The Gaelic order went unrecognised in modern Scots Law and civil administration, even ahead of the enforced Anglo-Scottish Union of 1707. Thereafter, it disintegrated due to hostility and Crown repression.

It is not that Gaelic is either alien or peripheral to the Scottish heritage, but its historic legacy is concentrated in the West Highlands, Argyll, Galloway and the Hebrides, with only the scantiest impact elsewhere. Therefore, it is more accurate to speak of Gaelic as "an" rather than "the" historic language of Scotland. Historically, Scots were forced to co-habit alongside other races, Celtic and non-Celtic alike. The most dominant were Welsh-speaking North Britons in the Central Valley and Southern Scotland; Picts settled in the eastern areas north of the Firth of Forth, while Northumbrian Angles settled in the south east and Lothians. Additionally, there were the Norse influences that embraced the Orkneys, Shetlands, Northern Highlands, and even touched

Gaeldom's hinterland of the Outer Hebrides, as denoted by the Norse name of Hebridean town, Stornoway. All have left a mark on contemporary Scottish society, but as the others have to a greater or lesser degree been absorbed into a recognisable Lowlands culture, as Professor C.W.J. Withers's study concluded, Gaeldom proved to be the most enduring, and also most resistant to historical anglicisation.*(45)

The introduction of Gaelic to Scotland is a subject that has long divided historians. In a land that was Pict-dominated at the time of the Roman invasion of Britain, evidently a mutation and displacement of previous masters and tribes occurred over the ensuing four hundred years. Professor John Duncan Mackie, late of the University of Glasgow, concluded that the gaelicisation of Scotland – as far as it went – was a natural process of migration from the northern part of Ireland dictated by a mixture of commercial, military and missionary factors from the second to the fifth centuries AD.*(46) As a result, the Gaelic language entered mainstream life in the Hebrides, Highlands and West Coast. Mackie's conclusion concurs with conventional wisdom, and has the benefit of being sustained by available evidence. Conversely, contemporary Scottish broadcaster and archaeologist, Neil Oliver, while not challenging Mackie, is less emphatic about the essence of the Irish link, instead seeing the language and Gaelic order as having emerged already in the Scotland of pre-Roman times.*(47) It is difficult to be definitive, but Mackie makes a more compelling case.

Mackie, along with another reputable Scottish historian specialising in Gaelic history, the late John Bannerman, offers substantial evidence of large numbers of Gaelic-speaking Scots migrating from their historic clan lands in North East Ulster to the Western Scottish Highlands, specifically modern Argyll, from the first century AD onwards.*(48) This migration followed on from existing Ulster-Scottish links, based on both sides of the Sea of Moyle, such as the ancient Gaelic kingdom of Dalriada – earlier mentioned. According to the great Celtic saga, '**Ruraiocht**', the exploits of Ulster's famed Gaelic warriors, the Red Branch warriors, including the legendary Cuchullian – hound and defender of Ulster from the fort at Emain Macha (Armagh), abound with accounts of crossing the Sea to the brethren in Alba (Scotland). Later, sixth century Christian evangelisation of Scots was undertaken by the Northern Irish monk from Tir Conail (Donegal), Columcille (Columba), who later founded a Celtic church that in time embraced all of Scotland. The subsequent triumph of the Gaelic language, clans, Brehon code and customs followed the ensuing conquest of the Picts, and was completed by the first recognised King of Scots and Picts, Kenneth MacAlpin in 844 AD.*(49) It is significant that Colmcille's missionary centre on the Inner Hebridean island of Iona, which subsequently became the burial place for a succession of Scottish kings up to the Reformation.

Thereafter, and variously sustained by a combination of aggression and missionary zeal, the Gaelic clans assumed an expanding profile into the Southern Lowlands and modern Border territories, complete with their language and political/social system. This expansion continued up until the reign of Malcolm Ceann Mor and his saintly English wife, Margaret Mary, in the 11th century. By then, as noted by Mackie, a mixture of military defeats and the entry of Norman French forces, along with enforced alliances aimed at protecting southern interests, meant the slow decline of the Gaelic chieftains and their restriction to the Highlands and Hebridean heartland.*(50)

The arrival of Norman marauders from the South meant different linguistic influences swiftly permeated the ruling elite of Medieval Scotland, thereby hastening the slow marginalisation of Gaelic and its cultural corollaries. Gaelic was not so much displaced as supplanted at the Scottish Court with, first, Norman-French, and later, English. As professors' Withers and Kenneth MacKinnon have each recognised in their respective studies, a combination of military and commercial forces, plus shifting political authority in Medieval Scotland, caused the gradual anglicisation of the Southern Lowlands, which was to extend over most of the slowly-urbanising burghs, exempting the West Highlands and Hebrides, throughout the next three centuries.*(51) At the same time, Bannerman noted that among the ordinary population Gaelic experienced a slow demise, and was still widely spoken among Lowlands Scots, as well as their Highlander fellow countrymen, by the time of John Knox's mid-16th century Calvinist-Presbyterian Reformation.*(52)

7. *Gaelic Decline:* Identifying the Gaelic decline in early-modern Scotland is a complex task, and one expertly covered by Bannerman and Withers in their respective historical treatises. For the purpose of this book, it is enough to say that by the time of the Anglo-Scottish Act of Union (May 1707), Scotland's Gaels were confined to the Highlands, Hebrides and Galloway in the South-West, although prior to the 18th century small Gaelic communities had emerged in, first, Edinburgh and, later, Glasgow. Elsewhere, as yet another of Glasgow

University's distinguished late historians, Professor George Pryde, observed, Scotland, with a total population of barely 1,200,000 – less than a fifth of that of England – had developed a commercial culture and political order based on mercantilist trade.*(53) There was also a separate Scottish legal system; and – by the standards of its day – advanced educational programme, with parish schools offering literacy and numeracy to all, along with universities in Glasgow, Edinburgh, St Andrews and Aberdeen – which boasted two universities To an extent, Scottish education was based on Calvinist principles, prioritising literacy so as to make each child fluent with Scriptures. It also permeated law, commerce and even the Church, which was subject to Crown patronage. Indeed various scholarly studies by Scotland's distinguished historian, Professor/Sir Tom Devine, catalogue the extent to which Calvinism in the communities fashioned social practice.*(54) Significantly, long before 1707, Scots-English had replaced Gaelic as principal language of both the Edinburgh establishment and ordinary Lowlanders. None of those factors bode well for the Gaelic language, nor did subsequent trends towards urbanisation, industrialisation or democratisation.

An additional problem for Gaeldom was the low status of the language in the Highlands after 1700. This reality was reflected in a marked preference by many Highland chieftains for adopting English and Edinburgh Scots-English culture in place of indigenous Gaelic, a practice that percolated to kinsmen with depressing effects. MacKinnon also noted a tendency for migrating Highlanders to conceal their Gaelic roots by adopting anglicised names and speech forms.*(55) Such was the hostile political atmosphere in the Lowlands following the Jacobite insurrection of 1745.

The legacy of that Jacobite defeat at Culloden of April 1746 proved devastating for the Highlands clans generally and Gaelic language in particular. Pryde, Withers and Bannerman in their respective accounts each tell how the Gaelic order was swept away in the climate of Crown-sponsored hostility, aimed at all sections of Highland Gaelic society which was then held synonymous with Jacobitism. The 1746 Disarming Act prohibited Highland dress (kilts), and though not specifically barring the Gaelic language, nevertheless it was targeted at the Gaelic clans who had lately supported the

Young Pretender, Charles Edward Stuart, and resisted the political rule of the Crown and Edinburgh administration. Although that repressive statue was repealed in 1782, by then de-gaelicisation was well under way in the Highlands and Hebrides, leaving consequences that are self-evident up to and including the present day. Indeed one fundamental and irreversible legacy of the Highland chieftains' defeat at Culloden was that it spelt the death knell of Scotland's Gaelic tongue as a popular spoken language in all but its most secluded heartlands of the Highlands and Hebrides.

The post-Culloden repression of Highlands Scotland followed a similar pattern to Crown polices in Ireland of the same time, notably cultural anglicisation, as a weapon to enforce political submission. Other related causes of decline included the Highland Clearances, itself a notorious practice of 18th and 19th century Highland landlords who forced tenant crofters off their holdings to make way for the more profitable infusion of sheep. This repressive saga caused the enforced depopulation of the Highlands and Hebrides to the order of over 400,000 crofters and cottiers; and as with the Irish potato famine of the 1840s, remains embedded in contemporary culture as a grievous injustice perpetrated by Crown-sponsored landlords against ordinary crofting Gaels. Those clearances also saw a mass migration towards the growing urban centres of Glasgow, Edinburgh, Dundee and the cities of England … all in search of work and basic survival. Like the Irish potato famine of 1844-49, Highlands Scotland too experienced its own potato famine throughout 1846/47, struck by the same destructive fungus, Phytophthora Infestans, which wreaked havoc throughout the West Highlands and Outer Hebrides, effectively hastening drastic depopulation. Altogether, a combination of clearances and famine produced a mass of emigration to the colonies of the expanding British Empire; Australia, New Zealand, USA and Canada. The latter country held a particular attraction to tens of thousands of displaced Gaelic-speaking Highlanders and Hebrideans, as is evidenced by the strong Gaelic traditions of contemporary Nova Scotia and Cape Breton Island – a theme developed and analysed to the full by the scholarly Professor Devine.*(56)

There were domestic factors at play. Not least among the latter was the nature of Scotland's emerging educational system, based on Calvinist principles of ensuring each child's capacity for reading the Scriptures. This meant extending literacy to every Scottish village without penalising the poor, and indeed the 'Lad o' Pairts' – personified by the national bard, Robbie Burns, a ploughman's son from Ayrshire – was a model for the social mobility offered by the evolving educational system. However, this code of Presbyterian egalitarianism did not extend to a purposeful defence of the Gaelic language, far less incorporating Gaelic into the school medium. As outlined by MacKinnon, the dominant attitudes of the 19th century Anglo-Scottish Unionist establishment linked Gaelic to Jacobite ideals, which was politically threatening.*(57) Additionally, there was the low educational status of Gaelic, which was decried in Edinburgh's urbane circles as a backward language of primitive society in the Highlands, Hebrides and Ireland. In those circles, the view prevailed for utilising economic and educational developments to assist Gaelic towards a peaceful demise. MacKinnon recounts that the use of education and schools to rid Scotland of what one hostile inspector contemptuously referred to as "*... the Gaelic nuisance ...*" was blatant and Crown-sponsored.*(58)

Anti-Gaelic prejudices were overtly reflected in the Education Act (Scotland) of 1872, which Kenneth MacKinnon noted:

"*.... was passed without recognition that the Highlands was an area of particular linguistic significance within a national educational system. No specific references to Gaelic were contained within the Act.*"*(59)

The Act created school boards in each parish and burgh, and to those bodies were transferred all schools created under parliamentary authority by an earlier act of 1838. These included charitable schools run by various Presbyterian groups and societies, specifically The Society for the Propagation of Christian Knowledge in Scotland (SSPCK), General Assembly of the Church of Scotland, Free Church of Scotland and the Gaelic Schools and Sunday Schools Societies. Previously, the Free Church – formed by breakaway from the Church of Scotland, 1843 – with its dominant Highlands and Islands base, and SSPCK had actively proselytised in the Gaelic tongue, thereby ensuring for it a regular medium of usage. Actually, the Free Church, along with the Gaelic Bible translation and special metrical Psalms, provided a valuable kernel for Gaelic speakers and preachers, which was used in the education of Highlands and Hebridean children throughout the 19th century. However, the 1872 Act swept away even the peripheral place of Gaelic in the Highlands educational structure. Under the new regime, Gaelic was actively discouraged in schools, while the appointment of English-speaking teachers was common, even in monoglot Gaidhealtachd districts. Indeed, so vindictive was the de-gaelicisation educational policy that a further corollary of the 1872 Act was the unsavoury practice of whipping native-speaking children with the 'maide-crocaidh', a stick on a cord, as punishment for communicating in their mother tongue on school premises. MacKinnon noted that the law of the 'maide-crocaidh' was deployed as an instrument of terror against Gaelic school children throughout the late 19th century and well into the 20th century, with its use being continued in certain schools on the Isle of Lewis –Scotland's largest Gaidhealtachd – until the mid-1930s.*(60)

8. **_Stirrings of Revival_**: Punitive anti-Gaelic measures prevailed right up to the 1950s, and did not stop with the phasing out of the 'Maide-Crocaidh' regime. This also included English-only educational instruction, with Gaelic literature denied and the language being subject to constant ridicule by visiting inspectors and other lead figures, none of which did much for the esteem of native-speaking children.*(61) Not until 1918 was any Scottish educational reform initiated that gave a modicum of recognition to the role of Gaelic in schools, both as a subject and medium for learning. Such modest concessions as were hard-won resulted from the diligent lobbying of three significant, if relatively-new Gaelic interest groups. One was **An Comunn Gaidhealach**, founded in 1891, and which emerged as Scotland's equivalent to the Irish Conradh na Gaeilge in that it undertook high profile and influential lobbying on various Gaelic issues over the next 125 years. Another was the Gaelic Society of Inverness, which also campaigned for Gaelic interests. The third was the Gaelic Society of London, founded by Highland and Hebridean migrants to preserve the language and culture in the Capital, while also lobbying its interests to public representatives and government. All three organisations provided an influential voice for Scottish Gaeldom throughout lean times, but unlike Ireland, the Scottish groups concentrated on education, the role of Gaelic in the churches and the cultural domain, while firmly avoiding the political front.

As regards numbers, like Ireland, Scotland's Gaelic-speaking population was not easy to quantify in the 19th century. This was partly due to the reluctance of many native Gaelic speakers to admit their normal medium to Census enumerators, for reasons previously discussed. There was also a difficulty about identifying monoglot Gaelic speakers in the Highlands and Hebrides, as distinct from bilingual Gaels both there and all over Scotland. For the most committed and dedicated of Scottish Gaels, there was the overriding reality of Gaelic's decline, as typified in a letter to the Lord Advocate:

"Even the most ardent lover of Gaelic cannot fail to admit that the possession of a knowledge of English is indispensable to any poor islander who wishes to learn a trade or to earn his bread beyond the limits of his native isle".*(62)

Furthermore, only after 1881 did the official Census seek information about Gaelic-speaking practices among the Scottish population over 3 years of age, unlike Ireland where it began in 1851. In 1881, some 231,594 persons were listed as first medium Gaelic speakers, out of a total Scottish population of 3,425,151. By 1951, Gaelic speakers had declined to 95,447 (out of 4,826,814), and by 1961 to 80,978 (out of 4,892,882).*(63) Predictably, on the records of Withers, the Gaidhealtachd of the 1880s included large parts of Arran, Bute, parts of Sutherland, Ross-shire, Inverness-shire, Isle of Skye and the islands of the Inner Hebrides, along with Scottish Gaeldom's heartland in the Outer Hebrides of Lewis, Harris, Barra, Mingulay, South and North Uist, Benbecula and the outlying St Kilda.*(64) Additionally, MacKinnon has shown evidence of a temporary, if also isolated 18/19th century Gaidhealtachd in the South West region of Galloway, composed predominantly of migrant Ulster (Glens of Antrim) Gaelic speakers, who co-existed alongside the mainstream Scottish population in a rural area embracing the towns of Stranraer and Dumfries.*(65)

By 1951, Scotland's entire Gaidhealtachd had contracted drastically. The Galloway Gaidhealtachd had long gone, while in the West Highlands only a few small villages remained native-speaking. In the Outer Hebrides, the remote St Kilda – located 150 miles off the West Coast – was finally evacuated in 1930, thus dismembering a very old and long-established Gaidhealtachd with a way of life that had survived for many centuries largely because of its isolation. Indeed by 1960, the only reasonably-sized Scottish Gaidhealtachd could be found in Skye and the Outer Hebrides, with Stornoway emerging as unofficial Gaelic capital of an otherwise Anglicising Scotland. It is significant that this Hebridean Gaidhealtachd was to prove a crucial reason for the subsequent creation of a unique Gaelic local authority, Comhairle nan Eilean Siar (Western Isles Council), and saving of the Western Isles, with its 29,000 population, as the smallest Westminster division in the UK parliament.

Significantly, during the last three decades of the 19th century, there emerged a degree of radical assertiveness on the part of Gaels and crofter activists. Resistance to evictions, formation of the Highland Land League, action against tyrannical landlordism, crofter reform campaigns and the launching of Gaelic lobbyist organisations – like An Comunn Gaidhealach – all testified to a growing self-confidence then sweeping Highlands/Hebridean popular culture of the time. Though the level of contact between the two Gaelic worlds then, as now, was minimal, actually, events in Ireland had not gone entirely unnoticed across the Sea of Moyle, and there was tacit encouragement from sister organisations such as Conradh na Gaeilge, Cumann Luthcleas Gael and the Irish Land League. Yet both Pryde and Devine in their different accounts of the period indicate that Highlands/Hebridean groups were less politically potent than their Irish counterparts.*(66) This was partly due to a lack of numbers, partly regional limits to the appeal of Gaelic culture in Scotland, and partly the modest nature of Scottish demands. Whereas An Comunn Gaidhealach (ACG) was mainly concerned with achieving legal recognition and educational provision for Scottish Gaelic, as has been shown earlier, by 1910 an increasing body of Irish Gaelgeoiri viewed language and cultural revival as symmetric partners with nationalism on the road towards achieving political nationhood.*(67)

Actually, An Comunn Gaidhealach's antecedents were quite different to the Irish groups. As was shown by ACG's official historian, Frank Thompson, the organisation's formation in 1891 owed much to the Scottish aristocracy and professional class's reluctance to allow the language to die.*(68) ACG was never a grass roots association, and its launch and funding was as much due to the efforts of local peers, along with Presbyterian church figures, businessmen and even sitting Liberal and Tory politicians, all of whom figured on its Management Committee. (For a full list of ACG leadership personnel, see Footnote 68). Early names included Sherriff J. MacMaster Campbell, along with first President, Lord Archibald Campbell, Provost Dugald MacIsaac, ex-Provost Maclean, and Lochaber's Church of Scotland Minister, Rev Dr Stewart. So too was the first Secretary, a certain Mr John Campbell, a Solicitor from Oban, while first treasurer was a Mr Donald Mackay, an Accountant, also from Oban.*(69) Conversely, grass roots input to ACG central direction and policymaking from native speakers, especially crofters and their spokesmen, was very limited.*(70)

Significantly, in the early years, the principal task in hand was organising an annual Gaelic Mod, which first happened in Oban on 13th September 1892, and was repeated for the next two years at the same place before finally making Glasgow in 1895 and Perth in 1896. By promoting the Gaelic cultural profile, ACG leaders believed they might wrestle concessions from the Scottish Office such as a Gaelic policy in Highlands schools, while doing something to protect the 231,000 Gaelic speakers still functioning at the time of the organisation's launch. As a result, a "respectable" image for both ACG and the Gaelic language and culture were deemed essential perquisites towards achieving progress. Hence there followed the enlistment of aristocrats and even Royal figureheads as patrons. There had always been Royal interest in Gaelic since the reign of George IV in the early 19th century. Actually, Queen Victoria, throughout her lengthy reign of 62 years, and loving Highland Scotland, to the point of arranging for the construction of Balmoral Castle in Aberdeenshire, donned Highland dress, learned Gaelic, hosted Ceilidhs and was regularly entertained by Gaelic singers at the castle. In 1912, ACG received a congratulatory letter from the new King, George V, and during the Great War, 1914-18, aside from staging concerts for returning Scottish military units and disabled soldiers, ACG devoted its energies towards knitting socks for soldiers and fund raising for ambulances.*(71)

It is noteworthy that despite a nascent interest in Gaelicism and Scottish Home Rule from 1880 onwards, early Scottish nationalists did not prioritise the Gaelic language on similar lines to the Irish. Indeed, as recalled by both Pryde and Devine, Scotland's early home rulers tended to be Liberals with the addition of some Socialists.*(72) In fact, whatever may have been the radical rhetoric, both those parties were essentially United Kingdom constitutional reform forces. As for the Scottish nationalist movement, Dr Jack Brand observed it was slow in reaching birth and muted in its programme.*(73) In contrast to Pearse, MacNeill, De Valera and Plunkett, there was a marked disinclination among Scottish nationalist pioneers to embrace Gaelicism on account of its marginal appearance to mainstream Scottish society in Glasgow, Edinburgh and Dundee; a close identification it was feared might limit the nationalist appeal in areas of potential electoral strength.

Another factor which discouraged the embrace of political nationalists was the appearance of servility by many outlying Gaidhealtachd communities to local lairds and petty aristocracy. The willingness of the few propertied Gaels to vote for the laird's candidates and to embrace his calls to arms in times of war, along with aristocratic sponsorship of local Mods (festivals of Gaelic music, dancing and recitation) rather depressed urban radicals. Yet such was also the climate in which An Comunn Gaidhealach and its allies lobbied the Gaelic interests to government at Edinburgh (where the Scottish Office had relocated) and London.*(74) As Brand was to elaborate, within the embryonic Scottish nationalist movement over its first 30 years there was an enduring faction that felt more inspired by the Irish nationalists, and thus the cautions of ACG seemed misplaced, while the spectacle of local embrace was unpalatable.*(75) Those tensions were to simmer in the ranks of Scottish Gaelicism and Scottish Nationalism for another half century.

Two other factors are noteworthy. Both are drawn from the writings of Tom Devine, with each going some way towards explaining why Scottish Gaeldom faced a less hostile establishment in London and Edinburgh than was true of its Irish counterparts of the time. First, with Jacobites firmly crushed by the failed 1745/46 uprising, and post-Culloden repression of Highland dress and the Gaelic language now revoked, by the latter 19th century there followed something of a national renaissance in the Scottish search for a new identity embracing many instruments and myths of the old Gaelic order, inclusive of the highlands pipes, kilts, poetry, ceilidh dancing and ballads, though not, significantly, the language. It was all about cultivating a national character based on the emblems, dress and sagas of a Gaelic Scotland that in truth only ever partially existed, but was encouraged by such improbable patrons as Queen Victoria – who had eagerly embraced the Highlands, especially after Prince Albert's premature death - and the novels of Sir Walter Scott.*(76) In this reborn Anglo-Gaelicised Scotland, by necessity, there had to be some accommodation of the Gaelic language, itself still then a mother tongue for large parts of the Highlands and Hebrides. Second, Devine emphasises that the Highlands and Hebridean Scotland provided a major kernel of manpower recruitment for the British Army, whose services in the overseas colonies and in the Boer War and Great War struck a chord with the wider British public and political class alike. Indeed the appearance of Highlands regiments marching to war attired in traditional kilts and bonnets, led by pipers, and with so many Gaelic-speaking soldiers was gleaned by onlookers everywhere.*(77) This sympathetic imagery of the Gaelic homeland was skilfully exploited by An Comunn Gaidhealach in their lobbying of the British government and Scottish Office on educational and cultural affairs then. Also, Devine, points out that ACG were careful to avoid the militant posturing of Conradh na Gaeilge, whose links with political Fenianism were all-too-evident. Such would not have suited Scotland.*(78)

Multiple reports of Scottish martial courage and valour, not to mention tragedies, also reached the same public. Perhaps the gravest tragedy of all was the sinking of the troop carrier, HMY Lolaire, on New Year's Day, 1919, when it struck a rock at around 2.00am on entering Stornoway Harbour. The ship, that had the previous day set out from the Kyle of Lochalsh, was carrying mainly naval and military personnel returning home from the War. Those men, who had survived the conflict and Spanish Flu, stood little chance in the stormy waters of the Minch, and though some 47 men were rescued, alas, a total of 201 Hebridean servicemen perished in the inhospitable waters of the North Atlantic that night. Public awareness of that great tragedy had the effect of generating sympathy in England for the Scots generally and Gaelic-speaking Hebrideans and Highlanders particularly.*(79)

Yet, interestingly, over the first quarter of the 20th century, as a result of the lobbyist activities of ACG and the London Gaelic Society, there was a general easing of erstwhile anti-Gaelic prejudices by various wings of the lairds' Scottish educational and political establishment. In 1915, came the introduction of a state secondary schools examination in Gaelic. Following on from ACG's further efforts, the 1918 (Scotland) Act included a mandatory Gaelic clause, which though proving ineffective as far as initiating Gaelic medium education went, nevertheless marked a beginning of the slow Gaelic incorporation to Scottish education. Even the Gaelic Mods and Feisean, organised by ACG, came to enjoy a rising esteem far and beyond the Highlands and Hebrides, and were patronised by an ever- rising pool of Scottish Establishment figures. Among the latter, was a certain Elizabeth Bowes-Lyons, whose marriage to the Duke of York, later King George VI, rendered the Consort's throne in 1936.*(80) As Queen Mother, following the King's premature death in 1952, Her late Majesty was a regular attender at ACG's National Mod and, televised, Grand Gaelic Concert throughout the 1950s and '60s, and also patronised many associated Gaelic cultural projects.

From those initial green shoots, other developments followed over ensuing decades, which are covered in later chapters. However, it is enough to say that by the end of World War 1 – which had taken a particularly high death toll among Highlands and Hebridean manpower – servicemen returning to the area found an unprecedented degree of seething discontent. The Isle of Lewis alone had lost over 1,000 men (out of a total population then of around 28,000), divided between soldiers, Merchant and Royal Navy seamen. The whole Highlands and Hebrides were rapidly depopulating, as tens of thousands left in search of employment in the Lowlands cities, while others emigrated to Canada. There was popular agitation by crofters in pursuit of land rights, and various other campaigns waged by fishermen, ex-servicemen and tenant workers. Indeed such important historical events have in recent decades become the stuff of televised drama to contemporary audiences by popular artistes like '7-84', a radical Highlands/Hebridean musical theatre group, headed by the distinguished, late Gaelic singer/actor, Simon Mackenzie, from the Isle of Harris.*(81) Their many performances were shown by Channel 4 in the 1980s and '90s.

Although the emphasis by ACG and its sister bodies was placed on lobbying rather than radical action, the plain fact was that as a result of past social injustices against the language and its people, by 1920 the Highlands and Islands, like the rest of Scotland, had become radicalised to a degree previously unknown. Yet Scottish Gaeldom depended on a functional Highlands/Hebridean social infrastructure, which under the twin pressures of economic depression and migration/emigration was visibly disintegrating to the point where the language's very survival looked most uncertain. Accordingly, unlike Ireland, where there at least beckoned the prospect of independent nationhood, the Scottish Gaels would have to fight their battles, confronting enemies and wooing allies alike, all within the confines of the British state. There existed no such appetite in Scotland of that time for the kind of independence sought by Sinn Fein and their Gaelic League allies in Ireland.

Therefore, in the moderate and non-confrontational methods pursued by ACG and the wider Scottish Gaelic lobby throughout the 20th century, it needs to be understood that their priority was the **survival of the Gaelic tongue**. If that meant focusing on education, drama, churches and culture, not to mention wooing Scottish aristocracy and Royalty, in contrast to Irish nationalist politicking, so be it! Such was the reality of Scottish Gaeldom's historic weakness, and thus its battle for survival.

FOOTNOTES and REFERENCES

1. A significant observation, quite startling to many on the outside, is that notwithstanding a few recent initiatives, generally communication lines over the past century between Gaidheal na h-Alba (Scotland) and Gaeil Uladh (Ulster), and indeed the whole of Ireland, have been surprisingly minimal. There has been little interaction and scarce sharing of common cultural properties over that time, and hence the barest understanding of each other's respective political conditions. – One of the few prominent figures to address the gap is the accomplished Scottish Gaelic ballad singer, Arthur Cormack, from the Isle of Skye, who has been a regular guest performer in Belfast and around Northern Ireland. He narrated his experiences and impressions in a discussion with this author, 31st October, 1997, at the Scottish National Gaelic Mod, Inverness.

2. Katharine Simms, Chap. 2; Nicholas Canny, Chap. 3; and R.F. Foster, Chap. 4; Oxford History of Ireland, (1992), Eds. R.F. Foster.

3. Jonathan Bardon – Chaps. 3, 4 & 5; A History of Ulster (1992).

4. R.F. Foster – Chaps 2, 3, 5 & 7; Modern Ireland 1600-1972 (1988).

5. (i) D. Figgis – The Gaelic State in the Past and Future (1917).

   (ii) K. Nicholls – Gaelic and Gaelicised Ireland in the Middle Ages (1972).

6. Bardon (1992); Chap. 8.

7. Ibid.

8. P.S. Robinson eds. 'The Language in Seventeenth Century Ulster Scots'; (Ulster Folklife), 1989; pp 86-99, Michael Montgomery.

9. Mairi Robinson – The Concise Scots Dictionary (University of Aberdeen, 1985).

10. P.S. Robinson – 'The Anglicisation of Scots in Seventeenth Century Ulster'; pp 50-64, Studies in Scottish Literature (1991).

11. Another worthy piece of Scots-Lallans enquiry literature is John Hewitt's – Rhyming Weavers and other country poets of Antrim and Down (1974).

12. Information cited in Reg. Hindley – The Death of the Irish Language: A Qualified Obituary (1990); Chap. 2, pp 14 -16.

13. Hindley (1990); Chap 2, pp 15-20.

14. Hindley (1990); Chap 2, pp 14-20.

15. HMSO figures cited in Hindley (1990); Chap 2, pp 15-20.

16. Also see: Tomas O'Fiaich 'The Language and Political History'; in A View of the Irish Language, ed. B. O'Cuiv (1969).

17. This picture is corroborated by literature from Conradh na Gaeilge, plus the records of historians like B. O'Cuiv, T. O'Fiaich and A. Hepburn, and 1911 Census figures from HMSO.

18. Hindley (1990); Chap. 3, pp 21-26.

19. Joseph Crehan, S.J. – 'Freedom and Catholic Power', Studies, 40, pp 158-166, 1951.

    Oliver Rafferty, S.J. – The Catholic Church and the Protestant State; Nineteenth Century Irish Realities (Dublin 2008).

20. Ultramontanism was the name given to a Catholic school of thought during the 19th and early 20th centuries which held that all power and civic institutions in Catholic societies should be subordinate to papal veto under doctrinal concepts of Christ the King and Papal Infallibility. It was thoroughly autocratic and illiberal, and associated with the era of Popes' Pius IX, Leo XIII, Pius X, Benedict XV, Pius XI and Pius XII, 1860-1958. Ultramontanism was effectively replaced by the new, open orthodoxy enunciated by the Second Vatican Council (1962-65), convened by Popes' John XIII (1958-63) and Paul VI (1963-78).

21. Brian Murphy – Forgotten Patriot: Douglas Hyde and the construction of the Presidency (2006).

22. Owen McGee – Arthur Griffith (2015); Chap 4, pp 81-86.

23. Taking Ulster as a case example, the Edmund Rice Christian Brothers and De La Salle Brothers, both of whom established secondary and grammar schools across the province in the early years of the 20th century, adopted Gaelic games and Irish Language Studies for their schools. So did diocesan

grammar schools - many being de facto junior seminaries - like St Malachy's College, Belfast, St Columb's Derry, St Patrick's Armagh, St Patrick's Dungannon, St Colman's Newry and St Patrick's Cavan. See - the range of historical booklets produced by those colleges celebrating their various establishment anniversaries.

24. Roger Blaney Presbyterians and the Irish Language (2012, Belfast).

25. Risteard Giltrap The Irish Language in the Church of Ireland (1990, Dublin), pp 96-42.

26. See earlier research by this author: V. McKee – Gaelic Nations: Politics of the Gaelic Language in Scotland and Northern Ireland in the Twentieth Century (1997).

27. James Hunter The Making of the Crofting Community (3rd ed., 1987).

28. A.C. Hepburn – The Conflict of Nationality in Modern Ireland (1990); O'Fiaich/O'Cuiv eds (1969).

29. Treorai Oifigiuil/Official Guide, 1992, Cumann Luthchleas Gael/Gaelic Athletic Association – Croke's letter reprinted in full, pp 92-93.

30. Eoin MacNeill's 'Appeal to the Clergy of Ireland', cited in Brian O'Cuiv 'The Gaelic Cultural Movement and the New Nationalism'; Kevin B. Nowlan (Eds.) The Making of 1916: Studies in the History of the Rising (1969, Dublin).

31. Padraig Pearse, though a qualified barrister, actually devoted his energies to establishing and managing Gaelic medium schools in Dublin, a role he maintained right up until his premature death by execution following the failed Dublin uprising of April 1916.

32. See Hindley (1990), Chaps 3 & 10; O'Cuiv, eds., (1969). Also, see Ambrose Macaulay (2016).

33. Bardon (1992), Chaps 3 & 4.

    A.T.Q. Stewart – The Narrow Ground: Aspects of Ulster, 1609-1969 (1977), Chap. 1.

    Padraig O'Snodaigh – Hidden Ulster, (1973).

34. Stewart (1977), Chap. 3.

35. Bardon (1992), Chaps 5 & 6.

36. Maolchalaim Scott 'When Planter was the Gael'; Fortnight Supplement (Belfast, 1993).

37. The anti-Catholic Penal Laws were enacted by the Crown following the triumph of William of Orange at the Battle of the Boyne in 1690, and were directed at the Catholic population of Ireland and Britain. For an informed examination of those statutes and the protracted campaign for their repeal, see: Ambrose Macaulay – The Catholic Church and the Campaign for Emancipation in Ireland and England (2016).

38. Macaulay (2016), Chap 1, pp 32-40.

39. (i) Patrick J. Clarke History of a County Down Townland: Drumaroad, (2004) Chaps 2 & 3.

(ii) A cross at Drumnaquoile, erected in 1953 and blessed by the RC Bishop of Down and Connor, Most Rev. Dr Daniel Magean, commemorates the Franciscan missions to East Down in Penal times.

40. Seamas MacGiolla Fhinnein (Anglicised - J.B. MacAleenan) 'Teagasc Criostai Ui Ghripin'; *Unpublished M.A. thesis, Dept of Irish Studies, University of Ulster, Coleraine, 1990.*

41. Seamas O'Casaide The Irish Language in Belfast and County Down (1930).

Also, see a published compilation of learned essays by Dr Maurice Hayes, Dr Roger Blaney, Mr Cathal O'Baoill, Dr Brian S. Turner and Mr Leslie Burnett in '*Language and Cultural Heritage of Down District*', marking a seminar on community relations and shared cultural traditions hosted by Down District Council, Down County Museum, Downpatrick, 27th April, 1991.

42. Among the better historical compilations must be: Feis na nGleann: A Century of Gaelic Culture in the Antrim Glens; Joint Eds – Dr Eamon Phoenix, Padraic O'Cleireachain, Eileen McAuley & Nuala McSparran (2005, Stair Uladh, Belfast). This masterful collection of specialist essays offers a valuable insight to the history of Gaelic speaking, Gaelic traditions, Gaelic games and distinguished Gaelgeoiri in the Glens of Antrim, the neighbouring Route (Ballycastle, Loughgiel & Dunloy) and Rathlin Island.

43. Phoenix (Eds) et al (2005), Chaps 4, 6, 7 & 8. – Dr Phoenix's profile of Francis Joseph Biggar is especially enlightening.

44. William Croft Dickinson   A New History of Scotland (1960); Vol. 1, Chap. ii.

45. C.W.J. Withers   Gaelic in Scotland, 1698-1981: The Geographical History of a Language (1984).

46. J.D. Mackie   A History of Scotland (1964), Chap. 1, pp 16-31.

47. Neil Oliver   A BBC History of Scotland: A look behind the Mist and Myth of Scottish History (2009) Chaps 1 & 2.

48. Mackie (1964); Chap 2, pp 23-35. – John Bannerman   Studies in the History of Dalriada (1974).

49. Mackie (1964); Chap 3, pp 35-62.

50. Ibid.

51. Withers (1984); Chaps 1-3. – MacKinnon (1991); Chaps 2 – 3.

52. Bannerman (1974); Chap 3.

53. George S. Pryde   Scotland from 1603 to the Present Day: A New History of Scotland, (1962) Vol.2, Chaps iv and v.

54. See Tom M. Devine   To the Ends of the Earth: Scotland's Global Diaspora, 1750-2010; (2011, Penguin Books, London), Chapters 1 & 5; - Also, T.M. Devine (2006), Chaps 9 & 11.

55. MacKinnon (1991); Chap 4, pp 54-60.

56. Tom M. Devine   The Scottish Nation 1700-2000 (2006); Chap 11, pp 235-245.

57. MacKinnon (1991); Chap 4, pp 54-60.

58. MacKinnon (1991); Chap 5.

59. (i) Ibid.

60. (i) MacKinnon (1991), Chap 6 p. 75.

   (ii) The late Mr Murdo Macdonald, a native Gaelic speaker from Point, Isle of Lewis, and past pupil of Baybel Primary School, Lewis, in the late 1930s and early '40s, while acknowledging that he had been spared the 'Maide-Crocaidh' regime, nevertheless confirmed reports from older siblings and neighbours who had all been subject to this barbarous instrument of anglicisation. Mr Macdonald (a long-standing personal friend of this author) later proceeded to a career as a Gaelic and English teacher in Aberdeen, as well as occasional writer, and widely viewed as a reliable commentator on 'times past' in the Outer Hebrides. – Discussion with author at Mr Macdonald's (RIP) late residence in Deeside, Aberdeen – 30th October, 2006.

   (iii) Similar reports were communicated to this author in discussions with the late Mr Calum Macleod (November 1993) and Mr Donald John Maciver, also deceased, April 1997. Both gentlemen – one a successful engineer, and the latter a Gaelic teacher, writer and educational planner – were Lewis natives, school children of the 1940s generation and first language Gaelic speakers.

61. MacKinnon (1991); Chap 5, p. 74.

62. J. Ramsay   Letter to the Lord Advocate of Scotland on the State of Education in the Outer Hebrides (1863, Glasgow) – cited in Devine (2006), pp 400-401.

63. HMSO, Census Returns for Scotland, 1841-1971.

64. Withers (1984); Chap 6.

65. Kenneth MacKinnon 'The Scottish Gaelic Speech-Community – Some Social Perspectives' (1985 academic conference paper, details provided in Bibliography) and in Scottish Language, no. 5, 1986.

66. Pryde (1962); Chaps. xiv and xxiii. - Devine (2006); Chaps 18 and 19.

67. MacKinnon (1991), Chaps 5-7. – Also, Wilson McLeod Gaelic in Scotland (2020, Edinburgh, EUP), Chap 3; and Brian Murphy Forgotten Patriot: Douglas Hyde & The Foundations of the Irish Presidency; (2016, Collins Press, Cork); Chap 9.

68. Frank Thompson History of An Comunn Gaidhealach: The First Hundred Years (1992, ACG, Inverness).

69. Thompson (1992), Chaps 2, pp 12-20.

70. (i) Patrons of An Comunn Gaidhealach were: The Duke and Duchess of Sutherland; Marquis of Breadalbane; Marquis of Lorne; Very Rev. Angus Macdonald, RC Bishop of Argyll and the Isles; Professor Mason of Edinburgh; Professor Blackie; Professor MacKinnon; Mr John Mackay, CE, Hereford; and Mr Hector Maclean, Islay.

   (ii) President: Lord Archibald Campbell; Vice-Presidents: - Rev. Dr Stewart, Nether, Lochaber; Magnus Maclean, Glasgow; Provost MacIsaac, Oban; Mr Peter Macleod, Glasgow; Rev. Dr Norman Macleod, Inverness; Rev. Dr Blair, Cambuslang.

   (iii) Executive Council: Professor Campbell Black, Glasgow; Dr Farquhar Mathieson, London; Mr MacNicol, Dalmally; Rev J. MacNeill, Cawdor; Dr N.M. Campbell, Oban; Rev. Alex Duff, Oban; Mr Maitland Malcom, Auchnacraig, Mull; Councillor Munro, Oban; Mr Bailie McCowan, Oban; Cllr Campbell and Mr H.G. Clements, Oban; Mr Donald Mackay, Ledaig; Mr George J. Campbell, Solicitor, Inverness; Mr Malcom MacFarlane, Paisley; Mr John Mackay, Kingston, Glasgow; Mr William Jolly, HMI; Mr Henry Whyte ('Fionn'); Mr Duncan Reid, a Glasgow teacher of Gaelic; Mr T.D. MacDonald, London; Mr J.G. MacKay, Portree, Skye; Mr Alexander MacDonald, HMI, Glasgow; Mr Alexander Carmichael, Edinburgh; Mr Neil Macleod, Edinburgh; Mr George Henderson, Oban; Mr W.A. Cameron, journalist with Oban Times; Mr George Henderson, Oban.

Sources: a/ ACG minutes, foundation meeting, 30th April, 1891. b/ Thompson (1992), Chap 2, p.14.

All told, An Comunn Gaidhealach looked the soul of respectability, in stark contrast to the nationalist elements underpinning and eventually dominating its Irish counterpart, Conradh na Gaeilge.

71. King George V's telegram of 15th September 1912 to An Comunn Gaidhealach on the occasion of their National Mod read: *"The King congratulates the Highland Association upon celebrating the 21st anniversary of its foundation, and upon the work which it has achieved in the cultivation of the Gaelic language, literature and music, and the encouragement of Highlands industries. His Majesty trusts that this week's Mod will be in every way successful"*. – Reprinted in Thompson (1992), p. 36.

72. Devine (2006); Chap. 14, pp 299-328. – Also, Pryde (1962); Chap XXIII

73. Brand (1978); Chap. 11.

74. Ibid.

75. Ibid.

76. Devine (2006); pp 400-401.

77. Thompson (1992); Chap 3.

78. Devine (2006); Chap 23.

79. See John Macleod   When I heard the Bell: The Loss of the Iolaire (2010, Birlinn, Edinburgh).

80. The Scottish National Mod now enjoys Palace patronage as the *"Royal" National Mod*.

81. (i) Interviews (1991 & 1992, Stornoway) between this author and the late Mr Simon Mackenzie.

    (ii) It needs to be understood that though Highlands and Hebridean orientated, in fact the '7/84' theatre group was Glasgow-based. I am grateful to Mr Arthur Cormack for clarifying this fact.

Chapter Two

1921-66: GAELDOM'S STRUGGLE FOR SURVIVAL!

Aims: This chapter aims to trace and analyse the emergence of two Gaelic revivalist movements, each defined by the particular conditions of political developments and culture in Scotland and Northern Ireland. A desperate struggle for survival by Scotland's Gaelic lobbyists was matched by an Irish Gaelic movement forced by circumstances to align itself with political nationalism. The different character of each movement is considered alongside the elements of successful retrenchment that both adopted at the time.

---

1. *Overview:* The 50 years that followed World War 1 saw a partitioned Ireland with a pro-Gaelic Free State and hostile pro-British North, alongside Scotland, where Gaeldom fought to develop its micro role in an urbanised and largely indifferent civic, cultural and political environment. Such a position prevailed until the mid-1960s, by when mildly encouraging breezes started blowing for the Gaels of Scotland. Conversely, in Southern Ireland a pro-Gaelgeoir agenda contrasted starkly with the Northern Ireland Unionist administration's suppression of those remaining pockets of an enfeebled Gaeil Uladh.

To say the least, those were bleak years for the Gaelic language and culture in both nations of the British state, with the result that Gaeldom's very survival looked uncertain. This phase represented the nadir of Gaeldom's fortunes in both Scotland and Northern Ireland. Over that period, the steady decline in native speakers in each of the two countries was accentuated by a failure to make major headway in the vital areas of education, publishing, the arts and broadcasting. Only a new social climate in the 1960s, bolstered by assiduous lobbying in Scotland and a slow willingness by nationalists in Northern Ireland to critically engage with the Unionist state, paved the way for the minimal but positive changes that followed. Kenneth MacKinnon identified those years as a "...l ong dark night" for Scottish Gaeldom, while Liam Andrews's colourful essay about Ulster Gaeldom's suppression under Lord Craigavon's Unionist administration, exclaimed "*... The very dogs in Belfast will bark in Irish*".*(1) At the same time, MacKinnon and Aodan MacPoilin each acknowledged the mid-1960s as marking significant turning points for Scottish and Ulster Gaeldom, with grudging rapprochements occurring in both countries.*(2)

Scotland experienced a substantial drop in Gaelic speakers numbers, with a declining Gaidhealtachd, as shown by linguistic cartographer, Professor C.W.J. Withers.*(3) Although minor openings occurred in education, arts and the media towards the end of the 1950s, nevertheless Scottish Gaels appeared to be an increasingly marginalised and diminished community, restricted to the West Highlands and Hebridean heartlands, and with a future that looked bleak.

Ireland fared little better, in either jurisdiction! Notwithstanding a thesis of decline documented in Reg Hindley's tendentious 1990 study, the reality is that the Free State policy of state-sponsored Gaelicism had manifestly failed to either stem decline in the Gaeltachtai or stimulate large-scale revivalism among the wider body of Southern Irish people.*(4) It took more than just constitutional recognition and grants to Gaelic cultural organisations and native speakers, to halt long-running decline in Ireland's Gaelic language patterns. Northern Ireland's position was especially bleak, with Ulster Gaeldom forced into a political ghetto by unrelenting hostility from successive Unionist administrations at Belfast, headed by Lord Craigavon, J.M. Andrews and Lord Brookeborough, 1921-63.*(5) Afterwards, the inclusive outlook of reforming Premier, Captain Terence O'Neill, ushered in prospects of change, but also encountered grave obstruction from Unionist die-hards.

The Stormont establishment's ethos was explicitly Unionist, anti-Catholic and anti-Irish. Therefore, Ulster Gaelicism, the Gaelic League and Gaelic Athletic Association were of necessity linked to nationalist political opposition to the state. After all, the Gaelic language and culture were denied recognition and outlets in education, arts and media, thereby forcing the alliance with nationalism. In any case, native-speaking Gaels had finally become extinct in Northern Ireland by the late 1940s, leaving Donegal (and Omeath until 1983) as surviving remnants of traditional Ulster Gaeltachtai in contemporary times, a point lamented by the late Belfast Gaelgeoir writer and nua-Gaeltacht co-founder, Aodan MacPoilin.*(6) It says something positive of Mr MacPoilin's Gaelgeoir commitments that he dedicated his entire life towards reviving Gaelic in education, publishing and the arts, often working alone, until finally drawn into the public sphere in semi-official bodies like ULTACH Trust, whose creation and profile marked the cultural reappraisal to which the British government pledged itself – in collaboration with the Dublin government - in the 1985 Anglo-Irish Accord and subsequent Belfast Peace Agreement of 1998.

MacPoilin's life-long labours, and those of other Belfast Gaelgeoir activists like Mr Gearoid O'Cearalainn, Dr Gabrielle Maguire, Dr Gordon McCoy and Mr Liam Andrews, underlined the stern challenges facing Ulster Gaels throughout that bleak era. Their efforts eventually bore fruit in post-1985 years.

2. **_Irish Free State/Republic of Ireland_**: It is significant that despite adverse experiences of Ulster and Scottish Gaels throughout the 50 years from 1921 until 1971, the Gaelic orthodoxy of the infant Irish Free State was greatly advanced, albeit with mixed results. Among key proponents were first education minister and Gaelic League co-founder, Professor Eoin MacNeill; first Dail President and leading statesman, Eamon De Valera; and the Gaelic League's scholarly founding father and first Irish President, Dr Douglas Hyde. All three, along with other nationalists, held strong political commitments to language revival; a cause borne from pre-independence days, which they earnestly followed to give institutions of the new Irish Free State a marked Gaelic identity.

The Oxford Irish historian, Professor Roy Foster, summarised the process:

"Outside the schools, Gaelicizing the new state was a preoccupation – the kind of process typical of many post-colonial states, highly sensitive to the influence of a once-dominant neighbour".*(7)

This comprehensive Gaelic programme was wide-ranging and vigorously applied to an extent that delighted large sections of the population, though irritating Southern Unionists (ie. mainly Protestants), whose numbers in 1922 constituted 11% of the population.*(8) In the first decade after independence,

Irish language teaching was made compulsory in all schools, and later introduced as a mandatory subject in Intermediate and Leaving Certificate exams, established in 1924. A range of Gaelic-learner textbooks and literature were widely disseminated in schools and libraries, with generous help from successive Irish governments. Basic Gaelic fluency became a requirement for entry to university, teaching, broadcasting (established in the late 1940s), An Garda Siochana (police), civil service and local government. Later, University College, Galway (UCG) went further in adopting a Gaelic fluency requirement for all entrants, while scheduling many lectures in the native tongue. Indeed the whole ethos of education was structured to meet a specific goal:

"... to revive the ancient life of Ireland as a Gaelic state, Gaelic in language, and Gaelic and Christian in its ideals".*(9)

A highly influential voice behind the proposed synthesis of Catholicism and Gaelicism in the new Free State was Jesuit cleric, Rev. Professor Timothy Corcoran, of University College, Dublin, whose imposing plans were reflected in a contribution to the journal, Catholic Bulletin:

"The Irish nation is the Gaelic nation; its language and literature is the Gaelic language; its history is the history of the Gael. All other elements have no place in Irish national life, literature and tradition, save as far as they are assimilated into the very substance of Gaelic speech, life and thought".*(10)

Corcoran's vision veered closely to the extreme parameters of militant Gaelicism. Yet it also reflected a desire among elites to construct a Free State where Faith and Fatherland merged to generate an identity counterpoising all that had gone before under British rule, and in stark contrast to James Craig's autonomous British Ulster. With the benefit of hindsight, it may be questioned whether this xenophobic line really served either Irish nationalism or Gaelic causes well in the long run? As is shown later, it minimised common ground between Ireland's two states, while proclaiming a political angle to Gaelicism that both fed Unionist objections and marginalised Ulster Gaelgeoiri.

The initial 1922 Free State constitution – an eminently democratic instrument, nationalist in aspiration, but peppered with allegiances to the British Monarch, as required by the Treaty - had enunciated a generous Gaelgeoir programme. It had enabled the Cumann na nGaedheal government to pursue the kind of Gaelic policies nationalists on all sides expected of an independent Irish government.*(11) Yet it was De Valera's constitution of

1937, Bunreacht na hEireann, that went further in proclaiming the Free State formally bilingual, asserting Gaelic primacy in all public documents, papers and communications. It needs be added that in contrast to Irish Catholicism, the Church of Ireland proved a reluctant partner in state Gaelicisation. Notwithstanding the active presence of its own Irish Guild, with an indefatigable campaigner in Miss Neili Ni Bhriain, who edited the Gaelic Churchman, and its esteemed patron, Dr Douglas Hyde (Gaelic League founder), Church of Ireland authorities and their Irish Times (old Unionist daily) and Trinity College allies, proved outspoken critics of the new policy of compulsory Gaelicisation in education and the civil service. As institutions nourished under British rule and headed by Anglophile elites, it was inevitable that they would not willingly acquiesce in the Gaelic transmogrification of the independent Irish state. Actually, Giltrap's historical account shows the Church of Ireland to have been a house divided, but one containing a vigorous Gaelic lobby insistent on reconciling itself to the new cultural conditions pertaining in the newly-independent Free State.*(12)

In 1926, the Cosgrave government announced the creation of a number of Colaisti Ullmhuchain or Preparatory Training Colleges as an instrument for the furtherance of its pro-Gaelic social and educational policy. The primary aim was to train up qualified and competent Irish language teachers, civil servants and other fluent functionaries. One such college was allocated to the Church of Ireland, under the aegis of its Dublin Archbishop. Accordingly, Colaisti Moibhi came to life at a location in Glasnevin, North Dublin; a development welcomed by the Church's Irish Guild, underlined in a 1927 edition of Gaelic Churchman:

"The preparatory school instituted in Glasnevin for pupils professing our form of the Faith is the hopeful beginning of a work we would fain see carried out in a spirit of whole-heartedness".(13)

By then, Irish was compulsory in all Free State primary schools according to the Education Department, with the added obligation, where possible, to teach other subjects through the medium of Irish-Gaelic.

Elsewhere, the range of Gaelic language and cultural organisation eligible for extensive funding from the Irish state was impressive. They included Conradh na Gaeilge, Gael Linn, Cumann Luthchleas Gael (GAA) and traditional Irish musicians, Comhaltas Ceolteori na hEireann, all of whom were generously supported by successive Dublin governments more or less from the inception of the Irish Free State. Irish arts and drama were also state-sponsored, with additional grants awarded to enable students to spend time in the Galway and Donegal Gaeltachtai to improve Gaelic fluency.

To a degree, in the early years there was some playing to the gallery of Irish voters between William T. Cosgrave's Cumann na nGaedheal and Eamon De Valera's anti-Treaty rival, Fianna Fail, with pro-Gaelic policies that augmented the nascent Irish nationalism.*(14) After all, many had shared a common Gaelgeoir lineage through the Gaelic League and Gaelic Athletic Association in pre-independence days, not to mention comradeship in the GPO at Easter 1916 and thereafter in British prison cells. Among that generation existed a deep reverence for the executed Easter Week leaders, many of whom like Pearse, Plunkett, Casement, MacDonagh, Clarke, Ceannt and MacDiarmada had been ardent Gaelgeoiri in their time.*(15) All those factors – political, psychological and cultural - combined to produce the first real policy consensus in the developing Saorstat Eireann/Irish Free State.

As much as that agenda indulged competing nationalist parties of the Free State, its long term application served to highlight differences between both jurisdictions of a partitioned Ireland. Not only was the Gaelic Catholic South, so beloved of Cosgrave, and, later de Valera, counterpoised by a pro-British, Protestant North headed by Unionist Prime Minister, James Craig (Viscount Craigavon), who, according to one biographer, Patrick Buckland, viewed Gaelicism as an appendix to Sinn Feinism, but it also meant Gaeil Uladh's stalwarts being thrust in a wholly different political environment to that of their Free State brethren.*(16) Given the reality of different conditions in both jurisdictions, Gaelic organisations like Conradh na Gaeilge, plus trade unions and professional bodies, were forced to facilitate autonomous Northern divisions in order to achieve viable progress under existing circumstances.

Actually, Southern Gaelgeoiri operated in a friendly, if austere, society, with abundant good will and public sponsorship. Conversely, Ulster Gaels, projecting an Irish identity – in language, sports and cultural pursuits – were for decades forced to brave multiple obstructions from a Belfast political establishment which begrudged recognition and even periodic protection such as might reasonably have been expected from civic authority in any functional democracy.*(17) Theirs was a hard struggle, and one not always understood either in the South, Scotland or mainland Britain, where stereotypes fuelled by assorted naivete, indifference and plain ignorance predominated to a level barely creditable in an advanced social entity as the British Isles.

Ever since 1922, successive Dublin governments have attempted to stem economic decline and depopulation of the Gaeltachtai by a mixture of socio-economic intervention, provision of educational facilities and payment of a small annual grant, Deontas, to native Gaelic speakers. Regrettably, the onset of partial industrialisation and commercial development meant it was towns and cities like Dublin, Cork, Limerick, Galway and Waterford that offered jobs and progression, not the rural Gaeltachtai anywhere. Indeed local fisheries and farms struggled to maintain an existence, while the younger people deserted in large droves for the towns or in many cases, abroad. Such trends wreaked devastation on the Gaeltachtai, both in collapsing numbers of native speakers and also through an absence of viable infrastructure conducive to survival.

All this happened despite the creation of a Gaeltachtai ministry – with full Cabinet status – in 1956. The latter was charged with halting depopulation and encouraging economic regeneration, particularly outside investment, but in the event the Gaeltachtai was not revived in viable economic form. There were individual initiatives, such as that of the late Fr James MacDwyer, who encouraged a fisheries co-operative in Gleann Cholmcille, Donegal, during the late 1960s and '70s, but despite achieving early success, those efforts proved unable to stem general decline. Even the launch of Radio na nGaeltacht in 1972, while boosting the profile of the language, did little to halt depopulation of native speaking areas. Indeed whether the Government's "rescue" plan actually enhanced the language in the long term, or unwittingly created a self-serving interest lobby within civic structures, is a topic for ongoing debate?

Figures were not encouraging. In 1911, the British Census identified 17.6 per cent of the entire Irish population as Gaelic-speaking at any level.*(18) By 1926, the Free State Census (covering only the 26 counties) put the numbers of native speakers alongside learners and second language speakers at 540,000 (19.3 of the population), itself an optimistic estimate, albeit one that squared with official government policy. The figure had increased to 716,240 (27.2) by the 1961 Census; 789,429 by 1971 (28.3), and 1,018,413 (31.6) by 1981.*(19) A substantial majority of those figures cover second language Gaelic speakers (ie. students, civil servants, teachers, voluntary functionaries, plus learners and voluntary enthusiasts etc), while reliable estimates of first language Gaelic speakers in the Irish Republic tally on 70,000 … at most.

Two other factors provided sobering reflections, both for the early Free State and Conradh na Gaeilge campaigners.

First was an emergent report in 1926 by a commission established to investigate the state of the language. Among other things, the report found that between 1881 and 1925, Gaelic -speaking in the Gaeltachtai, – covering a total of 7 partial and full native-speaking communities across the Free State – was down to 257,000 persons. Of that figure, over 110,000 lived in Gaeltacht districts. Plainly over the period 1881-1925, Gaelic speaking across the Free State had declined by 41%.*(20) Similarly depressing figures had emerged about language teaching in Irish schools, with the main problem identified as a severe scarcity of qualified and Gaelic-fluent teachers for the primary sector, including those schools located in the Gaeltacht areas.*(21) This problem was eventually addressed by the establishment of Colaiste Ullmhuchain (Preparatory Colleges), in which native speakers were trained to become teachers across the range of schools in the Irish Free State/Republic.

Second, by the mid-1920s, there was some evidence of popular enthusiasm for the language starting to wane. Crucially, a sharp decline had occurred in the number of Gaelic League branches from 819 in 1914 to 139 by 1924.*(22) Cultural historian, Terence Brown, attributes the trend to a popular sense of goals attained, with the state now entrusted with the tasks previously sought and prioritised by the Gaelic League in the days of British rule.

"It may be indeed that a cultural movement of the kind that the League had been, like the religion of the dispossessed, really thrives under pressure and that the elevation of the language to semi-official status in the state was a concealed disaster". *(23)

Very significantly, Brown noted the League's Ulster division, Comhaltas Uladh, as enjoying a much greater level of member enthusiasm, while not experiencing branch closures as afflicted their Southern counterparts.*(24)

Brown's unsympathetic treatment of the cultural nationalist leanings of early Cumann na nGaedheal and Fianna Fail ministers appears misplaced (especially where he likens them to cultural racists) *(25), and directed at winning cheers from the British and Ulster Unionist establishments, plus anti-Gaelic so-called 'modernists'. Yet his observation of dogmatic Gaelgeoir revivalists demanding enforcement of linguistic sanctions, which had the long term effect of damaging Gaelic appeal among the school population and wider Irish (Southern) public over decades since 1922, bears some merit. Apart from reflecting on trends in independent Southern Ireland, it also invites sharp introspection by proponents of the Gaelic League on strategy, if not aims.*(26) Such a duty begged of Brian O'Cuiv's scholarly study in 1969, but for whatever reason seems to have been either overlooked or plain blocked.*(27)

As always, comparisons between Gaelic promotions in the Free State/Republic over its first half century and divided Ulster are appropriate, and in this instance very telling. It is to that task that this book addresses its attention.

3. **_Northern Ireland: Unionist Hostility!_**   It has already been shown in Chapter 1 how the dominant Unionist character of Northern Ireland made Gaeldom's prospects look bleak from the outset in 1921.

Hostility towards the Gaelic language and culture by successive Belfast administrations was partly due to the Unionist sense of political and cultural Britishness, something that Gaeldom's historic legacy contradicted. Despite the relative political neutrality of Gaelic League founder, Dr Hyde, and a distinctive school of Gaelic linguists, many of them liberal Ulster Protestants like Joseph Biggar and Margaret Dobbs, the reality was that by 1922 most mainstream Unionists viewed Gaelicism as an appendix to Sinn Fein.*(28) Most tellingly in Unionist eyes, the association of Gaelgeoir lobbyists with political nationalism, as in the South in pre-independence years, made the two synonymous. Hence for the half century of its existence, successive Stormont regimes pitted the stance, resources and authority of the Northern Irish state against Gaeldom. No cognisance was taken of the historic roots of the language, nor its Scottish dimension, with which many Ulster Protestants might have identified. Plainly, the Gaelic language, along with related cultural and sports activities, was treated as subversive, unwelcome in state schools, blacked out of state broadcasting, and denied recognition and funding for its arts and cultural projects. Typical of the attitude was Prime Minister, Lord Craigavon's speech to the Stormont Parliament on 24th March, 1936, defending the termination of the Gaelic teaching grant.

"What use is it in this busy part of the Empire to teach our children the Irish language? What use would it be to them? Is it not leading them along a road which has no practical value? We have not stopped the teaching; we have stopped the grants ...amounting to £1,500 a year ... because we do not see that these boys being taught Irish would be any better citizens of the Union or Empire".*(29)

After Craigavon's death in November 1940, a slightly more tolerant breeze permeated Stormont. The latter permitted occasional variations from the Craigavon rule, such as the creation of a Celtic Studies department in 1952 at Queen's University, Belfast, and similar units at St Mary's and St Joseph's Catholic training colleges, Belfast in the early 1960s. Additionally, there followed a few Gaelic subject broadcasts from BBC Northern Ireland, but those were significant for their scarcity.*(30)

Otherwise, the anti-Gaelic quest of Belfast's Unionist administration throughout most of the Stormont years (1921-72) proved unrelenting. The Ard Scoil Ultach/Ulster Gaelic College, based in Belfast – which trained Irish language teachers – was denied both subsidies and recognition of its certificates by the Stormont Department of Education. The Department was headed in the early years by Lord Londonderry.*(31) Subsequently, the surviving minimal payments available for Gaelic language teaching in Northern Ireland's primary schools were further curbed by Craigavon's government, effectively forcing Gaelic language provision onto voluntary time and usually off-curriculum.*(32) An application from the Catholic Bishops to make Irish-Gaelic a compulsory subject for RC student teachers was refused by the Minister of Education in 1929. Schools, specifically Catholic schools (which were state-assisted but Church-managed), were directly affected by Stormont's anti-Gaelic agenda. State (i.e. Protestant) schools did not offer Gaelic in their curricula, nor was it taught in the Protestant grammar schools in Belfast or elsewhere in Northern Ireland. Predictably, Gaelic games, cultural activities, drama and arts were also banished from the Protestant schools curricula over the same period.

In April 1923, the first Stormont Education Minister, Lord Londonderry, issued a circular, titled: 'Instruction in Irish in Public Elementary Schools in Northern Ireland. *(33) This directive limited the time for teaching the Gaelic language to 90 minutes per week, allowing it as an alternative to History, and restricting its usage as an ordinary subject to pupils of third grade and above. Gaelic could be taught as an extra subject outside school hours to children of third grade and higher, and fees would be paid to qualified teachers who gave at least 40 hours annually of Gaelic classes as an extra subject.*(34) However, in 1926, shortly after Londonderry's departure from Stormont, the teaching of Gaelic as an extra subject was restricted to Grades 5, 6 and 7 (Primary Schools), which effectively limited Gaelic learning to senior classes.*(35) The latter had the consequence of impeding the Gaelic League's efforts at encouraging Catholic schools to teach children Gaelic from the early years onwards.

1926 saw the withdrawal of grants for the teaching of Irish-Gaelic as an extra subject at Grades 3 and 4. Finally, in 1933, all grants for Gaelic primary teaching were withdrawn by the N.I. Ministry of Education. When in February 1927, the Education Minister refused a Comhaltas Uladh delegation's request to teach Gaelic to classes below the third grade, he justified it on the grounds that Gaelic was "... *a dying language ...*".*(36) By 1933, according to estimates of Belfast Gaelgeoir educationalist, Dr Gabrielle Maguire, some 10,500 Northern children were learning Gaelic at primary school, amounting to 14% of Catholic pupils and 5% of the total N.I. primary school population.*(37) Aside from Lord Craigavon's raw outburst to the Stormont Chamber, the ostensible reason for ending the grant was the heavy financial strain on the public purse at a time of national austerity. Yet the Parliamentary Secretary, Mr Robb, also opined that primary school was not an appropriate place for the teaching of Gaelic, and further suggested that many Catholic schools had not availed of the grant.*(38) Taken together, Robb's statement with Craigavon's tirade, exemplified the hostility of Ulster Unionists towards the role of Gaelicism in Northern Ireland.

Significantly, the same hostility permeated higher education. Not only was the opening of a Celtic Studies Department at Queens University, Belfast, delayed until 1952, but also the professorship of Celtic Studies at the same institution had been left empty since the death of Dr John O'Donovan in 1861 until 1945.

Unionist hostility was further pitted against Gaelic games, which were denied public sponsorship and kept off-screen by BBC Northern Ireland and Ulster Television until the late 1960s. So also were ceilidh dancing and Irish music similarly curtailed, while Gaelic arts and drama were marginalised with little or no funding. This treatment of Irish culture by the Stormont establishment – directed then at some 35% of the N.I. population, it needs recalling – furthered the Nationalist alienation, a phenomenon steadily noted by political scientists in the 1960s, such as Richard Rose, based at Strathclyde University.*(39) One consequence was to ensure Ulster Gaeldom's dependence on nationalist political backing, while Gaelic sports and cultural activities and the language were fostered through Catholic schools and voluntary organisations like the Gaelic League and G.A.A.. Indeed as Dr Jennifer Todd noted, Gaelicism defined the cultural life of Northern Ireland's nationalist community throughout the Stormont years and for long afterwards.*(40) Specifically, this meant Gaelic sports clubs, Gaelic language groups, Ceilidh music, Gaelic arts and drama groups predominating in nationalist areas, as well as being actively promoted by the Catholic Church and its schools system. Those schools, along with some Catholic areas of West Belfast, South Down, South Armagh, West Tyrone, South Derry and the Glens of Antrim became cradles of Gaelic culture.*(41)

The Gaelic writers, Scott and McCoy, noted that maintenance of a Gaelic identity came at a hefty price when one remembers minimal resources being available, while also operating in a jurisdiction where the attitudes of civil authority varied between indifference and outright hostility.*(42) This factor has been scarcely acknowledged by many political scientists, journalists and other observers. It is significant that the former Stormont Nationalist Party and its allies were the sole political sponsors of Ulster Gaelgeoiri, assisted by very occasional subventions from the Dublin government and southern leadership of all-Ireland Gaelic organisations. Throughout the 1970s and '80s, even the so-called cross-communal Alliance Party was rarely heard to complain about the political marginalisation of Gaelic culture and the Irish language by the Northern Ireland Office and administration. Nor had this situation changed greatly by the 1980s or '90s. The SDLP (Social Democratic and Labour Party), more recently Sinn Fein, and always the Catholic church were/are principal sponsors for the language and culture to a Northern Ireland Office that since 1985 has dropped the hostility, but only very gradually shown any spirit for recognising the Gaelic identity of the North's nationalist people.

4. ***Gaelic Survival Efforts***: As a result of Stormont hostility, Conradh na Gaeilge and, latterly, sister bodies like Gael Linn, offered some limited help with language instruction and summer scholarships to the Donegal Gaeltacht (by competition at various county feiseann), thereby maintaining a rudimentary Gaelic presence in Northern Catholic

schools.*(43) However, not until the post-1945 expansion of third level education, inclusive of Belfast's new St Joseph's RC teacher training college and the 1950s/60s development of secondary schools, did the language move beyond the few existing Catholic grammar schools where it was taught and examined by a reluctant Northern Ireland Education Ministry. In those conditions, there were limits as to how far voluntary energies of Gaelgeoir teachers and cultural enthusiasts could plug gaps.

Marginalisation of Gaelic and the nationalist people went further than education and broadcasting. The 1949 N.I. Public Health and Local Government Miscellaneous Provisions Act made illegal the use of Gaelic street/road names, even in areas where such innovations were welcomed by local people. Then followed the 1953 Flags and Emblems Act (N.I.), that effectively barred public displays of the Irish tricolour.

Unionist hostility betrayed an ignorance of Gaeldom's place in the Ulster cultural heritage. The Donegal Gaeltacht, an established and well-known entity, was certainly not alone. Indeed there was the prevalence of Gaeltachtai across all nine Ulster counties up until the early 19th century, and the survival of smaller native-speaking communities like Rathlin Island and the Antrim Glens, Sperrin villages in Counties Derry, Tyrone and remote districts of South Down into the early 20th century. But Gaeldom had long impacted on the Celtic cultural renaissance across the province. As early as 1795, a Gaelic magazine, 'Bolg an tSolair', had functioned in Belfast, while the Belfast Harpers Society and Ulster Gaelic Society each provided documented festive events in the native medium.*(44)

Significantly, reliable accounts from reputable historians like O'Snodaigh and O'Fiaich suggest that late 19th century Northern Gaelic revivalism was prevalent among liberal Presbyterians, who constituted the largest educated social group of those times, and were in any case more conscious of the Scottish dimension than later generations of Orange leaders would have wished.*(45) In particular, Dr Phoenix et al pays particular attention to the efforts of Ulster Protestant Gaelgeoiri figures like Margaret Dobbs, Ada McNeill and Joseph Biggar, whose prominence in early Ulster Gaelic League circles was augmented by substantial contributions to the resurrection of Feis na nGleann/Antrim Glens Feis in 1904.*(46) Roger Casement, of the Easter 1916 uprising, was also among those lead figures. It is further significant – as noted by Phoenix – that while some Protestant Gaelgeoiri, like Casement, were converted to the independence cause, others like Dobbs remained lifelong Unionists.*(47) The Glens Feis has continued on an annual basis ever since 1904, attracting an ever-greater profile and media focus over those decades, and is generally recognised by Gaelgeoiri across the four provinces as being among the premier events of its kind.*(48)

Specific traits of native speaking in County Down were noted by Roger Blaney in a specialist paper. Blaney estimated the number of native Gaelic speakers in Down in 1911 at 2,432, of whom over a third, 897 (36.9%), were located in the rural Downpatrick area, while the other block of 725 speakers (29.8%) hailed from rural areas around Newry.*(49) Given that both areas were predominantly Catholic and nationalist, this can hardly have been a surprise. Down Gaels too had their annual cultural gathering, Feis an Duin; which began in 1903, but took off in a big way when run from St Patrick's Gaelic Park at Newcastle (Co. Down) over the next 90 years. Among distinguished figures delivering the famous Feis an Duin oration was Eamon de Valera, then Leader of the Fianna Fail Opposition in Leinster House, in June 1950. Along with former foreign minister and Armagh native, Frank Aitken, De Valera made the trip northwards to Newcastle, where his presence resonated variously with the area's moderate Catholic majority, though less so with the nervous Protestant minority.*(50)

A most unlikely patron of Feis an Dun in the early 1950s was Co. Down's leading land-owner, Mr Gerald Annesley, then in residence at the family seat of Castlewellan Castle. Although scioned from impeccable Anglo-Irish roots with a title and Lords seat, Annesley – never an Anglophile or Unionist – cocked a snoop at the Establishment by, first, running as a Nationalist candidate in the 1951 Westminster election in South Down, and, second, providing generous financial aid to the Gaelic League for the annual Feis an Dun.*(51) Notwithstanding his family's Church of Ireland affinities, Annesley also proved an equally generous benefactor of local Catholic charities, and to his everlasting credit, helped fund construction of the acclaimed R.C. Church of Mary of the Assumption, Newcastle, Co. Down, modelled on the Liverpool RC Cathedral and opened in 1966.*(52)

Returning to the late Victorian/early 20th century position, surprising was the prevalence of local Protestant Unionist establishment figures listed as subscribers to the then-definitory Irish Lanes Dictionary. They included Captain JP Allen of Hollywood (near Belfast), Dr R.S. Lepper of Carnalea and

Rev CK Pooler, Strangford (all Down). Other patrons included former British Prime Minister, Arthur J Balfour, Sir Charles Brett and the Marquis of Bute – all staunch Unionists.*(53) None of those figures would have associated with Home Rule campaigns, let alone the independence cause. Yet in the liberal spirit, then permeating sections of the Anglo-Irish establishment, rescuing the Gaelic Language – in its Irish and Scottish forms – was seen as a noble action unlikely to weaken either the Union or Empire.

5. **_Gaeil Uladh:_** Given the hostile conditions of the Unionist state, generally speaking, most all-Ireland Gaelgeoir organisations moved to facilitate the special circumstances of their Ulster brethren. Such bodies as the Gaelic League, Gaelic Athletic Association, Gaelic dramatists, musicians, educationalists and others developed autonomous Ulster sections, were   briefed to seek the best results in the exceptional conditions of partition.

Conradh na Gaeilge(Gaelic League) was central to the language campaign, both in Ulster and the rest of Ireland. In the years before partition, it had an executive dominated by nationalist-minded Presbyterians and other liberal Protestants, whose contributions to and financial support of the Feis Beal Feirste (Belfast Feis) – the first of which was held in 1900 – and Feis na nGleann (as previously discussed) were both valued and unique. At the same time, the great majority of Ulster rank and file Gaelgeoiri were nationalist Catholics, many of whose parents and forbears had arrived in the city from west of the Bann and also the poorer Connacht counties, semi-starving and desperate for work in the factories, linen mills and shipyards. Those rising Catholics numbers proved the crucial factor in determining the religious-political demography of Belfast before and after partition. Significantly, and despite the best efforts of Conradh na Gaeilge, it was the political influence of Orangeism that impeded popular Gaelicism from growing among working-class Protestants.*(54)

In 1926, Comhaltas Uladh was constituted as Northern division of Conradh na Gaeilge, with the specific aim of directing its lobby and comprehensive manpower towards securing the best deal for the language in the North. Notwithstanding the hostile political climate, Comhaltas Uladh proved a remarkably obdurate body, meeting various challenges. First among those was funding Irish-Gaelic teaching in Northern primary schools.

Comhaltas Uladh raised monies by voluntary effort, while receiving occasional grants from the Dublin government, enough to meet shortfalls caused by Stormont's withdrawal of its minor grant. Comhaltas also sought to popularise Irish learning by youth scholarships and summer colleges in the Donegal and Omeath Gaeltachtai, while organising voluntary language classes, publishing learner materials and associated educational activities. The annual Feiseann occurring across the Ulster counties in Belfast, Antrim Glens, Newcastle, Newry, Derry and Dungannon together acquired substantial popularity over the decades after World War 1, and even more following World War 2. Their significance lay not just as Gaelic cultural and sports events worthy in themselves, but also in the politics of Northern Ireland as popular assemblies of nationalist Ulster people celebrating their Gaelic-Irish identity, and thereby counterpoising the official Anglo-Unionism cultural agenda of Stormont and Westminster. This was politics playing out to the full in Northern Ireland, and enlightening for all with eyes to see from different perspectives!*(55)

There was another dimension to the development of Comhaltas Uladh, notably protection of Ulster's own unique Gaelic traditions against being subsumed by Free State authorities quest for standardising the Galway dialect. Significantly, the latter impetus came from two seemingly disparate sources. One was the Belfast Gaelic League, which was anxious to protect the role and status of its then-struggling Ard Scoil (Gaelic College), plus the growing network of Ulster Feiseann and county Gaelic League committees. Given that there still existed small native-speaking communities in rural Tyrone, Glens of Antrim and the Sperrins long after partition, this caution was soundly rooted. The other came from outside the modern Ulster Province, namely Louth in modern Leinster, where Omeath still harboured a long-rooted Gaeltacht and an infrastructure lasting right up until 1982.*(56) Historically, Louth belonged to Ulster, and it was the Ulster dialect that survived in Omeath, while the entire county of Louth also formed a part of the Roman Catholic Arch-dioceses of Armagh.

As earlier indicated, throughout the decades from the late 1920s to mid-1960s, Comhaltas Uladh continued to lobby successive Stormont Education Ministers for concessions, but to little avail. The Gaelic teaching grant was not restored, nor was Gaelic teaching accommodated in the curriculum, or the Ard Scoil Uladh's Irish language teaching certificates recognised. Some modest success was however achieved in the late 1950s with developing assorted voluntary Gaelgeoir activity in nationalist West Belfast. A range of voluntary language classes took root in the community, attracting several thousand adult learners. Other ancillary groups emerged, such as a Gaelic cycling club with its own magazine, '**Roth**' (Wheel). There was also a Gaelic swimming club, two Catholic prayer groups, 'Cuallacht Mhuire' and 'Realt', both of whom held their meetings in Irish. A Gaelic writers club emerged, 'Cleit'; while a Gaelic drama group also emerged in the mid-1950s, and the Belfast Gaelic Choir performed regularly at the National Welsh Eistedfodd over that period. The long term affiliation of a new Gaelgeoir community augmented the Comhaltas profile, thereby ensuring the Gaelic survival and subsequent resurgence in an urban environment.*(57) This in turn sowed the seeds for the Shaws Road and Gaelscoil initiatives in 1970/80s West Belfast, leading eventually to the modern Gaeltacht Quarter: - which is examined in Chapter 7.

The role of Ard Scoil Ultach (Ulster College), Belfast, assumed significance over this period. It had become principal centre for the propagation of the Ulster Gaelic dialect, and as such complemented the special aims of Comhaltas Uladh in keeping alive that same variant. Previously, the presence of Southern teachers in many Belfast schools, whose tutoring was in the Connacht and Munster dialects, raised fears among some Belfast Gaelgeoiri about future recognition of Ulster's distinctive Gaelic traditions. The Ard Scoil and Comhaltas Uladh ensured that such concerns were addressed. Moreover, the special contribution of Cumann Chluan Ard (Clonard, Lower Falls), along with the support given by Redemptorist priests at the local monastery, augmented the process with vibrant Gaelic learning and developmental programmes across Belfast.*(58)

A prominent figure in Gael Uladh, with direct connections to the Omeath Gaeltacht, was the indefatigable Gaelgeoir priest, An Athair Lorcan O'Muiri (Fr Larry Murray), whose lifetime of service to Faith and Motherland are memorably recalled by Liam Mac An Tsagairt.*(59) O'Muiri's Gaelgeoir agenda of those times embraced straightforward Anglophobia, and sought to replace the English language and so-called "British games" e.g. Soccer, Rugby and Hockey in schools and the community with Gaelic-Irish alternatives. Operating from a sheltered Free State, O'Muiri achieved some success, but as a strategy for mainstream Gaeil Uladh, militant Gaelicism was an unrealistic non-runner. It clashed directly with the culture of the Northern Protestant majority, and was not universally popular among Southern Gaelgeoiri. Many leading Southern schools like Blackrock and Belvedere promoted the Irish language, but that did not stop them from playing Rugby and Soccer and staging Gilbert & Sullivan operas. Yet the Gaelic Athletic Association, with its bar on "foreign" games and members attending those events, was a collaborator in this questionable cultural programme. Ultimately, it proved counter-productive, and plagued the Gaelic image among Irish people for decades, culminating in the 1938 Douglas Hyde episode – an event best forgotten, but covered in Appendix 1.

6. ***Gaeltacht Beal Feirste****:* Maguire's account of Belfast Gaelgeoiri focuses on the 1950s 'Fal' group, which operated at the forefront of so many city Gaelic activities.*(60) 'Fal' essentially constituted a loose collection of Gaelgeoiri, whose zest for the language and culture led them to develop an increasingly comprehensive network of Gaelic organisations covering language, drama, music, poetry, learners, recreation, prayer, economic and, latterly, education. The monthly 'Fal' magazine, 'Dearcadh', acted as a forum for the group, as well as outlet for members frustrations and concerns.*(61) One such concern was the absence of a national Gaelic language press anywhere, South or North, itself lamented fulsomely in the issue of August 1954. Significantly, a remedy for this gap emerged some 25 years on, from the initiative and labours of Belfast Gaelgeoiri, as shown later. Maguire further noted a gathering view among leading figures in the late 1950s of the need for developing a permanent new Gaeltacht, with its own socio-economic infra-structure.

Given the lack of state support, or even recognition, without social and economic self-reliance, Belfast's Gaelic survival looked unlikely.*(62) This view drew inspiration from the success of community leaders at attracting jobs and industry to the Donegal Gaeltacht. Later, in the 1960s and '70s, a special appreciation developed of the endeavours of Donegal priest, Fr James MacDwyer, whose driving of fishing and farming co-operatives in Glen Columcille parish aroused national attention. The creation of a Southern Gaeltachtai ministry in 1956, and later RTE television with its Gaelic output, encouraged a consensus everywhere that each Gaeltacht needed viable economic roots and social institutions to survive.*(63)

Accordingly, attempts were made by 'Fal' activists at applying the Donegal model to Belfast, and adapting it to local conditions. This experience came with little initial success, but despite the early failures, lessons were learned and the dream of building a new Belfast Gaeltacht survived into the 1980s when it finally achieved reality. Yet the pain of early failed experiments was considerable among all those involved. An Irish Credit Union functioned briefly, as did an Irish medium shop. One member sold his business in Belfast and invested sales proceeds in a craft enterprise in the Donegal Gaeltacht. Alas, the whole venture failed. When no rescue package was forthcoming, the project ended in disillusionment. Maguire argued that those setbacks served to strengthen Gaelic obduracy.

"Each achievement, whether long-term or fleeting, each plan which remained on some committee table, each unsuccessful attempt represented, at the least, a contribution to a community's self-assertion of its Irishness. They prevented the ideal of an Irish-speaking nation from slipping into oblivion. Sometimes it was propelled forward. Sometimes it just kept ticking over. It never quite died. What Irish speakers were determined to prove ... was that the Irish language was a viable and satisfying medium of communication in... society."*(64)

In reality, by 1965, only in West Belfast was there any growth in Ulster Gaelgeoir activity. Elsewhere, the picture was one of pessimism about the language's future, both for the surviving Gaeltacht and for Gaelic learners. The Ulster Gaeltachtai had been greatly diminished over the preceding 45 years since partition, and no longer functioned as a living entity within the six counties of Northern Ireland. A combination of political hostility from the Belfast Unionist administration, educational neglect and a chronic local economy in former Gaeltacht areas had caused population defections and boosted English as the language of the new economy. So too was Gaeldom a hostage to political realities in Northern Ireland, where its appeal was limited to the Catholic community and nationalist political sponsorship.

Only in a very limited way did Ulster Gaeldom benefit from a new liberal climate that rendered some improvements for Scottish Gaelic brethren in radio broadcasting, education, publishing and public funding. Actually, the late 1960s and subsequent decades did bring some improvements for Ulster Gaeldom, but less as a result of an enlightened new climate as more the political struggles of nationalists over that same period. More later!

7. _Gaidheil na h-Alba/Scotland's Gaels - in Decline!_ To say that the period 1921-66 marked a grave depression for Scottish Gaels would be an understatement. Notwithstanding encouraging signs emerging in the late 1950s/early '60s, the picture was otherwise a bleak one for both the declining Scottish Gaidhealtachd and its champion, An Comunn Gaidhealach.

After World War 1, the return of surviving soldiers in large numbers to their Hebridean and Highlands homes did not spell any meaningful revival in what was the country's only cradle of native Gaelic speakers. Indeed, quite the opposite occurred. The decline in numbers over the next 45 years put at risk the very survival of the Hebridean and Highlands Gaidhealtachd. Census figures showed native-speaking numbers to have dropped from 136,135 to 95.447 in the period 1931 to 1951, and again to 80,620 by 1961.*(65) The causes were self-evident. A weakened Hebridean economy, along with depressed crofting and fisheries industries – as described comprehensively in separate accounts by Devine and Hunter *(66) – ensured a population haemorrhage to the mainland, England and abroad.*(67) Similar conditions prevailed in the few remaining Gaidhealtachd pockets of the West Highlands over the same period, with the result that by 1960 Highlands native speakers had disappeared from all but a few outlying villages. Only the efforts of determined Gaelic activists kept the language alive in those areas of decline.

Otherwise, the effects were to prove devastating to the already embattled Gaelic language in Scotland. A contracting Gaidhealtachd meant poor morale among remaining dwellers, declining socio-economic infrastructure in the Highlands and Hebrides, reduced educational need, population imbalance and a generally uncertain future for Scottish Gaeldom. The latter was especially applicable, given the increasing pressures for anglicisation in the business and educational worlds as the twentieth century progressed to its second half.

In Scottish education, despite the modest openings acquired through the 1918 Education (Scotland) Act, with its mandatory but ineffective Gaelic clause, Gaelic remained a marginal subject, offered only in areas where demand was compelling. The frank truth is that Gaelic went untaught in most Scottish schools until the 1960s, and even found itself downgraded in the Highlands and Hebrides, where the Gaidhealtachd, though in decline, might have justified some investment in Gaelic teaching. Significantly, there was no

Gaelic medium education anywhere, including the Hebridean Gaidhealtachd, a factor that did little to raise the status of Gaelic among native speakers in Skye, Oban, Lewis, Harris and South/North Uist(s) and the wider population alike. While respected cartographers like Professor Charles Withers demonstrated how anglicisation had mutated the image and character of the Highlands and Islands, there seemed little appetite among public policy makers for effecting anything more than token changes to Scottish education where Gaelic was concerned.*(68)

Gaelic publishing and written works were scarce to the point of non-existent. Until the establishment of a publicly-assisted Gaelic publishing venture in the 1960s, almost the only new books emerging were Presbyterian catechetical tracts and occasional academic texts. The creation of a Gaelic quarterly, Gairm, which ran to some 200 issues and was succeeded by 'Garth and Seal', showed some level of progress. Yet there were virtually no popular books of any kind appearing, nor did a Gaelic language newspaper exist to cater for the Gaidhealtachd communities or second language Gaels. By the early 1950s, so poor was the provision of literature and low its educational recognition, that Scottish Gaeldom appeared set for a slow, if undignified demise, caused by a combination of ignorance, indifference and neglect.*(69)

Nor was there any meaningful Gaelic arts activity, far less public assistance for Gaelic drama or musical projects. Only the Mods (festivals), organised by An Comunn Gaidhealach, provided a mirror of Gaelic cultural life to the wider population, and even the Gaidhealtachd communities themselves. The National Mod (which acquired royal patronage in the early 1960s, largely due to the late Queen Mother's interest) taking place each October at shifting venues around Glasgow, Edinburgh, Perth, Stirling, Inverness, Skye, Oban and Stornoway, marketed Gaeldom's cultural showpiece of the year, and was patronised by royals. Its stature rose from the 1960s onwards, and in time came to attract television coverage and public funding to the point where it now numbers among the major events of Scotland's cultural calendar. Yet such elevated status was some way off in the negative climate of the 1940s and early '50s. In fact many developments were needed over the ensuing period when vital foundation stones were laid in education, arts, drama and politics.

Religion, especially Presbyterianism, provided some solace for Gaelic speakers. Professor Donald Meek in a paper published in 2000 for a joint Irish/Scottish forum at Queens University, Belfast, emphasised the historic part played by the Scottish Society for the Propagation of Christian Knowledge (SSPCK) in publishing Gaelic scriptural literature for dissemination among ordinary Presbyterian worshippers.*(70) This was not so much an exercise in stemming de-gaelicisation as more promoting the Gospel to humbler folk in their native tongue. However, it had the effect of encouraging both main Presbyterian churches, namely the Church of Scotland and the Free Church of Scotland (formed by secession from the Established Church in 1843), plus the Free Presbyterian Church of Scotland (a dissident faction who seceded from the Free Church in 1893), to nurture Gaelic as a principal medium of worship and preaching throughout the Protestant northern Outer Hebrides – including the islands of Lewis, Harris, North Uist, northern Benbecula and St Kilda – along with Skye, Tiree, Oban & the Inner Hebrides. For all effective purposes, as Meek showed, ministers' appointments in Hebridean and West Highlands churches required a working knowledge of Gaelic in those years.*(71)

As for the Scottish Catholic Church, aside from its large Irish immigrant community in Glasgow and Clyde Valley, indigenous communities were few and scattered across Highlands villages, plus the southern Hebridean islands of Barra, South Uist, southern Benbecula, Eriskay and Mingulay. Although the RC Diocese of Argyll and the Isles made a point of assigning Gaelic-speaking clergy to those parishes, in fact the use of Latin for Mass, hymns and other services rather negated Gaelic in church except for preaching sermons.*(72) However, reforms emanating from the Second Vatican Council (1962-65), promulgated by Pope John XIII, and continued by his successor, Paul VI, opened the way for Mass and services in the indigenous tongue, thereby encouraging the use of Gaelic liturgy, prayers and music in Hebridean and Highlands churches.*(73)

Another blow was dealt to the Scottish Gaidhealtachd in 1930 by the final abandonment of St Kilda, the most western and remotest of the Outer Hebrides. Located some 150 miles off-coast in the Atlantic, for centuries St Kilda had existed as a small self-supporting fishing/farming community, entirely Gaelic-speaking, Presbyterian and managing without modern conveniences such as electricity, motor cars and telephones. Unfortunately, as obdurate and proud as the last 130 St Kildans were, their remoteness proved the community's undoing. The customary drive for education and employment sent most young islanders to the Mainland and abroad, while many families came to depend on remittances from loved ones working in Glasgow and elsewhere. Constant loss of population, virtual disintegration of family structures, and the isolation of the dwindling community made it impossible to save.*(74) The final transfer of remaining St Kildans in 1930 had a depressing air of inevitability belying the reality of a remote Gaelic world that simply could not function in the 20ᵗʰ century. Now, the wild-life sanctuary and decaying houses are all that remains of that once-vibrant Gaidhealtachd, whose tragic abandonment wreaked demoralisation on Gaels elsewhere.*(75)

8. **_Scottish Political Developments_**. In stark contrast to Ulster Gaeldom, and indeed all-Ireland's combined Gaelic movement, Scottish Gaeldom remained tactically separate from Scottish nationalism. As the political scientist, Jack Brand, observed, because Scottish Gaels were more marginal in numbers and scope that their Irish counterparts, nationalists thus kept a distance.*(76) Scottish nationalists were reluctant to risk alienating urban voters in the Lowlands towns and cities -on whom the then-struggling Scottish National Party depended – by projecting a peripheral Highlands and Hebridean image that Gaeldom exuded. Although the early SNP leadership of Roland Muir and John MacCormick made positive gestures of support for Gaelic revivalism and its interests, actually the reality was less sanguine. Muir and MacCormick had devised a concept of Scottish identity that transcended regional character in favour of modern nationhood, but within that same vision only a marginal place was accorded to Gaelic.*(77)

Some other nationalists argued against the SNP developing associations with Gaeldom; among them the literary socialist republican, Hugh MacDiarmid, who prioritised a Scots-Lallans renaissance ahead of a Gaelic revival.*(78) MacDiarmid maintained that because Lallans enjoyed a popular Lowlands base, rooted in national heritage, it should be adopted as principal medium of literature and symbol of nationhood. Actually, many Gaels considered this thinking to reflect the ignorance and antipathy prevailing in large sections of Lowland society towards the Gaelic language and culture.*(79)

Dr James Hunter's authoritative history of the Highlands and Hebridean crofters links the latter's struggles to those of Scottish Gaeldom in the late 19ᵗʰ and 20ᵗʰ centuries.*(80) Spoken Gaelic was commonplace in those areas where crofting prevailed; hence its character was defined by Highland Land

League campaigns for social justice. Significantly, this legacy endured for the ensuing hundred years, and remains an indelible feature of folk culture in contemporary Gaeldom – something to which the musical and theatrical

The only nationalist movement to truly embrace Gaelic revivalism was the short-lived 1920s Scots National League. This movement was never large, numbering fewer than 1,000 members in a few branches around Glasgow, Edinburgh, London, Liverpool, Hamilton and Dunfermline. Brand observed:

"...the Scots National League (SNL) was descended from, even if it did not embody, the traditions of Gaelic cultural independence movements. It was clear that a great deal of the inspiration was Irish."(82)

Hunter's comparisons of struggles by Irish and Scottish Highland Land Leagues of the late 19th early 20th centuries, both operating in agrarian economies and confronting exploitative landlords, also bear serious reflection. So also was the exasperation felt by Scotland's nascent nationalists with the track record of the Liberals comparable with similar dissatisfaction felt in Ireland also towards the Liberals and elements of the Irish Parliamentary Party.*(83)

Independence through social and cultural emancipation, inclusive of a revived Gaelic identity, had as far back as the 1880s aroused the interest of John Murdoch, a Scot who had worked in Ireland in earlier decades, but retired to Scotland to edit *The Highlander* from Inverness. Under Murdoch's editorship, the paper actively propagated the twin causes of land reform and Gaelic revivalism, both of which were familiar themes in Ireland of the same period. It is significant that as Irish separatist ideals were encouraged in the 1890s by the infant GAA and Gaelic League, so did Murdoch advocate self-government for a re-Gaelicised Scotland. Later, the emergent Highland Land League – which managed to get MPS elected from some Highlands constituencies – pursued a staunchly pro-Home Rule policy. This situation led Brand to further observe:

"The cultural awakening of the Highlands was to be the basis of a national awakening for Scotland.... It was from this background that the link emerged between the Gaelic cultural movement and demand for self-government."*(84)

John Murdoch, was perhaps the most cerebal forerunner of a brand of Gaelic nationalism later propagated by the Scots National League throughout its short independent existence. Yet two other major figures dominated the SNL during those years. One was a writer and Catholic convert, Ruaraidh Erskine of Marr, second son of Lord Erskine, and whose two passions were Catholic evangelism and Gaelic revivalism. Both passions, Erskine espoused with a vigour that bore tribute to the Jesuits whom he so admired in his spiritual life. The other lead figure was something of a sober political pragmatist, but no less fervent in his commitment; playwright and businessman, William Gillies. Together, Erskine and Gillies made for a formidable duo, who each in their own ways left an indelible mark on the emerging school of Scottish nationalism.

Erskine founded various journals targeted at the Gaelic-speaking and Gaelic -sympathising Scottish intelligentsia. Most prominent of his initiatives was Guth na Bliadhna ('Voice of the Year'), which was published in Gaelic and English, and ran from 1904 until 1925.*(85) His editorials evoked positive images of Gaelic history, institutions and folk culture, while also propagating a distinctive anti-imperial message. Typical of his line was the following commentary:

"The English are making frantic endeavours to enlist the sympathies of the young people of these islands on behalf of their overgrown empire. But the trend of modern politics is, fortunately, in the opposite direction to that in which the friends of 'expansion' would like us to oblige the minds and consciences of our children to proceed".(86)*

Essentially, Erskine's strategy had been adapted from Sinn Fein in Ireland. Hence, though by 1914 he was advocating federal Home Rule, by the end of the Great War he had moved to a position of complete independence, which he maintained for the rest of his life.*(87) Erskine's significance lay in his role as an advocate and publicist for the infant nationalist movement generally and Gaelic revivalism particularly. As was reflected in various speeches and writings (often delivered in hostile conditions), Ruaraidh Erskine saw Scottish Gaeldom's future as inextricably linked to the progress of Scottish self-rule initiatives, which were then at an early stage. Moreover, Erskine shared the faith of Irish counterparts as Eamon De Valera, Eoin MacNeill and Padraig Pearse, none of whom saw a healthy future for the Gaelic tongue under Crown rule. Also, all lamented the negative image of Gaelic, as symbolising a suppressed nation, and believed that any national resurgence should prioritise a revival of positive Gaelic identity. Yet the hard reality for Erskine was that while such ideas had prevailed among Irish nationalists, conversely nothing of the kind was even contemplated in Scotland. He was a long way ahead of his time, even for the likes of nascent Scottish home rulers, and most certainly the cautious Gaelic lobbyists of An Comunn Gaidhealach.

William Gillies proved to be a sound organiser, whose efforts gave the SNL a viable corporate existence. Like Erskine, Gillies had spent time in Ireland, and later served as a full-time organiser with the Highlands Land League. At the time of the Easter Rising (April 1916), Gillies was among the few non-Irish to openly support the rebels, for which he and Erskine were savagely berated by numerous critics within and beyond Scotland. Following Gillies's return to business in London, he worked assiduously to cultivate support for political nationalism along Sinn Fein lines among Gaelic and ex-patriate Highland organisations in London and at home. He lobbied heavily, debated openly, and produced leaflets and promotional materials that were widely disseminated on the Gaelic and Highlands political circuit. Gillies also launched a London Gaelic choir, initially as a front for Scottish and Irish Land League meetings. Happily, that same choir flourishes today, over a century later!

Eventually, in February 1920, Gillies succeeded with getting the first branch of SNL formally launched, and over the next three years other branches emerged, with the result that throughout the early 1920s the SNL voice was heard, albeit with limited appeal. Plainly, it was too radical for post-1918 Scotland, where military culture was heavily ensconced in a population over 35% of whose menfolk had recently borne arms against the Kaiser and his allies. Most importantly, the Gaelic lobbyists of An Comunn Gaidhealach and the various Highlands clubs of Glasgow, Edinburgh and London had, unlike their Irish counterparts, deftly avoided the nationalist political embrace. All such factors left SNL rather marginalised from both the political and cultural mainstream.

It is beyond the scope of this book to evaluate Scottish nationalist parties, other than how they relate to the Gaelic language in Scotland. The Scots National League, as Brand recounts, was significant for its advocacy of Gaelic revivalism, and rather little else.*(88) It wielded only a minor impact on the embryo Scottish nationalist movement, then experiencing its birth pangs, and wider debate on Scotland's future. The League eventually merged with other nationalist groups to form the National Party of Scotland, from which the modern Scottish National Party (SNP) emerged in 1934. In terms of legacy, the SNL's self-styled role as '*Keeper of the Gaelic Conscience*', arguably, ensured a place for Gaelic in future nationalist programmes? Yet even on the latter count, there are those who would argue that it more was the patient lobbying of ACG and its allies down the years which ensured a Gaelic profile in recent times, and especially after the advent of Devolution in 1999. Either way, the organisation of Erskine and Gillies can more definitely be credited with raising Gaelic awareness in a way that shook the Scottish establishment and Lowlands civic society to the point where some concessions were forthcoming.*(89)

9. ***Cultural mini-renaissance***. Notwithstanding the ongoing crisis of declining Gaelic speakers and an ever-contracting Gaidhealtachd, actually the period was not without developments. Those occasional green shoots did not stem regressive trends, but in so far as they aided an embattled culture, slowly Gaelic became a more esteemed and recognisable culture, which boosted morale. In his memoirs, the late Donald Stewart, Scottish Nationalist MP for the Western Isles 1970-87, and previously Provost of Stornoway, alluded to representing an historic culture itself far from defeated. Though not a fluent Gaelic speaker, Stewart felt that defending Gaelic interests went with the job, and as shown later, made an individual effort with a Private Member Gaelic Miscellaneous Provisions Bill in 1981.*(90)

This sense of being part of a great Gaelic nation was the force that drove so many Gaelic minds in politics, literature, drama, broadcasting and education. There was also a desire to maintain the position of Gaelic when Scots-Lallans and even English literature were bidding for the nationalist soul in Scotland, as observed in the mid-1960s by the cerebal D.D. Murison, Editor of the Scottish National Dictionary.*(91) Gaeldom was not without its enemies, even in nationalist political circles, and thus morale was helped by each development.

As far back as 1931, at the 40th anniversary of An Comunn's formation, stock-taking of the state of Scottish Gaelic had generated a very sober atmosphere. That year's Census results showed Scotland's Gaelic-speaking population to have fallen to 136,135 a decrease of 15,024 on the 1921 Censual figure, by some 14.2 per cent. Welsh speakers' numbers had remained steady, while Irish-Gaelic figures had increased by an encouraging 31.2 per cent.*(92)

An Comunn's historian, Frank Thompson, with a mind for the major waves of 1920s emigration, mainly to Canada, commented wryly:

*"**The gloom which descended on 212 West George St, Glasgow {ACG's HQ}, was understandable with the decrease explained away by a loss of the Highland population by emigration furth of Scotland. The percentage decrease in the 'Gaelic' Counties of Sutherland, Ross and Cromarty, Inverness and Argyll was 7.2.**"*(93)

The records show An Comunn having developed a structured organisation over the decades following World War 1. By 1931, it had a full-time Glasgow head office, with active branches across the Highlands and Hebrides, as well as London and Nova Scotia. The Mods had become a recognisable annual event with aristocratic and royal patronage, thus raising the profile. There had also been some movement of Gaelic into education, journalism and the Scottish Academy of Music, with the latter offering occasional scholarships to Gaels. Also, ACG's journal, 'An Gaidheal', was a widely-read and respected voice for Scottish Gaeldom, albeit one that steered away from the political radicalism of its Irish and Welsh counterparts. Yet the numbers had continued to decline, and while much of this could be attributed to both emigration and migration, in the 1930s the view developed among radical elements that the Gaelic lobby needed to inject more fire into its own voce. However, notwithstanding debates and dissenting tendencies, the official line of ACG remained one of co-operation and lobbying of the Councils, broadcasters and Scottish Office.*(94)

From the late 1930s onwards, there had occurred a modest Gaelic renaissance in the literary world, with publication of the celebrated poetry of Sorley Maclean (Somhairle MacGill Eain) and George Caimbeul Hay in various themes, styles and forms. This resurgence further extended to Gaelic drama, leading in 1952 to the launch of a literary journal, Gairm. In 1958, there followed the introduction of Gaelic medium education to select island primary schools in Invernessshire. This was a pilot scheme by Inverness County Council, and was introduced with limited short term goals from an office containing as many 'begrudgers' as enthusiasts.*(95) Yet its eventual success, while increasing demand for expansion, also set the pace for further developments in Hebridean and West Highland schools during later decades.

Gaelic broadcasting also experienced a slow birth, as noted by Kenneth MacKinnon in his account of the post-war Gaelic mini-resurgence.*(96) As far back as 1923 BBC Home Service Radio introduced a three-hour weekly Gaelic slot in broadcasts to Scotland. Though by no means a major breakthrough, yet having a Gaelic voice on air marked a beginning, and was followed by the creation of a Gaelic Department at BBC Scotland in 1935, thereby paving the way for further developments over ensuing decades. The Gaelic writer, Domhnall Iain MacLeoid, regards 1964 as a pivotal year, when Fred MacAulay became Head of Gaelic Broadcasting at the BBC.*(97) Not only was airtime increased, but under MacAulay content was widened to cover Gaelic learning, Gaelic music, arts and commentary, as well as laying plans for further development in Gaelic radio over times ahead. In 1979, came Radio nan Eilean, while 1985 saw the launch of Radio nan Gaidheal, Scotland's first nation-wide Gaelic radio. Making a positive presence on radio and, later, television was essential for Gaels in a battle for proportional parity of esteem, and this point was recognised by ACG in the manner of its own tactical planning.

Elsewhere, the road to professionalisation was increased by grant aid received by An Comunn Gaidhealach from Highlands local authorities. The latter allowed ACG in 1965 to appoint a full-time director and public relations officer, notably the talented LSE graduate, Donald John Mackay. This move enabled the organisation to build professional liaisons and key contacts at all levels of government in Edinburgh and London such as ensured the Gaelic voice was heard in vital areas of policy making. It was also welcomed by many leading Gaelic educationalists and other proponents.*(98) The move also set in motion the momentum for developing a range of specialist lobbying bodies, which has since become a major characteristic of the workings of Scottish Gaeldom.

Educational esteem was further enhanced in 1966 by the initiation – albeit with public aid – of a Gaelic historical dictionary at the University of Glasgow. – Publication still awaited 54 years on! – Aside from the importance of a developed academic profile, this event generated ever more progress in Gaelic literature output over the next few years. It also enhanced the esteem of Gaelic and Celtic Studies as both taught and research subjects within the university, which in turn boosted course recruitment.

Notwithstanding the few recent attainments, by 1966 – the year when Harold Wilson's Labour government won a sweeping electoral majority – Scottish Gaeldom had reached a cross roads, where its future looked uncertain. Native speakers had been reduced to their lowest ever; the Gaidhealtachd was visibly contracting, primarily to the Outer Hebrides; and encroachment by Anglicising forces in education, commerce, the arts and media risked the very future of the traditional Gaidhealtachd and Gaelic revivalism. Despite positive developments, Gaeldom lacked a decent number of influential supporters in local government and the Scottish Office, while ACG's policy of seeking friends in all political parties meant it could rely on no particular party.

It is very telling that in the nationalist literature of the time, there seemed little recognition of the Gaelic language or its place in Scottish cultural life. A prime example would be a commentary on nationalist movements across the British Isles by Scottish radical, Tom Nairn. Though published in 1977, in fact the preponderance of material was clearly based on the evolving SNP and sister movements of the 1960s, as with nationalist parties in Wales, Ireland and the English regions, leading its author to conclude that the break-up of the British state was both inevitable and near.*(99) What is significant is that Nairn virtually ignored the Gaelic roots of Scotland's heritage and identity, and rather like his much-admired favourite, Hugh MacDiarmid, found little about Gaelic that was worthy of inclusion in a modern cultural agenda.*(100) Small wonder that some – though not all – leading Scottish Gaelic figures, like the late Donald John Maciver, steered a distance from political nationalism and the SNP.

Otherwise, in an environment where there was scarce political support, where broadcasting, arts and publishing outlets were few, and where Gaelic medium schooling was in its infancy, there was little for Scottish Gaels to celebrate. So too was there an issue of low esteem that both confounded the best efforts of redoubtable reformers while permeating even the junior ranks of ACG. It was against this decidedly pessimistic background that the skills, knowledge and judgement of Scottish Gaeldom's best brains in An Comunn Gaidhealach were deployed over the next two decades in what amounted to a battle for survival.

As much as ACG came under criticism for political timidity and dependence on establishment favour from radical Gaelic groups throughout the 1950s and '60s, the fact was that ACG had spearheaded the Scottish Gaelic revival for the past 75 years.*(101) ACG was operating in a climate of decline, and yet so many facilities required for effective revival, namely schools agenda/teaching, broadcasting, sponsored arts, music and drama, enlightened local government policies and investment in the Gaelic economy **could only be obtained by the patient lobbying undertaken by An Comunn over the period**. Accordingly, in this author's view, it is appropriate to credit achievements from previous years, plus glimmering hopes for decades lying ahead, to the sturdy efforts of An Comunn Gaidhealach. Indeed An Comunn proved to be the vanguard in a Scottish Gaelic movement that for all its troubles by 1966 had managed to avoid its own oft-predicted demise. However, it remained to be seen whether or not Scottish Gaeldom had a future, and if so in what form? *(102)

FOOTNOTES and REFERENCES

1. (i) MacKinnon (1991); Chaps 6, 8 & 9.

   (ii) Liam Andrews, Chap. 3, (title and narrative), pp 49 -95, in <u>The Irish Language in Northern Ireland</u>, Eds. by Aodain MacPoilin (1997, Belfast).

2. (i) MacKinnon (1991); ibid.

   (ii) Aodain MacPoilin, Chaps 2 and 6, in MacPoilin, Eds., (1997).

3. Charles W.J. Withers   <u>Gaelic Scotland: The Transformation of a Culture Region</u> (1988); The Gaidhealtachd 1698-1981, Figures 1.3 (p 38) , 1.4 (p 39) and 1.5 (p 40).

4. Hindley (1990); Chaps 3 (pp 21 -43) & 11 (pp 179 – 221).

5. See Jonathan Bardon (1992); Chap 11, pp 466-552.

6. MacPoilin, Chap 2, pp 31 – 49, in A. MacPoilin Eds (1997).

7. Foster (1988); Chap. 21, p. 518.

8. See Foster (1988), Chap 21, pp 533-535. By 1981, that figure had dwindled to around 4% as a result of variable factors impacting heavily on Southern Irish Protestants; i.e. inter-marriage with Catholics, relocation to the North and emigration to Britain.

9. Quotes from National Pastoral Conference on Primary Instruction policy document; Meeting at Dublin, 6th January, 1921.

10. Quoted, Terence Brown – <u>Ireland: A Social and Cultural History, 1922-79</u> (1981), p 63.

11. Foster (1988); Chap. 21, pp 516-526.

12. Risteard Giltrap   <u>An Ghaeilge in Eaglais nah Eireann – The Irish Language in the Church of Ireland</u>; (second edition, 2019, Dublin), pp 1908-202.

13. <u>Gaelic Churchman</u> (Journal of Church of Ireland Irish Guild), Ed. June/July 1927.

14. Ibid. – Also, see O'Cuiv, eds. (1969). – Note: In 1926, De Valera headed the relaunch of the old anti-Treaty forces in a new movement, Fianna Fail ('Soldiers of Destiny'). Later, in 1933, following their election defeat, Cumann na nGaedhael merged with the Army Comrades Association and short-lived Centre Party to form Fine Gael ('United Irish') under the leadership of W.T. Cosgrave.

15. In particular, Pearce was an avowed exponent of language revival, evidenced by the foundation of his two Gaelic medium schools in the Dublin area, something he hoped would mushroom in a sovereign Irish state. Macdiarmuid, a teacher and native of County Leitrim, had been a full-time organiser for Conradh na Gaeilge. Both were executed for their part in the 1916 Dublin uprising.

16. Patrick Buckland - James Craig (1980), Chap. 3, pp 50-89.

17. During periodic bouts of Unionist/Nationalist tension in Northern Ireland from 1921 until the 1990s, GAA sports premises and Catholic-owned businesses and social premises were regular targets for Loyalist attacks, sometimes with tacit collusion from elements in the Royal Ulster Constabulary and B Specials. – See Foster (1988), Bardon (1992) and Phoenix (1992).

18. HMSO, Census of Ireland, 1911.

19. Irish Census records 1926-2001, Irish Public Office Records, Dublin.

20. See Report of Irish Government on the condition of An Gaeilge within and beyond An Gaeltachtai (1926).

21. Ibid.

22. Terence Brown Ireland: A Social and Cultural History, 1922-2002 (2004); figures quoted in Chap 2, pp 43-44.

23. Brown (2004); Chap 2, p.44.

24. As what might be best described as conventional wisdom indicates, for the greater time covered by this book, 1918-2018, the passion of Gaelic linguists, cultural and sports campaigners in the Northern Six Counties far exceeded that of Southern counterparts. See for example: Eamon Phoenix et al, Centenary Publication of Feis na nGleann (2005). Doubtless the

repression of a Unionist state helped harness the energy and direction of Northern nationalists, for whom Gaelicism in general amounted to an expression of identity.

25. Brown (2004); pp 50 – 54.

26. Brown (2004); ibid.

27. O'Cuiv (eds.) 1969.

28. This view is confirmed by all major historians and Gaelgeoir writers, including Foster (1988), Brown (2004), Bardon (1992), O'Cuiv (1969), O'Fiaich (1966 & 1969), Phoenix (all) and MacPoilin (1997).

29. Record of Stormont House of Commons debates, 24th March, 1936, HMSO and Public Records Office, Northern Ireland.

30. Not until the late 1960s and 1970s did BBC Northern Ireland or Ulster Television give any kind of proportional coverage to Nationalist culture, Gaelic games, music/drama or other aspects of Irish identity – and the changes were dictated by the Troubles.

31. See McKee (1997); Chap. 2, pp 34-36.

32. Ibid.

33. File Ed 13/1/78; Public Records Office, Northern Ireland.

34. Ibid.

35. This was the same Charles Stewart Henry Vane-Tempest-Stewart, Seventh Marquess of Londonderry, cousin of Winston Churchill, and a scion of one of Britain's grandest and wealthiest aristocratic families, whose fortune had been made in ownership of the Northumberland coal mines. In the 1920s, his family also owned a stately home on the North Antrim Coast, Garron Tower, later to become St MacNissi's College, a Catholic boys grammar school. Londonderry's policy plan, had it been implemented might have ended the Northern Ireland Catholic Schools sector. Yet in 1926, Lord Londonderry – who privately despised Unionist tribal politics as narrowly parochial – abandoned Stormont for Westminster, specifically his hereditary seat in the House of Lords. Later, he developed his passion for the RAF, and was appointed Air Minister in Ramsay MacDonald's

National Government, 1931-35. Thereafter, Londonderry, an inveterate anti-Communist, admirer of German culture and friend of German revival, argued passionately for an appeasement policy towards Hitler; a view that squared with a large section of the British aristocracy of the 1930s. In 1936, Londonderry received at his Mount Stewart (North Down) stately residence the-then German Ambassador to London, Joachim Von Ribbentrop – who was executed for War Crimes at Nuremburg in October 1946. Londonderry, though not a collaborator, was nevertheless damaged by his pre-war associations with the Nazis, and died in February 1949, a lonely and rather discredited figure. – See Ian Kershaw – <u>Making Friends with Hitler: Lord Londonderry and Britain's Road to War</u> (Penguin 1990).

36. File Ed. 13/1/516; Public Records Office, Northern Ireland.

37. Gabrielle Maguire <u>Our Own Language; An Irish Initiative;</u> (1990) Chap 2.

38. File Ed. 13/1/878; Public Records Office, NI..

39. Richard Rose <u>Northern Ireland: A time of Choice</u> (Macmillan, 1976).

40. Jennifer Todd 'Nationalist Political Culture in Northern Ireland' – Paper presented to the UK Political Studies Association Annual Conference, 12-14th April, 1988, Plymouth Polytechnic.

41. Todd PSA Paper (1988), plus McKee (1997), Chaps 2 & 3.

42. Gordon McCoy and Maolcholaim Scott, eds., Aithne na nGael/Gaelic Identities(2000) Chap 1, pp 8-11.

43. Gabrielle Maguire <u>Our Own Language: An Irish Initiative</u> (1991), Chap 3, pp 34-49.

44. O'Snodaigh (1973), Chap 3 ; also Bardon (1992), Chap 9. Phoenix's essay on Belfast philanthropist and Gaelgeoir, Francis Joseph Biggar, (2005, Phoenix et al, Eds), Chap 8, pp 65 – 78, is also very instructive.

45. Tomas O'Fiaich 'The Language and Political History'; in Brian O'Cuiv (Ed.) <u>A View of the Irish Language</u> (1969); and O'Snodaigh (1973).

46. See Phoenix and O'Cleireachain et al (Eds), Feis na nGleann (2005).

47. Ibid.

48. Ibid.

49.

    (i) 'The Irish Language in County Down since 1800' – Dr Roger Blaney – Report to The Irish Committee Seminar/Coiste na Gaeilge; Tables 2 & 3, Proceedings Report, Downpatrick, 27th April, 1991. Report kindly supplied by Downpatrick Museum's now-retired Curator, Dr Brian S. Turner.

    (ii) Another important and scholarly source is Ciaran O'Duibhin's impressively-researched pamphlet - 'Irish in County Down since 1750' (Cumann Gaelach Leath Chathail, 1991).

50. See report, <u>Mourne Observer</u>, 5th June 1950.

51. See <u>Mourne Observer</u> election reports of South Down count, October 1951.

52. Private information received from local Church sources.

53. Proceedings, Irish Committee Seminar (1991), pp 13 & 14.

54. MacPoilin eds. (1997); see Chap 1 by editor himself, and Chap 2 by Liam Andrews.

55. Reference – The Feiseann competitions and assemblies for Gaelic language, music, Ceilidh dancing, poetry, recitation and History. While open to schools and competitors of all persuasions, in practice it was Catholic schools and candidates who provided the vast majority of participants. – This author holds fond personal memories of winning numerous awards for Irish History at the Feis an Duin (Down) and Feis na nGleann (Antrim) in the 1960s and '70s.

56. For the sake of clarification, this author refers to the Ulster Province only in its historical framework to include the six Northern counties of Derry, Antrim, Down, Armagh, Fermanagh and Tyrone, along with three Southern counties of Donegal, Monaghan and Cavan. Attempts by Unionist and English politicians and cultural policymakers to redefine Ulster as the Six Counties statelet, created in 1921, complete with Unionist flags and emblems, are not recognised by this author.

57. Maguire (1991) – Chap 2, pp 30-33.

58. Ibid.

59. Liam Mac An Tsagairt /Father Larry Murray (1983). Pamphlet has long gone out of print, and is not readily available. This author is most grateful to Dr Gordon McCoy for kindly making a copy available.

60. Maguire (1991); Chap 2, pp 29-33.

61. *Dearcadh* – Journal of the Fal Group in 1950s Belfast; author was granted privileged access by sources in Conradh na Gaeilge.

62. See MacPoilin (1997) Eds. – by author/ed. Chaps 2 (pp 31-49) and Chap 6 (pp 171-191).

63. Ibid. – It needs adding that the late Aodan MacPoilin was a lead figure in the development of the West Belfast nua-Gaeltacht at Shaws Road.

64. Maguire (1991); pp 31 & 32.

65. UK Census figures, HMSO Scotland, 1931-61; also cited in V. McKee, Contemporary Politics (1995), p. 94.

66.
    (i) James Hunter (1987), Chap 11, pp 198-207

    (ii) Tom Devine (2006), Chaps 17 & 18.

67.
See (i) Ken MacKinnon (1991), Chaps 4, 5 & 6.

    (ii) Withers (1984), Chaps 7 & 8.

68. Charles W.J. Withers   Gaelic Scotland: The Transformation of a Cultural Region; (1988) Chap 7, pp 402 – 407 and pp 412- 417.

69. Mackinnon (1991); Chaps 4, 5 & 6; also McKee (1997), Chaps 2 & 3.

70. Donald E. Meek 'God and Gaelic: The Highlands Churches and Gaelic Cultural Identity' in Aithne na nGael/Gaelic Identities, eds. G. McCoy and M. Scott; Chap 3, pp 28-48.

71. Ibid.

72.

    (i) Meek (2000), pp 42-43.

    (ii) Sample of reports, 1955-65, <u>Scottish Catholic Observer</u>.

73. Ibid. Also, the author's personal position as an active lay Catholic ensured access to Islands clergy and numerous Church documents.

74. See MacKinnon (1991); Chap 4.

75. See Withers (1988); Chap 6, pp 351- 389.

76. Brand (1978); Chap 11, pp 182 – 190.

77. Ibid.

78. Ibid.

79. Discussions over 1993 with the late Messers' Donald John Maciver of Lewis and Comhairle nan Eilean Siar and Simon Mackenzie of Harris and 7/84 Gaelic acting and musical Group.

80. Hunter (1987); Chaps 11 & 12. Also, see Withers (1988); Chaps 6 & 7.

81. The untimely death in 2008 of Harris-born Gael, Simon Mackenzie, himself a personal friend of this author, robbed Scotland of one of its most talented Gaelic actors, dramatists and singers – widely admired and genuinely mourned across the Scottish nation and abroad.

82. Brand (1978); Chap 11, pp 182-183.

83.

    (i) R.E. Foster (1988); Chap 16, pp 373-400.

    (ii) Tom Devine (2006); Chaps 18 & 19.

84. Brand (1978); Chap 11, p 183.

85. 'Guth na Bliadhna' – all editions, 1904-20. Seen by author.

86. 'Guth na Bliadhna' – Vol. 2, No. 1, p. 28.

87. See a sample of issues, 'Guth na Bliadhna', 1916-20.

88. Brand (1978); Chap 12, pp 182-188.

89.
    (i) The contributions of Torbid Cambuel, Robert Dunbar and Donald E. Meek to the McCoy & Scott eds publication (2000) suggest that they would each challenge any such claims from SNL admirers.

    (ii) The late Donald John Maciver of Stornoway, Isle of Lewis, a senior and highly respected Gaelic administrator, writer and educationalist, clarified to this author his personal view that nationalist political lobbying had brought few benefits to the Gaelic renaissance. Discussions – Stornoway, August 1993, and Inverness, October 1997.

90. Donald Stewart   A Scot at Westminster (1994), Chaps 19 and 21.

91. D.D. Murison   'Nationalism as expressed in Scottish Literature', Government and Nationalism in Scotland: An Enquiry by Members of the University of Edinburgh, Ed. by J.N. Wolfe (1969); Chap 12, pp 187-199.

92. See results, Census tallies for Scotland, 1921, 1931, 1951, 1961 – HMSO, Edinburgh and London.

93. Frank Thompson (1992) Centenary History of An Comunn Gaidhealach; Chap 3, p 61.

94. Thompson (1992), Chaps 3 & 4.

95. Confidential discussions with ACG officials, plus two leading Gaelic educationalists, whom the author was requested not to name.

96. MacKinnon (1991); Chap 7, pp 98-108.

97. Domhnall Iain MacLeoid   Dualchas an Aghaidh nan Creag – The Gaelic Revival 1890-2020 (2011, Inverness), p. 52.

98. Among lead Gaelic figures openly expressing relief at increasing professionalisation were Donald John Maciver, Murdo Macdonald and Dolina Macleod, all of Lewis, while similar sentiments were echoed by the late Simon Mackenzie of Harris.

99. Tom Nairn   The Break-Up of Britain (1977); see Chaps 1 & 3.

100. Nairn (1977); Chap 9, pp 329 – 363.

101. Given the diversity of opinion among activists and observers, it is but fair to intimate that this author's positive sentiments about the role of An Comunn Gaidhealach are not universally shared by everyone connected to the Scottish Gaelic world.

102. This author is most indebted to Professor Wilson McLeod of Gaelic/Celtic Studies Dept, University of Edinburgh, for time and trouble taken to clarify a multitude of points arising in preparation of the first two chapters of this book. Professor McLeod's vast scholarly expertise is matched only by the gentleman's personal kindness.

Chapter Three

1965-86: A MODEST DAWN BECKONS!

Aims: This chapter will be concerned with cataloguing and analysing the changing political climate that so favoured the skilled lobbyist strategy adopted by An Comunn Gaidhealach under the pivotal leadership of the late Donald John MacKay. The progress of Scottish Gaeldom over the 1960s, '70s and '80s is highlighted, along with results in broadcasting, education, arts and economic investment. So too was the hand of central government examined for its effects on overall Gaelic development. By contrast, Gaelic Ulster was rather less endowed with sympathetic patrons or assistance from government in either Belfast or London. The struggles of Gaelic spokesmen and their political allies, not to mention nationalist disaffection with the standing of government, will be the principal stuff of this evaluation. Also crucial shall be an analysis of the search for long-term solutions to the civil conflict, and growing dialogue between the governments of London and Dublin, culminating in the 1985 Anglo-Irish Accord. The latter's enhancing effects on the condition of Gaeil Uladh will be considered against the background of political nationalism's ascendancy.

1. **_Overview:_** Until now, whatever differences prevailed, Scottish and Irish Gaeldom were affected by a depressing spiral downwards in each of their fortunes. A combination of falling Gaelic-speaker numbers, contraction of the traditional Ulster Gaeltachtai and the Scottish Gaidhealtachd, failed efforts at reviving economic and social infra-structures, was matched by limited success with schools, broadcasters and the arts and literary worlds of Belfast and Edinburgh, plus a scarcity of effective political patrons. All those factors combined to devastate Gaeldom's language and culture in both places, with little salvation in sight.

Yet with the benefit of hindsight, it is possible to see the mid-1960s as something of a turning point in Gaeldom's decline. From then onwards, green shoots began to emerge. Though tenuous, especially in Northern Ireland, those developments were sufficient to augur positively for the survival, if not recovery of the Gaelic language in both countries.

The key to survival was Gaeldom's incorporation, however weak or conditional, within the civic cultures, and especially educational systems, of each country. In the latter process, Gaelic made some headway as a language of broadcasting, cultural projection and specialist literature. The Gaelic survival and its application to education and the wider cultural arena was predicated on an insistence upon public, specifically government recognition of its place, with the assumption of public assistance to follow. In that respect, the different images of Gaelic in Scotland and Northern Ireland, along with their political sponsors, proved to be of prime importance in determining the attitudes of public policy makers, and ultimately UK government. This helped shape the fortunes of Gaeldom differently in the two countries.

The relatively apolitical An Comunn Gaidhealach, with its sister bodies in Scotland, represented the principal face and voice of Scottish Gaeldom. With its orthodox political direction and distance from radical nationalists, ACG's dominant Presbyterian character, aided by a patriotic pro-British record of support during both world wars, along with abundant aristocratic, establishment and even royal patrons, ensured a positive response from successive British governments. This in turn meant appropriate benefits following in state funding, openings in broadcasting and some educational favour over the ensuing decades. A non-threatening political image was just one factor, albeit a significant one. Other gains from the period resulted from skilful lobbying, information-sharing, networking among all parties and government, positive profiling in media and consummate projection of cultural events like the Royal National Mod to the widest audiences in Scotland and Westminster.

Conversely, the fiercely anti-Gaelic prejudices of Northern Ireland's Unionist establishment in Belfast, meant Gaeil Uladh (ie. Gaelic Ulster) being marginalised and forced into continuing reliance on Nationalist political sponsorship, along with periodic moral support from Dublin governments. Either way, Gaeil Uladh's appeal was limited to Northern nationalists, their schools, youth groups and Catholic community organisations, with public funding severely curbed. Yet, Bob Dillon's 1965 pop song rang true: "**..Your**

old road is rapidly changin' ...The times, they are a changing"! – Nowhere was this shown to be more true than Northern Ireland. The 1960s and '70s proved to be cataclysmic in many respects; political, social and cultural. Hence with existing power structures under direct challenge by, first, civil rights campaigners and, later, republican paramilitaries, it was inevitable that the entire Nationalist agenda would be open for change, including the cultural. Given the prominence of the Gaelic language and culture in Nationalist affairs and identity, its profile was elevated in the direction of inclusivity and reform, with the eventual result of boosting Gaeldom's general esteem in Ulster civic society.

This chapter poses two questions, each of prime relevance to developments occurring over the period. Neither achieves conclusive answers, but each merits consideration against the general backgrounds for Scottish and Ulster Gaeldom set against developments elsewhere.

First, how far was the Scottish Gaelic mini-renaissance a product of the natural evolution of events stretching back to the 1930s Gaelic literary revival? The same question begs of the 1950s Gaelgeoir mini-resurgence in Belfast and elsewhere throughout Northern Ireland? Second, to what degree was that mini-renaissance in both countries fashioned by the new liberal climate of the late 1960s? Was Gaeldom a beneficiary of the same international tide that ushered in civil rights for American blacks, scorned the US bombing of Laos, Cambodia and Hanoi, and encouraged a humanitarian approach to the tragic quest of Nigeria's Ibo peoples' vain struggle for an independent Biafra?*(1) The late and highly respected Scottish social historian, Professor Arthur Marwick, saw a definite trend in 1960s challenges to the established order taking place across the world, and especially in former imperial nations where there existed disaffected cultural, ethnic and religious minorities.*(2) That being so, Gaeldom in Scotland and Northern Ireland can hardly have been exempted from this phenomenon. Another eminent scholar of post-war Britain, Professor Peter Hennessy, argued the relaxation of restrictions on cultural minorities to have been an inevitable corollary of a new liberal climate that permeated Britain as much as other nations.*(3) Professor Tom Devine, concurs with Marwick and Hennessy, seeing attainments by the Scottish Gaelic lobby, along with radicalising traits among Gaelic groups in Belfast and Glasgow/Edinburgh to have flowed naturally with developments trends elsewhere in both countries.*(4) The prevailing consensus was therefore one of inevitability.

Addressing those questions and their underlying theme requires an in-depth evaluation of cultural influences underpinning Sixties social developments. In particular, connections between small and minority cultures and Schumacher's "**...small is beautiful...**" theory merits assessment, as does the link between political and cultural rights within the British state. In essence, such an inquiry falls more properly within the province of sociologists... which this author is not! However, empirically-guided observations from the contemporary historian ..which he tries to be.. may go some way towards addressing the question?

With the benefit of hindsight, it may be said that the late 1960s liberal climate encouraged a more generous view of Gaeldom's claims to a proportional share of educational, arts and cultural resources in both Scotland and Northern Ireland. Modest advances achieved in Scotland may be traced to the adroit lobbying, bridge-building and winning of friends by An Comunn Gaidhealach, for which, as shown in Chapter 2, developments were already apace by1964. Further attainments throughout the 20 year period from 1966 onwards followed on from those earlier seeds. In Northern Ireland, it may be safely noted that in the mid-1960s a thawing process was underway by the Unionist establishment towards the culture, if not language of Gaeldom. There can be little doubt that the reforming Unionist Prime Minister, Captain Terence O'Neill, with his policy of inclusiveness proved beneficial towards Gaelic interests ... at least in the short term. For example, among the modest successes of Ulster Gaels experienced the beginnings of inroads to education and broadcasting.

Actually, the impact and consequences of O'Neill's policies have been debated by historians, and indeed it is not universally accepted that he was accommodating nationalism, as more acting to kill it off by kindness.*(5) Furthermore, as shown by Bernard Conlon's thesis on American influence over Northern Ireland's civil rights movement, assertions of political liberties translated into demands for parity of esteem for oppressed cultures.*(6) This demand was initially heard during the late 1960s, but had to await the 1985 Anglo-Irish Accord before acquiring official status. Meanwhile, the Ulster Gaelic lobby was left striving for whatever concessions could be extracted from a reluctant Stormont administration and — following Direct Rule's introduction after March 1972 — from the Northern Ireland Office.

An examination of the experiences of both Gaelic lobbies shows the apolitical Scottish Gaels to have gained most from a British state that did not feel threatened by its political sponsors. Therein lay the greatest difference between the two schools of Gaeldom, something imposed by the events of history, and which defined their different directions.

2. **Scotland**: As earlier indicated, advances made by the combined forces of Scottish Gaeldom over the years, 1966-1986, occurred on several fronts. An Comunn Gaidhealach, as the principal lobbyist group and with a professional director in place by 1965, had developed an expertise in liaisons with a variety of public bodies ranging from the Scottish Office, MPs of all parties and local councils to the BBC, universities, publishers and arts organisations. The overall result was to generate a positive climate of opinion towards the Gaelic language and culture among assorted sections of the Scottish political and public sector establishment, who had previously displayed variable hostility and indifference. Thanks to the increasing media and arts profile, Gaelic cultural projections, like the now-famous and televised National Mod, drew popular audiences across the whole of Scotland, which in turn enhanced the Gaelic image and ushered other benefits to follow.

The new climate so long in coming, was evident by the mid-1960s. Building upon popular expressions of Gaelic culture through the Mod and Gaelic music of figures like the late Lewis singer, Calum Kennedy, its other advances extended to the worlds of publishing, the environment and local government.*(7) Significantly, it was assisted by a sympathetic, if also cautious Scottish Office, whose pro-Gaelic policy was continued under successive Labour and Conservative governments of the 1960s /70s. Doubtless the political neutrality of An Comunn Gaidhealach, along with its insistence on maintaining a strict distance from all party alignments, boosted its credibility as a sectional lobbyist group.

As a result, by 1970, and even more ten years later, all four major Scottish parties – Labour, Unionists/Conservatives*(8), Liberals and Scottish Nationalists – had each adopted positive policies towards Gaelic's place in Scottish society. This domestic 'consensus' was to prove an invaluable aid to subsequent ACG campaigns for Scottish Office funding of Gaelic Medium Education in the Highlands and Hebridean Gaidhealtachd. So too did it consolidate ACG in its representations and established its pole position in dealings with broadcasters, churches, schools and local councils for greater priority for Gaelic in their respective areas. Given the steady decline in Gaelic-speaking numbers, recorded by each passing Census, ACG had to tread a delicate course.*(9) Their major strength lay with the appeal of Gaelic cultural and heritage bonds, not its electoral capacity. Indeed such efforts might have proved less productive had Gaelic been aligned with political nationalism, as happened in Northern Ireland. Yet the absence of a campaigning dimension also left Scottish Gaeldom quite dependent on Scottish Office good will, along with the positive support of various bodies composing Scotland's press, local government, churches and civic society.

As will be shown later, by joining forces with the Scottish political, educational and cultural establishment, An Comunn Gaidhealach risked losing some of its erstwhile independence, although in-house historian, Frank Thompson, questions whether ACG was ever truly detached from the elite patrons heading the organisation.*(10) Equally, Tom Devine noted the radical tactics of late 1960s nationalist-Gaelic group, Siol Nan Gaidheal (Seed of the Gael), marching with kilts and bagpipes and utilising Gaelic to the full.*(11)To some degree, the radical tendencies, while ephemeral and short lived, nevertheless showed up signs of irritation within Gaelic ranks at the price being paid for progress. Those activists looked admiringly towards the Welsh language Society and their sisters/brothers across the Sea of Moyle in Gaeil Uladh for inspiring profiles of effective Celtic radicalism.

This transition pertains to what political scientist, Wynn Grant – writing on pressure groups – defines as the "insider" versus "outsider" group scenario.*(12) Grant argues that while groups benefit from public sector favour through policy gains, they also lose their detachment, and become tied to the very establishment on whose patronage their purpose depends. Developments of the kind can and often do lead to internal rifts, with ensuing charges of "compromisers" and "betrayal" being heard among dissenters, in turn generating secessions and rival group formations. While An Comunn Gaidhealach was spared the more extreme experiences, nevertheless its edge got blunted, thereby leading to occasional frictions and formation of a short-lived rival, Comunn na Canain Albanaich, a 1970/80s militant campaigning body modelled on the Welsh Language Society. Yet, notwithstanding the alternate strategies of radicalism versus co-operation, an examination of Scottish Gaeldom's advances over the period 1966-86 shows impressive progress. Very significantly, with the LSE-trained Donald

John Mackay in post as ACG Director by 1965, the whole mode of operations assumed a welcome level of professionalism that ushered in several major achievements whose durability was to remain Mackay's lasting memorial.*(13)

3. **_Broadcasting_** marked one key area of development from that era. With a Gaelic unit operating at BBC Scotland since 1935, modest foundations had facilitated Gaelic music, learners, sport and current affairs programmes. Yet – as recounted in Chapter 2 – it was Fred MacAulay's emergence in 1964 as head of Gaelic Broadcasting at BBC Scotland that ushered a major breakthrough for Scottish Gaeldom. The expansion of content covering drama, religious and schools' broadcasts, Shinty, poetry, arts and music was augmented by an increasing quota of hours that boosted the Gaelic profile. Most importantly, it was MacAulay who put in place the foundations for what in 1979 became Radio nan Eilean; broadcasting to the West Highlands and Hebrides. This was followed in 1985 by Radio nan Gaidheal, Scotland's first nation-wide Gaelic broadcasting station, operating from studios in Stornoway, Inverness, Skye and Glasgow.*(14) Another important development was the long-running Gaelic learners radio series, 'Can Seo', commenced in 1979 by BBC Scotland in conjunction with An Comunn Gaidhealach, from which learner tapes were marketed throughout Scotland and beyond. The radio initiative was aimed at servicing the needs of each Gaelic community. It also squared with a positive new climate among broadcasters, favouring provision for minority cultures. As a result of the successful learning programme, a Gaelic learners association was established.

Thereafter the push for An Comunn was to break into the expanding world of television. By 1979, the two IBA companies operating in the Highlands and Islands, STV and Grampian Television, raised their profiles by opening studios in Stornoway. From there followed a progressive level of Gaelic broadcasts, not the least of them being the highly popular Calum Kennedy's 1980s musical series on Grampian TV from Aberdeen studios, plus ever-increasing coverage of the National Mod on all channels. Eventually, in 1992, the first Gaelic soap opera appeared, 'Machair', starring late Gaelic actor/singer, Simon Mackenzie, from Harris. Meanwhile, as recounted by Thomson and MacLeoid, expanded Gaelic broadcasting proved conducive to sustaining hope and morale among Scottish Gaels as they struggled to cope with falling numbers and minimal economic infra-structures in the Gaidhealtachd.*(15)

The emergence of the Hebridean Gaelic Rock group, 'Runrig' (founded 1973) was also to have enormous significance for Gaelic cultural esteem given the band's success in the 1980s and '90s on the national and international stage. This Gaelic musical renaissance generated other Gaelic groups like 'Na h-Oganaich' and 'The Lochies', while introducing to a nationwide audience the consummate musical talents of Donnie 'Large' Macdonald, not to mention Skye-based ballad singer, Arthur Cormack, and his occasional Lewis-collaborator, Eilidh Mackenzie. Also, the adoption of lead 'Runrig' figure, Donnie Macleod, as Labour parliamentary candidate to challenge Liberal Democrat, Charles Kennedy, in Skye and Cromarty in the Westminster election of April 1992 (a contest that Kennedy won!), added further dimension to the band's profile. Overall, Scotland's Gaelic cultural revival was being driven by assorted young talent, itself well geared towards utilising technology and the broadcasting stage to a degree not previously attempted by earlier generations.

4. *Gaelic Publishing* achieved substantial growth over the period. In 1952, a new Gaelic magazine, 'Gairm', emerged, edited by Glasgow academic, Derek Thompson, and Finlay J. MacDonald; and this magazine was to appear quarterly over the next fifty years. According to MacLeoid:

"...Gairm... **proved to be the seedbed of a new Gaelic literary revival, enabling a succession of writers to develop their skills and feeding the growing demand for modern reading material in Gaelic**".*(16)

Other developments followed. In 1968, the Wilson government redeemed a pledge to provide annual subsidies for Gaelic books through the creation of the Gaelic Books Council, thereby facilitating publication of 37 new Gaelic titles in the first year. This compared with a previous national average of 3 new Gaelic titles per year. To Kenneth MacKinnon, this multiplicity of output by Gaelic authors was evidence of how the benign British state could prove a force for good when encouraging Gaelic talent.*(17) In

1970, the programme of state-aided Gaelic publishing took another step, with the launching of the Highlands Book Club/Club Leabhar. From then until 1980, Club Leabhar produced seven Gaelic – English bilingual titles each year. Its successor Gaelic publisher, Acair, has a head office in Stornoway, itself a propitious location that speaks for itself. Along with the 1970s reforms that launched a Gaelic local authority in Stornoway, the Hebridean concentration has quite elevated the town's place as principal administrative centre of Scotland's Gaidhealtachd.

Perhaps it is useful to remember that in the post-1918 dawn of Gaelic literary renaissance, distinguished figures like Sorley Maclean and Iain Crichton Smith … to name but a few … by the merits of their respective works had drawn attention to the paucity of publishing outlets for Gaelic literary talent. To many imaginative figures within and beyond the Gaelic world, this gap highlighted the poverty of Scottish Gaeldom in that talent was being starved of recognition. Moreover, it meant the opportunities for coming generations of Gaelic writers, poets and dramatists needed swift improvement. The case for action was overwhelming. Accordingly, with expanded broadcasting, plus new cultural and literary infrastructures in place, Gaeldom's cultural demise was being addressed.*(18)

5. ***Local Government and Administrative Reform:*** This proved to be a major area of development on several inter-linked fronts, each connected with administrative reform, educational initiative and the generation of Gaelic-friendly environmental changes. While by themselves none fundamentally altered the precarious condition of Gaelic in the community, cumulatively each went some way towards inaugurating a positive climate where the sturdy efforts of the Gaelic voluntary organisations were matched by the positive intervention of government at Edinburgh and Westminster. The credit list is impressive.

First, was the1969 Local Authorities (National Mod) Scotland Act, that began as a Private Member Bill from Liberal MP for Inverness and Lochaber, Russell Johnstone. This law empowered local councils to provide discretionary financial support for funding the National Mod, which by then had become Scottish Gaeldom's most prominent cultural show-piece, not just to audiences in Scotland but across Europe and North America. It was passed with cross –

party support at Westminster and a chorus of approval at home. This reform was augmented by another enabling Scottish local authorities in the Highlands and Islands to erect Gaelic road signs with government aid. However, the value of that reform was rather undermined by the minimal take-up rate by Highlands councils over the period.

Third, but perhaps most significant of all such reforms was the creation in 1975 in the Outer Hebrides of a single-tier Gaelic purpose local authority, Comhairle nan Eilean Siar – Western Isles Council, whose boundaries squared with those of the parliamentary division of same name. This initiative came out of local government reforms initiated two years earlier by the Heath government (1970-74), and replaced the previous division of the jurisdiction between Inverness and Ross-shire councils. The council covered the islands of Lewis, Harris, North and South Uist, Benbecula, Barra, Vatersay, Mingulay and Eriskay, with the central administration in Stornoway. With a combined population of 29,000, Comhairle nan Eilean Siar emerged as the third smallest local authority in the UK. Very significantly, serving the principal Scottish Gaidhealtachd, the new Council had a specific remit to operate as a bilingual Gaelic/English local authority, using Gaelic as a main language of communication and promotion.*(19) From that base, other developments followed through partnership between the Council and a range of educational, learner and community organisations. *(20)

Fourth, was a key initiative aimed at tackling economic revival of the Gaidhealtachd through the creation of a regenerative authority to work in tandem with local councils and the Scottish Office for encouraging investment, protecting local industries and bringing fresh industry. Emerging from earlier development initiatives like the Scottish Development Council and Highlands Development League, plus Highland Fund, all of which sought to halt emigration abroad and migration to Glasgow, Edinburgh and England by aiding local businesses, and set against the depressing 1961 Census figures (listing barely 81,000 Gaelic speakers), there was a clear case for major government action to rescue the Highlands and Hebrides from innate poverty. It had long been championed by leading figures like Sir Alexander McEwen, ex-Provost of Inverness and advocate of harnessing the Highlands hydro-electric potential; the author, Sir Compton Mackenzie (whose works included 'Whiskey Galore'); Presbyterian Gaelic scholar, Rev Tom Murchison; and the academic, Professor E.L. Hilleary, whose earlier 1938 report had accused government of serious neglect of the Highlands. In his celebrated centenary history of An Comunn Gaidhealach, Frank Thompson, rightly asserted that language decline could not be disconnected from the key issues of crofting, fisheries, land usage and local industry, most of which were in chronic condition.*(21) Similar sentiments were aired by James Hunter in his treatise on Crofting decline*(22), while the late MP, Donald Stewart's, memoirs emitted grave concerns for the Hebridean economy.*(23) In contrast to a later generation of Europhile Scottish Nationalists, Stewart saw little merit in the European Economic Community, whose impositions he blamed for savaging the Western Isles fishing fleet on whom so many Hebridean homes had depended.*(24)

The eventual creation by statute in 1965 of the Highlands and Islands Development Board (HIDB) followed, with Sir Robert Grieve as its first Chairman. Its briefing was to stimulate the region's socio-economic regeneration, which would prove beneficial to local people and businesses. For Gaelic organisations, this meant grant provision for publishing, arts, Gaelic learning and festivals, not to mention local industry, thus rendering HIDB, and its successor organisations Highlands and Islands Enterprises (HIE), invaluable patrons of Gaelic.*(25) In 1984, HIDB appointed and funded the post of Gaelic Language Development Officer, who in turn produced a far-reaching Gaelic development policy that was enthusiastically adopted by the Board. Among other things, the latter resulted in the provision of financial assistance to Comhairle nan Sgoiltean Araich (Gaelic Playgroups Association) for the purpose of recruiting staff and acquiring a headquarters. The Board also funded a Gaelic Leaners body, Comunn an Luchd-Ionnsachaidh, whose profile and capacity grew considerably over ensuing decades. Overall, by helping Gaelic pre-school children and also adult learners, along with its assistance to industry and the regional economy, HIDB's record positively impacted on Gaelic in the Highlands and Hebrides in a way that was without precedent.*(26)

It is important to acknowledge that the Scottish experience was by no means unique. There were precedents in Southern Ireland and Wales. Thompson recalled ACG's attention having focussed on experiences in the Irish Republic of Gaeltarra Eireann. The latter body by 1965 had assumed responsibility for the economic management and linguistic development of Gaeltacht areas in Western Ireland. Gaeltarra Eireann had adopted a wide range of activities in its schedule, which included assistance to service industries like computer companies (an infant technology then), hotels, tourist enterprises, gardening, fish farming and agricultural schemes. The disadvantages of Gaeltacht communities were lessened by provision of essential economic infrastructure, plus new factory innovations and managed housing. It is significant that Gaeltarra Eireann's operations were matched similarly by developments in Wales, where that country's half-million Celtic speakers were also engaged in a survival battle against the assorted forces of encroaching anglicisation. Their principal government-funded body was the Mid Wales Development Agency, and in rural North Wales, the Welsh Development Agency. Similar incentives had been offered by sister authorities in Southern Ireland and Wales, such as giving preferential recruitment to Celtic speakers and extending maximum assistance to projects founded by Celtic speakers. As was documented by Thompson, Gaeltarra success had become evident by the mid-1960s through increased employment on Gaeltarra-assisted enterprises – from 680 in 1967 to 4,200 in 1978.*(27)

The apparent success of Gaeltarra Eireann, along with that of its Welsh counterparts, became the models closely noted by the new HIDB and its advocates in the early years.

Although HIDB's creation was welcomed by a consensus of Gaelic and Highlands/Islands organisations and public representatives, within the broad Gaelic movement there was some unease over the lack of formal commitment to Gaelic. For one thing, no known Gaelic speakers were appointed to HIDB's governing council, which opened its headquarters at Inverness in November 1965. Also, though the HIDB's founding mantra was to assist an economic regeneration of the Highlands and Hebrides, which implicitly meant aiding Gaelic language voluntary groups ... among other bodies from the region, this did not formally commit the Board to supporting Gaelic. Such concerns were reinforced by the Chairman, Professor Sir Robert Grieve's open scepticism about the Gaelic language future in Scotland; a view that did little to endear him to the Gaelic lobby. This also had the effect of presenting An Comunn Gaidhealach with another challenge, notably to robustly assert the place of Gaelic as a priority for the new Board. As it happened, the appointment of a new ACG Director, former colonial servant and industrial executive, Donald John Mackay, himself a native Gaelic speaker from North Uist, spelt the beginning of a fresh era for both ACG and Scottish Gaeldom. As Frank Thompson noted, with reference to the "..gaelicising of HIDB":

"It was on this front {HIDB} that HIDB's new full time Director was to spend much of his time and effort". *(28)

The fact that so much was achieved over that momentous decade both in terms of an extended Gaelic profile and becoming part of Scottish civic society, plus internal reforms and revamping of ACG, says much about the immense drive, sound judgement and executive skills possessed by Mackay. His whole approach prioritised modernising the organisation, its structures, membership and appeal to Gaelic speakers, central government and the arts and broadcasting establishments. It was also propitious that such a gifted professional was available to An Comunn Gaidhealach just when Gaeldom's very survival was in doubt, and so many quaint old traditions needed ditching in order to meet the challenges of the age.

> **6.** *Educational Reforms and Expansion:* the period 1965-86 was momentous for many developments in Gaelic education. Perhaps one of the most far reaching innovations occurred in 1972 with the opening of the Gaelic F.E. College, Sabhal Mor Ostaig, at Sleat, Isle of Skye. Indeed the old adage about little acorns spawning oak trees is applicable to this establishment, which has emerged as an icon symbolising the enduring character of Scottish Gaeldom.

Over 48 years since 1972, the college has developed into a Scottish Higher Education institute, and is affiliated to the University of the Highlands and Islands. In the process, Sabhal Mor Ostaig has emerged, arguably, as the most elevated college of its kind in the entire Gaelic world. Additional to the multiple courses offering degrees, diplomas, school qualifications and other certification, the college is a leading trainer and assessor of Gaelic Medium teachers, and has generated an important niche in the growth of Gaelic Medium units across Scotland. Additionally, the college has become a centre for Easter and Summer residential courses for Gaelic learners, while also running courses for mainstream learners, plus local and distance programmes. So too have many Gaelic drama productions and musical initiatives been brought to life at this college, which has hosted conferences and debates among different Gaelic associations, public and voluntary, as well as scholars and activists, from across Scotland. A full evaluation of its contribution to the Gaelic revival is offered by historian, Roger Hutchinson.*[29]

Another significant development has been the expansion of Gaelic in the curricula of Scottish secondary schools. This process originated in the post war years, but took off robustly in the 1960s, '70s and '80s, by when Gaelic entrants for Scottish Ordinary and Higher Certificate examinations had quadrupled. The progress was aided by the enhanced status of Gaelic, resulting from an expansive broadcasting profile, as well as the growth in Gaelic literature and cultural projection to an ever-wider body of students. Those same students provided the nucleus of undergraduate recruitment for the Celtic Studies degrees provided by the universities of Glasgow, Edinburgh and Aberdeen, and from which initiatives emerged over ensuing years in writing, drama, education, further research, Gaelic arts and political projection.- See Chapters 4 & 6.

A further long-lasting development was the laying of foundations in the 1970s for what became the Gaelic Medium Education programme. This scheme began formally in 1985, and was funded largely by the Scottish Office and supportive local authorities It was developed in conjunction with the visionaries of An Comunn Gaidhealach and its band of Gaelic educationalists, whose ideas were channelled into firm policy plans over preceding years. Gaelic Medium planning entailed creation of Gaelic immersion units in select schools – based on parental demand - in the Highlands and Hebrides.*(30) It aimed at encouraging the development of language skills and ensuring continuity among native speakers, whose children might otherwise have been forced to accept an English medium education outside the home. From An Comunn's viewpoint, the introduction of Gaelic Medium teaching in primary, and later select secondary schools, was welcomed not just for the expansion of Gaelic teaching units, but also because it boosted the profile of Gaelic linguistics, arts and education among the wider Scottish public.*(31) It also represented an advance by Gaels in the educational world, from where future initiatives in secondary and further education might be developed. -See Chap 6. for more data.

Finally, another couple of developments followed, enduring in their effects and based on the principle of extending Gaelic in the community. From 1975, a Gaelic/English bilingual project operated in 20 Outer Hebridean primary schools under the combined aegis of the Scottish Education Department, Comhairle nan Eilean Siar (Western Isles Council) and Jordan Hill Training College, Glasgow, affiliated to University of Strathclyde. The programme aimed at developing the leading ambiance of Gaelic in Gaidhealtachd schools across the Western Isles, and proved a valuable forerunner of Gaelic medium education in the future.*(32)

There was also the Bernard Van Leer Educational Foundation (a Dutch educational research charity), that funded research into plans for developing Gaelic into wider school curricula and in the community, drawing upon expertise of Gaelic teachers, lecturers and adult education tutors, such as Annie MacSween, a native Gaelic speaker and teacher in the Nicholson Institute, Stornoway, and Gaelic researcher/writer, David Mackay, also from Lewis.*(33) In 1978, thanks to a grant from the Van Leer Foundation, research units of three years duration were opened at Ness (Lewis), Harris and South Uist, which enabled a blending of ideas and pragmatism into workable proposals. This followed on from the 1976 campaigning book by David Mackay, envisioning a literacy goal, which facilitated debate, exchanges with the educational establishment and further development.*(34) – More about this important area of development will follow in Chapter 6.

7. *Political Developments:* Political developments of various kinds occurred over the period. While none spelt major changes in themselves, nevertheless the cumulative effect served to augment the increasing Gaelic resurgence in Scottish society, in turn making a solid case to Scottish policymakers.

There occurred at the Westminster General Election of June 1970 the return of former Stornoway Provost, Donald Stewart, as Scottish Nationalist Member for the Western Isles. Stewart was a highly popular local figure with a strong commitment to extending rights and facilities for Gaelic speakers, and in the process had defeated the incumbent Labour Member, Malcolm K. Macmillan, who had held the seat since 1935. As events showed, Stewart's election proved timely for his willingness to champion ACG at Parliament.*(35) In February 1981, Stewart produced the Gaelic (Miscellaneous Provisions, Scotland) Private Member Bill, which sought to achieve statutory recognition for Scottish Gaelic, as well as defining the right to Gaelic Medium facilities, following the Welsh pattern.*(36) However, the bill fell victim to a Conservative filibuster, led by Douglas Hogg, but as noted by MacKinnon's historical commentary, many provisions have since been adopted.*(37) The latter point was also noted with some satisfaction by Stewart in his memoirs.*(38)

Notwithstanding the hostility of Hogg and other, mainly English, soulmates, actually the period was also significant for the Scottish Conservatives positive embracement of Gaelic. That this happened was in no small way due to the Tories' perception of the Gaelic lobby as politically innocuous, and thus deserving of modest aid. Indeed under Edward Heath's progressive leadership, as noted by cultural/race relations expert, Professor Zig Layton-Henry, a new mood of multiculturalism, shedding the colonial and traditional white Tory image, was on the ascendant among party policymakers.(*(39) This was not a trend much favoured by Enoch Powell or others of the Tory Right, but nonetheless constituted an important element in Heath's new Progressive orthodoxy of the time.*(40)

This climate enabled an accommodation to be made with An Comunn Gaidhealach and its sister bodies in the mainstream of Scottish civic life. It also meant the Wilson government's pro-Gaelic policies were substantially continued by Edward Heath after succeeding in the UK General Election of June 1970. Equally significant was a positive affirmation to An Comunn's delegation by the incoming Conservative Secretary of State, Gordon Campbell. It is likely that alongside Heath's One Nation agenda, Scottish Gaeldom's gradual incorporation of arts, literature, education and broadcasting over previous years had encouraged Conservative acquiescence. So too did the "happy coincidence" of new Chancellor, Iain Macleod - son of Lewis parents, and a redoubtable Tory One Nationite - boost the Gaelic profile in Tory ranks. Unfortunately, Macleod's sudden death within weeks of his appointment in July 1970 dealt a severe blow to Tory and Gaelic interests alike.*(41)

One immediate benefit of Conservative good will was the Scottish Office agreement to fund a full-time Director for An Comunn Gaidhealach in the Outer Hebrides. This appointment was enacted in 1971, with the new Director commencing from an office in Stornoway. Given developments in local government, education, arts and broadcasting, which had boosted the Gaelic profile, it was judicious for the Conservatives in office to be aiding Gaeldom's development. Yet such pragmatism was predicated on the view of Scottish Gaels battling to save a valued heritage and identity, and being bereft of long-term political dimension. Indeed it is timely to contrast generous assistance to Scottish Gaels by the British establishment of the early 1970s with the plight of Ulster Gaelic brethren, being linked to Irish nationalism, battling fiercely with the Tories' Ulster Unionist allies – who in August 1971 had interned nationalists - as the Stormont regime edged closer towards its final hurrah.

Over the ensuing period, with further developments spawning the growth of Gaelic pre-school groups, Gaelic learners and the Feiseann movement, the mood among Gaels moved towards consolidating and furthering such achievements as had occurred over recent years. MacKinnon noted a general desire to replace the hitherto monopoly of An Comunn with something more dispersed along the lines of specialism.*(42) At the same time Macleoid estimated that by 1980 Scottish Gaeldom had achieved survival – a presumptuous view given the 1971 Census figure of 88,892 Gaelic speakers, at best confirming only the overall decline having slowed – and needed to prepare for a mini renaissance.*(43) Different papers appeared, and there was an important conference staged in 1985 at Sabhal Mor Ostaig, which prepared the way for an eventual report on a national policy for Gaelic – a subject more adequately covered in Chapter 6. Meanwhile, in 1984, as recounted earlier in this chapter, the Highlands and Islands Development Board had initiated a Gaelic development programme which included the appointment of new salaried officers in vital areas. Perhaps its most important initiative of the period was to facilitate the emergence of a specialist national advisory body, Comunn na Gaidhlig (CNG), the consequence of whose role was to effectively supersede An Comunn, and with a publicly-funded headquarters at Inverness. It was CnG, with its semi-official status and closeness to the Secretary of State, that assumed the lead role as principal organ of Scottish Gaeldom, although An Comunn Gaidhleach was left to run the National Mod, while also retaining its publicist role.*(44)

8. *Generally*, whatever may have been the price paid in lost independence, by 1986 the previous Anglicisation of the West Highlands and Hebrides had been cumulatively reversed, at least in part. Census figures for 1961-81, while showing reducing native speakers' numbers, nevertheless also indicated the decline to have slowed; i.e, 1961 – 80,620; 1971 – 88,892; 1981 – 79,307.*(45) Significantly, Census figures of the time overlooked increasing numbers of Gaelic second language speakers and learners, whose purpose had been revived by various developments occurring over the period in question.

While numbers of second language Gaels of that period are hard to quantify, there is creditable data available on more contemporary Gaelic learner levels. According to a 1995 report by the author, John M.K. Galloway, commissioned by Comunn na Gaidhlig and supported by the Scottish Gaelic Learners Association/ Cumann an Luchd-Ionnsachaidh, there were some 8,000 Gaelic learners located throughout Scotland.*(46) A majority were located in the area of Greater Glasgow, among largely, if not exclusively second and third generations of migrant Highlanders and Hebrideans, with proportionate numbers found elsewhere in Scotland and among Scottish communities abroad. Quite how this figure stood over the period 1966-86 is impossible to ascertain, due to an absence of data from that time? However, it is safe to assume that foundations for the1990s were rooted in developments achieved in earlier years. – See Chapter 6 for more data.

Undoubtedly, the expansion of learner and actual speaker levels boosted the Gaelic profile, laying solid structures for the development of Gaelic education, the arts, broadcasting, music and publishing. Inevitably those foundations enabled future developments, and in the process encouraged a new self-confidence that accompanied the rising esteem of Scottish Gaeldom from the mid-1960s onwards. If that progress was achieved at the price of less autonomy and muted political independence, then given the increased benevolence of the Scottish political and administrative establishment, it seemed like a price worth paying.

9. ***Northern Ireland:*** The progress of Gaeil Uladh was significantly less promising over the early period 1966-86, although by the mid-1980s events in Northern Ireland had experienced a degree of political progress that augured positively for nationalists in their cultural renaissance. As always, cultural affairs in Northern Ireland connected closely to political developments, and for as long as the North was governed by an anti-Gaelic regime from Stormont, prospects for Gaeil Uladh looked grim.

Three factors defined the Ulster Gaelic dilemma of the time. First, given the polarisation, documented in earlier chapters, there was the ongoing Unionist monopoly of political power, lasting until Stormont's abolition in March 1972 – ironically at the hands of a British **Conservative** Prime Minister, Edward Heath.*(47) For as long as Unionists controlled local and central government in Northern Ireland, as well as the Civil Service, broadcasting, the arts, higher education and public bodies, Gaeldom, being of necessity tied to sponsorship of nationalists, was subject to Unionist exclusion. Thus Gaelic sports, Gaelic arts and the Gaelic language all experienced exclusion from mainstream civic life of the North in a manner not greatly different from Craigavon's day. Notwithstanding green shoots of a liberal Unionist dawn characterising the premiership of Captain Terence O'Neill (1963-69), in fact O'Neill's progress was thwarted all the way by his own Right, with his leadership forcibly terminated in May 1969. In any case, there were limits to how far O'Neill's reforms extended, and Gaeldom was not greatly included in his outreach to the Nationalist community.

The actual events and conditions of the O'Neill period are evaluated by a plethora of scholars ranging from Brendan O'Leary & John McGarry, to Professor (now Lord) Paul Bew, Henry Patterson, Richard Rose and the late Queens University academic, Professor Cornelius O'Leary.*(48) Dr Jonathan Bardon's evaluation of the period is also worthy of a serious review.*(49) While perspectives differ from person to person about the purpose and effects of O'Neill Unionism, there was no denying its inadequacies to nationalists, and also the suspicions aroused among Unionists, not least the firebrand preacher and later North Antrim MP, Rev Dr Ian Paisley.*(50) Accordingly, it was inevitable that among the ranks of civil rights campaigners of the late 1960s and early '70s were a range of Gaelic language, sports and cultural activists. The divisive Stormont system had effectively forced nationalists into protests of political, rather than cultural, assertion, of which the civil rights campaign, 1968-72, represented the most poignant example.

Second, Unionists at all levels of government were explicitly hostile to Irish culture, resenting the Irish identity as a threat to the Union and "..Ulster way of life". *(51) Hence, aside from the anti-Catholicism, redolent of many Unionist sections, the scarcest regard was shown for Irish cultural pursuits, and none for the Gaelic language. Moreover, following the introduction of Direct Rule, for the first 15 years the Northern Ireland Office proved an indifferent overseer of Gaelic interests, as ungenerous as its Unionist predecessor. Only with the Anglo-Irish Accord at Hillsborough in November 1985, did a more positive attitude emerge, with an enlightened attitude towards funding the Gaelic language and cultural pursuits.

Third, the Ulster Gaelic lobby was hampered by the absence of a traditional Gaeltacht within the Sic Counties. This situation marked a contrast to Scottish Gaeldom, where an established, albeit small, Gaidhealtachd existed in the Hebrides and West Highlands. By contrast, Ulster Gaelgeoiri pleas for funds and legal provision, emphasising heritage and cultural identity factors, were largely ignored by a government that lacked sympathy for any aspect of the Gaelic agenda. Small wonder that Northern Irish society remained so ossified, with nationalists and their Gaelic advocates openly displaying the deep alienation from both Unionists and British government that became the stuff of Hillsborough reforms post-1985.

> **10.** ***Green Shoots:*** Yet from the late 1960s onwards, there emerged green shoots, auguring cautious hopes among Ulster Gaelgeoiri for the future. Those were due, partly, to voluntary initiatives by Gaelic language and cultural activists more than the active hand of government; and partly a slowly-reforming political climate within Northern Ireland, aided by intense interest in the North's affairs in Britain and abroad following the proliferation of civil rights marches, along with ensuing riots and violence over 1969/72. That period also witnessed a slow and grudging, but definite shift in official attitudes, such as enhanced the efforts of various Gaelgeoiri operating under the broad label of Comhaltas Uladh. Given the language's place within a broad Irish cultural movement, also including Gaelic sports, music, drama and literature, it is noteworthy that language developments were accompanied by modest progress in other areas. The effect was to boost confidence and self-reliance of Gaeil Uladh, sustaining it through the greatest-ever political crisis afflicting Northern Ireland's divided and strained society since partition in 1921.

Signs of that mini-resurgence were to be found on several fronts. First, as shown in Chapter 2, the opening of a Celtic Studies department serving St Mary's and St Joseph's Catholic training colleges (Belfast) in the mid-1960s, enabling the training of Irish language teachers to meet the growing demand from ... it must be acknowledged ... mainly Northern Catholic schools. Queen's University, Belfast, already had revived its long-dormant Chair of Celtic Studies in the immediate post-war years, thereby attracting multiple Gaelic scholars and students. Significantly, by the late 1960s, the New University of Ulster, with its principal site at Coleraine, had facilitated the introduction of a Celtic Studies Department. The latter offered degrees in Irish and other Celtic cultural and linguistic codes, while going some way towards meeting the demand for Ulster-dialect-trained teachers in the growing network of Northern Irish schools offering Irish both at exam level and cultural development.

Previously, there had been a reliance on Southern-trained Irish teachers, whose Gaelic dialect belonged to Connacht, which had been used in Dublin's public communications and schools programme. Now, with Gaeil Uladh slowly re-emerging, the Ulster Gaelic dialect was saved from virtual extinction. Additionally, and very significantly, the slow Ulster Gaelic renaissance had the effect of boosting Gaelic's progress within the North's educational system, while raising its profile and esteem, something which Gabrielle Maguire's account of educational developments in that period documents in some detail.*(52)

Third, the reputation for scholarly excellence acquired by the University of Ulster over the first two decades was beyond dispute. In a department headed by such leading Gaelic scholars as the late Diarmuid O'Devlin, former Chairman of Derry County GAA during the mid-1970s, and Gaelic educationalist and SDLP politician, Sean Farren, there arose a zest for sponsoring research in all areas of Irish studies, as well as hosting visionary conferences and seminars, validating new teaching programmes and promoting an awareness of Gaeldom's scholarly past. Indeed it is fair to add that by 1985, the Irish/Celtic Studies Department at the University of Ulster had enhanced its standing to a level comparable with Celtic Studies departments in other Irish universities, plus those of Scotland and Wales. Again, such developments, though modest, enhanced the confidence of Gaeil Uladh activists.*(53) Among other things, the latter helped stimulate a battle for parity of esteem for the Gaelic language and culture against an entrenched Anglophile culture so beloved of the Unionist establishment and their British Tory backers. Not until the 1985 Anglo-Irish Accord did that objective reach fruition.*(54) - More in Chapter 5.

Fourth, it was events on the ground that bade well for Gaeil Uladh. In education, growth in the numbers of Gaelgeoir teachers and students actually following Irish language courses in Northern schools and colleges was reflected in the rising numbers of exam candidates. By 1970, a record number of 2,348 candidates sat N.I. Exam Board Advanced and Ordinary Level Irish Studies across the Six Counties. Throughout the 1970s and '80s those figures remained consistently high, being second only to French, and commanding higher uptakes than Spanish, German and Italian studies. What is also significant is that in the 1970s and '80s for the first time, many state Further Education colleges like the former -and enlarged - Belfast College of Business Studies and Belfast College of Technology – merged in the 1990s to form Belfast Metropolitan College- began offering Gaelic to meet local demand, both for part-time evening students and to mainstream students pursuing full time and retake courses.*(55) Provincial FE colleges like Downpatrick and Newry institutes, along with Foyle (Derry) and Omagh, also offered similar courses to students in areas with a consistently high demand. So also did Gaelic football and Hurling clubs emerge in each of those colleges, plus Belfast College of Business Studies (which also boosted a Gaelic Cultural Society), throughout the 1970s, itself representing a break with the erstwhile practice of avoiding Gaelic sports and the Irish language.*(56)

Fifth, 1969 saw the laying of initial foundations for what became Gaeltacht Beal Feirste – Belfast's new urban Gaeltacht. In that year, the first Gaelic-speaking family moved into a small housing site purpose-built by a local Gaelgeoir development company, De Brun and Mac Seain Ltd, in Shaws Road, Andersonstown, West Belfast. Some assistance had been forthcoming from Comhaltas Uladh, but most funds had been generated through voluntary fund raising, along with donations from well-wishers across the rest of Ireland.*(57)

The general aim was to build housing, educational and social infrastructure for the support of a Gaelic-speaking community, most of whose families were drawn from among second-language Gaels. In Chapter 2, the background to Gaeltacht Beal Feirste was examined, along with their organisation, Teaghlaigh. This included the disappointments of the mid-1950s 'Fal' initiative (covered earlier); the chief lesson having been learned that despite its romanticism, rural Donegal (so admired in Belfast) was light years away from Belfast in terms of population, social environment and economic infrastructure. Therefore, any prospect of success in Belfast required the creation of a Gaeltacht based on the community and infrastructure of Belfast alone. While it was recognised that a Gaeltacht anywhere needed viable economic roots and distinctive social institutions to survive, the sober reality was that a prospective Belfast Gaeltacht needed to be built around the culture, environment and economy of Belfast and its people. Hence it was to that task that a number of leading Belfast Gaelgeoiri like writer, Gaelic educationalist and executive administrator, Aodan Mac Poilin (recently deceased), and, later, the youthful Gaelic language activist and founding editor of Gaelic newspaper, *La*, Gearoid O'Caireallain, plus other Ulster Gaelgeoiri, dedicated their lifetimes' labours over the next half-century.*(58)

Whatever may have been the hurdles, in fact throughout the 1970s and early '80s there occurred a steady growth of the urban Belfast Gaeltacht. By

1985, a dozen Gaelic-speaking families were settled in the Shaws Road Gaelgeoir housing development, and this figure kept rising over the ensuing decade, with the result that unlike the 1950s 'Fal' effort, this showed signs of a sustainable project. Indeed the emergence of a viable urban Gaeltacht in West Belfast had become a definite reality by 1985.

Sixth, in line with other developments, Belfast's first Gaelic Medium primary school - Bunscoil - opened its doors at Shaws Road in September 1969. Initial enrolment was 9 pupils, but steadily the intake increased, as did community interest and financial support of the venture. For its first 15 years, the school operated independently, through fundraising in Belfast and appeals to benefactors everywhere, and of course parental fees where they could be raised. As recounted by Maguire, the parents also had to deal with an attempt in the mid-1070s by anti-Gaelic elements in the North's Department of Education to outlaw their Gaelic Medium venture; and were rescued by the intervention of a sympathetic N.I.O. education minister, the now-deceased Lord Peter Melchett.*(59) By persevering and developing premises and increasing numbers, the Bunscoil both survived and spawned a Gaelic Playschool group, that managed to develop its appeal.*(60) By Spring 1984, when the Northern Ireland Department of Education finally announced the granting of Maintained Status to the Shaws Road Bunscoil, with accompanying financial support, there had already emerged a small network of other Gaelic Medium primary and nursery schools across Belfast, Derry and other nationalist areas of the North. Chapters 5 & 7 will carry more detailed information about the expanded Bunscoil and Meanscoil (secondary school), as they developed, but initial significance lay in the foundations laid during this early period.

Seventh, a related development in West Belfast came with the launch in 1981 of Preis an Phobail (Peoples Press), later renamed La, the first, and to date only, Gaelic language newspaper in Ireland with a nationwide (ie. all-Ireland) circulation. It began initially as a weekly, but in 1984 upgraded to a daily paper, before distribution and digital pressures forced management to revert to an enlarged weekly.*(61) Maguire noted that by 1985 it had become a matter of pride to Ulster Gaelgeoiri that notwithstanding all its disadvantages, in fact Belfast was publishing the only all-Ireland newspaper in the native language.*(62) As shown in Chapters 4 & 5, La proved to be an important influence in the Belfast Gaeltacht throughout the 1980s and '90s. The paper sponsored Belfast's various Gaelic cultural and educational initiatives, while also serving as a publicist for the Gaelic community, whose esteem was boosted by positive profiles and sympathetic news coverage.

Regrettably, the pressures on *La* proved unremitting. A combination of high production and distribution costs, added to falling newspaper sales everywhere, meant La was unable to compete in a digitalised market. Much to the chagrin of its spirited editor, Gearoid O'Caireallain, the paper was forced in December 2008 to cease publishing after the all-Ireland grants authority, 'Foras na Gaeilge', ceased its grant-aid. Its closure proved gravely injurious to the morale of Belfast's Gaeltacht. By then, the success of the Gaelic Medium schools project, along with increasing Gaelic learner figures, and the opening of a new Belfast Gaelic cultural centre on the Falls Road, Culturalan McAdam-O'Fiaich, enabled the disappointment to be borne.*(63) Yet its loss proved especially painful for those Gaelic language activists like O'Caireallain – himself subsequently victim of a Stroke in 2014, that forced his withdrawal from active life - who had devoted their lives to the paper's development.*(64) At its height, La had boasted 3,000 daily sales, but following its sale to the Andersonstown News in 2006, with leading Sinn Fein figure, Mairtian O'Muilleoir, taking over as editor, the paper became dependent on a grant from the all-Ireland-funding body, Foras na Gaeilge. When that ceased, the paper's last lifeline disappeared, leaving O'Muilleoir and his people no alternative but to cease publication. While a serious effort is currently underway to find a replacement title for the defunct La, all sources acknowledge that the best achievable option for the future would be an on-line paper.*(65)

The period 1966-86 was also noteworthy for the slow opening up of Northern Ireland's broadcast media to Gaelic sports and culture. Actually, the successes of Northern counties in national Gaelic sports competitions – especially the legendary feats of Down's Gaelic Football team that lifted three All-Ireland senior titles in 1960, '61 and '68, being the first Northern county to bring the famous Sam Maguire Cup across the border – boosted confidence among Ulster Gaels, while strengthening demands for access to the airwaves. It was a measure of their success that the victorious Down team of 1968 was for the first time ever welcomed to a civic reception at Belfast City Hall by the liberal-Unionist Lord Mayor, Alderman William Geddes. There was also the success of the Antrim Senior Hurling team that in 1969 lifted the All-Ireland Intermediate Hurling crown, and whose footballers also won the national U-21 crown.*(66) In 1968 BBC N.I. showed the All-Ireland Senior Gaelic football final second half, and Down's successes were applauded on BBC news coverage of the time. All these openings amounted to ".. small beer" - so to speak- but in so far as they opened up state broadcasting to Gaelic sports, such marked a positive beginning on which later developments were based. Yet even those modest pickings evoked protests from the Protestant Unionist (later Democratic Unionist) Party of Rev Ian Paisley, whose wife, Eileen (now a peer) led a picket on Belfast City Hall while the Down team was being entertained by Alderman Geddes.*(67) Civic Inclusiveness, a key O'Neill goal, was viewed by Paisley as a ".. betrayal of Ulster's Protestant British heritage..".

Significantly, those late 1960s Gaelic games broadcasting experiments created precedents for cautious developments over ensuing years. Both BBC N.I. and BBC Radio Ulster (founded 1975) and independent stations, Ulster Television and Downtown Radio (launched in 1976) were offering a creditable results and match reports service each week by 1977, along with coverage of the top games. Yet it took another ten years before live coverage of principal games was introduced, by which time Gaelic sports – with all Northern counties challenging for major honours at all-Ireland level, along with Queens University – had become ever more integrated in Northern Ireland's cultural and sports culture.*(68)

11. **_Continuing Hurdles:_** While developments in language, schools, an embryonic urban Gaeltacht in West Belfast and the opening up of broadcasting and limited government grants to Gaelic sports all represented a major advancement on the pre-1965 position of little or no Gaelic games coverage on air, substantial gaps remained. This was particularly true of broadcasting games and language events.

First, despite the popularity of Gaelic games among the Northern nationalist community, and the presence of some 350 GAA-affiliated Hurling, Gaelic Football and Camogie clubs in the six counties, media coverage throughout the 1970s and '80s never truly reflected the intensity of that activity.*(69) For example, the broadcast media gave minimal attention to the successes of Northern counties like Armagh, Tyrone and Down at Croke Park in the 1970s and early 80s, while even the historic centenary GAA Congress of 1984, staged at Queens University, Belfast, was largely ignored by BBC N.I.. This task was left to the nationalist press, while state and independent broadcasters remained largely offside.*(70) Notwithstanding modest developments, the frank truth is that up until the late 1980s, Gaelic games and the Irish language did not figure on the British establishment's "politically-acceptable" agenda. Progress was therefore slow and grudging, while all along any new initiatives encountered the most fierce proscriptions from Unionist-dominated Councils like Larne and Craigavon, while few Gaelic arts proposals ever found their way onto-air.*(71)

Second, Gaelic language coverage was exempted from the thawing process. By 1985, there were no regular Gaelic medium programmes of either a utilitarian or educational kind on offer from BBC N.I or the independent TV or radio channels. Nor did the cultural activities – including musical fleadhs, ceilidh dancing festivals, Gaelic drama etc of groups like Comhaltas Ceoilteoiri na hEireann, nor the GAA's annual Scor talent competitions – receive broadcasting coverage. Indeed that very issue was pursued relentlessly on live air by a young male caller to BBC Radio Ulster in March 1976, when a senior executive addressed listeners' questions on the first anniversary of Radio Ulster's launch. This factor was highlighted by nationalist politicians, and figured prominently in a collection of commentaries edited by MacPoilin (1997), demonstrating the grievance felt across the board. Moreover, it contrasted sharply with regular grant aid and broadcasting offered to An Comunn Gaidhealach and associated activities by BBC Scotland and independent broadcasters.

Third, Northern Ireland's broadcasters lacked any **clear** policy for providing a quota of programmes in the Irish language or coverage of Gaelic sports and cultural activities. This resistance prevailed despite the popularity of Irish Gaelic Studies in schools and the North's two universities, plus St Mary's & St Joseph's Teacher Training College, Belfast. So too was minimal attention accorded to the growing profile of Comhaltas Uladh generally and its network of sister groupings, who provided voluntary language classes at venues across Belfast and the rural towns of Northern Ireland, as earlier documented.

12. ***Generally***, the experiences of Ulster Gaelgeoiri proved less favourable than those of their Gaelic counterparts in Scotland. Over that same period, Scottish Gaels had experienced real advances in broadcasting, publishing and education. Indeed Scottish broadcasters had shown a less grudging attitude towards An Comunn Gaidhleach's pleas for a Gaelic programmes quota and learners service. Again, as

documented previously, similar favour had been shown towards Gaelic learning and teacher employment in Highlands and Hebridean schools, while Gaelic community organisations in the Isle of Lewis, South Uist and Bara had been favoured by the Highlands Development Board and Comhairle nan Eilean Siar with grants and staff support.*(72) Such was an inevitable reflection of the two political environments of Northern Ireland and Scotland respectively, and it is difficult to see how things might have been different, even in a less fractious period in post-partition Ulster. Yet those were the two lines of distinction drawn between both Gaelic nations.

It also needs adding that Gaelic developments in Northern Ireland over the period 1966-86 were affected by the political and social upheavals occurring then. Civil Rights campaigns of the late 1960s, along with realignment of the nationalist parties into the SDLP in the early 1970s – evaluated so aptly by Dr Enda Staunton in his treatise – with Sinn Fein joining the campaign by the early 1980s, guaranteed a politicisation of Ulster Gaeldom to a degree not not previously seen since partition.*(73) It also introduced a new and broad pan-nationalist agenda aiming at securing **parity of esteem** for Irish culture within the civic environment of Northern Ireland. The latter agenda embraced proportionate funding and legal entitlement for the Gaelic language in education, broadcast media, cultural and community affairs, the law courts, public administration and recognition by government.

In essence, Irish nationalists sought similar rights for Irish Gaelic from a hostile Stormont administration, and its reluctant Northern Ireland Office successor, as were being simultaneously accorded to Scottish Gaels by the Scottish Office and local councils. That cultural parity question generated an issue for relentless agitation by nationalists in Northern Ireland, and was supported to some degree by successive Irish governments from Dublin. It was not just a question of resources and political even-handedness, but for nationalists the issue struck at the very heart of a long-running quest for recognition of their **identity**.

The historic November 1985 Anglo-Irish Accord – agreed by the British Conservative government of Premier Mrs Margaret Thatcher and the Irish Fine Gael/Labour coalition of Dr Garret Fitzgerald (Taoiseach) and Mr Dick Spring (Tanaiste) – produced for the first ever time by London a seminal acknowledgement of the legitimacy of Irish nationalist identity and cultural/political aspirations. Martin O'Brien's dissertation on the Accord tends, along with many other commentaries, to focus on the political ramifications, but there was most certainly positive succour for the cultural nationalists of Gaeil Uladh from this treaty.*(74) An extension of the latter was an acceptance of the need to remove existing impediments to recognition and funding of Gaelic culture and the Irish language in Northern Ireland. To that extent, the Hillsborough Accord (so-called) represented a substantial advance on all previous developments. It also provided grounds for serious hope in the assorted ranks of linguists, cultural activists and Gaelic sportsmen comprising Gaeil Uladh.

How far those hopes were actually realised, and the reactions that they incurred, forms the next part of Gaeil Uladh's contemporary historical narrative.

FOOTNOTES and REFERENCES

1. There are many good general commentaries on international affairs and ethical issues of the twentieth century. My vote goes to Charles W. Kegley and Eugene R. Wittkopf <u>World Politics: Trend and Transformation</u> (8th edition), Macmillan (Basingstoke) and Bedford/St Martin's Press (Boston, USA), 2001. A much-accoladed treatise, edited by the late Professor A.H. Halsey, and concentrating on British social changes throughout the past century, is also worth reading: <u>Trends in British society since 1900</u> (1972, Macmillan, Basingstoke).

2. Arthur Marwick <u>Culture in Britain since 1945</u> (London, 1991); <u>Cultural Revolution in Britain, France, Italy and the United States, 1958-1974</u> (1998).

3. Peter Hennessy - A remarkably prodigious and award-winning journalist, who turned academic in mid-career to take up the Chair of Contemporary History at Queen Mary College, University of London. From an abundance of well-reviewed books, articles and papers, perhaps Professor – now Lord — Hennessy's scholarly series on the social and political history of post-war Britain is most relevant to this enquiry:

    <u>Never Again Britain 1945-1951</u> (London, 1992);
    <u>Having it so good: Britain in the 1950s</u> (London, 2007);
    <u>Winds of Change: Britain in the Early Sixties</u> (London, 2019).

4. The range of Sir Tom Devine's many scholarly publications on the politics, growth and strains of his country's development in modern times are exceptional. Scotland's most outstanding living historian, Sir Tom's treatise, <u>The Scottish Nation</u> – already covered – (1999) is virtually definitive, as is <u>Scotland in the Twentieth Century</u> (Co-editor and contributor), 1996, Edinburgh University Press.

5. For an insight to the different perspectives held of the O'Neill premiership, see:

    Jonathan Bardon – <u>A History of Ulster</u> (Belfast,1992), Chap14, pp 622-690; Roy Foster (1988), Chap 23, pp 579-586; and Michael Farrell – <u>Northern Ireland: The Orange State</u> (London, 1976) There is also the late Captain O'Neill's own account of his premiership; <u>The Autobiography of Terence O'Neill; Prime Minister of Northern Ireland, 1963-1969</u> (London, 1972).

6. Bernard Conlon <u>The Northern Ireland Civil Rights Association; Comparative Perspectives</u>; Unpublished M.A. Dissertation, University of Ulster, 1984.

7. Calum Kennedy, popular Gaelic singer, song writer, theatre owner, broadcaster and radio/TV personality was for some four decades the best-known Gaelic voice in and beyond Scotland. This Lewis native, with such a colourful personality (and even more colourful private life!) and folksy style, dominated Gaelic airwaves from the late 1950s until his death in 2006. Fourteen years on, continuing sales of Kennedy CDs of his memorable ballad compositions bears testimony to the man's enduring legacy.

8. See Election Manifestos, Scottish sections, for the UK General Elections of 1964, 1966 and 1970 – Labour, Conservatives, Liberals and Scottish National Party.

9. The 1951 Census showed a drop in Scottish Gaelic speakers from 136,135 in 1931 to 94,282 – a decrease of 31 per cent in 20 years. The figure for 1961 was down further to 80,978 – 1.64 of the total Scottish population. – No Census was held in 1941 due to prevailing conditions of War.

10. Thompson/ACG History (1992); Chap. 5.

11. Devine (2006); Chap 25, p. 600.

12. Wynn Grant <u>Pressure Groups, Politics and Democracy in Britain</u> (London,1995).

13. (i) Thompson/ACG History(1992); Chap. 5;

    (ii) MacLeoid (2011); p. 52.

    (iii) This author is also grateful to Professor Kenneth MacKinnon for his personal reflections and informed observations of the late Donald John Mackay.

14. MacLeoid (2011); p. 52.

15. (i) MacLeoid (2011), Ibid;

    (ii) Thompson (1992); Chaps 4 & 5.

16. MacLeoid (2011); p. 51.

17. MacKinnon (1991); p. 104.

18. Similarly qualified optimism emerges from reading of the accounts of Thompson (1992), MacKinnon (1991) and MacLeoid (2020).

19. Discussions and related documents. This author remains most grateful to the late Mr Donald John Maciver, Bilingual Adviser to Comhairle nan Eilean Siar and previously Head of Gaelic Studies at the Nicholson Institute, Stornoway, for his time and trouble to brief and clarify a litany of key points in a range of interviews: i.e. 15th August, 1991, 20th August 1992, 18th August 1993, 8th April 1994 and 30th June 1997.

20. V. McKee; <u>Contemporary Politics</u> (1995); Vol 1, No 1, pp 97-101.

21. Thompson (1992); Chaps 5 & 6.

22. Hunter (1987), Chap. 12.

23. Stewart (1994); pp 37-45, 'Backing the Fishermen', and pp 49-56, 'The Common Market'.

24. Ibid.

25. (i) Devine (2006); pp 579-581.

    (ii) MacKinnon (1991); pp 116 -121.

    (iii) MacLeoid (2011); pp 50-55.

26. (i) Withers (1998); Chap 7, pp 407-417.

    (ii) MacKinnon (1991); pp 116-123.

27. Thompson (1992); Chap 5, pp 98-102.

28. Thompson (1992), p.102.

29. Roger Hutchinson <u>A Waxing Moon: The Modern Gaelic Revival</u> (2005, Edinburgh)

30. In interviews with this author, the late Mr Donald John Maciver was at pains to point out that Gaelic medium and Bilingual education developed

an appeal over the initial 30 years to native-speaking parents beyond the Hebridean Gaidhealtachd. He identified migrant Gaelic couples in Glasgow and Edinburgh as regular take-up clientele for their children in local Gaelic Medium units. Many, but by no means all of those couples, had Hebridean and/or Highlands roots. Many others were just as likely to be Gaelic graduates from the universities and/or enthusiastic Gaelic learners eager to share a love of language and heritage with their off-spring.

31. Information shared with author in interviews with the late Mr Donald John Maciver.

32. Information initially provided in discussions with the author by Mrs Annie MacSween.

33. Ibid.

34. David Mackay   Breakthrough to Literacy (1976, Glasgow).

35. Stewart Memoirs (1994); pp 33-37.

36. Stewart (1994); Ibid.

37. MacKinnon (1991); Part 2, pp 117-120.

38. Stewart (1994); pp 33-37.

39. See Zig Layton-Henry, Eds. – Foreword by Sir Ian Gilmour MP Conservative Party Politics (London, Macmillan, 1980) - especially Chap 3.

40. For an account of the period from a contemporary historian's angle, see V. McKee – Forty Shades of Blue: Factionalism and Divisions in the Post War British Conservative Party from Churchill to Cameron (Takahe, Coventry, 2017), Chaps 4 & 5, The Tory Progressives and Rise of the Conservative Right.

41. See McKee (2017); Chap 5.

42. MacKinnon (1991); pp 108-121.

43. Macleoid (2011); pp 51-57.

44. MacKinnon (1991); pp 108- 118.

45. See UK Population Census results; 1961, 1971 and 1981; HMSO.

46. John M.K. Galloway – *'Estimation of the Number and Distribution of Adult Learners of Gaelic- Final Report'*; - Commissioned by Comunn na Gaidhlig, October 1995.

47. Suspension of the Stormont Parliament and executive by the British Premier, Edward Heath, was the final act to bring about the ending of the historic Conservative-Ulster Unionist alliance. - See McKee (2017), Forty Shades of Blue, Chap 5, pp 125-130.

48. Revisit Footnote 5, ibid. - Cornelius O'Leary & Ian Budge   Belfast: Approach to Crisis; A Study of Belfast Politics, 1613-1970 (Macmillan, London, 1973).

49. Bardon (1992); Chap 14.

50. Among the many biographies of the career of Dr Paisley, that of Ed Moloney & Andy Pollak, Paisley (Poolbeg, Dublin, 1986) is most instructive.

51. The late Merlyn Rees, former Labour Home Secretary and Northern Ireland Secretary in the Wilson and Callaghan Labour government of 1974-79, on early 1970s visits to Belfast outlined his utter exasperation at the code language used by Unionist politicians and their head office staff to emit ".. sheer anti-Catholicism". See Merlyn Rees – Northern Ireland: A Personal Perspective (Hard cover, 1985).

52. For authoritative account of developments in Gaelic education, see Gabrielle Maguire (1991); Chaps 2 & 3.

53. See McKee V. (1997); Chap 3.

54. This theme was prominently articulated in interviews with Mr Gearoid O'Caireallain.

55. Maguire data (1991); p 46. – Also, see McKee (1997), Appendix 3, p 122.

56. From 1974-77, this author was actively involved with organising Gaelic sports in in the Downpatrick and Belfast F.E. colleges, and also with the Ulster Gaelic Sports Vocational Schools division of Cumann Lutchleas Gael.

57. Information provided in discussions with Messers' Gearoid O'Caireallain and Cathail O'Donnaighle (1990s Gaelic educationalist).

58. Ibid.

59. Maguire (1991); Chap. 5, p 79.

60. Maguire; Chap. 5.

61. Ibid.

62. Discussions with Mr O'Caireallain, January 1994. Also, see McKee (1997), p 51.

63. Maguire (1991); Chap 4, p. 102.

64. Discussions with Mr O'Caireallain, 27th January, 2002. Though gravely disappointed by the earlier closure of *La*, nevertheless Mr O'Caireallain, by then medically retired due to ill health, maintained a remarkably robust optimism over the future of the Belfast Gaeltacht due to a series of positive developments. Not the least of these was the expanding Bunscoil movement, which had occurred over the previous twenty years. He continues to make a contribution through involvement in Gaelic drama and a regular programme on Belfast's Gaelic Radio *Failte*.

65. Discussions O'Caireallain/McKee, 27th January, 2020.

66. See McKee (1997); Chap 3, pp 51-54.

67. See press reports, Irish News, Belfast Telegraph and Newsletter – 12th October 1968.

68. 1971 was the year when the GAA abolished its infamous Rule 27, barring members from involvement with "garrison" (i.e. British games), at its Annual Congress, staged for the first time ever at Queens University, Belfast. A few weeks later, Queens University both hosted and won the prestigious All-Ireland Universities Gaelic Football tournament, Sigerson Cup, defeating University College, Cork, in the final. All those developments marked major progress for Gael Uladh, as it established its parity of expectation and achievement with both a hostile Unionist state and in competition with the Gaels elsewhere in Ireland.

69. McKee Contemporary Politics (1995), p 102.

70. Up until the 1990s, the Ulster GAA relied primarily on the Belfast-based *Irish News*, along with some independent and/or pro-nationalist provincial

papers for coverage of Gaelic games and Irish language activities in Northern Ireland. Other Dublin-based papers did offer fair coverage of inter-county games, but there were logistical limits to their capacity for covering Ulster Gaelic games and Gaelgeoir activities.

71. During the late 1970s, both Larne and Craigavon councils – each Unionist-controlled – tried stopping the playing of Gaelic games on Council pitches. In each case, the Courts intervened to force compliance with fair practice legislation.

72. Discussions with Gaelic educationalist and Lewis community historian, Mrs Annie MacSween, 18th December 2019. This author is most grateful to Mrs MacSween for kindly granting him access to a range of contacts and valuable policy papers.

73. Enda Staunton The Nationalists of Northern Ireland 1918-1973, (2001, Dublin) especially Part V, pp 212-285.

74. Martin O'Brien *'Margaret Thatcher and Northern Ireland – Special Focus on the 1985 Hillsborough Accord'*; Unpublished Master of Social Sciences Thesis, Queens University, Belfast, 1993.

Chapter Four

1986-99: SCOTTISH GAELDOM CONSOLIDATES!

Aims: This chapter assesses the various developments in Scottish Gaeldom's battle for survival in the last two decades of the 20th century. A series of new innovations in education, broadcasting, arts, teacher training, media, local government and the economy are charted, along with their impact on both the language and esteem of Scottish Gaels. At the same time, Donald John McKay's legacy of political neutrality and maximum co-operation with the government of the day had put Scottish Gaeldom in the role of establishment partner and a beneficiary. Whether this strategy was entirely consistent with An Comunn's roots as a voice of Highlands and Hebrides Gaeldom was and remains open to question? Although some Gaelic scholars take a critical view, this author questions whether there was any realistic alternative? Additionally, there was the debate over national devolution, and its implications for the future interests and capacity of Gaeldom. With the triumph of constitutional reformers in the 1997 Scottish referendum, the minds of Gaels turned towards making the most of a new, domestically self-governing Scotland. The focus here is devoted towards evaluating how far existing interests could be defended in a newly-devolved Scotland?

---

1. ***Overview:*** Having emerged from a bleak period during the earlier 20th century of fighting for survival, Scottish Gaeldom became primarily concerned with consolidating the few achievements gained in earlier decades. The Scottish lobby took full advantage of an inclusive new climate by pitching for allies, publicising its case, maximising opportunities, availing of extra funding and making the various hard-earned concessions work for them.

There cannot be any pretension of a level playing field between Scotland and Northern Ireland or that the hurdles encountered were of equal measure.

Frankly, the differences were both stark and rooted in their different histories and contemporary cultures. By 1986, Scottish Gaels, notwithstanding declining numbers of traditional speakers as recounted in Chapters 2 & 3, appeared to be winning its battle for survival. Additional to a growth in Gaelic arts, broadcasting, local government, publishing and education – all with Scottish Office aid – an ambitious new plan was being developed for publicly-funded Gaelic Medium and bilingual Gaelic/English units in primary schools in the Highlands and Hebrides, along with second-language groups further afield in Glasgow, Edinburgh and Perth. That story is taken up later and in subsequent chapters, with guidance from writers like the late Frank Thompson, Domhnall Iain MacLeoid and Edinburgh University academic, Professor Wilson McLeod. While each author has articulated his own perspective of the period, nevertheless the common theme in all three accounts pointed to progress in education, broadcasting and the arts, aided by increased public funding ... all happening since 1950.

By contrast, Irish Gaels, because of their alliance with political nationalism, enjoyed no such bounties. In fact any minor achievements as benefitted Gaeil Uladh came about entirely by their own efforts in the face of opposition from political Unionism, indifference from the Northern Ireland Office, distaste from the BBC and arts bodies, and even negligence from the unreliable "ally" as they viewed successive Dublin governments. In that respect, the experiences of the two Gaelic worlds could not have been more different.

This chapter will endeavour to make sense of the results of new Gaelic policies for Scotland, as well as evaluating the underlying political and cultural features.

The 13 years 1986-1999 represented a consolidation of policy attainments achieved over the previous 20 years. Significantly, in most areas there occurred further developments in just about all areas of activity, which, as indicated in earlier chapters, represented a vindication of the consummate lobbyist strategy long characterising An Comunn Gaidhealach, and so skilfully practised by ACG's eminent and first professional Director, 1965-70, the late Donald John Mackay.*(1) Mackay was not willing to wage political battles where they could not be won or forge alliances where the end result would be to make enemies needlessly. Instead he recognised that with such precarious speakers' numbers, the interests of Scottish Gaelic were best served by bridge-building with every potential policy-maker of whatever political shade in Edinburgh, Glasgow, Inverness and London. So also did he appreciate the prestige of 'Establishment' patrons like the late Queen Mother, who regularly graced the televised Grand Gaelic Concert that followed the annual National Mod, along with an assortment of aristocratic, artistic and political patrons of all parties, plus church leaders, Presbyterian and Catholic alike! By pushing for a prominent place for Gaeldom in Scottish heritage, and marketing it to a wide public, Mackay put Gaeldom beyond the reach of partisan-politics, thereby ensuring continuity of favour whichever party held office in London or Edinburgh.

Given the weakness of Scottish Gaelic in the 1950s and '60s, by way of a contracting Gaidhealtachd and declining numbers of speakers, history might well record the same Donald John Mackay of North Uist as having done more than anyone else to stem what looked in 1965 like the slow death of Scottish Gaelic. At the very least, Mackay ranks highly among those indefatigable champions of what looked then like a dying tongue; and it is appropriate that with a man who, sadly, appears largely forgotten by modern Gaeldom, his seminal contribution is asserted both for the sake of historical accuracy and posterity.*(2)

Another person whose consummate lobbying and developed network of connections pushed the Gaelic cause forward to a degree previously non-envisaged, especially in broadcasting and creation of a Gaelic television service, plus development of a new University in the Highlands and Islands, was Lewis native, John Angus Mackay. This tireless campaigner has been the subject of a deserving biography by Highlands political writer, Roy Pedersen, and was a product of the same Gaelic pragmatists school nurtured by Donald John Mackay.*(3) Pederson's account is both factual and balanced, and takes cognisance of his subject's struggle against personal disabilities of limited sight, hearing and autism. Those hurdles he overcame so as to make it his life's mission arresting the decline of Scottish Gaelic by the creation of durable institutions in education, broadcasting and Gaelic television.

2. ***Bilingual and Gaelic Medium Education*:** The introduction of Scottish Office Specific Grants for Gaelic Medium and Bilingual units, along with the government's funding of Gaelic pre-school education formed the core policy of the 1990s. Both programmes were assisted by the contemporary climate favouring Gaelic interests, which generated the necessary

political will for funding the policy. This ring-fencing policy sheltered Gaelic from the political fall-out that followed the Western Isles Council's embarrassing loss of an estimated £24m when investments in an Icelandic financial venture linked to the Bank of Credit and Commerce International (BCC1) collapsed in June 1991. Had that not been the case, doubtless Gaelic services, as happened other Council amenities, would have taken a substantial hit from subsequent Council economies.*(4)

It is significant that the prevalence of a Conservative administration at the Scottish Office during the 1980s right up until 1997 did not inhibit the progress of what was to be a major Gaelic reform. All the evidence points to the success of An Comunn Gaidhealach's political neutrality policy – as re-affirmed by Donald John Mackay – having rendered desirable results in that most Gaelic educationalists testified to the Tories having dealt even-handedly, even generously, with the Gaelic representatives from ACG and its sister organisations, as well as those from the municipal authorities and universities. Although it is left to Chapters 6 & 7 to deal with the specifics of Gaelic education in Scotland and Northern Ireland, in fact it was in these years that the early rudiments for immersion and bilingualism were laid. New units were opened, with help from the Bernard Leer Foundation, along with Comhairle nan Eilean Siar and Highlands Regional Council. So also was policy planning undertaken and cautious experimentation put in place in the 1990s, which in turn over time expanded into a more adventurous programme throughout the ensuing two decades.

Of course the creation of Comhairle nan Eileann Siar (Western Isles Council) in 1975 as a unitary local authority with a predominantly Gaelic-speaking population, along with other part-bilingual Highlands councils, augmented the process. Such reforms allowed for professional co-ordination of legitimate community demand, thereby providing a basis for further development in the future.*(5) It was the enhanced esteem projected by a new and openly pro-Gaelic local council, presiding over the country's principal Gaidhealtachd, that added extra power to the Gaelic education cause. Somehow, the Council's project seemed immediately relevant to the lives and cultural conditions of Hebrideans, and with Gaelic music, drama and broadcasting having already been promoted in a national context, this step towards Gaelic educational provision seemed consistent with the new momentum. Moreover, Comhairle nan Eilean Siar's willingness to facilitate a bilingual and Gaelic Medium programme, with involvement from leading Gaelic educationalists as Annie MacSween, Dr Findlay Macleod and the late Donald John Maciver, ensured reputable sponsors whose support would prove crucial over the years ahead.*(6)

That said, the Comhairle has not until now created any Gaelic medium schools within its own catchment area. Given that the Comhairle's remit covers Scotland's principal Gaidhealtachd, it is entirely understandable that prominent Gaels like former Bord na Gaidhlig Chair, Arthur Cormack, and Lewis nurseries campaigner, Finlay Macleod, have felt some disappointment with the local authority. Working with existing groups is one thing, but there was an expectation that the Comhairle might itself have given a more innovative lead.

Yet all things considered, by the late 1970s and early '80s, the Western Isles seemed far more ready for a major initiative in Gaelic education than had been the case for over a century. It remained to see just how the bilingual and Gaelic medium programmes would work, and would they stem a century of decline? The frank truth is that the project is an ongoing work, and at this time – i.e. Autumn 2021 – it is difficult to be definite with conclusive evaluations. That it has fed a climate of healthy Gaelic pride is beyond dispute, as well raising a large number of local school children into an educational immersion in their mother tongue. However, it remains to be seen whether the principal beneficiaries will be the families and communities of native Hebrideans and Highlanders, or instead will it be middle class Gaelic university graduates from Edinburgh, Glasgow and Aberdeen determined to educate their children through the mother tongue? This begs the question about whether in a zealous quest to further the cause of Gaelic revivalism, the new Scottish Gaelgeoiri have in fact generated a reinvention?*(7) On that subject, there remain divided views!

3. ***Creation of Comunn na Gaidhlig:*** Arguably, the most significant development of the period occurred in 1984 with the emergence of Comunn na Gaidhlig. This initiative emerged from a general feeling among leading Scottish Gaels that for all its achievements, An Comunn Gaidhleach (founded 1891) had lost direction and was failing to match the robust style of Gaeil Uladh in Northern Ireland or the militant Welsh Language Society, both of whom counterpoised Anglophile

establishments in Belfast and Cardiff respectfully. Something more than just organising the showpiece annual National Mod was required if reversing the serious decline in Gaelic speaker numbers - demonstrated by the Census poll of 1981 showing 79,307 first language Gaels – was to be achieved.

Pedersen's biography of John Angus Mackay noted that following the 1981 Census, alarm bells were sounded by the publicly-funded Highlands and Islands Development Board.

"In light of {Census figures} and following discussions with several prominent Gaels, Iain MacAskill, the pro-Gaelic HIDB Secretary, ... supported by the Board Chairman, Sir Kenneth Alexander, {sought} advice on how the Gaelic community could be supported to develop through the medium of its own language".*(8)

The result was HIDB's appointment in June 1981 of a specialist study group to advise on a plan of action for assisting developments in the Gaidhealtachd linked to the Gaelic language. Membership of this specialist committee was personal to each individual, and was purposely aimed at drawing upon a wide range of expertise and talent within Scottish Gaeldom. Membership of what came to be known as the '*Cor na Gaidhlig*' commission – from the title of its report – were: former ACG Director, the late Donald John Mackay (Chairman); Presbyterian minister and Highland Regional Councillor, Rev John MacArthur; Manager, BBC Radio Highland and Head of Gaelic at BBC Scotland, Mr Fred MacAulay; Scottish Gaelic teacher, Mrs Catriona MacDonald; Deputy Director of Education, Comhairle nan Eilean, Dr Findlay Macleod; Head of Gaelic at Inverness Royal Academy, Mr Duncan McQuarrie; and Education Director at An Comunn Gaidhealach, Mrs Cailean Spencer. The late Scottish journalist and broadcaster, Mr Martin Macdonald, was appointed reporter/secretary to the group, while senior Gaelic figures at HIDB, Messers' Bob Storey and Iain MacAskill were engaged as Assessors.*(9) – To say the least, this commission represented an impressive collection of the finest of Scotland's Gaelic talents, and set about its mandate with an equally impressive diligence. Scottish Gaeldom was fortunate in having so many well-connected patrons and men of outstanding ability at all levels – e.g. the mercurial Donald John Mackay – from Cabinet down to rank and file – a trait Pederson's book graphically highlights – and whose combined influence ensured good will from the UK establishment when finding solutions to problems that might have daunted lesser mortals.

A report titled 'Cor na Gaidhlig' (The Condition of Gaelic) was forthcoming in November 1982, and based on the previous 16 months of research, consultations and assessments of current conditions. Account was taken of several negative factors, including a refusal by council education officials to allow Gaelic teaching in schools, Highlands/Hebridean de-population, inward-migration by non-Gaels, an English mass media, and defeatist attitudes prevalent among so many Gaels. That said, there were encouraging signs; one being increased Gaelic broadcasting, another being the 1979 Celtic Film Festival staged in Benbecula, and growth of the infant Sabhal Mor Ostaig/Gaelic College on Skye. There was also an emergent pre-school Gaelic body, Comhairle nan Sgoiltean Araich, led by a radical campaigner, Finlay Macleod from Lewis, which sought instruction for infant Gaels in their mother tongue as the foundation for subsequent Gaelic medium primary and secondary schooling.*(10) Perhaps, most importantly, the commission observed a twin process of softening hostility towards Gaelic by numerous institutional bodies, while among students and Gaelic lobbyist groups support for political action was simultaneously growing.*(11)

The upshot of the 'Cor' report, was a full review of Gaelic's condition and representation by HIDB, followed by a major and lasting initiative taken to create a new publicly-funded body, **Comunn na Gaidhlig** (Committee of the Gaels), which emerged in 1984. As Pederson and MacKinnon both recall, CNAG, was tasked with adopting a **professional approach** to Gaelic development through directing and assisting bodies promoting Gaelic learners, education, arts, music, broadcasting, feisean, publishing, sports and festivals, plus the all-important lobby of government at Edinburgh and Westminster.*(12) Moreover, in contrast to ACG, which retained control of the National Mod and promotions, CNAG's professionalism was underlined by its constitution and composition. CNAG was in fact a partnership between HIDB, three councils – Comhairle nan Eilean, Highlands and Strathclyde – An Comunn Gaidhealach and the Scottish Office. Its office at Inverness and staff were publicly funded, while HIDB officers were seconded to assist CNAG's early transition. Very importantly, CNAG's emergence meant Scottish Gaels now had their own semi-statutory professional body, recognised by central government and the Scottish Office, whose voice was authentic. So did CNAG'S coming represent a realisation of the path-finding vision of its first Chairman, himself the famous 1960s ACG Director, the redoubtable Mr Donald John Mackay.

Although others brought the cause forward into the 1990s and beyond, nevertheless it was Mackay's strategy of unceasing networking and lobbying, while shunning street marches and radical action along the lines favoured by Welsh linguists (who numbered 21% of Wales's total population, as opposed to 1.8 for Scotland's Gaels), that defined CNAG's programme.

4. **_Gaelic Broadcasting:_** It is significant that the emergent Gaelic renaissance coincided with an increased role for broadcasting generally, which in turn had been skilfully adapted by CNAG advocates towards promoting the language earlier. This was as much a happy coincidence of fortuitous timing as any purposeful strategy by government or the Gaelic lobby, but in any case its potential was identified and utilised fully by the new CNAG leadership operating from head office in Inverness.

The biggest development of the period was the incorporation of Comataidh Telebhisean Gaidhlig (CTG) under the Broadcasting Act of 1990, with the genial Mr John Angus MacKay appointed Director. This same John Angus Mackay, acting under the aegis of the elder Mackay, secured from a reluctant London Thatcher establishment funding to the order of £9.5m for the facilitation of Gaelic programming in Scotland. This was done – as graphically recounted by Pedersen – through an intense and ultimately successful lobby of the Secretary of State for Scotland, Mr George Younger, and his successor, Mr Malcolm Rifkind, each of whom were impressed by the sheer professionalism and commitment of both Mackays.*(13) A London-based professional lobbyist firm was engaged to liaise with ministers, civil servants and Mps – at the-then princely cost of over £10,000 - by John Angus Mackay, with positive results following. So also did CNAG liaise regularly with the All-Party Westminster Gaelic Affairs Committee, itself including previously sceptical Tory MPs like Sir Nicholas Fairbairn and Bill Walker, as well as Labour's Messers' Calum Macdonald and Brian Wilson, and Highlands Liberal Democrats, Mrs Ray Michie, Mr Charles Kennedy, Sir Russell Johnson and Mr Bob MacLennan. (SNP Westminster strength then was restricted to 3 MPs!) *(14) The outcome was an inclusion of Gaelic television with extra funding in the 1990 legislation. Consequently, by 1991, there was a joint commitment between BBC Scotland and the IBA towards providing 300 hours of Gaelic programmes per year. In essence, the outcome represented a triumph for pragmatism and winning influence over radical protest!

By 1995, Gaelic broadcasting had reached 375 hours per year, which included various cultural, sporting (i.e. Shinty), religious, current affairs and Gaelic learners' programmes. This ever-increasing presence on-air had the effect of boosting confidence among Gaels, while stimulating a search for fresh initiatives that impacted positively on audiences in Scotland, Ireland, England and Canada. The long-running *'Can Seo'* series for Gaelic learners was repeated by BBC Scotland in Autumn 1993, and was followed by other learner programmes on IBA channels. Also, schools' broadcasts provided a learners' option, with the production of follow-up tapes marketed to individuals, voluntary groups, colleges and schools. This initiative had the effect of highlighting the increased profile of Gaelic in Scotland, thereby easing the transition to other developments in Gaelic drama, arts and musical coverage.

Gaelic broadcasting took a further step forward in the Autumn of 1992 when Scottish Television commenced the first-ever Gaelic soap opera, *'Machair'*. With most of the film scenes shot around the Isles of Lewis and Harris, and figuring talented Gaelic artistes like the late Simon Mackenzie from Harris and Lewis actor, Domhnull Ruadh, the series was welcomed by An Comunn Gaidhealach, Comunn na Gaidhlig and Scottish Gaeldom generally. It was followed across the Highlands and Hebrides, and parts of Glasgow by an estimated 500,000 viewers, enough to see off the numerous arrays of anti-Gaelic critics and be-grudgers .... regrettably, still prevalent in high places.

More generally, and as indicated in Chapter 3, greater television and radio coverage of Gaelic culture succeeded in bringing to national attention the cream of Gaelic talent. Professional singers like the late and very popular Calum Kennedy from Lewis, Catherine Ann McPhee (Barra), Arthur Cormack (Skye), along with genial instrumentalist, Blair Douglas (also from Skye), and the Gaelic rock groups, *'Runrig'* and *'Capercaile'* (from South Uist), were marketed to appreciative audiences throughout Scotland and beyond.

So too did broadcast coverage of the National Mod and associated events offer younger and non-professional Gaelic artistes the chance of recognition, with all the potential such held out for their future careers. The gifted Lewis traditional singer, Joanne Murray, herself a multiple Mod gold medallist, and fellow islander, Eilidh Mackenzie, lead singer in a family choir who proceeded to a professional musical career, were among those talents emerging from the Mods. Just as distinguished a figure was 1960s gold medalist, Mary Sandeman, who went on to have a British chart topper in 1981, under the stage name, 'Aneka', with 'Japanese Boy'. Indeed the glamorous Miss Sandeman became an icon for generations of aspiring young Gaelic performers aiming for a professional career. And there were others!

Even district choirs and local Gaelic drama groups – both central to community life in the Outer Hebrides – were able to enjoy an enhanced profile from the extended broadcast media. One such beneficiary was Tong Gaelic Choir from the Isle of Lewis, whose best known voice was the same Joanne Murray, already mentioned.*(15) Its successes at the National Mods of 1988 and 1989 resulted in substantial media coverage, including a slot on Calum Kennedy's Grampian television show, leading in turn to a subsidised invitation trip to Vancouver the following year to compete in the ex-patriate Canadian Gaelic Mod. From that trip, a commemorative musical tape was produced and widely distributed.*(16)

Overall, the advent of Gaelic broadcast media – including Radio na Gaidheal and Gaelic programmes on mainstream channels – meant a desirable utility for sustaining the language. That utility included everyday language usage, as well as outlets for cultural talent, Gaelic arts, educational medium, Gaidhealtachd churches, public affairs debates and other interests of the wider Gaelic-speaking and learner community across Scotland. This growing presence on air had the further effect of raising the Gaelic profile, and projecting Gaelic culture to urban and Lowland Scotland. Additionally, it enhanced the self-esteem of Highlanders and Hebrideans in their indigenous language and heritage. Doubtless the gathering climate of civic pride in Scotland's cultural heritage that had become evident since the 1970s, aided the process. However, such advantages were sustained by the comprehensive programme of Gaelic expansion in various areas of Scottish cultural life.

5. **_Gaelic Arts:_** Gaelic arts benefitted from the new era. The National Gaelic Arts Project / Proiseacht nan Eilean had been administered, with a Scottish Office grant from an office in Stornoway. Its briefing was to act as a co-ordinator for various Gaelic drama and arts bodies, of whom Naiseanta na h-Alba (DNA) was the principal youth organisation. It was also the most prominent name in Gaelic drama circuit and enjoyed easy access to leading planners and ministers in the Scottish Office. Such traits were not easily sold to radicals within ACG, as they appeared to indicate an unhealthy level of

establishment collusion. There was also the professional Gaelic theatre company, *'Tosg'*, based at Sabhal Mor Ostaig, Isle of Skye, and funded by the Scottish Arts Council. Its ever-growing profile in the press and broadcast media, as well as in Scottish schools, colleges and the universities, ensured another public outlet for Gaelic artistic talent which boosted its development and key personnel.

Additionally, the feisean – festivals of youth music, choirs, poetry, recitation and drama (similar to the Irish models, except events were non-competitive) – have developed in recent years to a level where they are now a regular cultural fixture across the Highlands, Hebrides and Glasgow. The swift development of the feisean movement may be underlined by the fact that as recently as 1985 only two local feisean were staged, one in the Hebrides and the other in the West Highlands. By contrast, over two decades with a serious organisational input from Gaelic activists and the involvement of leading Gaelic artistes, the results have been phenomenal. These events have now mushroomed to a degree where over 30 feisean occur across the Gaelic world. The result has been to popularise Gaelic music, arts and drama at ground level, while also generating new talent for the growing pool of Gaelic choirs and drama companies, not to mention Gaelic broadcasting.*(17) In the process, a dedicated organisation been created to promote the feisean movement, under the aegis of the publicly-funded umbrella body, Comunn na Gaidhlig – called Feisean nan Gaidheal. The latter's Director is the acclaimed Scottish Gaelic singer, Arthur Cormack, who operates full time and from an office in his native Skye.*(18) Having such a distinguished and popular figure at its helm has been no small factor in the feisean growth.

Publication in 2006 of a colourful history book of the movement's first 25 years showed confidence, plus a clear line of development. It is important to note that as valuable as Scottish Office funding has proven to be, the success of feisean activities is linked mainly to the voluntary energies and commitments of a network of Gaelic community activists throughout Scotland.*(19) In many respects, the feisean growth was a predictable corollary of the cautious Gaelic revival in Scotland. It offers an outlet for youthful Gaelic talent, and is closely geared to the development of children and teenagers whose standard of music, drama and recitation might not have quite reached Mod-levels, but nonetheless could be prepared for future such occasions. Willingness by the Scottish Office to invest public funds in young Gaelic talent also indicates a serious commitment to further development, along with implicit confidence of Gaelic's place in Scotland's national arts agenda.

Another dimension to Gaeldom's rising public profile is evidenced by the first-ever scheduled appearance of a Gaelic input to the official itinerary of the 1997 Edinburgh International Arts Festival.*(20) Although Gaelic arts had long featured on the Edinburgh Fringe, elevation to official status for some six concerts augured well for the language's future status and recognition. Moreover, having a role at Edinburgh, however belated, implied recognition from the Scottish cultural establishment. Subsequent Edinburgh festivals have built on that first appearance of 1997. This development should strengthen Gaeldom's future position for educational, literary and artistic purposes, with all necessary funding and political recognition, thus underlining Gaeldom's incorporation within the broad cultural framework of Scotland. - Such a positive change from times past when the Gaelic survival was in doubt!

6. _Press Advances:_ Another area of advancement was in the Scottish regional press. Though no enduring national Gaelic newspaper existed on a similar scale to the Irish language paper, '*La*', in Belfast, in fact for a period in the 1990s, there was a Scottish periodical called '*An Gaidheal Ur*'. Unfortunately, the latter was forced to close due to a lack of regular income from subscribers, advertisers and the Gaelic Arts Project; a fate that ultimately befell '*La*', but after a much longer battle and life time (see Chap 7). However, from the 1980s onwards several Scottish papers from 1980 onwards did facilitate Gaelic readers with columns and correspondents, plus reviews of Gaelic publications.

This gradual trend occurred in response to general lobbyist pressure from An Comunn Gaidhleach, but also the growing Gaelic profile in broadcasting, schools and the arts. There was a sense that Gaelic was slowly arising to meet the challenges of the 1980s and '90s in a professional and self-confident way such as had not been seen before. Moreover, it was public knowledge that the Gaelic language and arts were being supported by central government and the councils, and there was some Gaelic road signage; all of which boosted the image, enough to make press interest both likely and appropriate.

The titles facilitating Gaelic were, unsurprisingly, Gaidhealtachd-based or directed at Gaelic learner communities. The *Stornoway Gazette* had a Gaelic specialist page; it being targeted at the Outer Hebrides with its native-speaking majority.*(21) So too did the weekly Skye-based *West Highland Free Press*, edited by former Labour MP, Brian Wilson, himself a dedicated Gaelic enthusiast. The latter included a monthly Gaelic arts supplement, *An Canan*, while another monthly Gaelic supplement, *Guth na Gaidhlig*, appeared with the *Highland Free Press*. Other Gaelic-supporting papers include the *Inverness Courier* and *Oban Times*, along with the *Aberdeen Press and Journal*; covering Aberdeen, whose university boasts a major Celtic Studies department, with abundant Gaelic lecturers, students and researchers, plus ancillary staff, billeted throughout the city.*(22)

Later on, the convergence of 13 Highlands and Hebridean tertiary colleges into The University of the Highlands and Islands, with its vibrant Gaelic/Celtic Studies Division, also generated a convergence of Gaelic scholars on Oban, Inverness, Portree, Stornoway, Perth and Kinross. Those are the same places served by newspapers with Gaelic sections and writers, many of which, though not all, are deemed likely areas of Gaelic interest.*(23)

While the University was not formally established until 2011, with Princess Anne as first Chancellor, in fact its planning and academic preparations go back to 1992. Progress was closely monitored by regional, as much as national press, not least by a range of Gaelic commentators who saw real prospects for the development and nourishment of Gaelic educational, artistic, cultural and linguistic interests. How far those hopes have been realised is a subject for evaluation in Chapters 6 & 8? Suffice to add, press comment and establishment leanings have divided between supporters and be-grudgers with press paying a pivotal role ... like so much else of the developments in Scotland's Gaelic world.

Finally, additional to the regional papers' embracement of Gaelic linguistics and the culture, one national paper signed up to the same cause, *The Scotsman*. From the early 1990s, the latter engaged a weekly Gaelic columnist with a broad remittance for commentary on all issues affecting the progress and impact of Gaelic on Scottish life. His column was titled '*An t-Albannach*'. This adoption certainly offered a degree of kudos to the efforts of ACG, CNG and others. Conversely, at that time, the *Glasgow Herald* offered no such facility to the Gaels, notwithstanding the fact of Glasgow boasting a vibrant Gaelic community and Gaelic medium schools. Also, it must be added that several papers, e.g. *Scottish Daily Express* and *Daily Mail,* carried disparaging anti-Gaelic material, and discouraged readers from either regarding or supporting the Gaelic advances in media, radio, Arts or education.

Again, elevation of the language to the columns of respected national papers – where it happened – elevated the Gaelic image beyond regional and tribalistic visuals of bygone decades. With Gaelic now playing to a national audience, such developments encouraged pro-Gaelic activists in the Labour, Liberal and Scottish Nationalist parties to demand a national policy for the promotion of Gaelic as part of the modern Scottish identity.*(24) Significantly, Gaelic enjoyed a fair quota of supporters in the Scottish Tory Party, and indeed this record of tri-partisanship proved thoroughly conducive to the language's best interests in the decades immediately preceding and following constitutional home rule from Edinburgh.

This gain in turn led to a climate in the new millennium favouring Gaelic imagery in public signage, civil service documents, university and other institutional titles, such as projected an enhanced profile that relished Scotland's ancient bardic language. Even the Scottish police vehicles carried bilingual signs/notices, as does the modern British passport carry a Gaelic translation of title. How far that post-home rule phenomenon with its expanded imagery really boosted the language in terms of maintaining speakers and promoting its appeal to target groups is a question to be examined later in this book. All this occurred despite the 2005 Scottish Gaelic Language Act posturing sentiments of tolerance and cultural esteem.

7. *Gaelic in Local Government:* As indicated in Chapter 3, the creation in 1975 of a new unitary authority in the Gaelic-speaking Outer Hebrides provided the catalyst for further developments in so many different areas. There were of course other local councils in the Highlands and Inner Hebrides where Gaelic lobbying bore fruit in terms of grants and recognition, not least the Highlands Regional Authority. Yet the emergence of a purposeful Gaelic local authority was unique to all-Scotland and the UK as a whole, not to mention serving a positive tonic to the morale of An Comunn Gaidhealeach and its supporters in the broad Scottish Gaelic lobby.

This new departure in local government – itself part of a wider programme of fundamental local government reform across Great Britain - might have been arguable given the limited population of the Outer Hebrides, itself less than 29,000. However, given the scattered Hebridean community's historic dependence on crofting and fishing, and with the latter very much in decline, those characteristics underlined the homogenous nature of the community. Gaelic was perhaps the greatest unifying feature, and it was to a rescue of the language from its residual decline that the Council prioritised its energies.

Although by the mid-1970s crofting and fishing had greatly diminished, their importance to the Hebridean economy and social infra-structure was, and remains, vital. Such factors have been thoroughly evaluated in the historical context by James Hunter's authoritative history of Hebridean crofters.*(25) At the same time, replacements for the old pre-occupations had to be found, and this was a task challenging the energies of the new Comhairle nan Eilean Siar, acting in unison with the Highlands and Islands Development Board - and its successor body – bidding to stem de-population and rural decline. How well the Council managed that challenge is open to debate, but that it sought to defend the historic homeland of the Scottish Gaels as cogently as happened is established fact. This meant prioritising the place of the Gaelic language in schools, the community and voluntary organisations; a role for which the Council became a publicist and facilitator. It also meant working in tandem with other bodies to encourage home industries, e.g. Harris tweed and Hebridean crafts, plus local tourism, in the hope of keeping the Western Isles economy functional.

Another factor challenging Comhairle nan Eilean Siar is the unique geographical expanse of the Outer Hebrides; its strong religious traditions divided between the Presbyterian majority and Catholic minority, and a very scattered population in what is the UK's third smallest local authority. The population is mainly concentrated on the Isle of Lewis, whose principal town, Stornoway, is the de-facto Hebridean capital. From there, the Council operates its principal administration, while facilitating full Council meetings and those of its committees.

That dominance from Stornoway has inevitably provoked periodic tensions with the Southern Hebridean islands over such issues as health and educational resources distribution, but not to any major degree. The sturdy Calvinist character – of assorted Free Church, Church of Scotland and Free Presbyterians - in the northern islands of Lewis, Harris and North Uist, is well known, along with its uncompromising Sabbatarian and temperance agenda. The latter has long been counterpoised by an equally staunch Catholicism in the less-populated southern Hebridean islands of Barra, South Uist, Eriskay and southern Benbecula, where attitudes towards alcohol and Sunday opening are more relaxed. A Hebridean community, where hard Calvinism and traditional Scottish Catholicism have co-existed since the Reformation, held out prospects for grim divisions. So also were potential fault-lines in place over issues like Sunday closing of parks and pubs, plus islands' ferry and air services.

Yet somehow nothing of the kind actually happened. Notwithstanding occasional strains, actually the experience has been one of compatibility. The late Sir Compton Mackenzie vented social strains with his famous televised novel, 'Whisky Galore', but therewith the story with all its humour and literary licence gives way to the sober reality of Hebridean communal détente. Indeed given the assorted Presbyterian forces prevailing in Stornoway and the North, and the durable Catholic fraternity of the South, the avoidance of religious conflict ranks among Comhairle nan Eilean's positive attainments over the past 45 years since inception. Doubtless it was partly facilitated by a healthy desire among Hebrideans to work within their mixed community's parameters. Significantly, with Rev. Donald Macaulay (local Church of Scotland minister) as first Convenor and Fr Calum Maclennan, Catholic priest at St Mary's Church, Benbecula, as Deputy Convenor, a lead was given from the top!

Census figures for Gaelic speakers by 2001 are as follows: Lewis 56%, Harris 69%, Benbecula 56% (excluding the now-departed RAF base personnel), North Uist 67%, South Uist 71%, and the southern Hebridean islands of Barra, Eriskay, Vatersay, Scalpay and Berneray 68-75%. Other one-time Gaelic communities on the islands of Mingulay and the famous St Kilda were totally eroded by evacuations occurring earlier in the 20th century. It needs adding that even the Lewis Gaidhealtachd is undermined by Stornoway's position as a largely English-speaking town. This factor renders Stornoway comparable to Dublin of the past and its surrounding Anglicised Pale, something noted by linguists Marsaili MacLeod and Cassie Smith-Christmas.*(26) Furthermore, Stornoway's dominance of Hebridean commerce, municipal administration and education forced rural Gaidhealtachd dwellers to conduct normal business in English. As well as offering little incentive to outsiders to respect Gaelic as the primary medium of communication, the English ethos had an assimilative effect on upcoming Gaels from rural districts.*(27) Those factors might have damaged Gaelic more had not the new Comhairle nan Eilean Siar, supported by CNAG, adopted in 1986 an updated and comprehensive bilingual policy, with preference accorded to Gaelic.

8. **_Comhairle nan Eilean Siar_** – Publicist of Gaelic Revivalism! Although Comhairle nan Eilean Siar has critics among Gaelic activists and writers alike – being variously accused of lacking imagination and robustness – available evidence points to the Council having been a robust, if also pragmatic champion of its own Gaidhealtachd. Moreover, at the time of writing, with the Comhairle being less than five years off its first half century, such a view is based on a creditable track record of activity.

Of course it is for other academics more erudite than this author to offer their particular assessments, and one includes in that category the scholarly Professor Wilson McLeod, whose recently published treatise on Scottish Gaelic history of the past two centuries is authoritative to the point of definitive, meriting the attention of all readers with serious interests in the subject.*(28) Yet within its financial limitations, and despite all the criticisms, I found the Comhairle to have been an ongoing force for bilingual development.

Comhairle nan Eilean Siar's front-line bilingual campaign was adopted from the beginning and targeted three principal priorities.

First was the Council's own Gaelic projection. A preliminary bilingual policy was adopted in April 1975, with a Code of Practice following in November 1977, which was up-dated in October 1986.*(29) The latter committed the Comhairle to providing Gaelic medium for all educational, social, environment and cultural services. That goal was clarified from the start.

"**Is e run a phoilseasaidh … gum bithdeadh Na h-Eilean siar na coimhearsnachd da-chananan co-labairt gus am bitheadh an rogha canain aif muinnyir an aite anns gach suidheachaidh**". *(30)

"**The Council's policy is that the Western Isles should be a fundamentally bilingual community in which English and Gaelic are used concurrently as**

languages of communication, that people can have the choice.. in as many situations as possible".

From the beginning, many Comhairle staff have been fluent Gaelic speakers. Notices and communications are bilingual, as are records of plenary Comhairle meetings, along with those of committees, interviews and correspondence. Actual deliberations of the full Comhairle and committee meetings have been undertaken in optional mediums, but with a preference for Gaelic. Additionally, the special post of Bilingual Development Officer was created, to which current incumbent, former teacher and Lewis native speaker, Dolina Macleod, was appointed in 1985.*(31) Throughout the past 3.5 decades, Mrs Macleod patiently – and diplomatically – developed a programme of Gaelic primacy in Council affairs, while also ensuring the tedious task of translating Council documents and notices.*(32)

Second, Council environmental and tourist facilities were 'gaelicised'. Streets and roads were given Gaelic names, as were Council buildings and institutions, while the Council adopted a robust plan for encouraging and assisting local employers and voluntary groups, including the churches, to use Gaelic for their services and literature. Church attitudes have varied considerably. The strongly-placed Free Church has long used Gaelic for services, psalms and literature both in Stornoway and the rural Gaidhealtachd. Others such as the Church of Scotland, Free Presbyterians and modest Episcopalian church adopted optional Gaelic services. With Catholic authorities in the Southern Isles, Gaelic Masses had long been regular fare in Barra's two churches, plus those of Benbecula, Eriskay and South Uist. However, the small Jesuit-run chapel of Most Holy Redeemer, Stornoway, proved less eager, and only in Autumn 1992 did a monthly Gaelic Mass finally commence.*(33)

Third, priority was given to the development of Gaelic as both a mainstream subject and medium for learning in Hebridean schools. Gaelic education has long proved to be a major plank in the Council's bilingual programme, especially with a drive towards the provision of Gaelic Medium units. This programme included appointment of the first Bilingual Policy Adviser in 1975, the respected Gaelic educationalist, Dr Finlay Macleod, and in due course the Head of Gaelic Studies at the Nicolson Institute, Stornoway, Mr Donald John Maciver, took up position in 1989, bringing with him a lifetime's commitment to assorted Gaelic causes, including, later, the presidency of An Comunn Gaidhealach. More will be said about both those figures in Chapter 6, with each proving major policy initiators in their time. It is especially significant that both figures held strong commitments to the Gaelic Medium schools plan, which gradually emerged in the first 25 years after 1975. Additionally, in 1990 Comhairle nan Eilean's educational department created a new Gaelic Resources Database. This innovation was developed in liaison with other local authorities and Sabhal Mor Ostaig, Skye – then operating as a Gaelic F.E. College – and aimed at providing Gaelic resources to schools and colleges. By July 1997, the Database had built up over 8,000 records on Gaelic books, journals, videos, posters and music, and had become a prime utility to public and voluntary bodies, along with researchers throughout Scotland's broad Gaelic sector.*(34)

Generally, Comhairle nan Eilean Siar has proved an effective backer of Gaelic educational and cultural interests. Notwithstanding the Comhairle's critics, positive evidence speaks aloud. The latter includes hosting various international events for minority language groups, including the 1990 Stornoway conference for representatives from European minor language groups. Additionally, the Comhairle twinned with two bilingual Gaelic authorities in both parts of Ireland; namely Clare County Council from the South and Newry and Mourne Council in County Down.*(35) Moreover, the Council kept faith with its Gaelic policy, even in the embarrassing aftermath of the BCCI crash of 1991. Despite the loss of £24,000,000 investment capital, prompting a steep rise in local taxation, in turn generating pressures for cutting services, Gaelic education and cultural pursuits were not hit by the economies.

9. ***Politics of the Highlands and Hebrides:*** It is significant that until 1994 Comhairle nan Eilean Siar was one of the few remaining non-party councils in the United Kingdom.*(36) Although there existed active Hebridean Labour and Scottish Nationalist organisations, with smaller Liberal Democrat and Conservative associations, rivalries were restricted to elections to Westminster and, after 1999, the new Scottish Parliament. Until then, Council elections were characterised by local issues and contested by candidates on non-party slates. Even when political currents resulted in changes of constituency representatives – e.g. SNP loss of the Western Isles Westminster seat to Labour's Calum Macdonald in 1987,

followed by Macdonald's own defeat in 2005 to the SNP's Angus MacNeill – still the tradition of non-party local contests largely prevailed. However, in 1992, in response to the aftermath of the BCCI fall-out, Labour ran a slate of local candidates, which was later countered, rather successfully, by the SNP. Still, the preference for independents remained among Hebridean voters in local contests.

Further away is Skye, Lochaber, Easter Ross, Fortwilliam, Nairn, Moray, Caithness, Sutherland, Badenoch and Inverness. This whole sprawling area of 9.8 thousand square miles is governed by the Highlands Regional Council/Comhairle na Gaidhealtachd with its headquarters at Inverness. An estimated 12,000 native Gaelic speakers (from a total population of 236,000) are governed by this unitary 80 seat authority, which came into being in 1996 under the Local Government (Scotland) Act of 1994, replacing previous county authorities. Unlike Comhairle nan Eilean Siar, which returns one MP to Westminster and one MSP directly elected to the Scottish Parliament (since its creation in 1999), Highlands Council area elects a total of 3 Westminster MPs from single-member constituencies and 10 MSPs to Edinburgh.*(37) There are a couple of major differences between the two councils.

First, while the Western Highlands was a one-time kernel of Gaelic speakers in previous centuries, as testified by Withers and McLeod *(38), in fact numbers had dwindled to the fractions identified by HM Census enumerators in 1991 and 2001.*(39) Add those figures to the reality of large parts of the Eastern Highlands having no real Gaelic tradition, and it quickly becomes apparent that Gaelic fortunes were very much at the mercy of a regional authority where Gaels had little political 'clout'. Indeed Gaels were forced to rely on the lobbyist influence of An Comunn Gaidhealach and its sister bodies, plus positive sentiments and facilitative legislation enunciated by the Scottish Office.

Second, in contrast to the largely non-party Comhairle nan Eilean Siar, Highlands Regional Council has become politicised in recent years. Whereas in 1970s and '80s contests, Independents normally took some 80% of seats (eg. 1978, Independents won 40 of 47 seats, while in 1982 Independents took 42 out of 52), after 2000 Council elections featured a multi-party battle ground for Labour, SNP, Liberals and Conservatives, plus Independents. With an SNP-led coalition emerging in 2007, this ushered in further coalitions for running the Council, usually involving the SNP and Labour, but invariably involving independents. That said, with Gaelic interests having been embraced by all mainstream Scottish parties, the Gaelic lobby was not negatively impacted by political changes at the Council.

Similar conditions applied in other councils whose jurisdictions extend to the Highlands and Inner Hebrides; namely North Argyle & Bute and Perth & Kinross. In both the latter authorities, Gaelic speakers are few and scattered, and made only the most modest demands for Gaelic-medium education, public signage and funding of cultural events.

Overall, Highlands Council from its inception in 1996, and its Highlands Regional predecessor, proved supportive of Gaelic interests. The Council has long held a policy commitment to uphold the status of Gaelic in education, the arts and general community affairs, and this was followed assiduously. It appointed a Gaelic education director, Dr Donald John Macleod, who was previously Education Director at Comunn na Gaidhlig. Shortly after, the talented Dr Macleod produced an acclaimed discussion paper on the future of Gaelic Medium Education throughout Scotland.*(40) The latter was to eventually provide the basis for future Gaelic planning, and made no small input to the Gaelic Language Act passed by the new Scottish Parliament in the ensuing decade. – See Chapter 6.

Within the Highlands Region, the principal Gaidhealtachd – indeed the only one of any size - is the Isle of Skye. In 1996, Skye native speakers amounted to 58% of the population, with 5 Gaelic Medium primary units – within schools - catering for a total of 220 pupils, while a further 18 pupils were taught in local Gaelic nursery units. *(41) When Skye speakers are added to those of neighbouring Lochalsh, the overall figure for Gaelic speakers sits at 46% of the local population. Moreover, those figures have increased over the past 25 years in line with development and Gaelic expansion. Accordingly, while demand for Gaelic educational and cultural facilities is not so great as in the Outer Hebrides, it is still considerable.

Of course, being near to the mainland, Skye has long contended with an influx of affluent English speakers from the Lowlands and England, nick-named 'White Settlers', few of whom show much regard or even respect for the Gaelic language. Moreover, such people by their presence and affluence have had an undesirable impact on local house prices, forcing them up and pushing impoverished 'locals' off the island in search of affordable housing. So also have others of the same social group subtly lobbied against bilingual road signs and even sought to undermine the teaching of Gaelic in schools to which their children are sent.

Actually, to its credit, Highlands Council in the 1990s and beyond stood shoulder to shoulder with An Comunn Gaidhealach and Comunn na Gaidhlig in defence of Skye's Gaelic character. Aside from pressing through with bilingual signposts and aiding Gaelic medium schools, the Council also embarked on a campaign of safeguarding island crafts with grants and local preferences for to retain the Gaelic population. So too was generous help extended to the Feiseans, with local music & drama festivals and shinty tournaments.

Further safeguarding of that identity came from the location of two prominent institutions, both essential to the Gaelic world. First was the siting of a pro-active Radio na Gaidheal studio in Portree. Second was the presence of Sabhal Mor Ostaig, the Gaelic University college, which boosted the Gaelic profile ever further, making it something of a pillar in Scottish Gaeldom's slowly-developing world. Therefore, while broadcasting in Gaelic continues from Skye and the college retains its leading status in the Gaelic world, Skye's Gaelic character looks more secure. The Council has proved its metal in that process. However, the commercial Anglicising trends have not been wholly stemmed, thus requiring Gaeldom's defences being based on assorted foundations of Gaelic medium education, literature, arts and media. Anything less might not endure in the medium or long term.

10. **_Westminster Initiatives:_** As previously demonstrated, Scottish Gaeldom was not without supporters at Westminster. Notwithstanding the failure of Donald Stewart's 1981 Private Member bill – titled Gaelic Miscellaneous Provisions (Scotland) Bill – with its plan to rectify gaps in statutory recognition (which fell victim to English Tory filibusterers), in fact the Gaelic cause was kept alive, partly by the assiduous lobbying of An Comunn Gaidhealach and the Gaelic Society of London, and partly by the combined actions of sympathetic MPs located across the spectrum.*(42) In particular, the appointment of Brian Wilson as the Scottish Frontbench Labour team's Gaelic Affairs Spokesman, and following Labour's return to

government in May 1997, as Minister with the Gaelic Portfolio, augured positive prospects for Gaelic promotion.

As indicated earlier, an ad-hoc Commons Scottish Gaelic Affairs Committee emerged after 1987, comprising, among others, Calum Macdonald and Brian Wilson (Labour), Sir Russell Johnson and Mrs Ray Michie (Liberal Democrats), along with Sir Nicholas Fairburn and Bill Walker (Tories).*(43) This group held regular meetings in the decade 1987-97, and sought to generate a positive atmosphere towards the Gaelic language and culture, something its cross-party membership served to strengthen. This was to prove especially valuable during Committee stages of the 1990 Broadcasting Bill, which, as recounted by Roy Pedersen, facilitated Gaelic television with £9.5m funding and a statutory governing body.*(44) Yet it needs adding that despite modest gains, the process of declining numbers of native Gaelic speakers though slowed, was not stemmed. Nor, despite all the major campaigns, did CNAG, ACG, sister bodies, or indeed Comhairle nan Eilean Siar, succeed with halting slow Anglicisation of the Hebridean Gaidhealtachd, as shown by Census figures for the period. Given the vast socio-economic advantages enjoyed by English as a medium of commerce and media, not to mention its international appeal and telecommunications, perhaps it was unrealistic to expect that Gaelic could compete, even in its own cradle territory.

Still, the Hebrides remains the last real hope for Scottish Gaeldom, both as a native language and second language for learners. While government cannot by itself either stem or re-stimulate a language, nevertheless it can offer some protection in terms of statutory recognition and entitlements, as well as funding support. This was the process that led eventually to preparations for the passage of a Gaelic Language Act by the newly elected Scottish Parliament in its first decade. See Chapter 6 for details.

In anticipation of Home Rule, and with much encouragement from Wilson, Macdonald, the Liberals and SNP, Comunn na Gaidhlig took the initiative. A conference was called for Spring 1997, policy papers produced and a campaign initiated for secure status for the Gaelic language in Scotland. Moreover, the precise legal status to be accorded Gaelic by the new Scottish Parliament was an issue of particular interest to Comunn na Gaidhlig and its affiliate bodies.*(45) Given the sweeping referendum victory approving a Scottish Parliament of September 1997, Scottish Gaeldom looked forward to the transfer of policy making and legislation to the devolved new Edinburgh administration. It was also hoped that Home Rule would usher in a fresh era of co-operation where Gaelic interests would be secured by an elected Scottish Parliament that might prioritise the safeguarding of a vital component of Scotland's national heritage more effectively than occurred in Westminster days. How far that goal was realised after two decades of Home Rule will be evaluated in Chapters 6 and 8.

> **11. _Generally_:** – as Scottish Gaeldom reached the millennium, it appeared to have secured survival, albeit without achieving any great popular revival in Gaelic speakers' numbers. This attainment while modest was also realistic in its scope, and happened against the back drop of an all-encroaching Anglicisation of culture, language and social trends, to which Scotland was as subject as all other majority English-speaking nations. So also was it challenged by the computerisation of communications, language, literature and business methods ... much of which experienced growth over the last two decades of the 20th century. Nor were those challenges relaxed in recent decades since 2000. Put simply, Gaelic was pitting itself against some exceptionally powerful tides; raising issues which Dr Marissa Macleod & Dr C. Smith-Christmas, along with Professor Wilson McLeod, have each sought to address in their respective treatises.*(46)

Yet in challenging Scottish education to acknowledge its Gaelic dimension, while pushing Gaelic arts and broadcasting, and utilising a new Hebridean Gaelic local authority, the forces of Scottish Gaeldom had created a positive climate that enabled their voice to be heard. This success underpinned the professional lobbyist strategy of An Comunn Gaidhealach, and most especially that of its visionary director, Donald John Mackay. By avoiding confrontation and pushing the Gaelic appeal to a wide public audience and cultural establishment, Mackay's co-operation agenda represented a triumph of pragmatism over agitation. This was a view with which ACG's independent-minded late historian, Frank Thompson, largely concurred.*(47) In charting that strategy, Mackay was aware of the futility of a political campaign – Irish style – that lacked both numbers and potential for success. Whatever may have been his instincts, Mackay saw no merit in Quixotic campaigns. Nor, according to Thompson, did any of his immediate successors, all of whom followed the same pattern of cautious lobbying and networking where it mattered.*(48) It was not that Mackay or his successors lacked sympathy for Gaeil Uladh or the Welsh Language Society, both of whom were battling for their respective causes. However, Scottish Gaeldom was weakest of all the Celtic nations in numbers, and thus all the more dependent on good will and patronage.

All other developments emerging over the past half century were borne of the Mackay plan. The willingness of all mainstream Scottish political parties and their elected representatives to reform education, adapt the environment to provide for Gaelic inclusion, and the creation of Comunn na Gaidhlig with abundant government funding, along with positive attitudes adopted by newspaper editors and broadcasters towards Gaelic, proved cumulatively beneficial to the slow renaissance of Scottish Gaelic. It was a rebirth whose signs were self-evident. In the framework of "insider" interest groups, as charted by the English political scientist, Professor Wyn Grant. Those two groups, An Comunn Gaidhealach and Comunn na Gaidhlig, by virtue of their co-operation, links, personnel and influence, represented archetypal insiders, and benefitted accordingly through legislation and funding.*(49)

After the historic referendum of 1997 declared for Home Rule, and ensuing elections of 1999 produced a Scottish national parliament, there was a sense that the new arrangements had produced more than a constitutional change. Its tentacles embraced all aspects of Scottish political, cultural and civic life from across the Gaelic world. The eminent Scottish historian, Tom Devine, viewed " …. the devolution settlement … as more a process than an event..", with a future that looked exciting if also unpredictable.*(50) It was a future to which Gaidheal na h-Alba looked with nervous hope more than confidence?

FOOTNOTES and REFERENCES

1. This view was emphasised in a 2019 interview with Professor Ken MacKinnnon, plus two other senior figures from An Comunn Gaidhealach both of whom asked not to be named.

2. It is a measure of the late Donald John Mackay's immense legacy that to this day, over 20 years after his death in 2000, he is revered among a generation of elderly Hebrideans on his native North Uist, and on the Isle of Skye where he spent many years. A foundation to assist young Gaelic musicians and cultural artistes has been established in his memory. - Ref. Interview with Arthur Cormack, Organiser, Feisean nan Gaidheal and former Chairman, Bord na Gaidhlig 20-2-20.

3. Roy Pedersen Gaelic Guerrilla: John Angus Mackay, <u>Gael Extraordinaire</u> (2019, Luath Press, Edinburgh). – This book is strongly recommended to all serious observers of post-1980s survival struggles by Scotland's Gaels.

4. Ramifications from the financial collapse of an Icelandic bank where Comhairle nan Eilean Siar had invested large fiscal assets were painfully felt in services cuts throughout the Outer Hebrides over 1991 and '92. The affair led to the dismissal of the Council's Director of Finance, Mr Donald Macleod, in July 1991, the enforced resignation in August 1991 of Council Convenor, Rev Donald Macauley (accused of weak leadership), and early retirement of Chief Executive, Dr George Macleod, in 1992. See <u>Municipal Journal</u> of 19th July 1991, and coverage at the time in the <u>Herald</u>, <u>Scotsman</u>, <u>Stornoway Gazette</u> and <u>West Highland Free Press</u>. Also, in August 1992, this author was treated to a very frank and critical view of the Council's conduct by the-then Western Isles MP, Calum Macdonald.

5. Ref. Discussions with the late Donald John Maciver (August 1992 and October 1997), plus interview with Mrs Dolina Macleod, Bilingual Officer, Comhairle nan Eilean an Siar, August 1991, and follow-up correspondence 1990/91. Mrs Macleod was at pains to impress upon this author the official pro-Gaelic policy of Comhairle nan Eilean Siar, and ensured ready provision of official documents.

6. Discussions and correspondence with the late Donald John Maciver,1991-97. Also, Mrs Annie MacSween, discussions / correspondence December 2019.

7. Mrs MacSween, a Gaelic lecturer, linguist, policy planner and local historian from the Isle of Lewis, in discussions with this author, was decidedly underwhelmed about the place of Gaelic Medium education in terms of the survival and/or revival of Gaelic among ordinary crofter folk in the Highlands and Hebrides.

8. Pederson (2019); p. 85.

9. See Pederson (2019); p. 86.

10. MacKinnon (1991); Chap 8, pp 118-120.

11. Information gleaned from (i) Pedersen (2019); pp 86-88 and (ii) MacKinnon (1991); pp 118-122.

12. See (i) Pedersen (2019); pp 86-91 and (ii) MacKinnon (1991); pp 116 – 122.

13. Pedersen (2019) – Ibid.

14. (i) MacKinnon (1991); Chap 8. and (ii) Pedersen (2019); pp 88-97.

15. Joanne and her husband, Rev. Hugh Stewart (now a Presbyterian Minister at Uig, Lewis), were both personal friends of this author, and I enjoyed many social evenings with they and their families on Lewis. So much information about daily routines and challenges in this Scottish Gaidhealtachd was gleaned through friendship and sharing in the hospitality of their homes. There were other Hebridean – mainly Lewis – friends whom I made, but Joanne, along with the late Donald-John Maciver and his lovely wife, Alice, of Stornoway (also welcomed me to their home) were among the most forthcoming. So also did I benefit from numerous shared recalls by the late Mrs Peggy Maclennan, plus Joanne's mother, Mrs Catherine-Rose Murray, and sister, Catriona – all singers and stalwarts of Tong Gaelic Choir, Lewis. Other valued sources included Mr Murdo Macdonald (sadly deceased, Lewis/Aberdeen), Mr & Mrs Michael and Donella Bartlett and their family of Bru, Lewis, and Rev Donald Michael Macinnes, formerly of Bragar, Lewis, Presbyterian Minister at St Columba's Highlands Gaelic Church, Glasgow.

16. Discussions with Joanne Murray, 23rd August 1993, and Lewis Gaelic musician, Noel Eadie, 21st August 1993 – Stornoway. Also, further discussions with the late Murdo Macdonald, and Messers' Iain-Harry Maclennan and Donald Mciver (both sadly deceased of Callinish, Lewis), and his widow, Mrs Seonaig Maciver.

17. Discussions with Arthur Cormack, Mrs Dolina Macleod, Bilingual Development officer at Comhairle nan Eilean Siar and Mr Finlay Macleod of the Gaelic Nurseries Association, all of whom confirmed the pivotal role played by the Feisean movement in the cultural development of Gaelic school children in the Hebrides.

18. A combination of proven organisational skills, strong cultural commitments and the nationwide profile of a much-admired Gaelic singer, added to a rather likeable persona, made Arthur Cormack an ideal figure for leading the Feisean movement.

19. <u>Feis: the first twenty-five years of the Feis movement</u> – Edited Kate Martin – Published by Feisean nan Gaidheal 2006 (Meall House, Portree, Isle of Skye).

20. See official records of Edinburgh Festival 1997, and each year thereafter, for details of Gaelic projects.

21. The Gaelic columnist for the <u>Stornoway Gazette</u> throughout the 1990s and thereafter was Donald John Maciver, to whom this book is co-dedicated.

22. It is noticeable that Gaelic academics at the University of Aberdeen were among the most consummate contributors to the city's Press and Journal and local radio.

23. The upgrading of Highlands tertiary colleges to form University of the Highlands and Islands, though officially decreed in 2011, had long been a work in progress. Its inception was welcomed by An Comunn Gaidhealach and sister organisations, who, quite reasonably, viewed the new institution as a likely guardian and facilitator of the Gaelic language and culture. Amongst the constituent colleges was Sabhal Mhor Ostaig on the Isle of Skye, where a new generation of Scottish Gaelic teachers were trained ... under the University's auspices.

24. See McKee (1997); Chap 4.

25. James Hunter (1976); Chaps 11 & 12, pp 184-220.

26. See Marsaili MacLeod & Cassie Smith-Christmas (Eds.) <u>Gaelic in Contemporary Scotland: The Revitalisation of an Endangered Language</u> (2018, Edinburgh University Press), Chap. 12.

27. McKee (1997); Chap 4, pp 61-63.

28. Wilson McLeod <u>Gaelic in Scotland; Policies, Movements and Ideologies</u> (2020, Edinburgh University Press).

29. Bilingual Policy Update, Comhairle nan Eilean Siar, October 1986.

30. Ibid, p 1.

31. Correspondence V. McKee/Dolina Macleod, December – April 1990/91. Generally, I am most grateful to Mrs Macleod for the time, trouble and kindly spirit with which she rendered immense assistance with early research matters.

32. McKee V. <u>Contemporary Politics</u> (1995), p 99.

33. (i) Information on local Protestant churches obtained from Mrs Macleod, Joanne Murray and Rev. Donald Michael Macinnes – all three being devout Presbyterians.

(ii) Information on the Hebridean Catholic churches, especially Most Holy Redeemer RC Church, Stornoway (where this author was a regular worshipper on Hebridean visits), obtained from personal links and first hand observations.

34. Eirigh agus Soirbherachadh nan Meadhan Gaidhlig, May 1996.

35. McKee – <u>Municipal Journal</u> (1991) and <u>Contemporary Politics</u> (1995).

36. McKee (1997); <u>Gaelic Nations</u>, Chap 4, pp 64-67.

37. Highlands elections to the Scottish Parliament cover 3 single member constituencies elected on a first-past-the-post basis. The other 10 MSPs are elected as Additional Members from the entire Greater Highlands and Islands region, which includes Western Isles plus Shetlands and Orkneys.

38. (i) Charles W.J. Withers <u>Gaelic Scotland</u> (1988); Chap 7, pp 407 – 417.

    (ii) Wilson McLeod (2020) <u>Gaelic in Scotland</u>. See Chaps 1 & 2.

39. Census returns, Scotland, 1991 and 2001 – see HMSO London/Edinburgh.

40. 'Framework for Growth: A National Policy for Gaelic Education' – Comunn na Gaidhlig 1997. Prepared by Gaelic Education Action Group, headed by Dr Donald John Macleod, Gaelic Education Advisor to Highlands Council.

41. McKee (1997), Chap 4, p 81.

42. McKee (1997), Chap 4, p 68.

43. Ibid.

44. Pederson (2019); pp 92 – 117.

45. See Congress of CNG Campaign for Secure Status for Gaelic, CNG, Inverness, June 1997.

46. (i) W. McLeod (2020) <u>Gaelic in Scotland</u> – See final Chapter.

    (ii) M. MacLeod & C. Smith <u>Christmas</u> (2018); Chap 12 & concluding chapter.

47. Thompson (1992); See Chap 5, plus Chap 6, pp 126-137.

48. Thompson (1992); See Chap 6.

49. Wyn Grant <u>Pressure Groups, Politics and Democracy in Britain</u> (London, 1995); Chaps 2 & 4. Also, Wyn Grant 'Pressure Groups in Britain', <u>Social Studies Review</u>, October 1987.

50. Devine (2006); Chap 27, p. 663.

Mrs Annie Macsween: - Lewis born and bred, Gaelic local historian, retired educationalist, active Christian (Presbyterian) figure, and Her Majesty's Deputy Lord Lieutenant for the Western Isles.

Arthur Cormack: - Native Gael from Skye. Multi-talented Scottish Gaelic singer, television personality, Gaelic youth cultural organiser through the Feiseann movement, and former National Chairman of Bord na Gaidhlig; - statutory authority for the development of Gaelic in Scotland. Highly respected figure across Scotland and Northern Ireland.

Brian Wilson: - former Labour MP and Scottish Office Minister, who did much to pilot the Scottish Gaelic broadcasting legislation through Westminster immediately prior to devolution.

(Reprinted by kind permission of Stornoway Gazette)

Blair Douglas: - From Isle of Skye. Gaelic musician, and almost certainly the greatest instrumental talent in the Scottish Gaelic world. Many CDs, television, radio and concert appearances to his credit.

Calum Kennedy (sadly deceased); - Probably the best known and greatest of
Scottish Gaelic singers and entertainers ever. A native of the Isle of Lewis,
this colourful talent worked his way up to nationwide fame with abundant
recordings of Gaelic music and ballads, performed on television, in concert, at
festivals in Scotland, London and abroad to audiences everywhere. Owned his
own theatre in Aberdeen, presented a show on Grampian television, and
performed to HM Queen at the Royal Variety Concert.

(Photo courtesy of the Stornoway Gazette)

Donald John Maciver (sadly deceased, 2015): - Pivotal figure in Scottish Gaelic education and teacher provision; former head of Gaelic studies, Nicholson Institute, Stornoway, Isle of Lewis. Also a distinguished Gaelic poet and writer, crowned 'Bard' of National Mod in recognition of his immense Gaelic input.

The late and very distinguished Donald John Mackey: - Native of North Uist,
Outer Hebrides, educated at London School of Economics. Served as first ever-
professional Director of An Comunn Gaidhealach, 1965 - 70; during which time
he laid down the foundations for a consummate and lasting strategy for
promoting Scottish Gaelic at Westminster, Whitehall and St Andrews House,
Edinburgh. A most able and prodigious figure who left a lasting mark on
Scottish Gaeldom that remains to this day. Subsequently was Chairman of
Cumann na Gaidhlig, amongst many other roles. Widely respected in Gaelic and
government quarters.

(Photo courtesy of An Comunn Gaidhealach)

The late Donald Stewart MP, Scottish Nationalist member for the Western Isles, 1970 - 1987, who died in August 1992. Donald was sponsor of the 1981 Gaelic (Miscellaneous Provisions) Private Members Bill in the Commons.

(Courtesy of Rod Huckbody, Stornoway Gazette)

Gaelic medium schoolchildren on the Isle of Lewis, Outer Hebrides

(Courtesy of R. Huckbody, Stornoway Gazette)

Scottish Shiny game in action at Glasgow.

Shinty is the Scottish Gaels equivalent of Irish Hurling. It enjoys appeal among Highlands and Hebridean communities.

A Hebridean choir at the 1994 Scottish National Mod, Dingwall.

(Courtesy of Rod Huckbody, Stornoway Gazette)

Her late Majesty, Queen Elizabeth, The Queen Mother. A native Scot, widow of King George VI, and an ardent supporter of Scottish Gaelic events and campaigns. Patron of An Comunn Gaidhealach.

John Angus Mackay: - Hebridean native
Gael, who proceeded to eventually become
General Secretary of Cumann na Gaidhlig.
Played major role in winning Gaelic
television for Scotland from a reluctant
Westminster government. An unremitting
champion of Gaelic interests, labelled by
his biographer as 'Gaelic Guerilla'.
Awarded OBE by HM The Queen for
services to Gaelic.

Professor/Sir Tom Devine Kt OBE FRSE FBA: - Scotland's greatest living historian, with over 30 historical books to his credit. Also, broadcaster, researcher, author of numerous scholarly papers, lectures and articles, and acclaimed throughout the world as among the greatest Scottish and British academics of all time. Knighted in 2014 by Her Majesty, The Queen, for scholarly services to Scottish history.

St Kilda ... home to the St Kilda Parliament, held in the house on the left in this 1886 picture. The body consisting of 100 per cent Gaelic speaking island adult males, met daily to discuss appropriate communal tasks. St Kilda was evacuated in 1930.

(Courtesy of ACG)

Stornoway: - 'capital' of the Outer Hebrides and centre of the Scottish
Gaidhealtachd.

(Photo by Andrew Bennett)

The 1997 Annual Congress of Comunn na Gaidhlig, Inverness.

(Courtesy of Ewan Weatherspoon)

Chapter Five

1986-99: RESURGENCE OF GAEIL ULADH!

Aims: This chapter aims to identify and evaluate a new era of positive attainments for the Gaels of Ulster. Coming in the aftermath of the 1985 Hillsborough Accord - agreed between the governments of Mrs Thatcher and Dr Fitzgerald – and squarely aimed at ending the alienation of nationalists and Gaels by a series of reforms, essentially this era of entitlements and funding unfolded for Gaelic organisations and interests at all levels of Northern Ireland's civic society. While the overriding, albeit unstated, aim on all sides was to boost SDLP appeal among Ulster Gaels, as opposed to that of Sinn Fein, in fact this objective was not fully realised. Nor, as is shown, did the SDLP take proper advantage of the empowered role allocated by Hillsborough. Equally, Sinn Fein activists declined to accept their own exclusion, and instead adopted a very robust Gaelic profile over the period. All those factors were to play a big part in N.I. of the post-Good Friday Settlement of 1998. The chapter shall endeavour to deal even-handedly with the many and assorted factors dictating evets at that seismic junction of Northern Ireland's troubled history.

1. ***Overview:*** By 1986, the progress of Gaelic Ulster, though still retarded, had been boosted by the recently-signed Anglo-Irish Accord; the Hillsborough Treaty, agreed between British Premier, Margaret Thatcher, and Irish Taoiseach, Dr Garret Fitzgerald. Its specific wording pledged to "*... **foster the cultural heritage of both traditions ... and ... the avoidance of economic and social discrimination ...**".**(1) The concept of 'Parity of Esteem' for the Gaelic-Irish culture of the Catholic Nationalist community alongside the Anglicized/ Scots-Irish culture of the Unionist/Protestant community was to prove a major innovation, and one that endured over the next 35 years. This in turn led to fundamental civic changes to cultural,

educational and sports infrastructures in Northern Ireland. While Protestant / Unionist opposition to the Agreement over the next 18 months was widespread, robust and entrenched, it was directed more at Dublin's consultative role in future government of the North (which Unionists believed undermined the sovereignty of UK jurisdiction), not parity of cultural esteem, which though quietly resented, was not formally opposed.*(2)

In any case, the progress of Gaeil Uladh over the previous decade, though less than remarkable, was still considerable in several quarters, albeit far below the levels achieved by Gaidheal na h-Alba. However, as shown in Chapter 4, and the three preceding chapters, different political and cultural conditions prevailed in Scotland, where Gaeldom was not viewed as threatening the establishment. Northern Ireland provided a fundamentally different political and civic environment. The slow emergence of a new urban Gaeltacht in Andersonstown, West Belfast, headed by among others, the late Aodan MacPoilin, meant a number of families taking up residence in a purpose-designated Gaelic housing project. This had led to increased demand for Gaelic-medium schooling, with the self-sustaining West Belfast bunscoil finally attaining government recognition and funding in 1984, and other Gaeilge schools becoming operational by 1987. The latter meant increasing pupil numbers and facilities in search of similar status, along with meeting a demand for qualified teachers.*(3) It was to prove a long and difficult road over the ensuing decade, as will be shown.

Significantly, the Hillsborough Agreement never envisaged permanent resolution structures, nor did it enunciate long-term ambitions on resolving the political challenges facing Northern Ireland. As the late SDLP Deputy Leader, Seamus Mallon, recalled in his memoirs, the Agreement's main benefit was to offer prospects of progress. Access to a Gaelic cultural renaissance was one such option.

"The Anglo-Irish Agreement proved to be a real milestone and the beginning of new hope for Nationalists. For the first time, the British government was not overruled by the Unionist veto. Mechanisms for dealing with the deep alienation of Nationalists ... from the institutions of law and the state in Northern Ireland were to become more effective over the next decade and a half.*(4)

While Mallon was more immediately concerned with political reform than a Gaelic cultural renaissance, actually he recognised a mushrooming of Gaelic broadcasting, educational access, sports, language and arts as showing positive signs of change to ordinary people. In emerging from the shadows of past decades, Gaelic Ulster was slowly joining the mainstream, thereby auguring the prospect of better things to come. Major political reforms would await the 1998 Belfast 'Good Friday' Agreement, but in the interim a new dawn had risen for Gaeil Uladh, and one not conceivably reversible in the short or long term.*(5) Moreover, along with a perceived growth in nationalist numbers of the population, any such gains would be vigorously defended over times ahead.*(6)

2. *__Legacy of the Anglo-Irish Accord__:* The creation of a joint inter-governmental conference that included British and Southern Irish representatives for monitoring the Accord's provisions, ensured that Irish culture in the North now had an influential sponsor. It further meant a mechanism existed for ensuring the progress of Gaelic education, culture, music, sports and broadcasting, with public funding and other civic entitlements accruing on a scale hitherto unknown in Northern Ireland throughout its 65-year history, 1921-86. Unlike before, actual structures were created for pursuing concerns and resolving grievances.

One major advancement occurred in **broadcasting and coverage of Gaelic sport and Irish arts**. Over earlier years, there had been a mini-resurgence in coverage of Gaelic games and Irish arts and language activities. For example, all the mainstream broadcasters by the mid-1980s included coverage of Gaelic sport and cultural events, while appearances by Ulster counties at Croke Park in All- Ireland semi-finals and finals were covered live, specifically where it involved premier Ulster Gaelic Football counties, namely Down, Tyrone, Armagh and Derry, plus Donegal, along with Antrim and Down Hurlers.*(7) This process now found itself receiving fresh impetus from political reverberations of the Accord.*(8) An increased number of Gaeilge language programmes, arts, cultural and Gaelic sports reports on BBC Northern Ireland Television and Radio Ulster was followed by the emergence of an Irish Language Unit at BBC Radio Foyle, Derry, in the early 1990s. These developments opened up other options over ensuing years.

Extended Gaelic sports coverage and new inroads to Irish language and drama programming by the 1990s fundamentally changed the face of public broadcasting in Northern Ireland. This phenomenon, once established, led to a degree of legitimacy settling on the broad Gaelic heritage and culture, elevating it above the disputatious arena of previous times. The new climate owed much to the Accord, but was also boosted by a spirit of cultural inclusiveness which measured a particular impact on sport. Quite simply, the sight of Down's Gaelic footballers repeatedly mastering Croke Park to lift 5 All-Ireland senior titles between 1960 and 1994, along with the football teams of Derry (1), Tyrone (4) and Armagh (1), plus Antrim hurlers battling in the finals, was something even hostile Unionists could not begrudge, nor could managers at BBC Northern Ireland ignore. Just as Billy Bingham's Northern Ireland soccer team won (rightly) global plaudits for their feisty performances at the 1982 and '86 World Cups, so it appeared had Gaelic Ulster finally come of age with peak performances at Croke Park that made them the pride of all Northern Gaels. That mood of celebration of Ulster successes was reflected in a new broadcasting strategy, while sporting success among Northern Gaels boosted confidence among the wider nationalist community. The latter phenomenon, added to a growing Catholic graduate class that first emerged in the late 1950s, augmented the political confidence of nationalist politicians and their people.

Yet the positive civic spirit encouraged by the post-Accord climate had its limits everywhere, including broadcasting. As Gabriel Maguire noted in 1991, for all those fresh forays into sports and drama/music coverage, there were no scheduled Gaelic language programmes, nor had BBC Northern Ireland or Ulster Television (UTV) taken any lead in encouraging initiatives in that area.*(9) Nothing along the lines of Scottish television's 'Machair' soap either appeared or was planned, nor were there any Gaeilge learner programmes similar to BBC Scotland's 'Can Seo' series. Evidently, the practice of 1990s BBC managers in Belfast was to react rather than initiate! That said, the evolving climate of harmony and inclusiveness following from the April 1998 Belfast Agreement, and ensuing St Andrews Conference Accord of 2006, ushered in greater developments, but like the conditions generating them, their impact and legacies are the stuff of a later chapter.

Meanwhile, it must be acknowledged that not all Unionists accepted gracefully the new cultural pluralism adopted by BBC NI or UTV. Showings of Gaelic games, Gaeilge language and cultural events often took place against a backdrop of regular Unionist protests, couched in emotive phrases alleging that Gaelic broadcasts undermined the North's "British" and "Protestant" ways of life. Also, Unionist objectors frequently cited connections between Gaelic cultural aims and republican politics*(10), while also making the most of the GAA's-then disputatious Rule 21.*(11) While the protests appeared shrill, it is important to recall that only 30 years earlier – late 1950s & 1960s – similar prejudices prevailed at the top of BBC N.I. and UTV, and were used to keep Gaelic-Irish games and culture off-screen in Northern Ireland. To that degree, changing times meant changing policy.

The Hillsborough spirit of cultural inclusiveness was extended to **community arts funding** in the years following 1985. Over the next decade, Northern Ireland's Arts Council gradually increased its funding for Gaelic drama and related initiatives, moves that drew a qualified welcome from the Catholic secondary school sector, along with St Mary's Catholic Training College, Belfast, University of Ulster at Derry, and various community drama groups. Whatever may have been the ideal of all-inclusive Gaelic drama, in practice it was Catholic schools who hosted some 95% of participation. Thus for effective purposes Irish drama and the arts were viewed as Nationalist culture.

Another important innovation occurred in 1989 with the creation of the **ULTACH Trust** with the aim of promoting Irish/Gaeilge in the widest community structures of Northern Ireland. This body was initiated as part of the Cultural Traditions Group of the Northern Ireland Community Relations Council, and its sponsorship owed something to the Northern Ireland Office's desire to see the Irish language and culture promoted beyond traditional Nationalist boundaries. Its Director was the respected Belfast Gaelgeoir writer, poet, educationalist, broadcaster and Gaeltacht housing project co-founder, the late Aodan MacPoilin. Other trustees included former GAA President from Fermanagh, Peter Quinn, and ex-Ulster Unionist General Secretary and Belfast councillor, Chris McGimpsey. The Trust which operated from an office in Belfast city centre over 24 years, until its disbandment in 2014, was funded by grants from the Northern Ireland Office and the interest accrued from an investment fund. It took responsibility for grant-aiding voluntary language groups, Gaelic medium schools and publishing ventures. The original Northern Ireland Office grant of £65,000 was increased to £90,000 over 1996/97, and was augmented by a Dublin government grant of IR£20,000.*(12) Additionally, a foundation capital fund generated further income of £85,000 per annum, and after allowing for salaries and office costs, the Trust paid out over £100,000 in grants to Irish language groups and causes over 1996/97.*(13)

It needs adding that ULTACH Trust gave substantive assistance to new Gaelic Medium schools, to the point of some 50% of its total budget. This was partly because of the struggles for viability faced by the new Gaeilscoileanna ahead of formal public recognition and funding, and the admiration which they drew from senior Trust figures.*(14) Additionally, there was a recognition that those embryonic ventures may not have stayed the course without external help, and as O'Reilly and Maguire have each shown, parental economic capacity was decidedly limited.*(15) Thus the new inclusive climate emanating from the Hillsborough Accord enabled greater flexibility and licence to be taken with regard to what were viewed as "... deserving causes in the Irish cultural sphere". The principal caveat from both the Northern Ireland Office and Dublin was that help was extended to genuine Gaelic causes only, and none resembling Sinn Fein and/or IRA front organisations. To that extent, MacPoilin with his multiple experience, inspired confidence from all quarters, including the NIO, and his judgement, if resented by militant Republicans, was endorsed by ULTACH's paymasters.*(16)

Since the mid-1970s, NIO grant aid to the **Gaelic Athletic Association** had been steadily increasing. This process was itself the result of enlightened new attitudes within the NIO and BBC, along with the ever-increasing success of Ulster sides in all-Ireland premier competitions, as previously indicated. Doubtless the Hillsborough Accord accentuated that process, but it must also be acknowledged that certain GAA's practices, specifically its Rule 21 – barring RUC and British military servicemen from membership - worked against the Association's full incorporation to the civic mainstream. This situation was exploited by Unionist politicians, who viewed the GAA as a pro-republican body utilising sport for the purpose of fostering support for a united Ireland. – See Appendix 1 for a brief but substantive account of the GAA's part in the Gaelic revival.

Yet notwithstanding all the hurdles, positive developments were forthcoming. In 1977, the publicly-funded Ulster Sports Council appointed a full-time Hurling Development Officer – the first of its kind ever - whose primary role was to liaise with schools, colleges and Gaelic sports clubs over promotions, access to resources and enhanced profile.*(17) Later, other Gaelic coaching positions were created, with a mind for developing the games and their place in civic life. Significantly, in the course of joint negotiations, the Sports Council, broadcasters and N.I.O. all enjoyed cautious co-operation from the Ulster GAA and its affiliate county authorities, as well as the parent leadership at Croke Park, Dublin. This new relationship was borne partly of desire to keep a positive profile among Nationalist youth, and nervousness about losing out to Soccer which held ongoing appeal in many Catholic areas.*(18) There was also a desire to benefit from funding programmes of successive governments, recognising that with some adjustments to their rules, the GAA stood to reap a crop of grants and other aid from a wider British state that outside Northern Ireland had no real quarrel with Gaelic linguists, teachers, artists, writers and/or sportsmen/women.

As will be considered more fully in Chapter 7, over the period 1985-99 there occurred a steady growth in the numbers of Gaelic medium educational schools/units. Indeed as figures supplied by Conradh na Gaeilge and sister bodies highlights, the bunscoileanna and Gaelic playschool movement ranked as Northern Ireland's fastest growing educational sector in the 1990s. Yet until recently this sector received minimal, and in many cases, no state funding whatsoever. Righting the wrongs of a century's political exclusion was never going to be a quick process. That said, in the broader context, all the signs were that following the 1985 Hillsborough Accord, Gaeil Uladh, in its language, cultural and sporting forms were gradually being, if not exactly embraced, then at least admitted from the cold to an accommodation with Northern Ireland's inclusive new civic culture. This process was called the 'Green litmus test' by a senior member of the N.I. Community Relations Council.

Of course, such gains were not trouble-free, as was shown by the ongoing aggravations between Gaelic bodies and both the state and Unionist organisations, most particularly involving the GAA and certain of its questionable regulations. Nor significantly, did the various Gaelic organisations or their lead figures, renounce tacit associations or sympathies with political nationalism. Moreover, the pace of change did not satisfy everyone in Gaeil Uladh, and, predictably, a rift emerged between ULTACH people and the radical voices of Sinn Fein and *La*. -- More on this subject later.

3. ***Belfast's New Urban Gaeltacht and 'La':*** Another major development in progress by 1986 was a pilot Gaeltacht at Pairc Ross an Goill, Shaws Road, Andersonstown (West Belfast); itself comprehensively covered in the respective accounts of Dr Maguire and Dr O'Reilly.*(19) Each of those

researchers in their turn have addressed the various issues of legality, practicality and different logistical challenges confronting the pioneers of this ambitious project in Troubles-afflicted West Belfast. Not least among the latter were generating basic and affordable housing, along with primary infra-structures such as space, shopping, child play areas, schooling and work options which lent viability to a project representing the hopes and aspirations of a generation of Gaeilge-speaking families. This would require substantial input, not just from the Gaeilge pioneers, but also a sympathetic wider community who at the very least willed the venture's success. In that respect, political solidarity from Nationalist West Belfast went a long way towards facilitating the latter.

As previously noted, with the bunscoil having first opened in 1969 and the first Gaeilge-speaking family having taken up residence in 1971, by 1987 a track record of gradual attainment had shown itself. By then, the number of Irish-speaking households at Pairc Ross an Goil had increased to 16, which lent an air of permanence to the housing project, while across Belfast other Gaeilge-speaking couples and families were mushrooming, thus ensuring solidarity from which further aid emerged. So too had the first bunscoil stayed the course, seeing off legal threats and obstructions while fund-raising, and eventually winning recognition and finance from the Northern Ireland Department of Education. Other Gaeilge-medium schools were subsequently developing, along with Irish play-schools and Gaelic units within mainstream local Catholic schools, but still public funding remained an elusive target. Significantly, there was by then an embryonic Meanscoil – Gaelic-medium secondary school – operating from premises on the nearby Falls Road, which in 1987 was struggling to establish its viability and case for public funding.*(20) It was in this early period prior to any public funding that the quest for viability was at its most acute, and the vision of Gaelgeoir educationalists had to be augmented with practical and ongoing fund raising schemes led by Gaelic League activists. The establishment of a secondary Gaeilge medium school in Belfast was essential in order to meet expectations from a generation of Gaelic educationalists for whom there had to be a next stage for the increasing numbers of pupils emerging from the city's bunscoileanna. It was a formidable task that challenged Gaelic league activists, teachers, pupils, parents and the community ... all to the full.

Elsewhere, by 1997, with the urban Gaeltacht having expanded, albeit cautiously, the momentum for developing essential social infrastructures – e.g. playgroup areas, parent groups, Gaeilge-medium shopping and even the beginnings of employment sources - was aided by a Gaelic renaissance across West Belfast. Additional to mushrooming Irish-language classes staged by Conradh na Gaeilge and Gaelic community organisations, other major developments followed. Not least among the latter was the emergence in Summer 1984 of La as a national weekly, and for a brief period daily, Gaelic-medium newspaper which sold all over Ireland. It had emerged as successor to a previous Gaeilge journal, *Preas an Phobail*, published from West Belfast, but with a nationwide circulation. Under the committed editorship of the redoubtable Belfast Gaelgeoir journalist, Mr Gearoid O'Caireallain, the paper steadily built up a readership and profile in such a way as to ensure its place among leading Nationalist causes and institutions. It was assisted over the years by the Andersonstown News; another nationalist community magazine also operating from West Belfast, and whose publisher, Mr Mairtin O'Muilleoir (a prominent Sinn Fein figure) was a distinguished Gaelgeoir of fair reputation. The longstanding friendship between those old school friends led to Mr O'Muilleoir assisting Mr O'Caireallain with publication and other practicalities, such as enabled La to get through the early hurdles; a fact about which Mr O'Caireallain was entirely open, frank and appreciative.*(21)

La's raison d'être was as a political voice for the identity and aspirations of Ulster Gaelgeoiri in challenging the expressed hostility of cultural Unionism and indifference of the Anglophile establishment, as much as a forum for projecting the wider cultural activities of Gaeil Uladh. The paper also took a firm line in insisting on positive action for language and culture from a Dublin administration composed – as they saw it – of suspected 'Free State compromisers', with whom they were never entirely comfortable nor in political league.*(22) Those attitudes are rooted in the legacy of the Irish Civil War of 1922-23, particularly its hostility to republicans, but also in Dublin's 'luke-warm' support of Northern nationalists throughout the Stormont years, as well as the general isolation of Gaelic Ulster. Such suspicions continued to permeate North/South politics in the 1980s and '90s. Indeed within *La* ranks there prevailed more than a shade of Sinn Fein's hostility to the Southern establishment, whose main political parties, especially Fianna Fail and Fine Gael, they regarded – with good reason, it needs adding – as perfidious and self-serving.

La's emergence as All-Ireland's leading Gaelic language newspaper stimulated other initiatives in West Belfast's Gaelgeoir community. Additional to the growing Bunscoileanna movement, a Gaelic Arts and Cultural centre called the Culturlan Macadam/O'Fiaich – named in memory of 19th century Presbyterian Gaelgeoir, Robert McAdam, and Armagh Gaelic cleric and scholar, Cardinal Tomas O'Fiaich, who died in 1990 – emerged in the 1990s on the middle-Falls Road on the site of a de-commissioned Presbyterian church. By 1997, the Culturlann was facilitating a number of Gaelic enterprises. They included *La*'s offices, Meanscoil Feirste (Belfast's then-developing Gaelic medium secondary school), an Irish book store, shop, café, reading rooms, Gaelic theatre and recording studio. All those services were – and remain – bilingual, with Gaeilge as the preferred medium. Significantly, all services operated – from the beginning – on a commercial basis, and grew up in response to demand from Belfast's and the North's wider nationalist community.*(22)

The organisation and funding of the Culturlann highlighted the inclusiveness policy of the Northern Ireland Office following the Anglo-Irish Accord. Premises were leased from a Catholic diocesan agency, Springfield Association, but from 1991-97 the annual rent bill was met in full by the Northern Ireland Department of the Environment. As for 'tenant' organisations operating within the centre, they met their own running costs, while also paying rent to Culturlann management. After 1997, the DoE grant was exhausted, and Culturlann Management sought alternative funding from amongst others, the Northern Ireland Arts Council.*(23)

Overall, the experiences of *La* showed an intermittent dependence on public funding sources, albeit with a capacity for survival in hard times. La's editor, Gaearoid O'Caireallain, himself an avid Republican of the radical school, nevertheless maintained his paper's formal independence from Sinn Fein.*(24) The paper was run under the direction of its editor, and overseen by a broad-based board of directors. However, that did not spare the paper in 1989 a British government accusation of being "a front for Sinn Fein". After moving around different locations between 1986 and 1988, *La* settled on the Old Conway Mill in the Lower Falls area, sharing premises with the Irish Language action group, Glor na nGael.*(25) When the latter's funds were suspended in 1989, on the directive of the then Northern Ireland Office Minister, Dr Brian Mawhinney (himself hailing from a Belfast Unionist background), *La* lost its grant. Mawhinney argued that the Conway Mill was a centre of IRA activity, and declared it to be "... out of bounds for public funding". Although Mawhinney's claims squared with widespread Unionist prejudices at the time, the minister never actually produced any firm evidence for his assertions beyond so-called "intelligence reports".

In any case, Glor na nGael's cause was taken up by a wide range of nationalist campaigners, including (predictably) Sinn Fein, but also the SDLP and, interestingly, Irish government. So also did a number of Church sources (encouraged by Cardinal O'Fiaich and his Gaelgeoir colleague, Fr Raymond Murray) pursue the case, along with some trade unions.*(26) Eventually, NIO funding of both La and Glor na nGael was restored in 1991, by which time the newspaper had moved to a permanent premises at the developing Culturlann premises.*(27) Thereafter, the relationship of La with the NIO prevailed in a spirit of uneasy cordiality.

Throughout the 1990s, the paper operated as a small business, which in 1994 had a combined staff of six, including editorial staff along with a commercial manager. Revenue came from a variety of sources such as sales and advertising, along with external subsidies, that included an NIO grant in kind for computer equipment and a smaller sum from Bord na Gaeilge, the Republic's then-statutory Irish language authority. An ACE grant from the Northern Ireland Department of the Environment enabled La to hire a temporary official – creating subsequent ACE posts – during 1993-94.*(28) In January 1994, La was selling 1,000 subscription copies per week; 500 by subscription in Dublin, 300 in Belfast, and the remainder in various locations around the country. Significantly, it had a greater appeal among second language Gaels, achieving only modest sales in traditional Gaeltacht areas.*(29) In the past, La had faced competition from Anois, the Dublin-based Gael Linn paper, which until 1995 was subsidised by the Irish government. However, loss of funding forced Gael Linn to close the paper – amidst public consternation in the South – but enabled La to pick up many Anois readers. It amounted to a 'dog-eat-dog' scenario, from which La, as the more radical and independent journal – and rooted in the political scions of Gaeil Uladh – emerged the stronger force.

By July 1997, notwithstanding the launch of another Irish Government-sponsored Gaeilge paper, Foinse (Galway-based), La appeared to have emerged ever-strengthened. The paper boasted a full weekly readership of 4,000, almost half of that figure being sold in the Six Counties, with 800 in Belfast alone. Outside Northern Ireland, the largest point of sale for the paper then was Dublin.*(30) Indeed by mid-1997, Gearoid O'Caireallain felt confident enough to comment positively:

"La and the Culturlann provide a community function for Irish-speakers in West Belfast and further afield. The paper gives literary impetus to Gaelgeoiri visions of a parallel society in the Six Counties; one in which state services and its infrastructure are provided within the medium of Irish."(31)

Such confidence seemed justified at the time, but over the course of the post-millennium decade proved somewhat premature. By then, the cold winds of renewable state-subsidies, on which *La* had come to depend, began blowing in a negative direction.

4. ***'Parallel Society'*** Not that the "parallel society" vision was confined to *La* or Gaelic Medium education! Actually, in the mid-1990s it made inroads to a number of economic and vocational areas across the Six Counties. Several local employment and business initiatives gathered force among Belfast's Irish speakers throughout the decade, of which *'Forbairt Feirste'* emerged as the most prominent. Founded in 1994 as an economic agency, and modelled on the Welsh body, *Menter-Y-Busness*, it aimed to identify and utilise prospects for Gaelic speakers. The organisation was led by Belfast Gaelgeoir, Jake Mac Siacais, a redoubtable figure and former Republican prisoner, who had previously worked at the *Andersonstown News*, and over time developed a small network of soul mates assisting his various projects.*(32)

Forbairt was funded by the Northern Ireland Training and Employment Agency, and created two Gaeilge-medium training courses; one in Media Studies and the other in Business administration. There was also by 1997 a clear plan at Forbairt to establish a technical-business division at the Meanscoil Feirste, which augured positively for the future training of Gaeilge-speaking business operatives and even entrepreneurs. This development further reinforced the presence of computer technology in the Meanscoil, itself no minor consideration in a school that until public funding was forthcoming much later, was otherwise gravely cash-strapped.

It was hoped on all sides that these innovations could act as path-finders for other initiatives to follow. In the event, results proved mildly encouraging, if also slow, and a reminder to Forbairt's people and Ulster Gaelgeoiri generally, if indeed such were ever needed, just how steep would be their task of achieving acceptance for Gaeilge in Northern Irish civic society with its preponderant Unionist and Anglophile cultural roots.*(33) Those longstanding hurdles did not disappear overnight.

The overriding Forbairt goal was to prepare Belfast's Gaeilge speakers for running their own businesses, and to win as much financial and technical aid from government as they could manage. The latter involved adopting modern training methods and gaining access to cutting edge IT, such as would be necessary for making an effective impact in the 1990s and post-millennial Northern Ireland. With a mind for what had happened to the ill-fated 1950s 'Fail' efforts between Belfast and Donegal, the assorted forces of Gaeil Uladh generally were resolved to follow a path of hard-headed realism that acknowledged the need for all initiatives to be self-reliant and economically viable. Forbairt's purpose and strategy followed in that very same direction of realism.*(34) Significantly, its progression ensued over the next decade, so that by 2010 the concept of viable Ulster Gaeilge businesses looked like a reality, albeit on a smaller scale to that originally envisioned. (See Chap. 7) This positive trend fed off a climate of optimism and growing Gaelgeoir corporate competence.

During the mid-1990s, several positive developments had occurred. There had been the creation of a dedicated Gaelic technical organisation, Gaelchursai, with the aim of training technical and business Irish-speaking students. This body, acted as a sister organisation to Forbairt Feirste, and assisted many Meanscoil teenage students with 'A'Levels, B.Tech and HND courses. Its lead figure was Mrs Colma Mhic Aodha, and the organisation was mainly self-funded, with minimum help from the N.I. Office's Department of Communities, plus a small grant from the European Union.*(35) Additionally, there followed liaisons with Gaelgeoiri elsewhere, notably with a pilot group in South Derry, headed by Messers' Niall O'Cathan and Liam Flanagan. The latter, with its emphasis on a local Gaeltacht following similar lines to the West Belfast initiative, eventually blossomed in the post-millennium decades into a Maghera village Gaeltacht complete with bunscoil and housing project.

Foras na Gaeilge's creation as a statutory body in 1998 was to have far reaching effects for funding and policy initiatives within all walks of Gaeil

Uladh. Appointed jointly from North and South, and funded by both the Northern Ireland Office and Dublin government, this body contained a number of high-profile appointments on both sides. As will be later shown, it also presided over some momentous decisions that in turn sparked off grave tensions between Ulster Gaelgeoiri and the Dublin establishment, such as over the termination of La's lifeline grant in December 2008.*(36) However, in the first instance, Foras provided funding for a Gaelchursai-led 2-year business training course for prospective Gaelic entrepreneurs; with 16 candidates in total, 8 each from the North and South of Ireland. Forbairt's Director, Mr Jake MacSiacais, told this author that he regarded the success of that pioneer course as "*… pivotal to the development of Irish language technical training, because for the first time Gaels demonstrated adroit business skills to a hostile Unionist macro culture and cynical Education Department.*"*(37) To Mr Mac Siacais, this phenomenon amounted to parity of esteem in action where it mattered, namely in the work place and training zone.

Another aspect of the 'parallel society' was the expansion of Gaeilge medium primary schools, about which something has been said already and will be carried on in Chapters 7 and 8. Further expansion into the secondary sector represented both confidence and development on a scale that had not been seen before, and augured positively for the future of this initiative. Equally, with the growth of La and adoption of a positive pro-Gaelgeoir policy by the *Andersonstown News*, headed by Mr Mairtin O'Muilleoir. Also included were Gaelic activist brothers, Messers' Seamas and Sean Mac Seain, plus copy editor, the late Mr Sean Mac Aindreasa; and there were knock-on effects elsewhere.*(38) Expansion depended on momentum, and given the sequence of events occurring across Belfast and beyond, this owed much to an atmosphere of innovation in the Gaelic world.

Overall, by the time of the Belfast Agreement of April 1998, it was possible to detect clear signs of an embryonic 'Parallel Society' beginning to emerge. This was far from established, but foundations were being laid in education, business training, housing, arts, media and language learning. There was support from the community of West Belfast and elsewhere, but much more was needed in order to further that progress to the comprehensive levels it required so as to achieve stability. This struggle took place over the next few years of the new millennium with the return of a power-sharing administration to Belfast following the signing of the Good Friday Agreement of April 1998.

5. _**Rising Esteem of Ulster Gaels:**_ Undoubtably, by 1998 Belfast Gaelgeoiri particularly and indeed Gaeil Uladh generally had experienced a growth in esteem and confidence. The growth in Gaeilge medium education and the Gaelscoil movement was a definite marker, while the emergence of the first Gaeilge secondary school in the city enhanced that optimism. After all, Gaelic medium education had been denied to earlier generations under Stormont rule, and now it was starting to happen. Moreover, this development was envisaged as permanent in structure and character, with further prospects boding. There was also the slow growth in Gaelic-medium technical training under Forbairt Feirste, while the growth in Gaelic medium teacher training at St Mary's College, Belfast furthered those developments. Add to the latter, the ever-rising profile of Gaelic sports, arts, drama, literature and broadcasting, along with the comprehensive programme of language classes across Belfast and throughout the North, and the picture becomes clear. Plainly Gaeil Uladh were on the march, albeit still constrained by hostile political influences.

All the same, there was room for cautious optimism from the latter and further developments that occurred around the same time. Outside Belfast, a significant initiative emerged from the-then SDLP-dominated Newry and Mourne Council; itself partly symbolic and partly utilitarian, and reflecting the political character of this large nationalist community. In 1986, a specialist sub-committee, Coiste na Gaeilge, was established as an advisory forum to the Council's Recreation and Tourist Committee. Its task was to present viable proposals for the Council to adopt. The following year (1987), saw the creation of the post of Irish Language Development Officer, whose long-running initial incumbent, Mr Maolcholaim Scott, was a Presbyterian and son of a Lisburn Presbyterian minister. In 1990, the Council adopted an official name, with bilingual symbols, shield and selective notices. It pledged support for local Gaelic cultural and educational projects, and subsequently twinned with Comhairle nan Eilean Siar in Stornoway and Clare County Council in the south west of Ireland. An official calendar featuring the logos of all three councils was produced in celebration of the twinning. There followed a Gaelic arts programme, which included Gaeilge language classes, and Irish plays in Newry, a town long renowned for its abundance of local drama talents.*(39) Of course the prevalence of power-sharing at the Council helped the pro-Gaelic policy, but so also did a number of minority Unionist councillors also demonstrate a genuine interest in taking matters forward, eg. participating in exchange visits to the Protestant – dominated Comhairle nan Eilean Siar in Stornoway.

The Newry and Mourne experiment prompted other power-sharing Councils, e.g. Derry, Down and Dungannon, to explore comparable initiatives. However, by 1998, none of those authorities had advanced to the stage of adopting a full bilingual policy. Northern Ireland councils – of which there were then 17, before being reduced to 9 in a reorganisation in 2015 - lacked the capacity for major bilingual campaigns, and were confined to limited public functions of tourism, refuse collections, environment and planning. Unlike Scotland, Wales and England, due to a history of past Unionist cronyism, education, housing and social services were managed by appointed Area Boards, to which Councils nominated representatives, e.g. N.I. Housing Executive and Council. This drastic curb on local authorities' powers limited the scope for Councils taking any major role as Gaelic publicists along similar lines to Comhairle nan Eilean Siar and Highlands Regional Council in Scotland.

Other positive developments boosted the morale of Gaeil Uladh in the '90s decade. As already indicated in Chap 3, there were the sporting successes of Ulster counties, Down, Derry, Donegal, Armagh and Tyrone in All-Ireland Senior Gaelic Football competitions, with Antrim Hurlers also distinguishing themselves in 1989. Additional to those premier attainments, Ulster colleges like St Colman's, Newry, St Patrick's, Maghera, and Queens University, Belfast, each of whom won all-Ireland honours in the Hogan and Sigerson cups, while Crossmaglen Rangers, South Armagh, and Burren from Down, also carried off All-Ireland senior club titles. So did Loughgiel (Antrim) twice capture the coveted All-Ireland Senior Hurling Club crown. No longer were Ulster Gaels the poor relations of Southern brethren, and indeed by the millennium turn, Gaelic football's centre of excellence had shifted northwards to Ulster when twice the Ulster Football final had to be played at Croke Park (due to overwhelming crowds), and in 2003 the All-Ireland Gaelic Football final was an all-Northern affair between Armagh and Tyrone. Given the increasing practice of GAA clubs and County executives for appointing Gaeilge Language officers, and sponsoring learner classes across the province, it was self-evident more than ever before the degree to which Cumann Luthcleas Gael and its Irish language sister organisations were moving in tandem. Accordingly, sporting successes of county and club teams, themselves the pride of their communities, in turn encouraged a more adventurous approach to learning the language and nourishing Gaelic cultural pursuits in dance, music and the arts. It all amounted to a political exercise, as observed by Camille O'Reilly, in building a popular Gaelic cultural identity among the wider nationalist population.*(40) The same direction was also noted by Mac Poilin in an acclaimed collection of published essays. (41) Such developments counter-poised the Anglophile identity long favoured by the traditional forces of political unionism and the British establishment down the outgoing century. At the same time, it also reinforced the growing sense of Irish consciousness, encouraged most particularly by a nascent Sinn Fein, but also favoured by the moderate SDLP then led by John Hume.

Finally, there was the election in 1995 of *La* editor, Gearoid O'Caireallain, as President/An Uachtaran of Conradh na Gaeilge/ All-Ireland Gaelic League, a position he held for several years. Given Mr O'Caireallain's long-standing and high-profile role in the Gaelic world, not to mention his contribution to Gaelic journalism, this was an inevitable and, it needs adding, well-deserved elevation. It meant a key place for Ulster Gaelgeoiri in the affairs of Conradh na Gaeilge generally and campaigns for Gaelic language development and access particularly. Hosting of the Ard Fheis (Congress) in Belfast, as in 1997, along with other specialist conferences, ensured the presence of key figures whose speeches augmented the League's appeal and impact. Such was true of the 1997 event, which was addressed by the Lord Mayor of Belfast, SDLP Councillor Alban Maginness.*(42)

6. ***Evaluations:*** Without doubt, by the time of signing of the Belfast Peace Accord on Good Friday, April 1998, the fortunes of Gaeil Uladh had improved inexorably. The Gaelscoil movement was expanding with limited state aid; a meanscoil was functioning in West Belfast; ULTACH Trust was distributing funds to community Gaelgeoir groups and other deserving bodies; *La* was established as the leading Gaeilge paper across all-Ireland, with its editor now President of the Gaelic League; the new West Belfast urban Gaeltacht had passed the crucial formative years, and was being consolidated and expanded; An Culturlann McAdam/O'Fiaich was now functioning as a centre for Gaelic arts, education, cultural activists and linguists; and the Gaelic sports advances of Cumann Luthchleas Gaeil and its affiliated clubs and county organisations had succeeded to the point of elevating Ulster

Gaelic sport to premier status across Ireland. So too had
Gaeilge broadcasting on BBC N.I. expanded dramatically, with
a specialist Irish Language unit functioning in the Derry area.

Perhaps, most significantly, UK Census returns were showing an encouraging
trend among Ulster Gaels. The 1991 Census of Northern Ireland recorded
142,003 persons as having some knowledge of Irish Gaelic, with a further
70,000 acknowledged as holding oral and literate fluency.*(43) This figure
represented a fair proportion of the total number of UK Celtic language
speakers, covering Scottish Gaelic, Irish Gaelic and Welsh, which the UK
Census totalled at around 725,000 speakers.*(44) While it may be safely
deduced that many Northern Irish Gaelic language claimants were asserting
cultural identity, more so than authentic fluency in the language, nevertheless
the fact of such an appeal showed the extent to which Gaelicism had
permeated the nationalist political agenda.

Although the Gaelic trend had long-standing roots in the politics of Irish
nationalism, as highlighted by Eamonn Phoenix and Enda Staunton in separate
accounts, there can be little doubt that the 1985 Hillsborough Accord
facilitated its renaissance, indeed pushed its slow, grudging acceptance by
the Unionist cultural establishment of Northern Ireland over the years that
followed.*(45) There was no sense then of having sold Gaelicism – in
language, arts or sport – to the Unionist population at large, but rather having
forced Unionists and the Northern Ireland Office to acknowledge the
legitimacy and place of Gaelic in the North. The increased nationalist political
representation for SDLP and Sinn Fein after 1987 further augmented the
process *(46), with Gaelic-minded elected representatives being spokesmen
– and in some cases like SDLP Deputy Leader, Seamus Mallon – active
participants for a cultural cause that had now started to find its feet.*(47)
Gaelicism was not part of an 'integrated culture', but nor was it any longer
banished to the nationalist fringes and deprived of profile, legitimacy and
funding. In short, by 1997, Gaelic was on its feet and running in the North!

Another not-insignificant source of support was the Irish Catholic Church,
whose bishops, priests and religious orders (especially the De la Salle and
Edmund Rice Christian Brothers) the latter of whom ran many Catholic boys
schools, North and South, as well as northern RC church dioceses who ran
academic colleges in each county, e.g. St Malachy's Belfast, St Patrick's
Dungannon and St Colman's, Newry – many being former junior seminaries)
were key backers of the language, culture and Gaelic sports. Under leadership

from the Archbishop of Armagh (1977-90), Cardinal Tomas O'Fiaich, a native of South Armagh and acknowledged Gaelic scholar, the Church openly sought substantial progress on the Gaelic cultural renaissance ushered in by the Hillsborough Accord, and was a grave critic of attempts by Dr Mawhinney, his political advisers and civil servants to curb funding for Glor na nGael. O'Fiaich was no minor player in this process; he had many influential contacts abroad, and brought his personal esteem and weight of office to challenge Mawhinney and the NIO.

Overall, despite the advantages of Gael Uladh's renaissance, there remained a lingering suspicion among Gaelic language activists that institutional hostility was still intact among Unionist politicians and the British establishment. This was fuelled by underfunding of the Gaelscoileanna and Glor na nGael affair. Writing in 1993, the Belfast Gaelgeoir writer, Mr Pol O'Muiri, had this to say of Glor na nGael's strident approach, its intensive scrutiny and very public battle with Dr Mawhinney.

"Not surprisingly, with their track record, Irish speakers do not hold the authorities in great esteem. Their (NIO) hostility towards the language fluctuates from .. hostile to patronising to obstructive. The policy seems to be to do as little as possible, and when backed into a corner, to {fund} academic projects which, while worthwhile, do little to alleviate the daily struggle of so many other schemes." *(48)

A similar view on NIO prejudices came from Gaelgeoir activist and writer, Maolcholaim Scott.

"... no organ of government recognises the right to choice in use of the language. In practice, most, and this includes the majority of local authorities, prefer to exclude Irish Gaelic from their arts and heritage programmes, arguing that it does not have a 'consensus' or 'across the board support'. Few arts or heritage projects do, and this is an illustration that if Irish is politicised, that various branches of government and state-funded institutions are part and parcel of this; no language can be de-politicised, English least of all; what can be done is to ensure a broader range of participations." *(49)

Gaeil Uladh has long complained that its funding is considerably below that of Scottish Gaeldom, despite the evidence of larger numbers of participants, and the fact that the Gaelic heritage is a shared cultural inheritance with the rest of Ireland. Such claims are well documented by funding figures available. In 1991/92, Northern Ireland Office combined funding to Northern Irish Gaelic causes totalled £1,276,000, compared to £12,000,000 for their Scottish Gaelic counterparts.*(50) The figurer rather speak for themselves, and notwithstanding political progress, arguably showed a serious reluctance by the British authorities to embrace Gaeil Uladh much beyond the superficial.

This disparity in funding, access and policies of the British government, visa-viz the two national Gaelic communities, was to hold fundamental ramifications for the future of both lobbies over the ensuing three decades – as this enquiry goes on to document.

FOOTNOTES and REFERENCES

1. Anglo-Irish Accord, November 1985; co-signed at Hillsborough Castle, Co Down, concerning the future government of Northern Ireland. Principal signatories included: Right Hon. Margaret Thatcher (Premier) and Douglas Hurd (Northern Ireland Secretary) representing the United Kingdom Government, and Dr Garret Fitzgerald (An Taoiseach/Premier) and Mr Dick Spring (An Tanaiste and Foreign Minister) representing the Government of the Irish Republic. – Article 5a. – HMSO London/Belfast.

2. Unionist opposition to the Accord took on a major scale, involving mass rallies, protest meetings, processions, petitions from Unionist-led local councils, obstructive action at Westminster by Unionist parliamentarians, multiple meetings with ministers and the Prime Minister, a lengthy programme of non-co-operation with the Anglo-Irish Inter-governmental conference and its Secretariat at Maryfield, Belfast. Eventually, there followed the resignation en-masse of all 15 Ulster Unionist and DUP MPs in January 1986, each of whom stood again in 15 separate by-elections at the end of the month. In 14 contests, Unionist victories resulted, with the sole casualty being Jim Nicholson in Newry & Mourne, losing to the SDLP's Seamus Mallon.

3. See Gabrielle Maguire (1991); Chap 5, pp 67-84.

4. Seamus Mallon (with Andy Pollak) A Shared Home Place (2019); Chapter 6, p. 72.

5. So much progress was traced back to the new Irish cultural dawn generated by the 1985 Hillsborough Accord. This view represented a consensus, reiterated by numerous figures from GAA, Conradh na nGaeilge, Comhaltas, La, Irish arts and BBC figures interviewed.

6. The 1991 Census showed Catholic-Nationalist numbers to have grown to almost 41% of the total population. HMSO London/Belfast; Religion Report.

7. Down GAA was the top-performing Ulster county over half a century and the first to bring the All-Ireland Senior Gaelic Football trophy across the border; winning first in 1960, then '61, '68, '91 & '94, and beaten finalists to Cork in 2010. Tyrone won the senior trophy in 2003, 2005, 2008 and, most recently, in September 2021; and were beaten finalists in 1986, 1995 and 2018; while Armagh won in 2002, and were beaten finalists in 1953,

1977 & 2003. Derry, having lost the final of 1958, finally won the All-Ireland senior football trophy in 1993, while Donegal won in 1992 and 2012 while losing to Dublin in 2013. Antrim Hurlers reached two All-Ireland Senior finals; 1943 (lost heavily to Cork), and 1989 when they lost to Tipperary, but won the Intermediate trophy in 1970. – It says much of Ulster's dominance of Gaelic football across the whole island that the 2003 All-Ireland Senior final was contested by two Ulster counties, Armagh (holders) and successful challengers, Tyrone, led by their legendary manager, Michael Harte.

See: BBC Gaelic sports journalist and broadcaster, Jerome Quinn - Ulster Gaelic Football and Hurling: The Path of Champions (1993, Wolfhound Press, Dublin). Also, Donal McAnallen – The Pursuit of Perfection: The Life, Death and Legacy of Cormac McAnallen (2017, Penguin Books, UK). A touching but also searching biography by Dr McAnallen of his beloved and tragedy-ridden brother, the Tyrone Gaelic football star, Cormac, whose sudden death in March 2004 touched the entire Irish nation.

8. This was a point emphasised very clearly by Gearoid O'Caireallain (then Editor of La) in discussions with this author, January 1994.

9. Maguire (1991); Chap 4, pp 57-59.

10. During the 1970s and '80s, several Unionist-led Councils across Northern Ireland; eg. Larne, Craigavon, Ballymena and Belfast refused funding and facilities to Gaelic sports clubs, while Unionist MPs like the late Rev/Dr Ian Paisley repeatedly accused the GAA and IRA of acting in cahoots. – In 1976, an unsuccessful move was made by Democratic Unionists Society, at the Students Union, Queens University, Belfast, to block Union funding for both student GAA clubs (Gaelic Football and Hurling) and the ladies Camogie Club (Ladies Hurling) on the grounds of the disputatious Rule 21. See Gown (Student magazine), Autumn 1976.

11. The former Rule 21 barred GAA membership to RUC officers, British police officers and all British armed forces members. Over the course of a century, the rule was never consistently enforced, and additional to predictable Unionist hostility, it was bitterly denounced by liberal-minded GAA members; among them this author. See BBC N.I. *'Hearts and Minds'* current affairs broadcast 27th April 2001. Rule 21 was finally abolished

by a special Congress of the GAA in November 2001. – For more details about the GAA, see Appendix 1.

See Donal McAnallen <u>Forgotten Gaelic Volunteers: Ulster Gaelic Volunteers who fought in World War One</u> (2019, Cardinal O'Fiaich Library/Heritage Centre, Armagh).

12. See McKee V. <u>Contemporary Politics</u> (1995); p. 102.

13. Correspondence from Mr Aodan MacPoilin, Director - ULTACH Trust, 9th July, 1997.

14. See O'Reilly (1999), Chap 5; and Maguire (1991), Chaps 3 & 5.

15. Ibid.

16. The tensions between Mr MacPoilin and ULTACH Trust on one hand and the radicals of Sinn Fein and Conradh na Gaeilge on the other – who accused ULTACH of being unhealthily close to the Northern Ireland Office – were very poignant e.g. Belfast's Linen Hall Library for the launch of Gaelic Nations on 31st October 1997, Messers' Aodan MacPoilin and Gearoid O'Caireallain (Editor, La) traded abrupt exchanges at what was after all an official event of 1997 Ard dheis of Conradh na nGaeilge. Ref. Discussions with Dr Gordon McCoy, 30-11-19.

17. The incumbent was the late Mr Seamus McGrattan, retiring Secretary of Down GAA Hurling, Board, whose appointment was formally announced at the Annual Hurling Convention of Down GAA, Denvirs Hotel, Downpatrick in November 1976. This author attended the event, witnessed all relevant developments, and retains official GAA records.

18. Discussions with Mr Brian McAvoy, General Secretary, Ulster GAA Council – 21st October 2019, Armagh. Also, discussions with Dr Gordon McCoy and Mr Maolcholaim Scott, both of whom had worked with Conradh na nGaeilge.

19. O'Reilly (1999), Chap 5; and Maguire (1991), Chaps 3 & 5.

20. This author visited the Meanscoil Beal Feirste on 4th November 1997, to present copies of my then-recent publication, <u>Gaelic Nations</u>. I was indeed welcomed by a gracious Deputy Headmaster, Mr Feargus O'hEithir, who

gave me a clear explanation of the school's campaign progress and general development.

21. The distrust of Dublin and its compromising legacy was a prominent theme underpinning Sinn Fein's view of Southern administrations. See Gerard Murray and Jonathan Tongue – *Sinn Fein and the SDLP: From Alienation to Participation* (2005, Dublin).

22. Interviews with Gearoid O'Caireallain – January and July 1994.

23. Information provided by Gearoid O'Caireallain – Interviews January and July 1994.

24. O'Caireallain insisted that such a distance was necessary in order not to allow Unionists and hostile figures at the Northern Ireland Office any scope for establishing Gaelicism as the cultural handmaiden of Sinn Fein.

25. Discussions with Gearoid O'Caireallain – July 1994.

26. Fr – now Monsignor - Raymond Murray, priest of Armagh Arch-Diocese and close friend of Cardinal O'Fiaich, was a lifelong Gaelgeoir. He edited the Armagh Arch-Diocesan Historical Society Journal, and contributed to numerous Gaeilge publications elsewhere. Fair to say that during Cardinal O'Fiaich's tenure as Archbishop of Armagh, 1977-90, a positive approach was taken towards the place of Gaeilge as a language for the liturgy and music, and as a subject for diocesan historical and heritage enquiries. The establishment of the Cardinal O'Fiaich Memorial Library and Cultural Archive rather testifies for itself.

27. See McKee V. Gaelic Nations, p. 74.

28. Discussions with Gearoid O'Caireallain, January and July 1994.

29. Ibid.

30. Ibid.

31. Ibid, January 1994.

32. Interviews: Jake MacSiacais, Director Forbairt Feirste (25th & 28th Sep., 2020); Tarlac O'Branagain, Assistant at Forbairt, 18th 19th & 23rd Sep. 2020), and Mrs Colma Mhic Aodha/McKee of Gaelchursai, Beal Feirste, 23rd September 2020.

33. Interviews with Messers MacSiacais and O'Brainigan.

34. Ibid.

35. Interview – Mrs Colma Mhic Aoidha – confirmed by Messers' O'Branagain & MacSiacais.

36. Interview – Mr MacSiacais. Also, same point confirmed in discussions with Mr Gearoid O'Caireallain (2020) and Dr Gordon McCoy, 15th December 2019.

    Discussions with Mr MacSiacais.

37. Discussions with Mr Maolcholaim Scott, 6th September, 2020. – Note: Mr Scott worked for some 12 months in the 1990s at the Culturlann with <u>La</u>.

38. Discussions with Messers' MacSiacais and Scott.

39. McKee (1995); <u>Comparative Politics and Municipal Journal</u> (March 1991).

40. O'Reilly (1999); Chaps 2, 5 & 6.

41. Aodan MacPoilin in Aodan MacPoilin Eds.(1997); Chaps 2 & 4.

42. See <u>Irish News</u> (Belfast) reports, 3rd November 1997.

43. Northern Ireland Census, 1991, HMSO, Belfast (1992), p 159.

44. UK Census 1991, HMSO London.

45. (i) Phoenix et al (2005); (ii) Staunton (2001); Parts 2 & 3.

46. By 1992, the SDLP held 4 Westminster seats (ie. Foyle, West Belfast, Newry & Armagh and South Down), while Sinn Fein held Mid-Ulster and West Tyrone; there was also sharp competition for local council representation. The late Mr John Hume further held one of Northern Ireland's 3 European Parliament seats. Earlier, in January 1986, Mr Seamus Mallon had captured Newry & Armagh from the Unionists in a by-election, while in the following year's Westminster poll, the SDLP's Mr Eddie McGrady defeated the incumbent Unionist MP and former British Tory Cabinet Minister, Mr Enoch Powell (now deceased), in South Down.

47. The late and highly respected Mr Mallon was a keen dramatist and one-time Armagh county senior Gaelic footballer. – See <u>Mallon Memoirs with Andy Pollak</u> (2019); Chaps 1 & 6.

48. Pol O'Muiri <u>The Irish Review – An Ghaeilge</u> (1993, Belfast).

49. Correspondence – Mr Maolcholaim Scott to V. McKee, October 1st 1990

50. Figures produced by Conradh na Gaeilge and cited in <u>La</u>, November 1993.

Chapter Six

1998-2020: SCOTTISH GAELDOM'S EXPERIENCE OF DEVOLUTION

__Aims:__ This chapter will examine the experience of Scottish Gaelic interests and initiatives under the new constitutional instrument of a national parliament and executive, post 1997. Areas to be evaluated shall include education, Gaelic medium schools, Gaelic broadcasting, arts, drama, culture, public signage and funding, all of which were delegated to the new Edinburgh administration. Legal initiatives shall form an important part of this evaluation, most particularly the Gaelic Language (Scotland) Act of 2005, with its impact on the language's place in Scotland of the third millennium. So will the attitudes of the Scottish political parties be considered, as well as civil servants in the former Scottish Office, and how the existence of a Holyrood administration affected the various approaches of politicians and bureaucracy. In particular, the chapter will take account of the tactics and attitudes of anti-Gaelic elements in local government, the Parliament and public administration, in an endeavour to ascertain their level of influence. Those individuals championing the Gaelic cause in Scotland, and their campaigning records shall also be evaluated.

Although preliminary comparisons will be made with Gaeldom's progress in Northern Ireland, where devolved government followed broadly the same time period, albeit at a slower pace, detailed cross comparisons shall be held over until Chapter 8. It will take the experiences and evidence emerging from two decades of devolved rule in both countries to make an informed evaluation approximating to the realities of prevailing Gaelic conditions in each country.

---

1. *__Overview:__* By the time of the new Scottish Parliament's election and historic opening at Holyrood Palace, Edinburgh, by Her Majesty, The Queen, on 1ˢᵗ July 1999, there was a sense

in which Gaeldom, like all other major Scottish institutions, had reached a seminal crossroads. The past offered only a broad indicator as to what lay ahead? Scotland had long learned to bear with the policies of successive Conservative administrations from London, so long as the old Scottish Office softened their impact to make them more palatable to Scots. In many cases, as Professor Tom Devine reminds us, government policies generally from London were not always unsympathetic to Scottish needs, and with Gaelic a positive response had been forthcoming in several areas, not least broadcasting, arts and Gaelic medium education, provided the case was made by diligent lobbyists, not hostile agitators.*(1) Yet however hopeful might have been leading figures in An Comunn Gaidhealach, Comunn na Gaidhlig, the Gaelic Societies of London and Inverness, and various sister bodies in arts, education, drama, broadcasting and such like, beyond broad manifesto commitments there were no clear directions as to what road the new Labour/Liberal Democrat coalition, headed by a talented Labour First Minister, Donald Dewar, might take? It all looked very uncertain?

Few, if any of the new government ministers, including Dewar, were Gaelic speakers, or had any real experience of Gaelic culture. Nor were they known for holding unyielding Gaelic sympathies. The Scottish Left after all, as Wilson McLeod noted, had long held divided views about the place of Gaelic in modern Scotland, and overall had a less than distinguished track record in Gaelic promotions.*(2) Moreover, whatever positive sentiments may have been spoken on election platforms, there were abundant numbers of high-placed 'naysayers' in the Scottish Civil Service and local councils with sufficient influence to at least delay, if not thwart, Gaelic progress. It was by no means a 'given' that the modest degree of home rule legislated by the New Labour government of Tony Blair, and enthusiastically endorsed by over 76% of the Scottish people in the Celtic referenda of Autumn 1997, would unquestionably spell 'milk and honey' for the future of Scottish Gaeldom. Overall, Gaidheil na h-Alba faced a hard struggle to assert its place in the new Scotland – post-devolution.

Tom Devine noted that following the sudden death of Donald Dewar in October 2000, a succession of short-lived Labour First Ministers – namely Henry McLeish and Jack McConnell – proved weak and inept, and unable to give the level of national leadership required. Nor were the Liberal Democrats – Labour's coalition partners – headed by Jim Wallace, much of an improvement. Indeed only the opposition Scottish National Party came into its element after 1999, under the inspiring leadership of Alex Salmond. The SNP proved sufficiently robust and appealing to win power in the elections of 2007, which it has retained at subsequent elections variously as a minority and majority administration until this time of writing (April 2021). Despite losing an independence referendum by 55% to 45% in September 2014, the SNP did not lose its party appeal. Additional to strengthening its hold on Holyrood, the party swept the board at the Westminster election of 2015 when capturing all but three of Scotland's 59 seats – decimating its old Labour enemy in the process.

McLeod (W.), along with other writers like O'Giollagain et al and M. MacLeod & C. Smith-Christmas, all seemed to be of a common mind as to what should be the priorities for the new Holyrood administration's Gaelic policy.*(3) They included, first, a stemming of the declining numbers of Gaelic speakers; second, the extension of Gaelic medium education, and the creation of stand-alone Gaelic medium schools; third, the development of a Gaelic Language statute to define and protect Gaelic interests; fourth, the resolution of funding issues; fifth, progress on economic development for Gaidhealtachd areas; and, sixth, consolidation of the cultural profile. This ambitious programme needed to be addressed urgently if the language was to have any resonance with the new administration, such as would enhance its appeal to Scotland's Gaelic world.

It was not that Scottish Gaeldom had any hardline opponents among either the mainstream political parties, pressure groups or other influential elements of the Scottish or even British 'body politic' … so to speak. Conversely, its dilemma was its modest size and limited constituency. There were many civil servants, media elements, academics, councillors and, no doubt, MPs and local parliamentarians who felt the Gaels were punching above their weight, claiming a disproportionate share of resources, air time and public profile that defied their popular roots. Such naysayers were not so few, and their case had to be answered with rational arguments presented by creditable lobbyists and esteemed patrons whose tactics were both proportional and balanced. It was not a role for cranks or radical extremists, whose effects if let loose could have been very damaging to Gaelic interests.

One area where I must respectfully disagree with my scholarly friend and much regarded fellow Gael, Professor Wilson McLeod, concerns the role of professionals and aristocracy in An Comunn Gaidhealach. Professor McLeod, for reasons amply articulated in his acclaimed 2020 book, takes a somewhat disdainful view of the ACG's abundance of patrons from Scotland's higher social orders.*(4) He did not much like their privileges or the influence they wielded; something he felt amounted to keeping ACG and Gaeldom effectively tied to the Scottish social and political establishment.*(5) This is a a valid enough point of view, and on an issue that has generated recurrent strains within the broad Scottish Gaelic family, especially among young radical activists from Comunn na Canain Albannaich. The latter were more inspired by the direct action tactics of the Welsh Language Society and indeed Comhaltas Ulaidh in Belfast, and wondered why Scottish Gaeldom could not show more belly fire in its promotions? However, this author tends towards another interpretation, and one consistently stated throughout this book, as goes to the heart of my analysis.

The keywords for Scottish Gaels are about **numbers** and **survival**: - as basic as that! Over the course of a century, Scotland's Gaelic speaking numbers have fallen from 158,779 in 1921 to 88,892 in 1971 to 57,602 in 2011, totalling 1.1% of the whole Scottish population.*(6) This situation compares most unfavourably with Wales, where upwards of 20% of the 2.9 million Welsh people speak their mother tongue daily. Nor, despite the interest of some Scottish Gaelic advocates like Wilson McLeod and MacLeod M. & Smith-Christmas C. in Galway-based Gaelgeoir initiatives, does the Scottish situation remotely compare with Southern Ireland where constitutional support for the language is available, or Northern Ireland where despite adversities Gael Uladh's progress may be traced to hard campaigning by nationalist political parties and the Ulster Gaelic League. Plainly, and notwithstanding the spirited efforts of Scotland's Gaelic activists, the position of Scottish Gaidhlig is grievously weak to the point of acute. Developments in education, arts, music, broadcasting, literature, community affairs and local government …. there have been many, as indicated in previous chapters. Yet, as O'Giollagain et al concluded in 2020, those dropping numbers and creeping Anglicised encroachments to the Gaidhealtachd all contributed to create a crisis in Gaeldom's homeland and spheres of interest.*(7)

In those circumstances, the social class structure of An Comunn Gaidhealach and sister organisations was and remains of peripheral importance. Throughout the 20th century, Scottish Gaels have been engaged in a long-running battle for survival, and thus the use of lobbyist, rather than confrontational tactics, spear-headed by skilled networkers and policy advisors, and fronted by patrons from the professions and House of Lords, all amounted to clever politics by ACG, CnG and others. Ranged against sceptics in the Scottish Office, hostile Whitehall officials and 1980s Conservative governments not instantly sympathetic to the Gaelic cause, it is a tribute to the skills of distinguished lobbyists like John Angus Mackay (as recalled by his biographer, Roy Pederson) and the memorable Donald John Mackay that positive results in terms of grants and Gaelic TV authority were forthcoming. Those were the tactics that enabled Scottish Gaeldom to make a decent fist of its survival through from Westminster to Holyrood rule. Conversely, it is difficult to see how radical politicking could have fared any better? Now, it remains to be considered how the first 21 years of Scottish devolved government have impacted on the character and progress of Scottish Gaeldom?

> **2. *Gaelic Language Act (Scotland) 2005.*** Professor Wilson McLeod had this to say of the Act: "***The Gaelic Language Act is based to a considerable extent on the Welsh Language Act 1993 (and bears some resemblance to the Official Languages Act 2003 in the Republic of Ireland), but is rather less vigorous. Nevertheless, the Act is without doubt a landmark in the history of Gaelic policy in Scotland***".*(8)

Arguably, the most important initiative from the new Scottish Parliament to date has been the 2005 Gaelic Language Act. This legislation at Edinburgh followed on from the failed attempt back in 1981 by the late Hebridean MP, Donald Stewart, at Westminster to secure recognition for the struggling Gaelic revival with his Gaelic Miscellaneous Provisions Private Member Bill, which fell to Tory filibustering. Unlike the Stewart initiative of 24 years earlier, this law was the product of intensive lobbying by An Comunn Gaidhealach, Comunn na Gaidhlig, Gaelic academics and educationalists and other campaigners. The primary aim of lobbyists was to achieve legal recognition for Gaelic in Scottish society, and protection of its status with a public watchdog. At the Committee stages, there was debate about whether or not to accord Gaelic equal legal status with English, but in the end the Parliament settled on 'Equal Validity' – a nebulous concept whose precise meaning remains unclear?

Very significantly, the 2005 legislation was passed by the Holyrood Chamber with unanimous support from all Scottish political parties, including the Conservatives. Additional to the obvious advantage of securing actual legislation, the cross-party 'consensus' also ensured that Gaelic was not dependent on the favour of any one political movement, far less its electoral success. Among Gaelic advisers in the drafting process was Professor Robert Dunbar, Head of Celtic Studies at University of Edinburgh; Scottish-Canadian by background, married to a Hebridean lady, and originally a trained lawyer with a consummate skill for dealing with legislative issues connected to Gaelic. Dunbar's influence and scholarly input to the legislative process ensured more than most that a viable and positive statute finally reached the Parliament in a form both appropriate and watertight.*(9) Unlike the civil servants and public draughtsmen who were deemed 'neutral' – not all of whom had their hearts in the process – such could never be said of this modest Edinburgh-based professor. Frankly, Robert Dunbar was a wholehearted Gaelic advocate, with a life-long devotion to the Gaelic cause, and throughout those crucial months of 2004 and 2005 slaved prodigiously to render every aid for ensuring that a workable Gaelic law reached Scotland's statute book.*(10) This observation was noted from a range of discussions with figures from across the Gaelic world.

While most observers welcomed the passage of the Act, not all were enthralled with its prospects. As McLeod (W.) observed: "*... the Act does not actually contain any straightforward declaration of Gaelic's status. This is in contrast to the Welsh Language (Wales) Measure 2011, which unambiguously states that 'the Welsh language has official status in Wales'...The wording in the Gaelic Language Act is much more indirect: the phrase '..an official language of Scotland commanding equal respect with the English language'... is actually preceded by '... with a view to securing the status of Gaelic as..' a formula which suggests that that this status is aspirational rather than actual.*" *(11)

Another commentator, Eamonn O'Gribin argued that the Act falls well short of the status accorded to Welsh in a manner that makes it difficult to believe any substantial change will come about as a result of either the legislation or its emergent watchdog corollary, Bord na Gaidhlig (BnG).*(12) Time alone will determine whether such pessimism is justified?

The main provisions of the 2005 law were as follows. First, it defined Gaelic in Scotland as having 'Equal Validity' status with English, which fell somewhere short of actual parity of legal status, although it did offer a basis for ensuring that the public and private sectors made Gaelic provisions in their notices, resources and services. Second, the Act established a statutory development body, **Bord na Gaidhlig** (BnG) with a remit to consolidate the status of Gaelic as an official language of Scotland. Third, Bord na Gaidhlig was required to prepare a National Gaelic Language Plan on a five-yearly basis for the scrutiny and approval of Ministers of the Scottish Executive. Fourth, BnG was mandated to produce a framework and guidelines for both Gaelic Medium Education and Gaelic as a teaching subject for the Scottish Councils and Department of Education. Fifth, the Act placed a legal duty on Scottish public bodies and Anglo-Scottish cross-border public organisations carrying out devolved functions, to prepare and implement Gaelic Language plans where directed by BnG.*(13)

Frankly, 'Equal Respect' rather than parity of legal status is as about as far as the Act would proceed. As again noted by Wilson McLeod - Section 8 (10) requires that "... in preparing guidance (concerning Gaelic language plans) and giving advice and assistance (concerning the development of Gaelic), Bord na Gaidhlig must seek to give effect, so far as is both appropriate ... and reasonably practicable, to the principle that.. Gaelic and English ... should be accorded equal respect."*(14)

Probably the most significant innovation of the 2005 Act, aside from the aspirational statement of 'equal respect' between Gaelic and English, was the creation of Bord na Gaidhlig – replacing the earlier Bord Gaidhlig na h-Alba) with its range of attendant powers and responsibilities. This body had charge of developing and directing the National Gaelic Plan, although its terms are vague and its enforcement authority has rightly been viewed by McLeod (W.) as "weak and indirect".*(15) Also, though the Bord spearheaded the National Plan, Holyrood retained control over the process. In practice this meant key BnG officers working jointly with the Gaelic/Cultural Minister at Holyrood, but, significantly, with enforcement actions against 'laggers' resting solely with the Minister.

As a result of the legislation and creation of Bord na Gaidhlig, the positive climate boosted the language profile in several areas. In October 2009, it was agreed that Scottish Gaelic could be used between Holyrood ministers and officials of the European Union. This arrangement was confirmed by a deal co-signed by the-then British EU Permanent Representative, Sir Kim Darroch, and the Edinburgh administration. It did not actually confer official status on

Gaelic in the EU, but allowed for its acceptance in formal communications in EU institutions, conditional on the Holyrood government paying the translation costs from Gaelic to other European languages. This was essentially a boost for Gaelic promotions, and showed some positive results in terms of extending the language profile, as well as demonstrating implied support from the UK government. The latter point was emphasised in a 2009 interview given by the-then Secretary of State for Scotland, Jim Murphy, who talked about "... *raising the profile of Gaelic as we drive forward our commitment to creating a new generation of Gaelic speakers in Scotland.*"*(16) At last, Gaelic was out in the open with a fair wind at its back.

It is significant that the October 2009 agreement between the Scottish Executive and EU over language usage followed on from an earlier action by the UK government of Tony Blair in ratifying the Council of Europe's *Charter for Regional and Minority Languages* in 1999, something that its Conservative predecessor had refused to sign. The latter had placed an onus on signatory nations to reform practices to ensure fair and proportional access to resources and enabling legislation governing minority languages and cultures. In this instance, Scottish and Irish Gaelic, along with Welsh, were designated for affirmative action. Such provision had provided further impetus for the passage of the 2005 Gaelic Language Act, with the endorsement of the Westminster parties. All these reforms had boosted the Gaelic profile, but as we shall see, such was the smaller part of the challenge. The results that mattered were those on the ground, and nothing was guaranteed.

3. **Impact of Gaelic Language Act and Holyrood Executive on Scotland.** Passing the new law was one thing; implementing it was another. In particular, there were the thorny questions about declining Gaelic language speaker numbers, the contracting Gaidhealtachd, socio-economic retardation in native-speaking areas and the uncertainty surrounding development of Gaelic Medium Education and schools. As shown in previous chapters, by 2005 Gaelic arts, drama, music, publishing, television and radio had already been facilitated and indeed generously aided by central government. The major test now was how to apply the legislation and powers conferred towards raising speakers,

boosting Gaelic in schools, and defending the declining Gaidhealtachd.

(i) Bord na Gaidhlig was not a body whose creation was universally welcomed across the Gaelic world. While many leading Gaels endorsed its introduction as a necessary vehicle for leading the survival and re-growth of Gaelic in the communities and across the country, other Gaels viewed BnG as a bureaucratic arm of government. They doubted its independence and questioned its relevance.*(17) Yet a distinguished former BnG Chairman, Gaelic musician and Feisean na Gaidheal director, Arthur Cormack, felt the Bord's performance over 14 years vindicated its healthy purpose by constructive involvements with a range of public sector organisations ranging from Police Scotland, BBC Scotland, Scottish Universities, schools and colleges, and various departments of Scottish government to the municipalities, health boards and tourist authority etc.*(18)

The Bord operates from an office in Inverness, with 24 administrative, field and research staff, all funded from the Scottish Department of Culture. Bord na Gaidhlig's executive was composed of nominees appointed by the Holyrood Gaelic Affairs Minister, who were drawn from a range of creditable lead sources across the Scottish Gaelic world.*(19) They included the likes of Professor Robert Dunbar, of University of Edinburgh; Lewis-based Gaelic educationalist and local historian, Mrs Annie MacSween; former Director of Comunn na Gaidhlig and the Gaelic Television Committee, Mr John Angus MacKay; Gaelic academic and writer, Professor Ken MacKinnon; Lewis-native, but retired Edinburgh Police Inspector and President of An Comunn Gaidhealach 2007-2017, Mr Iain (John) Macleoid*(20); Western Isles Crofting Commissioner, Mr Murdo Maclennan; and Director of Careers Scotland and non-executive Director of the Scottish Government Strategic Board, Mrs Christina Allen – a classical example of what political scientist, Wyn Grant, defined as an "Insider Group".*(21) Positions were subject to re/appointment by the Holyrood administration, specifically the Gaelic Affairs Minister, and all carried a remunerative allowance.*(22)

Although BnG had its defenders, its critics were just as prominent, and … in the Grant model … tended towards the radical side of politics. It was gravely criticised for funding decisions, such as the early withdrawal of aid to

An Comunn Gaidhleach's monthly journal, *'An Gaidheal Ur'*, which operated from 1998 until its closure in 2009. Seemingly, despite the journal's positive profile, BnG had doubts about its long term financial viability. Frankly, closure came as a severe blow to the struggling world of Gaelic publishing.*(23) So also did the cutting of help to the Gaelic Pre-School organisation, *'Taic*/CNSA, whose radical but energetic director, Mr Finlay MacLeod (a Lewis native), had a lengthy and distinguished track record of developing Gaelic nurseries ever since the early 1980s. Mr McLeod had been a consistent Gaelic establishment critic from the start, and underlined his case by public utterances of disaffection with that establishment throughout the 1990s and post-millennium decade.*(24) He also accused the Bord of being a tame creature of political masters in Edinburgh rather than being linked to Gaelic community interests in the Highlands and Hebrides.*(25) Another such questionable act was the withdrawal of funding from the Gaelic Learners organisation, *'Cli Gaidhlig'*, which critics claimed undermined efforts at winning over new speakers. The budget was clearly not infinite, but economy choices sparked grave controversy, especially from those claiming that the Bord was not projecting a sufficiently radical image.

Given the mildly overlapping fields of activity, there certainly existed potential for tension. Yet Arthur Cormack was strongly of the view that BnG had a defined role of liaising with the various organisations whose Gaelic policies were subject to compliance with the Act, and the Gaelic Affairs Minister at Holyrood. This briefing was adequate for purpose, and Mr Cormack had no recollection of any 'territorial' clashes with other Gaelic organisations, most specifically Comunn na Gaidhlig. *"CnG had a specific role to co-ordinate and promote between the different Gaelic groups and authorities, whereas BnG was tasked to produce the National Plan and ensure compliance"*.*(26) Conversely, he recalled both bodies as rather complementing one another.*(27) Similar responses were forthcoming from Professor Ken MacKinnon and Mrs Annie MacSween, both of whom saw distinct but complementary goals for each of the principal Gaelic bodies in the public sector.*(28)

Interestingly, Comunn na Gaidhlig also had its head office in Inverness, almost next door to BnG, where it employed 9 full time administrative staff, plus a smaller quota of part-timers. Another congenial "neighbour" in that same Inverness district was An Comunn Gaidhleach, which employed 3 full time administrators and a small compliment of part time assistants. Mr Cormack's own group, Feisean na Gaidheal, also had a head office in

Inverness, along with a field office on the Isle of Skye, from where he worked primarily. An Feisean employed some 10 full and part time clerical and policy staff, plus numerous Gaelic language and cultural tutors engaged for fixed term purposes.*(29)

(Ii) Bilingual Public Signage: This issue had been rumbling on since the late 1970s when Gaelic road signs first appeared within the Highlands Council area, including Skye, Ardnamurchan, Moidart, Morvern and Assynt. Under the Road Traffic Regulation Act (Scotland) 1967, plus a successor statute of 1984, local authorities were required to get Scottish Office consent in order to erect bilingual signage of this kind. Normally, such requests aroused little objection, but problems arose once Councils applied for trunk roads. Civil Servants proved reluctant to co-operate. There was the case in 1999 of Holyrood Transport Minister, Sarah Boyack, refusing Highland Council's request to place bilingual signage on the A87 in Skye and part of the A830 near Mallaig, claiming "safety concerns". It later emerged that prior to the devolved administration's assumption of power, the Westminster Transport Minister, Calum Macdonald (significantly, a native Gaelic speaker representing Western Isles), had overruled Scottish Office civil servants to authorise the Highlands Council application.*(30) In 2001, Boyack finally changed course to grant authorisation for bilingual signage on both roads. Then in 2003, succeeding Holyrood Transport Minister, Lewis Macdonald (no relation!), announced bilingual signage for another eight trunk roads in Highlands and Argyll & Bute districts, underlining a new Holyrood policy of Gaelic road signage on main roads throughout the region, as well as those serving Glasgow and West Highlands ferry ports.*(31) This fresh practice appeared to underpin the Holyrood plan to project Gaelic culture, and in so far as it went was welcomed by An Comunn Gaidhealach and its allies. Yet the process was not without its problems. When the A9 main road from Central Scotland to Inverness was denied bilingual signage, Highlands Councillor, Dr Michael Foxley, made a public accusation of "institutional racism" against Gaelic prevailing within the civil service.*(32)

Overall, however, the effect of public signage initiatives was positive, and extended beyond the Highlands road system. By the turn of the millennium, there were already signs of a bilingual profile on the Scottish railways system, with Gaelic signage on the two Highland lines from Glasgow to Oban and Mallaig and from Perth to Kyle of Lochalsh and Thurso. There were fewer objectors with the railways than the road system, and after 2005, under pressure from BnG, bilingual signage appeared across the whole Scottish network of railways and stations. The use of Gaelic signage on main roads and railways, did much to boost the Gaelic profile to a hitherto un-accustomed Scottish public, plus appealing to the large numbers of visitors to the country.

With the passage of time, bilingual signage was extended to many other public organisations previously listed, while also embracing private bodies like churches, hotels, supermarkets, schools and colleges etc.*(33) This process amounted to a slow but steady growth in the gaelicisation of Scottish society, and beyond a predictable range of 'naysayers' – to be found everywhere – connected to a consensus of good will spearheaded by the mainstream parties, churches, trade unions and interest groups. CnG provided logistical support to private and public organisations requesting assistance with development of bilingual imagery, as did local Councils like Comhairle nan Eilean Siar and Highlands. The co-operation of BBC Scotland and independent broadcasters further aided the popularisation process. Indeed public bilingual signage proved the most effective addendum to a new and inclusive image of post-millennial Scotland where Gaelic ceased as a Highland foible, but instead registered as a valid form of national identity.

(iii) Terminology and Linguistic Development: As Gaelic became more formalised and with a higher public profile, the need for standardisation of dialect and terminology became obvious. This was an exercise as much about the status of Gaelic in post-millennium times as any serious effort at accommodating linguistic clarity and discipline. It was hoped, rather vainly, that Gaelic's earlier lack of polished finesse might be rectified by linguistic planning and boosting formal settings. In the event, nothing of the kind happened swiftly, although some planning initiatives were attempted and are ongoing.

An Comunn Gaidhleach had earlier staged some training in standard Gaelic for use on BBC Radio (just then opening Home Service radio waves to Gaelic) during the 1920s and '30s. The results had been modest. However, in the late 1980s, Sabhal Mor Ostaig, along with Comhairle nan Eilean Siar, had sought to produce an agreed Gaelic terminological database.*(34) This initiative ran into problems, especially when Radio nan Gaidhlig, was found to be pushing a particular dialect, much of which was not easily followed by native-speaking Gaels from parts of the Hebrides. In any case, as McLeod noted, the experience raised a case for updating terminology, but only within the context of a consultation of different dialects across the Gaidhealtachd.*(35) Gaelic success in the third millennium required some degree of consensus on linguistic dialectics,

Among the corpus initiatives planned was '*Faclair na Parlamid*', which amounted to a published dictionary of Gaelic terminology associated with the business of the Scottish Parliament and Executive. Following completion and adoption of the latter, further glossaries were attempted covering local government and public administration, as envisaged by the European Language Initiative 2011 and 2012. However, as McLeod noted, a lack of fluent Gaelic draughtsmen meant those dictionaries were somewhat lacking in quality and usefulness.*(36)

Overall, the task of defining terminology and standardising the dialects of the language, has been accorded scant priority by the Scottish Gaelic world. Low numbers were one reason, as was the sporadic nature of initiatives, but so also did mild tensions occur between Gaelic intellectuals in the various universities and native speakers in the Gaidhealtachd. Academics were regularly berated by grass roots Gaels like Lewis Gaelic educationalist, Annie MacSween.*(37) Mrs MacSween – herself a champion of Gaelic in the communities – has never concealed suspicions of the underlying consequences of Gaelic Medium education, which in her view seemed geared primarily towards meeting the identity questions of middle class graduates rather than facilitating school and language learning skills among crofter children.*(38) The same was true of terminology and harmonisation of dialects, which she felt held even less value. In a paradoxical way, Mrs MacSween's warnings were lent a fair degree of succour by the very sober warnings of impending crisis for the Gaidhealtachd laid out by Professor Conchur O'Giollagain and his colleagues in their published study of 2020.*(39) The latter led to a robust exchange of views in the Scottish press between the book editor and Gaelic policymakers, many of them like former Scottish Office minister, Brian Wilson, stern critics.*(40)

> (iv) General Climate: It needs adding that the Gaelic Language Act of 2005 was significant not just for the specific reforms relating to public signage and creation of a Gaelic watchdog authority, but also for the positive new climate that it ushered in. The latter generated a buoyant confidence among Gaels who foresaw a series of welcome reforms that enhanced their status and entitlements as never before, and which held out hope for better times lying ahead. Just as important was the realisation that the reforms carried cross-party consensus, and did not hinge on any party or alliance holding office at Holyrood. Gaelic had no declared enemies in Scotland's political mainstream. That factor was demonstrated by the continuity of Gaelic policy accompanying political change from the Labour/Liberal Democrat coalition to the SNP after elections in 2007.

Other developments included the expansion of Gaelic Medium education through specialist units in schools and establishing a stand-alone Gaelscoil in Glasgow. Along with the latter went the further development of Gaelic playgroups and the Gaelic parents body, as well as provision for the training of Gaelic teachers in colleges like Sabhal Mor Ostaig, which was by this same period scheduled to become an affiliated institute of the new University of the Highlands and Islands. There existed a general air of optimism among Scottish Gaels which permeated the entire arena of arts, education, broadcasting, drama, publishing, local government, political and legal advocacy. In no small way did the 1905 Act's passage serve to boost the profile and esteem of Gaelic everywhere, while opening new doors that had remained firmly shut to previous generations of Gaels.

The emergence of a Gaelic Television Authority in 2008 for managing the novel Gaelic television channel, BBC Alba, proved the crowning achievement of the decade to follow from the legislation. Its complicated genesis – as documented in some detail by W. McLeod *(41) – resulted from a mixture of political pressure and skilful representations by the Gaelic lobby, and based on previous structures in place from earlier battles of the 1980/90s, as recalled by Roy Pedersen.*(42) This development, along with Gaelic educational growth, deserves further examination.

4. ***Gaelic Television and Genesis of BBC Alba.*** The progression from Gaelic quotas and occasional programmes like 'Machair' (a successful Gaelic soap opera running from 1993 to 1999) to a formalised and stand-alone Gaelic TV channel that commenced broadcasting in 2008, initially at 7 hours daily, proved a momentous development both for broadcasting and the esteem of Scotland's Gaelic world. BBC Alba's gestation and delivery certainly came about under direction from the newly devolved Scottish Executive and its advisory bodies. Yet as Pedersen's account shows, the latter's genesis occurred during the last years of the Westminster Scottish Office.*(43)

Under reserved powers contained in the 1998 Scotland Act, broadcasting was retained by the Westminster government. However, after devolution, control of the Gaelic Television Fund transferred from the Scottish Office to the new Holyrood administration, inclusive of its share of an overall block grant provided by the Whitehall Treasury. This meant that effective policy-making authority for directing Gaelic broadcasting lay with the new Scottish DCMS, thereby making it a de-facto creature of the devolution process. Earlier, Tony Blair's Gaelic Affairs Minister in the Scottish Office, Brian Wilson, himself a Gaelic supporter and one-time publisher of the Skye-based *West Highlands Free Press* *(44), caused some surprise by announcing a cut of £1,000,000 (later reduced to half that figure) in the Gaelic broadcasting budget. Yet by this point, and with Gaelic eyes turned towards the Welsh-speaking S4C Channel (funded to the tune of £97m), momentum was accruing for the launch of a Gaelic Television channel in Scotland. This new "Spring" climate worked in favour of what was to become BBC Alba. As more widely observed by Tom Devine, that same climate was moving in the direction of a rediscovery of Scottish heritage and a new sense of national identity at all levels of Scottish society where "Britishness" was slowly giving way to "Scottishness".*(45)

Significantly, Pederson and McLeod (W.) each acknowledge the process to have been hard-driven by the zealous John Angus Mackay, utilising all connections and liaisons at Westminster, Whitehall and Edinburgh, and operating through Comunn na Gaidhlig and other Gaelic postings.*(46) In 1998, the Minister, Brian Wilson, delegated a senior civil servant, Neil Fraser, to write a report on the viability of a dedicated Gaelic television channel in Scotland. Very significantly, plans for Gaelic TV took place against the backdrop of emergent digital technology replacing the traditional analogue model, a transition that would likely involve many other changes. When reporting a few months later, Fraser endorsed the principle of a digital and coherent Gaelic television service, but, significantly, driven by "... a single Gaelic Broadcasting Authority".*(47) There were issues about the budget, and though declining to name an actual figure, nevertheless he drew poignant attention to the gaps prevalent in sums spent on Celtic broadcasting elsewhere, notably £96.9m for S4C in Wales, £18m for TG4 in the Irish Republic and £11.13m for Gaelic Television in Scotland.*(48) Rather tellingly, no figures were provided for the budgeting of BBC Radio Ulster's Irish Language Unit in Belfast, itself an issue of controversy as negotiations leading to the historic Belfast Agreement were then reaching their peak.

Following on from the Fraser Report, a new Gaelic Broadcasting Task Force was created under the chairmanship of the late Sir Alasdair Milne, with the goal of examining the technical, financial and social viability of a dedicated Gaelic TV Channel. Now, with a force headed by the former BBC Director General (retired to Scotland), herewith was evidence of the serious intention of government to meet this principal demand of the Gaels. Milne's report, coming in 2000, made recommendations that augured a potential new dawn for Gaelic broadcasting, as follows:

1. A stand-alone Gaelic Broadcasting Authority, modelled on SC4 (Wales), mandated to run and direct all mainstream Gaelic programmes.

2. A Gaelic television service to be made available on a 'free-to-air' basis on all digital platforms, but with digital satellite prioritised.

3. A new Gaelic Broadcasting Authority to be funded by a statutory formula that raised £44m per annum, with additional increments to take account of inflation. Although the Milne formula would have resulted in a quadrupling of current Gaelic broadcasting income, it still left Gaelic with less than half the Welsh budget, something only partially explained by the 60,000 first language Gaels compared to some 500,000 Welsh mother tongue speakers.

4. An estimation that under the new formula the capacity existed for over three hours daily peak-time broadcasting in Gaelic, which also meant increasing the numbers of Gaelic broadcasting staff increasing from 316 to over 800.*(49) This growth never quite happened!

Responses to the Milne Report were universally supportive within the Scottish Gaelic community, and indeed no gestures of opposition were forthcoming from any of the Scottish political parties, including Scottish Conservatives. There was a general feeling in various circles that a compelling case for a reformed Gaelic television service had been made, something reflected in the Scottish media at the time, not to mentions newspapers like the Scotsman, Glasgow Herald and Aberdeen Press and Journal. However, it was at the higher level of government, both with ministers and top civil servants, that the response was more muted, indeed lukewarm. Although the new Assembly had been created and elected, actual functions of executive government were then in the transition process. Broadcasting was a devolved function, but in 2000 London still held control of the portfolio, and the Blairite Minister, Dr Kim Howells, described the Milne proposal for a Gaelic Broadcasting Authority with an annual budget of £44 m. as "..not justified or acceptable..". Even Brian Wilson appeared to beat a retreat. However, McLeod (W.) noted that the principal excoriation of the Milne proposals came from civil servants in both the Scottish Office and Whitehall, who resented the fact that the Department of Media, Culture and Sport had to bear most of the expense of a second minority language channel, rather than BBC Scotland.*(50) Gaelic Television was at that time, as John Angus Mackay of Comunn na Gaidhlig, rather aptly described it: "… *a devolution orphan*".*(51)

Eventually, following a series of lobbies by CNG and other Gaelic publicists over the ensuing seven years, and with numerous interactions and compromises agreed between Whitehall and the new Edinburgh administration – vividly catalogued by Professor Wilson McLeod – the new BBC Alba was agreed in a document July 2007. A budget of £16.8m – about 37% of Milne's recommendation – was to provide a service of seven days per week, with seven hours of daily television, and provision for 1.5 hours daily of new programmes, later rising to three hours.

Significantly, this was also a time of political change; as the year 2007 saw the election of a minority SNP administration at Holyrood under Alex Salmond, which ousted the previous Labour/Liberal Democrat administration. Salmon also favoured the emergence of the new BBC Alba, which took to the air in 2008. There was a definite change in the political atmosphere, and while McLeod does not directly allude to the latter, clearly Gaelic Television was the kind of innovation that the First Minister (not himself a Gaelic speaker … like most of his party brethren!) was overtly encouraging in his vision of a new and culturally enhanced Scotland.*(52) Devine's thesis of a reborn Scotland, proud of its national heritage and in search of an inclusive identity, in which Gaelic had a valued place, was being vindicated by events in this latest chapter of the Gaelic renaissance.*(53) Even a stern SNP critic as Professor Tom Gallagher was forced to acknowledge in his 2016 text that the ascendant SNP under Alex Salmon, and, following the failed independence referendum of September 2014, Nicola Sturgeon, had been a positive force for reflecting rising popular support for a sense of national identity based on Scottish, rather than British, heritage.*(54) While keeping a strict equidistance from political alignments, nevertheless – and understandably – the Scottish Gaelic lobby were not slow to take full advantage of all such trends as favoured their position.

5. ***Gaelic Medium Education (GME).*** The process of Gaelic education was advanced by a series of developments occurring in the first two decades of the new millennium. While Gaelic speaker numbers – especially first language Gaels – dipped below the 60,000 figure in the previous Census of 2011, and CnG/ACG anxiously awaits the forthcoming 2022 Scottish National Census (delayed by 12 months because of the Covid 19 Pandemic), nevertheless there can be little doubt that Gaelic medium schooling has advanced both within and beyond the Gaidhealtachd, as has Gaelic learning. While the attainment of go-it-alone Gaelic medium schools have not yet been achieved – in contrast to the Gaelscoil movement of Gaeil Uladh (Northern Ireland) – nevertheless a combination of persistent parental demand, patient perseverance by Gaelic educationalists, support from politicians across the political spectrum, and generous funding by the Scottish state at all levels has rendered tangible, albeit modest results.

It also needs to be acknowledged that Gaelic medium education is not just about pupil learning, as vital as that is to the core objectives. It also raises questions about the training and provision of qualified Gaelic teachers, pupil numbers and teacher ratios, plus logistical questions over whether dedicated Gaelic medium units should exist within existing schools or be pursued in stand-alone Gaelic schools, and what might be their relevance to the wider community? Also, the perennial question arose over funding, and from which budget finance for Gaelic medium education might come? The attitudes, and in many cases prejudices, of senior civil servants, councillors and campaigners were paramount. In several areas of the Highlands, Glasgow and Edinburgh, the introduction of Gaelic medium education provoked heated local debates, and the attitudes of local newspaper editors and elected public representatives played its part. Objectors raised various issues about the best use of public money, while others questioned whether Gaelic immersion was conducive towards the children's best educational development.*(55) There was also an attempt by some Labour critics in Edinburgh to link Gaelic educational development to notions of a privileged minority, while others even accused Gaelic medium schools – rather like state-funded Roman Catholic schools – as contributing to educational apartheid in Scottish society.*(56) An example of the latter occurred in the first decade of the new millennium in Edinburgh, when parents seeking an expanded GME unit at Tollcross were confronted by the Council's Education Convenor, Mrs Marilyne MacLaren's expressed view that *"... it was difficult to see the value of Gaelic in a capital city when we are such a cosmopolitan people".*(57) Nor were such narrow prejudices unique to Edinburgh!

In his comprehensive account, Wilson McLeod addresses many of those questions graphically and with a balanced regard for the sensitivities they aroused in the various communities concerned. The reality was that Gaelic immersion education began with the Gaelic pre-school groups, whose merits were so passionately articulated by Mr Finlay Macleod; carried on into Gaelic medium units most of which were located within state primaries across the Hebrides, Highlands, Glasgow and Edinburgh; and with the ambition of progressing to secondary units contained within mainstream primary schools. This was very much the preferred route for Gaelic educationalists, but as ever was limited by available places and units. Until recently, go-it-alone Gaelic medium schools have been limited to one in Glasgow and another in Inverness, while attempts at such an innovation in Edinburgh ran up against formidable opposition such as prevented the effort from achieving fruition.*(58) Equally, attempts at creating a Gaelic secondary school movement have not as yet enjoyed much success, mainly due to lack of numbers and suitable teachers for making such a venture viable.*(59)

In terms of actual numbers, primary pupils enrolled in GME increased from 2,068 in 2005 to 3,467 in 2019, an increase of over 67% from the previous decade. However encouraging may be the growth, it represents on 0.9 of the national total.*(60) The numbers of primary schools facilitating

GME units in 2019 amounted to 59, the same figure as that for 1999-2000. Moreover, despite the passage of the Gaelic Language Act of 2005, McLeod noted no additional education authorities having introduced Gaelic Medium schools or units within schools in their jurisdictions; the last being Inverclyde in 1999. Actually, by 2019, 18 of the 32 Scottish local authorities did not offer any form of Gaelic Medium education in their primary or secondary schools; a figure that tallied with 1998.*(61) Only 3 Gaelic medium units opened after 2006, all three of them in Highland Council area; namely Nairn in 2006, Drumnadrochit in 2011, and Thurso in 2013. An additional GME unit was opened in Aberfeldy in Perth & Kinross in 2013.*(62) That said, by 2020, only 7 stand-alone Gaelic Medium primary schools operated across Scotland; 3 in Glasgow (1999, 2016 and 2020 respectively), 1 in Inverness (2006), 1 in Edinburgh (2013), I in Fortwilliam (2015) and 1 in Portree, Skye (2018).*(63)

Significantly, and despite the static position in providers, actual numbers of GME pupils increased. Between 2005 and 2019, numbers of GME primary pupils increased from 195 to 700; 90 to 375 in Edinburgh, and 96 to 225 in Inverness.*(64) However, in the principal Scottish Gaidhealtachd of Outer Hebrides numbers increased more hesitantly over the same period from below 500 to 731. What is rather more surprising is that despite its pivotal position in the Gaelic world, by 2020 there was no sign of a stand-alone Gaelic medium primary school in the whole Hebridean local authority area covered by Comhairle nan Eilean Siar. Seemingly, the authority was reluctant to embark on this initiative, preferring instead to develop its GME units in local primary schools, plus the Nicholson Institute in Stornoway. Doubtless money scarcity played a part, but so also was political will lacking.

Elsewhere, some critical focus may be fairly directed at Bord na Gaidhlig. The Gaelic Language Act of 2005 empowers the Bord to require good practice from all public and private organisations in relation to the language. Clearly this includes local education authorities. Yet it took some 12 years after its creation for the Bord to publish a Gaelic education statutory compliance document. Since then, a total of 11 previously non-compliant local authorities have begun publishing Gaelic plans, but BnG did not require an offer of GME in their schools as a condition for endorsing their plans. Indeed so weak were the commitments over commencement of GME, that none have actually done so. Needless to add, this record did little to commend the reputation of Bord na Gaidhlig among Gaels, either on the ground or among the Gaelic intelligentsia.*(65)

In the secondary sector, Gaelic medium developments have been of lesser magnitude. By 2019, across all-Scotland, a total of 1,423 secondary school students were taught through the Gaelic medium, a figure approximating to around 0.5 of the total Scottish secondary population. Yet the former Woodside School, Glasgow - now called Glasgow Gaelic School/Sgoil Ghaidhlig Ghlaschu - operating since 2006, with a 3-18 age range intake and with 343 enrolled secondary stream students in 2019 (total primary/secondary enrolment of 630), is the only stand-alone Gaelic secondary institution of its kind in Scotland.*(66) That said, it has not been possible until now for Woodside's full curriculum delivery to be run through Gaelic Medium, with up to 33% of subject teaching having to be done in English due to a lack of specialist Gaelic teachers. The same is true of Edinburgh, where 136 teenagers – mainly, but not exclusively graduates of the city's only Gaelic-medium primary, Bunsgoil Taobh na Pairce – are placed in the Gaelic medium stream of James Gillespie's High School/Ard-sgoil Sheumais Ghilleasbuig.*(67) There, about 65% of subject teaching is done through Mother tongue, with the remainder in English.*(68)

Nor have such problems been restricted to Glasgow. In the Nicholson Institute, Stornoway, non-availability of certain Gaelic subject specialists has meant the Gaelic medium unit being able only to offer about two thirds (10 subjects) Higher Certificate teaching in Gaelic. Given that the Glasgow school caters for the city's largest Hebridean and Highlander migrant community, and the Nicholson is the principal secondary school in the Hebridean Gaidhealtachd, those shortages gravely undermine the core aims of Gaelic medium education.*(69) Some help has recently been forthcoming from central government by way of a £700,000 grant to aid distance learning and IT-led subject development, but, though welcome, that in itself proved inadequate to purpose. The real problem lies with a shortage in Gaelic teacher training provision, and the general incorporation of Gaelic within the Scottish education system.

Actually, the Gaelic teacher training and provision question has been addressed, though with limited results until now (April 2021). The opening of a Gaelic teacher training unit at Sabhal Mor Ostaig, Isle of Skye, and the latter's affiliation to the new University of the Highlands and Islands was followed by the creation of Gaelic Teacher Training degrees by UHI and University of Edinburgh in 2014 and 2016 respectively. This innovation added to the long running Gaelic Teaching degree offered by The University of Strathclyde, and appeared in follow-up to BnG's teacher recruitment programme, 'Thig Gam

Theagasg'/'Come Teach Me'.*(70) Yet the sober fact was that of the four universities, the combined number of Gaelic graduates was usually under 40 each year, of which few were attracted to teaching. A small number of specific bursaries were offered each year by BnG as incentives to attract Gaelic teachers. However, the proposed expansion of those was ruled out by the Scottish Government, as was Gaelic's inclusion with the £20,000 bursaries for encouraging Maths, Science and Technology graduates into teaching. As for paying Gaelic medium teachers salary increments owing to the shortage, as McLeod commented: *"... this was deemed politically unacceptable"*.*(71) Like so many institutions, Gaeldom was also subject to political pressures of the time.

At the time of writing (2021), other options are being applied such as the Gaelic Immersion Course for serving teachers (GIFT) by Strathclyde University, with financial support from the Scottish Government. This scheme has gone some way towards addressing the shortage, but has been shown to be costly, and of necessity restricted to ten teachers in any school year – who are taken out of the classroom for intensive Gaelic development courses, while simultaneously having their salaries paid. Not all local authorities were willing to release teachers from classroom duty for 12 months, and not all headmasters/mistresses proved willing to licence absences for such a lengthy sabbatical. There has also been the ongoing question of teacher retention, which by 2010 saw almost one third of Gaelic-trained teachers quit Gaelic medium education for mainstream English teaching.*(72)

Amidst the problems, Gaelic educationalists were heartened by the publication of a study in 2010 by O'Hanlon, McLeod and Paterson, showing that students of GME consistently outperformed English-medium students in English reading and grammar.*(73) The effects of this report were twofold: First, the findings broadly confirmed those of an earlier study by Richard Johnstone at the University of Stirling in 1999.*(74) Second, together, both study reports enhanced the standing of Gaelic as a valid and positive force in the classroom, and one contributing to the educational well-being of its speakers and learners. This boost to Gaelic esteem was a vital asset to Gaelgeoiri everywhere.

6. **Summary:** The attainments of Scottish Gaels under devolved home rule were not inconsiderable, and clearly they took full advantage of all available opportunities. Old fears of a new

and hostile Edinburgh establishment emerging to curtail the Gaels' place and funds simply did not happen, and nor did Gaels sustain any injuries in the process of lobbying. Perhaps the hard-earned ground won during the Westminster years, such as Gaelic broadcasting and Gaelic medium education, had come to be accepted by the mainstream of Scottish society, and along with cross party support, plus influential royal, civic, educational and artistic patrons, Gaelic clearly has established its place.

The Gaelic credit account is substantial. A new Gaelic Broadcasting Committee and a Gaelic television channel, access to the air for a litany of Gaelic interests in culture, music, education, the arts, sports and political campaigners, plus the emergence of a growing army of Gaelic broadcasters, producers, educational and planning staff... numbered among successes. Those developments, though having roots in earlier years, nevertheless came to full fruition under an elected Holyrood administration. Most importantly, public money was found to finance those projects. Elsewhere, Gaelic Medium education had taken off through a growing number of dedicated schools and units within schools, which in turn projected demand for Gaelic teachers and literature, provided by the 4 Scottish universities offering Gaelic Studies degrees, both academic and in Gaelic teacher training.

Elsewhere, the Gaelic Language Act of 2005 conferred a fair number of entitlements such as the right of Gaelic education, funding of Gaelic festivals such as the National Mod, public signage and a body of mixed persuasion and enforcement in the form of Bord na Gaidhlig. The availability of rather generous grants for education, drama, publishing, enterprise investment and community culture, such as the feiseann and local Mod festivals ... all pointed to a level of development that both boosted the esteem of Gaeldom, but also the self-confidence with which the Gaels approached life.

Yet there was also a debit page to the account. Greatest among those was the continuing decline in native Gaelic speaker numbers. While slowing down from 30 years earlier, nevertheless Anglicisation continues its grim course, felling what remains of the lands of the Gael. Lately, there have even been signs of that most sacrosanct of Scottish Gaelic institutions, the Outer Hebridean Gaidhealtachd, contracting under assorted media, commercial and tourist pressures of Anglicisation. It is difficult to be optimistic given all the latter signs, but yet those stoic Gaels battle on heroically for survival.

In fairness, it must be conceded that the days of English and Edinburgh establishment oppression of Scottish Gaeldom are long gone. History has run its course in the 275 years since Culloden, but for all the major social reforms, economic, educational, democratic and industrial strides forward the world of the Scottish Gael has never looked so vulnerable as at present. Moreover, given the variety of party alignments of Gaels, it is a matter of debate as to whether or not Gaelic decline can be properly halted by any political institution, whether it be answerable to Westminster or Holyrood? Certainly, unlike their Irish brethren, Scottish Gaels continue to resist the embrace of any party, and activists of all parties can be found among them all. Such has been the strength of the Gaelic lobby ever since the formation of An Comunn Gaidhealach back in 1891 at what - from a modern perspective - looks like the most improbable surroundings of the Masonic Hall at Oban.

For certain, Professor Conchur O'Giollagain and his team of collaborative writers/researchers were, and with valid, albeit contentious reason, pessimistic about Scottish Gaeldom's future, as displayed from the title and content of their 2020 book.*(75) Whether or not the O'Giollagain' text can be justified or accused of excessive pessimism is a task awaiting a future researcher some 25 years ahead? What can be stated with reasonable confidence is that all those comprehensive battles in education, broadcasting, arts, publishing, political and environmental reform, into which Scottish Gaeldom has thrust itself before and since the introduction of devolution, represent an ongoing quest for survival. It remains to be seen whether and how far that battle will render positive results?

FOOTNOTES and REFERENCES

1. London governments' historical semi-benign treatment of Scotland – driven by a desire to keep Scots content with the Union – has long been a cogent theme of Professor Devine. See: T.M. Devine The Scottish Nation, 1700-2007 (Penguin, 2008), Chaps. 24, 24 & 27. – and – Independence or Union: Scotland's Past and Scotland's Present (Penguin, 20017); Chaps 7, 8.

2. Wilson McLeod Gaelic in Scotland: Policies, Movements and Ideologies (EUP, 2020); Chapter 7, pp 242-274.

3. Wilson McLeod (2020); Chap 7, pp 242-247. – Also- O'Giollagain eds The Gaelic Crisis in the Vernacular Community (Aberdeen 2020) and MacLeod M. & Smith-Christmas Gaelic in Contemporary Scotland: The Revitalisation of an Endangered Language (2018, EUP).

4. It is significant that Professor McLeod's scholarly 2020 book received the highly esteemed 'Fletcher of Saltoun' national award in recognition of its invaluable contribution to Scotland's contemporary and historical debate on the place of Gaelic.

5. A consistent theme of Professor McLeod (2020) – see Chaps 6 & 7.

6. See all UK government censuses, inclusive of Scotland – 1921, 1971 and 2011 (HM Stationary Offices, London & Edinburgh).

7. C. O'Giollagain et al (eds), 2020 – Chap 9, pp 419-435.

8. Wilson McLeod (2020) – Chap 6, p. 253.

9. Advice from accomplished singer and Gaelic activist, Arthur Cormack.

10. Ibid. Similar advice was forthcoming from Professor Ken MacKinnon.

11. Wilson McLeod – Chap 6, p. 253.

12. O'Gribin in Colin H. Williams Legislative Devolution and Language Regulation in the United Kingdom (Geolinguistics.org/geo 32 articles/GEO-32-Williams-art.pdf), Cardiff University.

13. See relevant provisions of 2005 Gaelic Language Act (Scotland) – HMSO Edinburgh & London.

14. Gaelic Language Act (Scotland) 2005, Section 8 (10) – cited in W. McLeod, Chap. 6, p. 254.

15. McLeod (W.) 2020 - Chap 6, p. 255.

16. 'EU green light for Scottish Gaelic'; (http://news.bbc.co.uk/1hi/scotland/highlands_and_islands/8294853. stm). BBC News Online – 7th October 2009.

17. Interview with Arthur Cormack, An Cathaoir- Bord na Gaidhlig, 2008-2012 – 19th January 2021 (Skype).

18. Ibid.

19. Information supplied by Arthur Cormack (Interview – 19th January, 2021) and Professor Kenneth MacKinnon (Interview, telephone, 18th September, 2020).

20. David Pollock   'John Macleod, Champion of Gaelic'! Obituary; *The Glasgow Herald* , 24th March, 2018.

21. Annual Report of Bord na Gaidhlig na Albannaich, 2010.

22. Correspondence – Arthur Cormack/Vincent McKee, 17th March, 2021.

23. (i) Annual Report of An Comunn Gaidhleach, 2009 (Inverness).

    (ii) McLeod W. (2020); Chap 8, pp 282 – 285.

24. (i) McLeod W. (2020); Chapter 8, pp 283 – 284.

    (ii) Discussions with Finlay MacLeod, 18th August 1993, Stornoway, and 14th October 1997, Inverness.

25. Mr Finlay McLeod's disaffection with the "Gaelic establishment" he vividly outlined in discussions with this author on 14th October, 1997 at Inverness.

26. Interview Arthur Cormack (19 01 2021).

27. Ibid.

28. Interviews – Professor Ken MacKinnon (18th September 2020) and Mrs Annie MacSween (3rd March 2021).

29. All information kindly supplied by Arthur Cormack (19th January 2021). Also, those figures are available from the annual reports of An Comunn Gaidhleach, Comunn na Gaidheal and Feisean na Gaidheal for 2019/2020.

30. For a full documented account of the road signage campaigns of the first decade of the new millennium, see McLeod W. (2020) – Chap 7, pp 270 -272.

31. Former Western Isles Labour MP, Calum Macdonald, is a longstanding personal acquaintance of this author, and I am familiar with his connections to the Gaelic language.

32. WHFP 2003; see also Scotsman 2002a.

33. Public signage in Signage in Inverness and Oban was a theme followed by this author in a previous publication. See Chap 4, pp. 64 (iii), (iv) & (v) – Gaelic Nations (1997) – V. McKee.

34. See Frank Thomson (1992); pp 134-137.

35. See McLeod (W), 2020 – pp 272 - 273.

36. Ibid.

37. Discussions with Mrs Annie MacSween 30th June 2020 and 4th December, 2020.

38. While in no sense an obstructionist, nevertheless Mrs MacSween vigorously presented her positions on different issues connected to education and language refinement at Bord na Gaidhlig, on which she served for several years in its first decade.

39. O'Giollagain eds. et al (2020) – See Chaps 4 & 5 on Gaelic usage among schoolchildren and communities in the Outer Hebrides.

40. Throughout July and August 2020, frank exchanges were run by Professor O'Giollagain and several critics, who included ex-MP and Gaelic Minister, Brian Wilson, in The Scotsman.

41. McLeod W. (2020); Chap 7, pp 267-270.

42. Pedersen (2019); pp 148-157, 193 – 2001.

43. Pedersen (2019); pp 170-182.

44. Brian Wilson was also author of an official history of Glasgow Celtic FC.

45. Devine (2008); Chap 27. – Professor Devine's belief that a popular celebration of Scottish identity and the prevalence of Scottish heritage had taken root in post-1999 Scotland is a constant theme underpinning the final chapter of his scholarly and highly acclaimed history of modern Scotland. Given the very thorough analysis characterising Devine's work – something acknowledged by leading commentators – his theme is worthy of consideration by all with a serious interest in the contemporary history of Scotland.

46. (i) McLeod W. (2020); Chap 7, pp 267-270.

    (ii) Pederson (2019); pp 161 – 182.

47. Neil Fraser - '*A Review of Aspects of Gaelic Broadcasting*' (Report to Scottish Office, 1998).

48. Ibid.

49. This author is most grateful to Professor Wilson McLeod for his detailed analysis of the Milne Report's financial and broadcasting implications. See McLeod (2020), Chap. 7, pp 267-270.

50. McLeod (2020); pp 267-270

51. Pederson (2019); pp 161 – 182.

52. (i) See SNP Holyrood manifesto, 2007 Scottish Parliament elections.

    (ii) Alex Salmond – 'Sabhal Mor Ostaig Lecture: Government plans for Gaelic'; -Delivered at St Cecilia's Hall, Edinburgh, 19th December, 2007.
    www.scotland.gov.uk/News/Speeches/First-/Minister/sabmorost07.

53. (i) T.M. Devine (2008); Chap 27.

    (ii) T.M. Devine Independence or Union: Scotland's Past and Scotland's Present (2016, Penguin), Chaps 8, 9 & 17.

54. Tom Gallagher – Foreword by Rt Hon. Alistair Darling <u>Scotland Now: A Warning to the World</u> (2016, Scotview Publications, Edinburgh); See Chapters 1 & 6.

55. Re. - Discussions on several occasions with former Gaelic Educational Bilingual Advisor, the late Donald John Macivor, at his office in Comhairle nan Eilean Siar, Stornoway, 1991-1993. Mr Macivor so kindly furnished this author with various follow-up documents related to the bilingual policies and developments of Comhairle nan Eilean Siar.

56. McLeod (2020); Chapter 7, pp 264- 267.

57. Cera Murtagh *'Balancing Act'*; <u>Holyrood Magazine</u>, pp 42-43, 31st January, 2011.

58. McLeod (2020); pp 264-267.

59. McLeod (2020); Chapter 8, pp 296 – 307.

60. McLeod; pp 296-297.

61. Ibid.

62. Data supplied, plus accompanying letter, by Mrs Joanne McHale, Education Manageress, Bord na Gaidhlig, Inverness, May 2020 – to whom this author remains sincerely grateful.

63. Ibid.

64. Figures released by University of Strathclyde (2006) and Bord na Gaidhlig, 2019.

65. Data and actions contained in annual reports of Bord na Gaidhlig, 2012-2020.

66. Figures released by Mrs Joanne McHale, Bord na Gaidhlig, May 2020. Also, Wiklopedia entry.

67. Information deduced from Wiklopedia entry and school website.

68. Information received privately from a student's parent.

69. In several interviews in earlier years with the late Donald John Macivor of CnES, Stornoway, he made clear his view that to be successful Gaelic medium education had to be total, and would be seriously undermined by the introduction of English-medium teaching, however necessary on account of teacher or resources shortages. As ex-Head of Gaelic Studies at the Nicholson Institute, Stornoway, Mr Macivor was certainly a voice of professional expertise.

70. Data released by BnG (2020), plus interpretation by McLeod (2020), pp 303-309.

71. McLeod (2020); p. 308.

72. Camilla Kidner SPICe Briefing, Education (Scotland) Bill, 2015.

73. Fiona O'Hanlon, Wilson McLeod & Lindsay Paterson – *'Gaelic Medium Education in Scotland: Choice and Attainment at the primary and early secondary stages'*; 2010, BnG, Inverness.

74. Richard Johnstone et al. *'The attainments of pupils receiving Gaelic medium primary education in Scotland'*; 1999, University of Stirling, Scottish CILT.

75. Conchur O'Giollagain et al <u>The Gaelic Crisis in the Vernacular Community: A Comprehensive Sociolinguistic Survey of Scottish Gaelic</u> (2020, Aberdeen University Press)

Chapter Seven

1999 - 2021: GAELICISM AND STORMONT – AN UNEASY CONCORDAT!

**Aims:** The signing in Belfast of the April 1998 Good Friday Peace Accord, its endorsement by the London and Dublin governments, along with the Clinton administration in Washington, proved a historic milestone for progress in Northern Ireland. While leaving it to greater scholars e.g. Professor O'Leary – to mull over the precise ramifications, there can be no denying the Accord's enormous significance for civic, cultural, religious and political life in all corners of Northern Ireland, and indeed all-Ireland, throughout the ensuing quarter century.*(1) In a noble endeavour aimed at replacing strife with civic harmony, and the creation of new equitable political structures based around power-sharing, all areas of life were impacted. The latter included culture(s), identity and issues of esteem; hence the pivotal prospects for Gaeil Uladh!

This final substantive chapter will examine the Belfast Agreement's impact on cultural parity of esteem, and thus Gaeil Uladh's place in Northern Ireland's post-millennial civic environment. The assessment shall cover Gaelic-language schooling at all levels, the language's place as a curriculum subject across the board, and its ramifications for drama, music, broadcasting, Gaelic arts and Irish community projects, such as feiseanna and the traditional musical fleadh festivals characterising nationalist communities like those of Castlewellan, Co Down, the Glens of Antrim and the Gaeltacht Quarter of West Belfast. Treatment by mainstream broadcasters of the Gaelic language, Gaelic music and drama, and Gaelic sports, as well as the state's accommodation of the Gaelic Athletic Association and willingness to grant-aid its comprehensive Gaelic sports programme, are further considered. This chapter will evaluate the extent to which political pressures from the two main nationalist parties played a part, and which, if either, party played the lead part. Those questions and others, including the broadened parameters encompassing new Gaelic activists like those in East Belfast, are addressed as far as possible.

It will be difficult to draw any lasting conclusions, but new and profound trends are noted and evaluated, both for immediate effects and long term legacies.

---

1. *Overview:* By 1999, as the political parties of Northern Ireland were gearing towards putting the Troubles behind and making the historic Belfast Agreement of April 1998 work, Gaeil Uladh were very much on the ascendant. Information and data listed in Chapter 5 seeks to document precise levels to which change had occurred. Devolution, based on power-sharing, was in the air, and planning by the Gaelic lobby, like all other sectional interests in the North, envisaged its impending restoration. This prospect held ramifications for Gaelic linguists, cultural activists, dramatists, poets, musicians and sportsmen/women, and there was a general air of optimism that the new system would succeed where Direct Rule had lost its way. Also, as much as progress had been modest until then, and in no way comparable to that of Scottish Gaelic brethren, the reality was that Gaeil Uladh expected to benefit from the combined green shoots slowly emerging ever since the 1985 Hillsborough Accord. With fair justification, those developments were widely expected to continue.

Nor was such optimism misplaced or exaggerated. Indeed the feeling that Gaeldom's exclusion was a historical wrong that the Belfast Agreement would correct in part, was implanted in the aspirations of a cross-section of Northern Ireland's nationalist people, now composing some 46% of the total population of just under 1.9 million.*(2). So was it reflected in the commentaries by press pundits, nationalist and republican political leaders like John Hume, Seamus Mallon and Gerry Adams, along with Catholic bishops and the-then All-Ireland Primate, Cardinal Sean Brady, at Armagh.*(3) Additionally, academics like Brendan O'Leary and Feargal Cochrane presciently noted those sentiments in their respective accounts, which gave grounds for hope all round.*(4)

Given the good will emanating from America and Britain, along with popular support from the government and people of the Irish Republic (who earlier had overwhelmingly backed the Agreement, while also effecting modest constitutional amendments in a 1998 referendum that replaced assertions of sovereignty over the North with *aspirations* towards unity), there was good reason to believe that the Agreement was guaranteed by formidable signatories. Additional to the latter, the support given in N. Ireland's separate 1998 referendum by clear majorities of Protestant and Catholic voters – though, significantly, not Dr Paisley's Democratic Unionists – augured well for times ahead. The new spirit appeared to permeate everywhere that mattered.

Evaluations of the 1998 Belfast Agreement's workings, plus corollaries like the 2006 St Andrew's Accord and 2010 Hillsborough Accord, are best left to the writings of Professor O'Leary, and to a lesser degree, Dr Cochrane.*(5) This account is primarily concerned with the _**impact**_ of the Good Friday Agreement on the progress and experiences of Gaeil Uladh. In that pursuit, particular attention shall be paid to three factors indicating the extent of the changes promised by the Agreement – notably:

(i)   The effects on Gaeil Uladh of devolved government at Belfast.

(ii) Attitudes of UK government towards Gaelic culture and the language.

(iii) The new civic forum of Northern Ireland: though acknowledging Gaeldom's place in terms of parity of esteem, not all sections of the former Unionist establishment genuinely embraced the transition.

Regarding its condition at the time of the Belfast Agreement, Gael Uladh, while denied the relatively favoured status of Scottish Gaeldom, nevertheless had achieved major gains. The latter had come about by a mixture of assertiveness, positive profiling and political support from the North's two nationalist parties and Church, plus Dublin. A look at the debit balance points to growing assets.

First, was the growth of the Irish language Gaelscoil movement in education, which was especially prominent in the primary sector. By 1999, over 5,000 primary pupils in 28 schools – bunscoileanna – and Gaelic medium units in mainstream schools were taught through the medium of Gaeilge, while a further 1,500 infant pupils were taught in Gaelic nursery schools across the North of Ireland. Further plans for expansion, along with grant aid, were in place.*(6) So too had Meanscoil Beal Feirste (Gaeilge secondary school) – now known as Colaiste Feirste – become a novel reality, initially on the Falls Road, Belfast, near to the Culturlann, but developed further over ensuing years. The training of Gaeilge-medium teachers had its base in St Mary's College, Belfast (affiliated to QUB) and the University of Ulster, where grant-aided programmes had developed to service the budding Gaelscoil sector. Second, the teaching of Irish language studies had mushroomed to include most Catholic secondary schools, plus a substantial number of technical colleges, inclusive of the enlarged Belfast Metropolitan College (formerly Belfast College of Business Studies and Belfast College of Technology) and its counterparts in Derry, Armagh, Omagh, Newry, Downpatrick, Dungannon, Ballymena, Lurgan and Enniskillen. This advancement included a dramatic rise in the numbers of students entering curriculum and competitive exams set by the Northern Ireland General and Advanced Examinations Authority, where by 2010 Gaeilge candidate numbers exceeded those taking Modern European languages.*(7)

Third, there had been an upsurge in the level of voluntary Irish language classes provided by Gael Linn, Glor na nGael and Comhairle na Ulaidh (Ulster division of All-Ireland Gaelic League) through community-based GAA clubs and Church (Catholic) parish halls.*(8) Data figures are supplied later in the chapter, but for the present it is helpful to note the general trends.

A further task will be to establish just how far Gaelic revivalism was driven by a general atmosphere of civic inclusiveness, doubtless augmented by the Good Friday Agreement of 1998, or whether it was driven by the political agenda of nationalism. In specific terms, how far was the Gaelic educational movement and Gaelic in the communities a triumph for Sinn Fein? Was that party's triumph in Council and Assembly elections, plus Westminster and Strasbourg polls, indicative of a general air of militant radicalism whose embrace had replaced previous 'moderation'? Given the republican aim of fostering an alternative society based on a nationalist-Irish identity and popular spoken Gaeilge, the question may be asked as to whether the Gaelscoil movement, Gaelic street signs and an ever-increasing profile of Irish-language programmes on BBC Radio Ulster, inclusive of a dedicated Gaeilge unit and the Irish language station, Raidio Failte, represented signs of the growing Gaelic revival, driven by a desire to challenge the British establishment with an indigenous and effective cultural weapon?*(9) The changes envisaged by Sinn Fein started taking off within a short distance of the Agreement's signatures and eventual ratification. It may well be asked what portents did this hold for the future?

Finally, Ulster Gaelicism has lately reached new levels with an emergent Gaelgeoir development in predominantly Protestant/Unionist East Belfast. Commencing in 2011, and on the initiative of a feisty Protestant Gaelgeoir,

Mrs Linda Ervine, a Gaelic group became attached to the East Belfast Methodist Mission, and, aided by public funding, appointed Gaeilge teachers and a cultural researcher. As a result, regular classes commenced, and later a local naiscoil was established, with intensive media interest following.*(10) The wider significance of this development needs to be seen against the backdrop of traditional Gaelic appeal to the Catholic Nationalist population, currently dominated by Sinn Fein. It is now to be considered whether those boundaries are to be exceeded, and if so what prospects this holds for the political direction of the Gaelic language in the North? Is it still a weapon in Sinn Fein's cultural armoury, as favoured by Republican Gaelgeoir, Feargal Mac Ionnrachtaigh, or is Gaeilge destined to move in a liberal direction as favoured by late SDLP figure Seamus Mallon and ULTACHT's Aodan MacPoilin?*(11)

Should the Belfast Gaeltacht Quarter be considered the primal centre of Gael Uladh's alternative Gaelic society, or more a tourist curiosity, rather like the Titanic Quarter? Those questions beg consideration in the context of just which direction has Gaeil Uladh taken and under which guise?

Other goals were targeted. Top priority was the passage of a statute of protection for the Gaeilge language and culture, something promised by the British government but resolutely opposed by Unionists of all shades. So also was there the disputatious street Gaeilge signage question. There were also questions about Gaelic access to Lottery funding, further development and aid to the Gaelscoil movement, expansion of Gaelic broadcasting and funding of the prime Ulster Gaelic sports stadium, Casement Park, in West Belfast. All those issues beckoned, and each in their turn generated debate at all levels of political and civic society in Northern Ireland. While Sinn Fein led the pro-Gaelgeoir agenda, it by no means monopolised the lobby, and what emerged rather reflected the broader school of Gaelic activism.

All those questions need to be seriously considered.

2. *Gaelscoil Movement.* Over the two decades of the 21st century, growth occurred in terms of actual numbers of first language Gaeilge students, along with a slow mushrooming of Gaeilscoileanna/schools across the North. As of August 2020, according to figures supplied by the Northern Ireland Department of Education and its specialist Gaeilge medium

authority, Comhairle na Gaeilscolaiochta, there were 30 Gaelic-medium schools in Northern Ireland, 28 primary, and two secondary schools. Of 10 Gaelic medium streams attached to English-medium host schools, 7 were primary and 3 were secondary.*(12) Also, according to the Northern Ireland Statistics and Research Agency, there were 17 Gaelic-medium nursery schools, and one Gaelic-medium stream within an English-medium host school.*(13) All told, a total of 7,064 Gaelic-medium pupils were enrolled at schools throughout the North, a figure that continues to grow.*(14)

It is important to recognise that N.I. government figures accounted only for state-recognised and funded schools and units. Additional to places listed, there are a number of private Gaelic medium schools struggling to achieve viability in terms of pupil recruitment and sustainability, vital criteria on which funding depends. They operated as independent schools, and were sustained by a combination of parental subscriptions (where affordable), fund-raising by supportive groups in their communities and aid from Foras na Gaeilge. Such arrangements had to be temporary, with state-recognition being heavily dependent on the good will of the Department of Education, as well as attainments of the schools. Inevitably, political pressure played a part too. In most pressure lobbies, as was acknowledged separately by Camile O'Reilly and Feargal Mac Ionnrachtaigh respectively, Sinn Fein led the drive.*(15) This factor underlines the hard commitment of Sinn Fein and its activists to the Gaelic language at all levels, something not remotely matched by the SDLP or indeed old-style nationalists with their pedestrian, even elitist approach.*(16)

Returning to the issue of state-funded Gaeilscoileanna, it might be useful to acknowledge the distribution of Gaeilge-medium schooling across the North.

Predictably, Belfast offers the scene of greatest development. By August 2020, a total of *14 established* Gaelic-medium *naiscoileanna/nursery schools* were functioning across the city, with *9 established bunscoileanna/primary schools* recognised/funded by the Department of Education for Northern Ireland.*(17) Sizes and recruitment varied, as did resources, but all conformed to a basic formula. Most schools operated in nationalist areas of West and North Belfast, but there was also one in the Ormeau area of South Belfast, while, as this script is written, a new naiscoil is coming to life under the indefatigable leadership of Mrs Linda Ervine in Protestant East Belfast.*(18)

Additionally, there is the North's largest and pivotal Meanscoil/Gaelic-medium secondary school, **_Colaiste Feirste_**, situated in West Belfast. In the course of three decades, Colaiste Feirste has grown from a loose set of classes hosted at the Culturlann to a modern and competitive Gaelic medium high school with 11-18 years intake, and a total of 850 students, with further intake capacity reaching up to 910. It is led by a devoted Gaelgeoir headmaster, Mr Michael Mac Giolla Ghunna, himself a Gaelic researcher, writer and sociologist of no mean distinction.*(19) Put simply, Colaiste Feirste is the flagship, pride and majesty of all segments composing Gaelic Ulster.*(20) It puts students through the normal GCSE and A'Level examinations, sending a quota every year to Queens University and other establishments of higher and further education across the North and all-Ireland.*(21) Moreover, the growth of Colaiste Feirste has meant the emergence in Belfast of a de facto structure of Gaelic medium schooling that facilitates Irish speakers from across the city and beyond from nursery straight up to adult years, preparing them for university and the world of work.*(22) So also has the growth in Gaelgeoir education been picked up by the media, and figured prominently in numerous press reports.*(23) & *(24)

In conversations with this author, Mr Mac Giolla Ghunna, expressed confidence in the prospect of a second meanscoil emerging in North Belfast within the foreseeable future. He believes growth in naiscoileanna and bunscoileanna numbers – some of whom were coming to Colaiste Feirste from East Down and South Antrim – all pointed to the viability of a fresh initiative in North Belfast. *(25) This overspill in numbers, he felt, might be better utilised in creating a new school, as opposed to a fresh site for Colaiste Feirste.*(26)

A second meanscoil exists in Dungiven, Co. Derry, with public funding, while 3 English host high schools facilitate Gaeilge medium units in the counties of Tyrone, Armagh and Down respectively. Such attainments in what was previously a hostile political environment are impressive.*(27) The effect has also been to boost morale among Gaeil Uladh activists at all levels.

Turning to rural counties, the picture is patchy, with, inevitably, the greater developments occurring in centres of nationalist population. There were 3 Antrim-based bunscoileanna in Glengormley, Glenavy and Ballycastle, with all 3 feeding off naiscoileanna (nurseries) in the area, plus a fourth one at Toome Bridge. Fermanagh has just one bunscoil and a single naiscoil, both based in nationalist Lisnaskea. County Armagh has 4 bunscoileanna; with one in the ecclesiastical capital, and others in Crossmaglen, Lurgan and Portadown respectively. A total of 3 naiscoileanna operate in Armagh, with additional nurseries at Crossmaglen, Keady, Lurgan and Portadown.*(28) Armagh also boasts the longest-running Gaelic-medium stream to be hosted in an English-medium secondary school, St Catherine's College. This venture began in 2002 with 10 students, and has since grown to 155 students of all ages and levels in 2021.*(29) The biggest intake until now is 49 students, and its Gaelic director, Mrs Catriona de Bleine, has high hopes for the Gaelic Stream's future.*(30) Undoubtably, the thriving presence of a local Gaeilge-cultural centre, 'Aonach Mhacha', has had an enhancing effect on Gaelgeoir morale in Armagh, as well as providing a focal point for the energies of Gaelic dramatists, linguists, poets and other Gaelgeoir cultural devotees across the county. *(31)

In Tyrone, there are 6 functional bunscoileanna, running at Carrickmore, Strabane, Omagh, Coalisland, Dungannon and Cookstown, plus 7 feeder naiscoileanna in those towns, and one further at Castlederg.*(32) Additionally, St Joseph's Grammar School, Donaghmore, itself an-English medium rural establishment in a nationalist area, currently hosts a Gaelic medium stream of 172 students, which has been developing with increasing viability.*(33)

In Co Down, a total of 4 bunscoileanna operate; one in the county town, Downpatrick, with additional schools at Castlewellan, Kilkeel and Newry. A further 5 naiscoileanna function at Downpatrick, Castlewellan, Newcastle, and Kilkeel, with 2 Gaelic nurseries at Newry. Additionally, St Malachy's High School, Castlewellan, has been hosting a Gaelic medium stream – growing from an original intake of 5 students in 2011 to the current figure of 149.*(34) The Gaeilge students enjoy a 50% teaching programme through the native tongue, and are mainly, but not exclusively, recruited from local bunscoileanna.*(35)

A total of 8 state-recognised and funded bunscoileanna are located in Derry City and across Co Derry, with a further 12 naiscoileanna functioning as feeders across the same area. Derry City has a full complement of 3 bunscoileanna, with a further 4 naiscoileanna feeders; other bunscoileanna are operational in Dungiven, Limavady, Maghera (2), Magherafelt and Ballinascreen, all supported by Gaelic nurseries. The naiscoileanna also extend to Coleraine and Swatragh, suggesting potential for further expansion in those areas. Very significantly, Dungiven boasts the county's only post-primary meanscoil, **Gaelcholaiste Dhoire**, which functions at Dungiven Castle.

Founded in 2015, and with a current student population of 272, this 11-18 intake school recruits from a total of 9 feeder bunscoileanna in the surrounding area, and being situated in mid-Derry – as opposed to the City – can viably offer places to students from around the county, plus neighbouring communities on the Antrim borders and Tyrone.*(36) Its present headmaster, Mr Diarmaid Ua Bruadair, heads a full-time professional staff of over 26, and is conscious of the need to compete with other secondary schools in public exams and the quest for university and apprenticeship places.*(37) The school had a difficult start, and secured public funding only after lengthy battles which relied on political good will from the Department of Education.*(38) Now it is functioning smoothly with a positive potential for the future.*(39)

The durability and growth of the Gaelscoil movement at both primary and secondary level should not be taken lightly. In earlier days, Ulster Gaelgeoiri were forced to endure a plethora of insulting discourse from Unionist politicians and their acolytes in education, civil service and the arts, which questioned its relevance and even intellectual merits. One leading DUP figure, Sammy Wilson MP, in an infamous outburst, descended to denouncing Gaeilge as "**... a leprechaun language**"! Clearly, the intemperate rantings of Wilson and his like has been shown up for the shallow bigotry that they are, not so much by adverse nationalist reactions as more by the gradual success of Gaelscoil education over the past 50 years ... ever since the opening of the first Belfast bunscoil in 1971.*(40) One result has been to provide two growing generations of Gaeilge-literate young people, amounting to upwards of 18,000 ... and growing. The facilities for further study at both universities and teacher training college, plus radio and various other Gaeilge organisations, ensure some positive prospects for Gaeilge graduates, trades and business operatives into the future. That growth looks set to continue over the decades ahead.

3. **Further Gaelic Educational Developments.** Additional to the mushrooming Gaelscoil movement, other developments have emerged over the past two decades to boost the profile of Gaeilge in education and training throughout Northern Ireland. So also has the face of Higher Education been changed with the arrival of a new generation of Belfast

Meanscoil graduates at Queens University, University of Ulster and elsewhere. To a certain degree, the whole picture speaks of an 'Alternative Gaelic Society' slowly emerging and growing from the ground upwards, based around popular demand for Gaelic education and services in radio, arts, sport and even housing/employment. This trend had its roots in the early Gaeltacht initiatives at Shaws Road housing development and the initial bunscoil movement of the 1970s, and has now progressed to its current levels.

Not the least of those developments has been the enlarged departments of Celtic Studies in Queens University, University of Ulster and St Mary's University Training College – all of whom have offered various Celtic Studies degrees, and in the case of St Mary's, training programmes with accredited teacher status to Gaeilge-medium students. Queens have an average of 20 students in final year degree classes every year, of whom some 50% are single –honours Irish students, while the other 50% combine Gaeilge with another language, eg. English or French, or a liberal arts subject, eg. Politics, History, International Relations, Sociology etc.*(41) Additionally, the Celtic-Irish Studies Division contributes to degrees in Modern and Medieval Irish Literature, although as Celtic Studies Head, Professor Micheal O'Mainnin , acknowledges:

"... the emphasis in our curriculum has been much more on Modern Irish (than on Celtic Studies more broadly) over the past twenty years"(42)

While St Mary's College is essentially a provider of trained teachers for bunscoileanna and the growing meanscoileanna across the North, its degrees are conferred by Queens University and recognised by the Northern Ireland Department of Education. This gives proper educational status to Gaelic graduates and a professional career structure to Gaeilge teachers in Gaeilscoileanna. Of course there is nothing new about St Mary's providing for student teachers specialising in Irish language teaching, as this has been on offer for over 70 years, but preparation of Gaeilge-medium teachers in dedicated Gaeilscoileanna is a recent innovation in line with the general level of Gaelic medium expansion across the entirety of the North.*(43) In September 1995, Gaelic medium education was introduced for post-graduate (PGCE) students for the first time, and for B.Ed. undergraduates the following year. Previous to that, B.Ed. students could specialise in Gaelic Language and Literature, but lacked access to training in Gaelic medium education.*(44) In

September 2000, St Mary's introduced a new degree in Liberal Arts, where, additional to core subjects, students could choose a specialist subject, one of which was Gaelic-Irish Studies.*(45) Figures listed below provide an indicator of the take-up rates of Gaeilge education at St Mary's, Belfast:

	Gaelic-medium Student Teachers	Gaelic Academic subject.
1992/93		55
1997/98	57	
2002/03	57	27
2007/08	62	20
2012/13	93	25
2017/18	87	29
2021/22	99	43

Figures kindly supplied by Mr Trevor Abbot, Academic Registrar, St Mary's University College, Belfast – 29th November, 2021.

What is interesting is the ever-increasing trend for more Gaeilge teachers for the expanding Gaelscoil sector, the figures having virtually doubled since 1999. Significantly, on current trends, and given the positive projections of Gaelic educationalists at all levels, it is likely that this growth pattern will continue to permeate Northern nationalist society for decades ahead.*(46)

Turning to **Gaelic technical training**, this too has undergone considerable growth since 1999. Under the aegis of Forbairt Feirste, itself operating from offices on the Falls Road, Belfast, a pilot scheme involving Meanscoil finishers – with interests in the trades, clerical, child care and beauty therapy etc – was given the initial green light by Enterprise SDLP Minister, Dr Sean Farren. The scheme was publicly-funded, and aimed at training participants in the trades while using the Gaeilge medium.*(47) Success at this level led to the establishment in 2002 of a partnership between the Gaeilge trusteeship body, 'I dtreo Fostaiochta', with Belfast Metropolitan College, which formalised the training programme, and ran it viably for nine years. This scheme was granted approval and funding by Stormont Communities Minister of the time, Mr Stephen Farry (Alliance). However, at the beginning of 2012, financial troubles at the 'Met' led to the college's withdrawal, and its temporary suspension. A replacement company was set up, which continues to run Gaelic-medium programmes for young pre-apprentice trainees in the trades of beauty therapy, hairdressing, secretarial and IT to this day.*(48)

The organisation that has taken over this vocational training is Gaelchursai, which is managed by Mrs Colma McKee. When interviewed, Mrs McKee estimated that since 2018, when Gaelchursai took up headquarters at the purpose-built centre, Aras na bhFal, at Broadway, around 300 trainees were active in the vocational programmes, with some 60 Gaelic-speaking trainees having taken on two-year apprenticeships.*(49) In the current year, 2021, this figure has risen to over 400 general participants and over 70 structured apprentices.*(50) The level of progress is self-evident.

Very significantly, at the time of writing, Gaelchursai has lodged an application with the Stormont Communities Minister, Mrs Deirdre Hargey (Sinn Fein), for approval and funding for a permanent Gaelic technical centre in West Belfast. Given ever-increasing demand, not just from Belfast-based recruits, but extending to Gaelscoil students from Down, Armagh and west of the Bann, such an application possesses great force and is likely to be approved in some form by the Minister.*(51) Additionally, some participants have recently been forthcoming from the East Belfast Turas project, and given developments with language and the naiscoil, this source looks likely to grow over times ahead.

4. ***Gaeltacht Quarter, Belfast.*** The recognition of a distinctive Gaeltacht Quarter in West Belfast, stretching from Castle St in the city centre to embrace the entire Falls, Whiterock, Ballymurphy, Turf Lodge and Andersonstown areas, is a major development.

This area, boasting some 83,000 people, is a flagship for Gaeil Uladh. It comprises a number of establishments and organisations whose relevance to the Gaelic renaissance has been of central importance. These include the

Culturlann McAdam/O'Fiaich, itself arguably the nerve centre of Gaelic Belfast; Conway Mill with its various Gaelic theatrical and cultural organisations, as well as commercial tenants; Cumann Chluain Ard, the leading Gaeilge language learning and speaking organisation, affiliated to Conradh na Gaeilge; Radio Failte, Belfast's independent Gaeilge radio station; Aras na-bhFhal, the Gaelic business centre on Broadway; Colaiste Feirste, the flagship meanscoil, plus a string of local bunscoileanna and naiscoileanna; Forbairt Feirste, the Gaelic technical training organisation; multiple Gaelic sports grounds for the playing of Hurling, Gaelic Football and Camogie, including the redeveloped Gaelic sports stadium, Casement Park, and Corrigan Park, head grounds of Ulster and Antrim GAA, with the Ulster body boasting 9 county associations and multiple local GAA clubs at all levels. Additionally, the Andersonstown News offices – a key supporter of Gaelgeoir interests - and Shaws Road Gaelic housing project, though located outside the official boundaries, nevertheless constitute vital segments of the West Belfast Gaeltacht.

Given the Northern Ireland/UK Census figures for 2011, putting Gaeilge speakers at 184,898 (10.65 of the total NI population) and 104,943 persons (6.05 of total population) with a working knowledge of Gaeilge, it is to be assumed from intensive Gaelgeoir activity levels that a much higher proportion of the Gaeltacht Quarter population speak the language than would be the case among the wider population.*(52) Reliable estimates put the approximate percentage of persons with a basic Gaeilge knowledge at over 50%, with some 31% of local persons having a working knowledge and use for Gaeilge. Given the concentration of Gaeilge schooling, Gaelic broadcasting and Gaelic arts/drama and sporting activity in West Belfast, those figures would appear to have a solid basis, erring only on the side of caution.*(53)

The Gaeltacht Quarter already figures in the four-part division of Belfast – alongside the Cathedral Quarter, Titanic Quarter and University Quarter – acknowledged by the City Council in its tourist promotions. As a result, in 2021 the Stormont SDLP Infrastructure Minister, Mrs Nichola Mallon, announced a full programme of bilingual signs on buses and road notices throughout West Belfast.*(54) Additionally, the bilingual facility is scheduled for extention to include bilingual messaging on the city buses operating in the Gaeltacht Quarter, which has delighted Belfast Gaelgeoir campaigners.*(55) Already a local system of Gaelic street signs has functioned for the past decade, but this was on a limited basis, and operated in the teeth of Unionist and NIO opposition.*(56) Now the Mallon plan – drawn up after extensive consultations with local bodies – looks set to change the face of the city's West, giving meaningful purpose to the concept of a Gaeltacht Quarter.

The very existence and development of the Gaeltacht Quarter testifies to two factors: First, is a growth of multiple Gaelic uses in education, arts, drama, radio, publishing and sports, as well as language learning and speaking. Second, is the extent to which the Gaeltacht Quarter in all its manifestations symbolises a dichotomy of cultural and political identity in Northern Ireland, quite different to, indeed counterpoising the British state.*(57) There is no pretension of political neutrality by either Gaeil Uladh or its various constituent affiliates towards the Northern Ireland state, nor indeed by the state towards Gaelic forces. Each counterpoises the other in terms of appeal and roots. Yet the cordial, if also uneasy co-existence of one alongside the other testifies to the degree to which the politics and cultural agenda of Gaeil Uladh has been accommodated by the state and its anglo-centred/unionist establishment. This might be said to represent a triumph for both the 1998 Belfast Agreement, not to mention its 1985 Hillsborough Accord predecessor. It also represents a recognition by all parties of the propriety of *'real politics'* as they had emerged since then. A fuller test might be pending with the imminent Irish Language Bill promised by the British government, regardless of Unionist objections?

This growing application of the Gaeilge language towards everyday usage by teachers, students, consumers, arts and cultural activists and sportspeople, complete with an ongoing struggle for the attainment of political and legal entitlement, gives it a unique footage in the wider European forum for lesser-used languages. The latter angle was meticulously explored by Daithi Mac Sithigh from Queens University (Belfast) Law Department in a widely-acclaimed paper, first published in 2018.*(58) Crucially, Professor Mac Sithigh noted that "ambivalence" had characterised the policy approach of successive British governments. They (i.e. HMG) were essentially reactors to the Gaelgeoir initiators; but for all the British insistence on their own good faith the process was compounded by an evident lack of constitutional safeguards that rendered every Gaelgeoir initiative – including the accumulated developments on which the Gaeltacht Quarter was founded – somewhat risky.*(59) Therefore to say that the Gaeltacht exists as an autonomous entity, sustained by intensive local political support, but bereft of creditable legal foundation from the British state, would be entirely apposite. Such are the realities of Gaelic life in Belfast.

Whether the passage of a much-heralded Irish Language Act – similar to Scottish Gaelic legislation of 2005 – actually strengthens Irish Gaeilge's legal entitlements and capacity remains to be seen over times ahead?

5. **_Gaelic Sports/Cumann Luthchleas Gael._** Whereas promoting the Gaeilge language required a strong educational push and fundamental commitment towards achieving Gaelic fluency, none of which were easily attainable among a people long used to conversing in English, with Gaelic sports the position was more relaxed.

Gaelic games – meaning Gaelic Football, Hurling and Camogie – had long held a genuinely popular appeal among mainly nationalist people of the North. As has already been outlined in previous chapters, the roots ran back over 140 years, and the modern GAA had long become an established player in the Northern cultural scene. Indeed the GAA was established in most Catholic schools and colleges, and also in the universities and colleges of higher education. Perhaps, most important was the establishment of GAA sports clubs in almost every parish and town hosting a sizeable nationalist population, which of course proved the grass roots base of the Association and its games. So too were the achievements of Ulster counties, colleges and clubs in various all-Ireland competitions both impressive and conducive to ever-greater confidence among the nationalist community of the North. - See Chaps 3 & 5, along with Appendix 1 (on the GAA) for further details.*(60)

By November 2001, the GAA – at a special all-Ireland Congress – deleted its discredited Rule 21 that had long denied membership to Northern Irish police officers, British police officers and all British military personnel.*(61) & (62) It was an illiberal regulation, rooted in an earlier era, but had clung on – with the support of Sinn Fein militants – for decades past its time despite pronounced opposition from a large section of its own membership, plus moderate nationalist opinion in the Northern and All-Ireland spheres.*(63) In this debate, notwithstanding the eleventh hour conversions of prominent SDLP figures like the late John Hume, significantly his party maintained a studied ambivalence over Rule 21.*(64) While there were courageous individuals who took a public stand, often braving the mockery of Republican militants, the reality is that the party dodged the issue where it could, and even harboured a number of defenders within its ranks.*(65) For certain, it gave little in the way of leadership to the nationalist community over the

GAA's Rule 21, like certain other issues, and indeed it becomes clear at least one reason why the party lost support among nationalist voters over the period 1998-2021, slipping behind Sinn Fein, and even latterly Alliance, in the polls after 2003.*(66)

Elsewhere, the GAA over the first two decades of the 21st century managed to achieve a virtual transformation in relations with the Northern Irish state. This meant receiving a plethora of grants and other benefits unprecedented in earlier decades of the GAA's icy accord with government in Belfast and its various political, cultural, sports, educational and media establishments. In return, the Association ended once-and-for-all its 80 year-long de facto boycott of the State, opting, in common with Nationalists and Republicans across the North, for positive engagement within the shared civic society of a newly-inclusive Northern Ireland. To a fair degree, this was about peace-building, but it went further to embrace various educational schemes covering shared cultures, beliefs and symbols, plus community regeneration. So also did it involve partnering with the two other mainstream sports providers, namely Ulster Rugby operating from Ravenhill stadium, and the Irish Football Association based at Windsor Park, both in South Belfast.

Its details are worthy of closer review. For some years since Good Friday, and more particularly since the 2006 St Andrews Accord, the GAA had increased its rapport with the Northern Ireland government. As already indicated, the first Gaelic sports appointment in modern times – largely public-funded and working as part of the Northern Ireland Sports Council – was that of a Hurling Development Officer in 1977. This proved to be a successful appointment, whose incumbent, the late Mr Seamus McGrattan of Portaferry, Co Down, remained and thrived until retirement. He was followed in the late 1990s by an expanded network of Hurling and Gaelic Football development officers over the next two decades. Very significant was the gradual incorporation of the GAA into a three-part sporting collaboration alongside Ulster Rugby and the Irish Football Association (IFA), which ensured the recruitment of qualified coaches in Soccer, Rugby and Gaelic sports, who were publicly funded and equipped for liaising with schools, justice programmes and youth organisations and where the emphasis was placed on development and skills training. These programmes were prioritised as a strategy of " ... positive peace-building ...", and the GAA, no longer encumbered by its divisive political bans, proved to be a major partner in the process – itself supported by the four principal Christian churches, most branches of civic society and all major political parties.

As of December 2021, a total of 10 Gaelic football, Hurling and Camogie coaches were engaged full-time by the GAA, with the bulk of their salaries paid from public funds. Additionally, Sport Northern Ireland, a public quango body, engaged a further Gaelic sports coaches, again with salaries heavily subsidised by the State.*(67) Comparable numbers of Rugby and Soccer coaches were also publicly engaged, and all the evidence pointed to positive working relations and co-operation being forged between all three bodies.*(68) Additionally, during the Covid crisis, clubs of all three associations organised mass numbers of volunteers to distribute food and medical parcels to homes across the North, including in remote rural communities where the GAA had a pronounced presence. So also were Gaelic sports grounds and social clubs opened up as vaccination centres, and widely utilised by their communities. There was also a programme of Covid management in prisons and youth clubs.*(69) This was another form of peace-building and co-operation, and one which the newly-devolved Northern Ireland government greatly valued.

Then there was the GAA stadium investment programme. Alongside the modernisation of Ravenhill Rugby ground and Windsor Park football stadium, the N.I. state has committed to assisting the redevelopment of Casement Park in West Belfast, home of the Ulster GAA. At the time of writing, Stormont Communities SDLP Minister, Mrs Nichola Mallon, has pledged £61,000,000 towards the re-construction of a modern 33,000 seater Gaelic sports stadium, with the GAA meeting an estimated £15,000,000 balance.*(70) It is anticipated that the new Casement Park, complete with its comprehensive facilities, will open by 2025 as the largest sports ground of any kind in Northern Ireland.

Generally, the GAA has made great strides forward over the past two decades since the signing of the 1998 Belfast Peace Agreement. From being an excluded force, distrusted by Unionists and viewed with suspicion by British administrators, frozen out by the N.I. political, media, educational and recreational establishments, it has now proved its appeal and capacity for sustainment. More significantly, having curbed its more self-exclusionary regulations (e.g. Rules 27 and 21 – see Appendix 1), the GAA took full advantage of the new post-Hillsborough (1985) and post-Good Friday (1998) climate, inclusive of the parity of esteem concept to maximise its gains. Through constructive engagement with the N.I. state, the GAA has reaped considerable financial and broadcasting rewards, along with a greatly extended profile. Dr Jennifer Todd, in a scholarly paper delivered back in 1988, noted that the GAA had long taken much solace as a popular agent, indeed active cultural exponent of nationalist political identity.*(71)

Yet erstwhile exclusions understated the Association's influence among nationalists, and as the latter became obvious to discerning British civil servants, especially after 1985, the process was ripe for a thawing of previous distrust and exclusion. Todd subsequently argued that Northern Irish Nationalist culture embraced "... *three inter-related concepts of nation, community and justice*".*(72) Central to that view was the place of Catholic communalism. There were more than faint strains of all three ideals prevalent in the Ulster GAA's perspective of its place in Northern society, but recognising the latter involved a process of discernment. That process is ongoing, with much remaining ground yet to cover, but its momentum is firmly established.

It remains only to add that given the overt synchronisation between the Gaeilge language and Gaelic sports in Northern Ireland over the course of its 100 years of existence, it is surprising just how sparse has been the attention paid by academics to the place of Cumann Luthchleas Gael/GAA in that marginalised Ulster Gaelic world. Sports profiling and cataloguing have been plentiful by both nationalist papers and the BBC, but curiously little focus has been directed towards analysing the place of Gaelic sports and the GAA in the process of forged political identities and as agents of momentum.*(73) Perhaps addressing that remiss has been a much needed task, albeit unintended, but yet adopted of a sense of necessity in the writing of this book?

6. ***Other Political Developments.*** The final part of this chapter offers reflections on political developments occurring over the two opening decades of this millennium. Specifically, some cognisance must be paid to the 2006 St Andrew's Accord negotiated in Scotland, along with the 2010 Hillsborough Agreement that set the pace for a promised new Irish Language Act. Up until now, it may be said that progress had amounted to piecemeal concessions wrenched by assorted wings of Gaeil Uladh from an unwilling Northern Ireland Office and its Unionist 'begrudgers' in the Civil Service and administrative establishment, the latter having managed in intervening periods between successive Stormont executives. That was certainly the view of Mac Ionnrachtaigh,

coming from a radical Republican perspective.*(74) By contrast, Cochrane avoided the language and cultural agenda, having little to say about either.*(75) Significantly, there was no defining legislation – other than the positive sentiments evoked by the 1998 Good Friday Accord – none of which were legally defined. Something more definite and substantial was required.

Two crucial developments occurred in the first decade of the 21st century, both of which had a major bearing on the progress of the Gaeilge language.

First, was the St Andrews Agreement of October 2006, emerging from a conference of all the major political parties in Northern Ireland staged at the old Scottish venue, just north of Edinburgh. By this time, Sinn Fein, headed by its Deputy Leader, Mr Martin McGuinness, had replaced the SDLP as dominant nationalist party in the Assembly and executive, and was thus in a position to exercise policy authority. Specifically, with the Royal Ulster Constabulary (RUC) having been dismantled and replaced by the Police Service of Northern Ireland (PSNI), and a discredited UDR having been replaced by an amalgamated Royal Irish Regiment, the process was sufficiently advanced for shared initiatives from Sinn Fein and the British Government. Sinn Fein, for its part, made an historic declaration of support for the PSNI. In response, the Northern Ireland Office offered a commitment to the introduction of an Irish Language Act. The latter was aimed at reflecting on the experiences of Wales and Scotland, and the NIO further pledged to work with an incoming devolved Stormont Executive to enhance and protect the language's development.*(76)

While analysing the comprehensive developments that followed on from St Andrew's belongs more properly to the scholarly labours of Professor O'Leary, nevertheless the conference enabled a return to devolved government in Belfast.*(77) Given Sinn Fein's prioritisation of the Irish language, there was considerable optimism about the prospect and benefits from a new enabling statute as promised by the British government at St Andrew's. However, with a novel power-sharing arrangement emerging from a government headed by Dr Paisley, and with Mr McGuinness as Deputy, progress was much slower than earlier hoped. Reform of the cultural programme was rather down the priority list behind basic government functions like policing and justice, which were then being intensely debated between Sinn Fein and the Democratic Unionists (DUP), the latter having lately replaced Mr David Trimble and his Official Unionists (UUP) in the elections of 2003.*(78)

Second, at a further conference staged at Hillsborough in 2010, transferring of Justice and Police from the NIO to Stormont was accompanied by a further government pledge of £20,000,000 for development of the Irish language.*(79) A proportional grant was also conceded to the Ulster Scots Agency and its language clients. From Sinn Fein's and Conradh na Gaeil's point of view, though still some way off the promised Irish Language Act, still further material benefits flowing from the British Treasury amounted to a windfall. Shortly afterwards, Gerry Adams, Sinn Fein President, announced that a large portion of this money would be passed on to the Irish Language Broadcast Fund; where it might boost the 75 hours of existing Gaelic programmes, including offering outlets to BBC N.I., RTE and the Gaelic TG4.*(80) In response, Stormont DUP Culture Minister, Mr Nelson McCausland, expressed satisfaction that developmental funds had also been allocated to the Ulster Scots Agency, of which he was a long-standing personal patron.*(81)

While the infusion of funding maintained the progress of Gaeil Uladh with its various projects, the reality was that the issue of a Language statute did not make progress through the Executive, and therefore no legislation followed. The DUP Culture Minister after 2007, Mr Edwin Poots, wanted either a pro-rata Ulster-Scots arrangement or no legislation at all. He was not prepared to sanction a stand-alone Gaeilge statute. Questions were constantly raised by DUP opponents over funding, speaker numbers, posting of signage in communities and public buildings, broadcasting and its use in courts and judicial procedures. Also, just how far would the terms of such a statute run, and would it have the backing of Westminster? This issue pointed to a need for agreement by parties composing the Executive, but the DUP remained implacably opposed to a new Gaeilge law, while the SDLP, Alliance and Greens critically supported such proposals.*(82) Predictably, the remnants of the Ulster Unionist (UUP) – with a succession of leaders over the period – were divided, and it must be added, irrelevant. Nor could there be an independent initiative from the British government while Stormont remained in place. Consequently, through the process of devolved Executive government, followed by collapse and short-lived Direct Rule, proposed legislation became the subject of inaction. The necessary level of consensus simply did not exist, and thus nothing of the kind was or could be forthcoming.

During the extended suspension of devolved government that lasted from January 2017 until December 2019 (almost three years), the question of a new Gaeilge law was emphasised as a poignant issue of division between Sinn Fein and the DUP. Only when the mammoth inter-party talks eventually produced agreement on a way forward that included **two publicly-funded posts** of Gaeilge Commissioner and Ulster-Scots Commissioner respectively did political conditions prove conducive to the restoration of devolved government. Even still, the issue of an Irish Language Act was purposely avoided until later in the 2020. The eventual agreement of First Minister, Mrs Arlene Foster, to a Gaeilge law produced deep divisions within her own DUP, bringing about her exit.*(83)

At this time of writing (13th December, 2021), all evidence points to a DUP unremitting in its opposition to an Irish Language Act. Notwithstanding the reduced Unionist share of demography, and with opinion polls auguring poorly for the party's electoral prospects in the impending Assembly poll of May 2022, it seems determined to carry that opposition to the wire, even on a reduced share of the vote. *(84) How far this opposition will proceed remains to be seen? Not only has a Gaeilge/Irish Language Act not been realised, but nor have the two Commissioner posts (Irish and Ulster-Scots) been filled. As of now, the impasse appears to be ongoing, with no obvious end in sight!

7. **_Foras na Gaeilge:_** A major development occurring over the past two decades was the creation, expansion and redirection of Foras na Gaeilge. This body was founded on an All-Ireland basis – operates in both jurisdictions and is jointly funded by the UK and Dublin governments – after the 1998 Good Friday Agreement, and took over responsibilities for promoting Irish language development from its predecessor in the Irish Republic, Bord na Gaeilge. Its principal duty was to co-ordinate and direct Gaelic promotions in both parts of Ireland by focusing on priorities, with the goal of contributing to a climate of communal reconciliation.*(85)

Foras has additional functions as an advisor to both governments in such areas as education, arts, public administration, policy making and boosting Gaelic-medium schools, as well as supporting community projects in both South and North. Operating from a Dublin headquarters, with offices in Belfast, having a budget of £9,700,000 and staff of 71 (2021 figures), Foras is co-sponsored by the Irish Republic's Department of Community, Equality and Gaeltacht Affairs (DCEGA) and Northern Ireland's Department of Culture, Arts and Leisure (DCAL).*(86) The composition has drawn critics, while Foras direction has drawn the ire of Ulster Gaelgeoiri campaigners.*(87) In essence, the alleged domination of Foras by appointees of the Dublin government caused concerns among Northern Gaels, especially Sinn Fein, whose historic relationship with the "... *Free State* ..." establishment had long been fractious and coloured by suspicion of Southern perfidiousness. Foras's axing of funding to La, the Belfast-published Gaeilge newspaper, causing it to close in December 2008, was an example in point. La's closure was followed in July 2009 by the closure of Foinse, an all-Ireland newspaper, following the further withdrawal of its grant. This move again drew grave criticism from Northern Gaelgeoir campaigners like Miss Janet Muller of Pobal and Mr Mairtin O'Muilleoir, former Sinn Fein MLA, Belfast councillor and publisher of La.*(88)

In the early days, some 19 Gaelgeoir campaigning groups were known to Foras, concerned with a range of promotional activities ranging from Gaelic arts, broadcasting, nursery and primary school development, voluntary language learning, Gaelic publishing, technical training and other similar roles. A total of 7 of the 19 core organisations were based in Northern Ireland, and together the 19 organisations received a combined figure of some £6,600,000 of public funding.*(89) Yet political pressures had mounted for stream lining aid to only viable causes managed by organisations commanding confidence from both governments. This led in 2014 to a decision by Foras to withdraw grants to all but **6 core-funded groups**. Significantly, none of those 6 core-funded groups are based in Northern Ireland, with two Belfast groups, ULTACHT and Pobal subsequently winding up. Others lost core-funding, including Iontabhas Ultach, Forbairt Feirste and Altram, and were thus forced to reapply for assistance to new schemes of funding devised by Foras. Another literary outlet, the 97-years old journal, An Ultach, had its £16,000 annual grant axed, leaving its future in serious doubt. At present, an on-line version of the journal is maintained, but at the time of writing the magazine was operating a shoe-string existence, with no security of tenure.*(90)

As for the interests which Foras continued to fund after 2014, they included youth, cultural and educational developmental groups: Colaiste na bhFiann, Gaeloideachas, Glor na nGael, Gael Linn and Art Oireachtas, along with the 128-year old campaigning body, Conradh na Gaeilge.*(91) Only Raidio Failte, based in Belfast, and An t-Aisionad, the Gaelic resources centre based at St Mary's University College, Belfast, had their funding retained by Foras.

Significantly, the favoured groups all had Dublin headquarters, and all were Southern-controlled, which did little to commend either the groups or Foras na Gaeilge to Northern Gaelgeoiri. Nor were the critics restricted to Sinn Fein. In a rare input from SDLP quarters, their-then Gaelic Affairs spokesman, Mr Dominic Bradley MLA, complained at a meeting of the Assembly's Cultural, Arts and Leisure Committee in October 2013 that Northern Gaeilge interests were being undermined by recent cuts to Irish language groups. He questioned the direction of Foras na Gaeilge's orientation, and suggested the recent progress of Gaeilge language and cultural movements in the North risked reversal.*(92) Mr Bradley's concerns were echoed more robustly by Ultacht's Mr Aodan MacPoilin, who argued that "... the voluntary sector in Northern Ireland will become no more than a bolt-on, or afterthought, to that of the South".*(93)

The prevalence of devolved government at Stormont, has meant Sinn Fein holding the Culture/Arts ministerial port-folio for some time under Caral Ni Chuilin. In turn this has put Sinn Fein in the embarrassing position of presiding over spending cuts to Irish language interests. The transition from poacher to game-keeper has meant the party being no longer on the outside demanding concessions from ministers. Instead, it is now a party of power, holding budgetary authority. In austere times, this dichotomy created conflicting loyalties, which have proved difficult to resolve. The issue remains ongoing!

8. ***Final Comments:*** Any assessment of this period is restrained by the uncertainties of what lies ahead, while also bolstered by experiences of the past two decades. The rocky journey that Northern Ireland has taken since 1998 is cause for optimism, but can only get smoother with the passage of time and the familiarity which its people and their elected representatives display in their expectations of efficient and stable self-government. Just where this whole process leaves Gaeil Uladh is rather uncertain? Yet, with all things considered, there are grounds for cautious optimism.

O'Leary continues his search for long-term civic and institutional goals, which however interesting, is a subject falling outside the realms of this enquiry.*(94) Underlying a scholarly analysis of past and contemporary conditions, he is of the view that all forces within the Northern Irish state are subject to legitimate constitutional authority, and therefore any quarrels such as Gaeil Uladh's perception of their own long term exclusion from Ulster civic society may only be redressed by democratic action.*(95) This liberal perspective is plausible, but not wholly palatable to some battle-hardened republican stalwarts among Gaeil Uladh, whose experiences have fashioned a different, albeit more radical perspective of the language and culture.

Mac Ionnachtaigh views the Gaelic language and culture as a suppressed institution, submissive to the historical oppression of all-Ireland by the English Crown down the centuries. *(96) Being a former republican prisoner, he makes no effort at concealing his view that the language must be a driving force for a new socialist and sovereign Ireland. It must also be the cultural faith radicalising a whole generation of militant republicans in struggle.*(97) Hence for that reason, just as the rather pedestrianised SDLP rather gave up on its earlier Gaelgeoir battles in the late 1990s, so did the militants of Sinn Fein take over. O'Reilly spoke fairly when noting that "... *Sinn Fein are the lead force driving all contemporary Gaelgeoir forces ...*" in Northern Ireland today.*(98)

And yet aside from political battles, Gaeil Uladh have certainly benefitted as never before from nationalist reassertion and post-Good Friday devolution. The ever-mushrooming Gaelscoil movement and dramatically-increased Gaelic profile on radio and television, plus advances of Gaelic sport and the GAA, all testify to a more beneficial and enlightened public stewardship from devolved government in Belfast as well as its Westminster overseer. Prospects for Gaelic education look encouraging, as do those for Gaelic arts, drama, music, culture and sports, as the political gravity slowly shifts in nationalists' favour. It is difficult to see those advances being reversed at any time in the future.

Yet engagement with the state - to some degree at least - has been the price paid by Gaeil Uladh in return for concessions and grant aid. Old notions of a nationalist boycott of Northern Ireland, discussed so vividly by Phoenix and Staunton in their respective accounts – no longer hold, as the pace of Gaeil Uladh quickens in their drive towards realising long held objectives.*(99) It looks improbable that current constitutional parameters will fit those changes, at least in the long term. That being the case, the development of Gael Uladh in the new Millennium could yet prove a centrifugal force in plotting the onward direction of the Irish nation.*(100) Time alone holds the answers!

FOOTNOTES and REFERENCES

1. Brendan O'Leary <u>A Treatise on Northern Ireland: - Vol. 3, Consociation and Confederation</u> (Oxford University Press, 2019); Chaps 3.5 & 3.6, pp 175-289.

2. For appropriate data cataloguing the slowly increasing population of Northern Ireland and growing percentage of Catholic nationalists, see the UK Censuses of 1991, 2001 and 2011, HMSO, Belfast and London.

3. See a selection of editorials, opinion pieces, features and news coverage in the <u>Irish News</u> (Belfast) – April 10th – July 30th 1998 – principal daily paper of the North's nationalist community.

4. See (i) Brendan O'Leary (2019); Vol. 3, Chaps 3.4 & 3.5, pp 87-175.   (ii) Feargal Cochrane <u>Northern Ireland: The Fragile Peace</u> (Yale, 2021), Chap 8, pp 225-261.

5. Professor O'Leary's scholarly three-part volume (OUP, 2019) on Northern Ireland offers the nearest thing possible to a definitive account in terms of facts, data and balanced evaluation of the roots and legacy of the contemporary Irish question. It is recommended to all readers with a serious interest in Irish/Northern Irish history and politics. By contrast, Dr Cochrane's 2021 book on the post-Good Friday state of Northern Ireland, while containing much merit, by virtue of its excursions into the realms of impressionism in later chapters, falls somewhat short of desirable standard. For a review of Cochrane, readers are referred to this author's website: www.laganwritingservices.co.uk.

6. See: http://www.comhairle.org/gaeilge/

   or http://www.comhairle.org/english/. --- cited in M.B. O'Mainnin & J.Carruthers 'Empowering Multilingualism? Provisions for Place-names in Northern Ireland and the Political and Legislative Context' – in – Robert Blackwood and Deirdre Dunlevy (Eds.) <u>Multilingualism in Public Places</u>, pp 59-87 (Bloomsbury Academic, 2021).

7. See O'Mainnin & Carruthers (2021).

8. In the early 1990s, Cumann Luthchleas Gael (GAA) across All-Ireland, including the Ulster counties, initiated a new requirement on each county committee for an elected Cultural – meaning Irish Language – Officer,

whose duty it was to promote Gaelic language and associated cultural activities as part of an overall blend of sport, language and cultural identity consistent with the aims of CLG/GAA. See Official Guide of CLG, Dublin.

9. Feargal Mac Ionnrachtaigh Language, Resistance and Revival: Republican Prisoners and the Irish Language in the North of Ireland (Pluto Press, London, 2013).

10. Discussions with distinguished Protestant Ulster Gaelgeoir writer and activist, Dr Gordon McCoy; 15th July and 2nd November 2021.

11. See Mac Ionnrachtaigh (2013), Chap 7, pp 156-189. – Also, Seamus Mallon (with Andy Pollak) A Shared Home Place (2019, Lilliput Press, Dublin), especially Chaps 13 & 14.

12. Figures kindly supplied by Comhairle na Gaelscolaiochta, (CNG Scoils) Belfast. Special thanks to Acting Chief Executive, Mrs Maria Thomasson, and Senior Researcher, Mr Tarlach Mac Giolla Bhride, both of whom went to extra efforts to provide the most up-to-date data.

13. Irish/Gaelic Medium Education 2020-2021, Key Statistics – figures supplied by the NISRA and Northern Ireland Department of Education, Belfast.

14. See https://www.education-ni.gov.uk/articles

15. See Mac Ionnrachtaigh (2013), Chaps 7 & Epilogue – and O'Reilly (1999), Chap 4.

16. Regrettably, this author felt disappointed by the weak and grudging responses of a variety of SDLP lead figures, including official Gaelic Affairs spokesman, Patsy McGlone MLA, to numerous enquiries. From 2018 to 2021, Mr McGlone saw fit to answer just one of five direct enquires, and that was to send this author a copy of his own article, which proved to be of marginal relevance. Regrettably, the party leader, Mr Colum Eastwood MP, showed even greater indifference. When pressed by this author to explain a supposedly 'new policy document' claimed on a Facebook posting in Spring 2021 by his junior colleague, Miss Ciara Hunter MLA, both Eastwood and Hunter ignored three separate requests for follow-up information. Presumably, Eastwood was endeavouring to minimise the impact of "empty spouting" by his lady colleague, choosing silence in preference to admitting that she had made empty pledges? Rather a deflating experience!

17. Information and data supplied by CNG/Mr Tarlach Mac Giolla Bhride, 2020.

18. Discussions with Turas tutor & researcher, Mr Aodan Mac Seafraidh, 19th October 2021, Belfast.

19. Discussions with Mr Michael Mac Giolla Ghunna, BA (Hons), M.A., Principal – Colaiste Feirste on 12th November 2021. All figures, data and projections for the next growth period were verified by the Principal.

20. Discussions with Mr Mac Seafraidh and Dr McCoy – plus information contained on Colaiste Feirste and N.I. Education Auth. websites: rmhicanlia963@colaistefeirste.belfast.ni.sch.uk

21. Discussions with Mr Mac Giolla Ghunna, 12th November 2021.

22. Ibid

23. It is worthwhile adding that the talented Michael Mac Giolla Ghunna, as well as being a distinguished Gaelic educationalist and pioneering headmaster, is also the researcher and author of a highly merited MA thesis (validated by Queens University, Belfast) analysing the Belfast Gaelic League in the last years of the 19th century – already cited earlier in this book.

24. See article by Robbie Meridith, BBC News N.I. Education Correspondent, 19th Oct., 2019: 'Colaiste Feirste: Belfast Irish medium school to expand by 50%'. https//www.bbc.co.uk/news/uk-northern-ireland-50099598.

25. Information provided by Mr Mac Giolla Ghunna.

26. Ibid.

27. Ibid.

28. Information supplied by Mr MacGiolla Bhride/CNG.

29. Discussions with Head of Gaeilge Stream, St Catherine's College, Armagh, Mrs Catriona de Bleine, 11th November, 2021. Also, data supplied by Mr Mac Giolla Bhride/CNG.

30. Discussions with Mrs de Bleine.

31. Discussions with Mr Gearoid O'Machail, Director of Gaelic Cultural Centre, Armagh/ Aoanach Macha, 11th November 2021.

32. Figures and information supplied by Mr Mac Giolla Bhride/CNG.

33. Website information, St Joseph's, Donaghmore, Co Tyrone. – Worth adding that this author approached the school directly for information, but despite phone calls and emails (Nov. 2021), the Headmistress, Mrs Geraldine Donnelly, declined to acknowledge or respond.

34. Figures kindly supplied by the Head of Gaeilge Medium Education Stream at St Malachy's High School, Castlewellan, Co Down, Mrs Ciara Pickering – 9th November, 2021.

35. Clarity of data and accompanying information provided by Mrs Pickering. Generally, I am most grateful to this same lady for her helpful advice on the St Malachy's Gaeilge project.

36. Figures supplied by CNG/Mr Mac Giolla Bhride.

37. See Mr Diarmaid O'Bruadair's statement on school website.

38. Discussions with Mr O'Bruadair who offered abundant general information about the school. This author is most grateful to Mr O'Bruadair, who is evidently a most diligent and conscientious headmaster, for kindly providing the full picture on his school.

39. The granting of recognition, with funding, occurred in the teeth of opposition from an alliance of Unionist opponents.

40. Full figures of schools and numbers provided by NISRA/Dept of Education, N. Ireland.

41. Information kindly provided by Professor Micheal O'Mainnin (Head of Celtic Studies, QUB) – correspondence with this author, 24th November 2021.

42. Letter from Professor O'Mainnin to author, 24th November, 2021.

43. St Mary's University College, Belfast, has provided a constant line of Irish-Gaeilge teachers in one form or another since the Second World War.

44. Information kindly provided in correspondence by Mr Trevor Abbot, Academic Registrar, St Mary's University College, Belfast, 29th November 2021.

45. Ibid.

46. Regrettably, and despite direct enquiries, officials at the University of Ulster dallied and dragged their heels about offering meaningful responses on Gaeilge take-up rates. One official suggested that such information was "private", while another recommended submitting enquiries under the UK Freedom of Information Act. Frankly, this author had neither the scope nor inclination for chasing obstructive time-wasters.

47. Discussions with Messers' Tarlac O'Branagain and Jake Mac Siacais, both of Forbairt Feirste, Belfast – 23rd November 2021. Also, Mrs Colma McKee, Manageress of Gaelchursai, a Gaelic technical training organisation with some public funding, Belfast, 23rd Nov. 2021.

48. Information provided by Mr Mac Siacais and Mr O'Branagain, 23rd & 24th November 2021.

49. Ibid.

50. Discussions with Mrs McKee of Gaelchursai, Belfast – 23rd Nov, 2021.

51. Ibid.

52. Information provided by Mrs McKee and Mr Mac Siacais 23rd & 24th Nov, 2021.

53. 2011 UK Census, Northern Ireland figures – HMSO London & Belfast. – Note: the figures for the 2021 Census are eagerly awaited, and widely expected to show increased Gaelic participation levels. Figures release anticipated for Autumn 2022.

54. Figures discussed with a range of lead Gaelgeoir figures in West Belfast, but the author accepts responsibility for the stated estimate.

55. See Department of Communities (Northern Ireland) website, October 2021.

56. Ref. Discussions with Messers' Mac Siacais and O'Branagain, 23rd & 24th Nov, 2021.

57. See McKee V. <u>Gaelic Nations</u> (1997), photographs.

58. For an outsider's perspective, see: Siun Carden – 'Post-conflict Belfast sliced and diced: The case of the Gaeltacht Quarter'. Divided /Cities/Contested States – Working Paper No 20; 2011, School of History and Anthropology, Queen's University, Belfast.

59. Daithi Mac Sithigh 'Official Status of Languages in the UK and Ireland' – Common Law World Review, 47 (1), pp 77-102, https://doi.org/10.1177/1473779518773642 (2018).

60. Ibid.

61. For details on GAA competitions and winners since the 1970s , see: Jerome Quinn <u>Ulster Football and Hurling: The Path of Champions</u> (Wolfhound Press, Dublin, 1993). Also, for a valuable record of the directions taken by Hurling and Gaelic Football players during the Great War, see: Donal McAnallen <u>Forgotten Gaelic Volunteers; Ulster GAA Members who fought in World War One</u> (Cardinal Tomas O'Fiaich Library and Archive, Armagh, 2019.).

62. By the time of Rule 21's abolition in 2001, just about all and every moderate nationalist and ecclesiastical voice across the four provinces of Ireland sought its removal. They included the late Messers' John Hume MP & MEP and Seamus Mallon MP (a former Armagh county footballer), President Mary McAleese (a Belfast native), An Taoiseach – Mr Bertie Aherne, Archbishop Sean Brady (former Cavan footballer) and the late & scholarly Cardinal Cathal Daly (a native of Antrim Hurling citadel, Loughgiel). Only Sinn Fein was campaigning for retention. It was also noticeable that within the GAA, the three southern provinces of Leinster, Connacht and Munster favoured removal, while certain counties in the North, ie. those with a strong Sinn Fein lobbyist presence like Tyrone, Antrim, Armagh and Derry, vigorously opposed removal. Conversely, Down (this author's native county), always the most moderate of the Six Counties - under the courageous leadership of Chairman, Mr Eamon O'Toole (a member of the family whose pub was ravaged by gun-toting Loyalist assassins in June 1994 at Loughinisland, Co Down), after fierce debate, was brought to favour the pragmatic way forward, and opted for removal. An earlier example of the general moderation of Down GAA was the election in January 1974 as County Chairman of Mr Anthony Williamson, a prominent Alliance Councillor on Newry & Mourne

Authority. Mr Williamson's election encountered dogged resistance at the County Convention - held in Newcastle (Co Down) - from pro-Republican activists led by the late Mr Gerry Fitzmaurice, but the outgoing Chairman, Mr Paddy O'Donoghue (RIP), himself a newly-elected SDLP Member of the Northern Ireland Assembly, flatly refused to allow Mr Fitzmaurice and his associates to either reverse the result or disrupt the Convention. Later, the GAA Central authority in Dublin gave a ruling of endorsement to the new Chairman's position, plus a vote of confidence to Mr O'Donoghue's handling of the event. - See reports – Irish News, Irish Press and Belfast Telegraph, 21st January, 1974; Mourne Observer and Down Recorder, 23rd January, 1974; Sighle Nic an Ultaigh – O Shiol go Blath (1990) Chap. 10, p. 396. Also, minutes of Down GAA Convention; 20th January, 1974, held at Donard Hotel, Newcastle. These facts were further checked from records held by Ulster GAA Secretary, Mr Brian McAvoy; tel. discussions 03/12/2021.

63. It is also worth noting that the 2001 Northern Irish Policing Report – undertaken by a Commission headed by former Conservative Cabinet Minister and last Hong Kong Governor, Mr Chris Patton, and which also included the much-acclaimed 1960s Down GAA Secretary and later Northern Ireland Community Relations Chairman, Dr Maurice Hayes (RIP) – recommended replacement of the Royal Ulster Constabulary by a new and more inclusive Police Service of Northern Ireland (PSNI), drawn from both communities and unarmed. The Patton Report – much to the pleasure of nationalists and unease of Unionists – was duly implemented by the Labour government of Messers' Tony Blair and Peter Mandelson. – See O'Leary, (2019), Sections 3.5 & 3.6, pp 175-289; and Cochrane (2013), Chap 8, pp 225 261.

64. At the GAA's 2001 Ulster Club Gaelic Football Championship final, played the day after the GAA Special Congress that voted to abolish the notorious Rule 27, Ballinderry (Derry) v Mayobridge (Down), the event was marred by hostile barracking from a pro-Republican section of Derry supporters. In response to Down's formal backing, the previous day, for the removal of Rule 21, Derry fans howled vile abuse at both the Down club and their fans throughout the match. Not a pleasant spectacle, and one witnessed first hand by the author. Significantly, despite negative press reports, the GAA declined to take disciplinary action. See Irish News match reports and news reports on BBC Radio Ulster.

65. This author was a relentless and lifelong critic of Rule 21, GAA. As far back as May 1976, his speech – as official Down delegate – to the GAA All-Ireland Youth Congress, held at Colaiste Naomh Mhuire, Dublin, attacked Rule 21 as "... sectarian, divisive, illiberal and self-defeating". That opposition continued over subsequent decades. See Opinion Piece Irish News, 19th April, 2001; debate with former Antrim All-Ireland U-21 football medal holder (1969), Mr Liam Turbett, Irish Sunday Life, 21st October 2001; Opinion Piece, Irish Post, May 2001; and televised debate with former Derry Gaelic footballer and later Sinn Fein N.I. Assembly Member, the late Mr Francie Brolly, BBC Northern Ireland, 'Hearts and Minds' programme, 26th April, 2001, Belfast.

66. To his credit, the late Mr Seamus Mallon's career was peppered with condemnations of IRA bombing outrages and murders, along with divisive practices on the nationalist side of Irish politics, of which the GAA's Rule 27 was held up as a prime example. Mallon had the credibility – unlike Hume – of being a retired Gaelic football college and county player in his youth. However, he lacked the authority of Hume's leadership within the SDLP. See: Memoirs - Seamus Mallon ... with Andy Pollak ... A Shared Home Place (2019) - Also, Gerard Murray & Jonathan Tongue Sinn Fein and the SDLP: From Alienation to Participation, Chap 13, (Dublin, O'Brien, 2005). – Further merit in the edited collection of essays by Dr Gordon McCoy with Mr Maolcholaim Scott – Aithne na nGael /Gaelic Identities (Belfast, ULTACH Trust, 2000).

67. In the final UK elections to the European Parliament of 2019, the SDLP Leader, Mr Colum Eastwood, was overtaken by Alliance's Mrs Naomi Long in the bid for Northern Ireland's third seat. See Election Results European Assembly, June 2019, Northern Ireland. Also, see results for Westminster, European, Stormont Assembly and Local Council elections from 2003 – 2019, HMSO London/Belfast.

68. Discussions with Mr Brian McAvoy, An Runai & CEO, Executive Council, Ulster Gaelic Athletic Association, Armagh head office – 3rd December, 2021.

69. Ibid.

70. Ibid.

71. See website, Dept of Communities, Northern Ireland, plus news reports throughout Autumn 2021 in <u>Irish News</u> and <u>Belfast Telegraph</u>. – Also, information passed by Mr McAvoy in interview 3/12/21.

72. Jennifer Todd *'Nationalist Political Culture in Northern Ireland'* – Paper presented to UK Political Studies Association Annual Conference, Plymouth Polytechnic, 12th - 14th April, 1988.

73. Jennifer Todd *'Northern Irish Nationalist Political Culture'*; pp 31-44, Irish Political Studies, 5, 1990.

74. Rather disappointingly, Dr Camille O'Reilly's 1999 book on the Irish Language in West Belfast (referred to previously) had surprisingly little to say about the role and significance of Cumann Luthchleas Gael, either in the context of Belfast or the wider forum of Gaeil Uladh.

75. See Mac Ionnaichtaigh (2013), Chap 7, plus Conclusion. The same anti-imperial/radical republican theme characterises the entire narrative of his book.

76. Cochrane – New Edition – (2021) has remarkably little to say about the government's thawing in its attitude towards Gaelic culture and the language. Given the priority accorded by the Good Friday Agreement to 'Parity of Esteem' for both cultures, Dr Cochrane's remiss seems strange.

77. Statement released by NIO, 13th October, 2013.

78. O'Leary (2019); Vol. 3, Chap. 3.6, pp 264-269.

79. N.I. Assembly Elections of November 2003; Results from HMSO, London and Belfast.

80. Statement released by NIO, 3rd February 2010. – Also, see article by Henry MacDonald, <u>Guardian,</u> 5th February, 2010.

81. News reports, <u>Irish News</u>, <u>Belfast Telegraph</u> and <u>Belfast Newsletter</u>, 3rd February, 2010.

82. Ibid.

83. SDLP, Alliance and Greens all enunciate formal commitments to an Irish Language Act, as proposed by Conradh na Gaeilge. See the websites of all three parties previously listed.

84. As was widely reported at the time, Mrs Foster's resignation as both DUP Leader and First Minister of Northern Ireland was hastened by disquiet among several of her own MLAs and party grass roots after she conceded the principle of an Irish Language Act. See news reports and analysis Belfast Newsletter, Belfast Telegraph and Irish News 14th June 2021.

85. A University of Liverpool Autumn 2021 survey found the DUP to have lost support among a third of their voters, and languished behind Sinn Fein at 20.6 of first preference votes. An earlier Lucidtalk Poll, commissioned by the Belfast Telegraph, put DUP support at 13.0, with the UUP at 16.2 and the hard-line Traditional Unionist Voice at 14.1. Sinn Fein received the backing of 23.5 of respondents. – Figures cited in article by Christopher Leebody, Belfast Telegraph, 5th November, 2021.

86. Dan Hull – 'A Summary of Proposed Funding Changes for the Irish Language Voluntary Sector: Recent Developments'; pp 2-4. Northern Ireland Assembly; Research and Library Service Briefing Paper; 67/11, 2nd June, 2011.

87. Ibid.

88. See summary of critics – Newry Times News; 30th October, 2013.

89. See 'Foras na Gaeilge' briefing paper, 17th January 2014. Also, Andersonstown News 18th January, 2014, plus constant new reports throughout that week in Irish News.

90. Ibid.

91. News briefing, Foinse, 11th March, 2014.

92. See current website of Foras na Gaeilge.

93. Ibid.

94. O'Leary (2019), Chaps 3.6 & 3.7.

95. Ibid.

96. News reports, Irish News and Belfast Telegraph, 11 & 12th March, 2014.

97. Mac Ionnrachtaigh (2013); Chaps 1, 2 & 7.

98. Mac Ionnrachtaigh (2013); Conclusion.

99. O'Reilly (1999); Chaps 6 & 9.

100. See Staunton (2001); Chaps 8 & 14.

   Also, Phoenix E. Northern Nationalism (Ulster Historical Foundation).

101. For an assessment of conflicting aims, see Mac Ionnrachtaigh (2013), Chap 7, and Seamus Mallon (2019), Chaps 13 & 14.

Mr Aodan Mac Poilin (sadly deceased): - Life-long Belfast Gaelic campaigner extraordinaire! Co-founder of West Belfast Gaeltacht housing project, writer, broadcaster, educationalist and Director of former public body ULTACHT Trust. Widely respected across both Irish Gaelic and N.I. Government circles.

The late Cardinal Tomas O'Fiaich

Archbishop of Armagh and Primate of All-Ireland, 1977 - 1990, and
previously President of St Patrick's University College and Seminary,
Maynooth, Co Kildare. Gaelic scholar, writer, broadcaster, researcher and
teacher. To many, O'Fiaich, a native of Crossmaglen, South Armagh, and
ardent Gaelic football supporter of his native Armagh, personified the
synthesis of Irish nationalism and Gaeilgeoirism.

Children being taught in a Gaelic medium Bunscoil in Ulster

(Courtesy of La)

Down Gaelic football team: - All-Ireland Senior Champions, 1960 & 1961. First Ulster county to bring the All-Ireland Senior Crown across the border, and paved the way for multiple Northern successes over the ensuing six decades. This success in Gaelic sport had the effect of stimulating morale and confidence among Northern Gaels, leading to a more robust campaign for reform and inclusion in so many areas of previous political and cultural exclusion in Northern Ireland over the years ahead.

(Courtesy of Down GAA)

An early gathering of Coisde Gael Uladh in Belfast, pre 1920.

(Courtesy of Linenhall Library, Belfast)

Forbairt Feirste / Gaelic Economic and Business Training Forum

In the 1980s and 90s, the use of spoken Gaelic at meetings provoked sharp conflict with the Northern Ireland Office. Since 2000, this body has played a major role in the development of Gaelic technical education and training. Head Office at Belfast Gaeltacht Quarter.

Gearoid O'Caireallain - Founding editor of La (former Belfast Gaelic daily), Gaelic dramatist, broadcaster, writer eand campaigner, and former President of All-Ireland Gaelic League/Conradh na Gaeilge, Pivotal figure in Gaeilge Uladh.

Feis na nGleann (Glens of Antrim): - Opening procession, led by piper, of the first Glens Feis, Cushendall, 1904.

(Courtesy of Ulster Historical Foundation, Belfast)

Dr Gordon McCoy: - Native of Saintfield, Co Down.
Probably the leading Protestant Gaeilgeoir in Northern Ireland. Writer,
researcher, tutor, broadcaster and campaigner. Actively involved as Gaelic
Affairs Officer - East Belfast Methodist Mission.

Early Hurling game, 1904 Feis na nGleann, Cushendall.

(Courtesy of Ulster Historical Foundation)

Meanscoil Feirste students with vice principal Mr Prionnsios O La Bhradha, 1997. Belfast's first Gaelic Medium secondary school has now been superseded by Colaiste Feirste (650 students) in West Belfast. Already there are advanced plans for the creation of a second meanscoil, this one to be sited in North Belfast.

(Courtesy of La)

Mrs Linda Ervine: - Feisty personality and founder of East Belfast
Gaelic Bunscoil. Originally of Ulster Loyalist political roots, but now
has embraced the Gaelic language and culture for her Protestant
brethren and the wider Ulster Protestant community.

Professor Eoin MacNeill: - Native of Glenarm, Glens of
Antrim. Co-founder of Gaelic League, historian at University
College, Dublin. Moderate figure in Republican circles and
Education Minster in Free State government, 1922 – 1925.

Roger Casement: - Former British Civil Servant and decorated humanitarian campaigner in Congo. Native of North Antrim and convert to Irish Nationalism through, initially, the Gaelic League. Executed by British authorities in 1916 for his part in the Easter Uprising. Remains returned to Ireland in 1965 for Irish State funeral. Ulster GAA principal ground named in his honour, Casement Park, Belfast.

Pupils on their way to classes at early Meanscoil, Beal Feirste, in 1990s.

(Courtesy of Irish News, Belfast)

Young ceilidh dancers, 1990s, Feis an Dun, Newcastle, Co Down.

Chapter Eight

CONCLUSIONS

1. Overview: This conclusion aims at drawing together all the main segments of evidence presented in the previous seven substantive chapters about divergent Gaelic language and cultural politics over the past century. Being a contemporary history work, its goal is to identify events and trends from the past 100 years so as to enable a better understanding of present day conditions some twenty years into the new millennium. Therefore, notwithstanding the welter of information offered, this chapter is purposely brief and evaluative in order to highlight the most salient points. Such a succinct approach might inform the reader on what the author considers the most relevant issues arising.

Specifically, this final section shall be concerned with three key questions.

First, given common historical origins in the North of Ireland and West of Scotland over previous millennia, and with a common language evolving, the question begs; **are modern Gaidheil na h-Alba and Gaeil Uladh similar creatures?** Actually, the historic roots of both Gaelic nations is a specialist subject best left to recognised Celtic scholars like Micheal O'Mainnin *(1) of Queens University, Belfast, and Wilson McLeod of Edinburgh University, to name but two.*(2) Another eminent authority with valuable published interests was the late Cardinal Tomas O'Fiaich, who in earlier days as a Celtic scholar of Maynooth Pontifical University, Kildare, contributed much on Gaelic-speaking missionaries.*(3) Yet both Gaelic worlds are recognisable, and it is proper for observers to discern the nature of each as it appears. Alternatively, another related question may be fairly posed? Do those two Gaelic forces counterpoise each other, imbued with different symbols and goals, while competing for slices of the same cake from a lately-insistent "beneficent" British state, itself haunted by memories of repression by predecessors?

263

Second, are the two Gaelic neighbours really "… worlds apart …"? Is it not the case that there exists scope for meaningful convergence through shared cultural pursuits in such areas as music, literature, sports, arts and drama? Indeed is there such thing as a distinct Celtic identity, on a par with Welsh or even the Afro-Asian and European ethnic identities that over recent decades have found a passive outlet within the wider concept of Britishness? Perhaps it is only in their historic direction that the Gaels of Scotland and Ulster diverged?

Third, how has the British state responded to the rise of Gaidheil na-h-Alba and Gaeil Uladh, especially in modern times? Why have the Scottish and Irish divisions been treated so differently; one as a legitimate cultural interest, and the other as a subversive threat to the political harmony of the British state? Given their diverse antecedents, was it ever realistic to expect any other response? Also, how far is it accurate to hold the UK government responsible for hostility where it occurred, in Scotland and Northern Ireland? International influences have also played their part in restraining the hand of UK governments against its Celtic peoples. There have been large numbers of sympathetic Irish and Scottish Gaels trans-located in England, USA, Canada and Australasia, resulting from the diaspora, a subject on which Tom Devine*(4) and Brendan O'Leary have each written at length.*(5) However, what would be interesting is to understand to what degree the pace of Gaelic assertiveness from foreign soils, and whether such campaigns made any difference?

Only by evaluating those three key questions can useful conclusions be extrapolated from the comprehensive evidence presented in the previous seven chapters. Admittedly, there occurs a degree of overlap in the ground covered, and the issues might on first sight appear rather basic. Yet there is a serious purpose in that anti-Gaelic 'naysayers' in Scotland and Northern Ireland strike their 'sting' through raising the most basic questions about the purpose and role of Gaelic in both countries, often adding insults along the way. Examples would include a former Education director of Edinburgh and Ulster Loyalist MP, Sammy Wilson (see Chaps 6 & 7).

Rather than regurgitating earlier assessments, or introducing new evidence, this conclusion is concerned with analysing existing information so as to offer general points of analysis that are credibly corroborated by the weight of material outlined in this book. That said, the process of evaluation carries a degree of subjective judgement, and inevitably differences will prevail among the author and readers as to specific issues and their prioritisation in this script. In those circumstances, as author I can only plead for the reader's forbearance and understanding, not to mention tolerance of diverse views.

2   **(i) *Gaelic Nations: Fact or Myth?*** At the end of a lengthy and comprehensive examination of the general subject, it has to be asked whether the two schools in any meaningful sense constitute a singular, or at least con-joined cultural entity? Is there any way in which the concept of a pan-Gaelic nation stretching across all-Ireland and the West of Scotland has validity or credible recognition? Are there common bonds knitting those two entities together, or, as per the book title, has the course of history and development of two modern nations cast the Gaels of Ulster and Scotland ***"... worlds apart ..."***?

Come to think, is this author alone in peddling a maverick thesis, both here and in a previous publication, when speaking of Gaidheil na h-Alba agus Gaeil Uladh & Eireann as composing diverse branches of a historic Celtic nation?*(6) Whatever may be the nature and characteristics of modern nation states, the roots of contemporary Scotland and both parts of Ireland are to be found in their common Gaelic heritage. The weight of evidence produced here, and cited from multiple Celtic scholars on whom this book has drawn, shows the reality of a diverse and historic Gaelic nation on both sides of the Sea of Moyle.

Kingdoms and petty clan duchies there were a-plenty, and so often ranged against each other. Yet the things that give people national identity – namely land area, language, economic circumstances, religion and culture – were well established by the early middle ages in both countries. Those traits remain the same so as to define both modern Gaelic nations. Moreover, the fact is that historically with music and Gaelic arts, sports like Hurling and Shinty, dress like the Scottish and Irish kilts, names, families, clans and chieftains, literature and a broadly similar language – albeit with diverse dialects – a primitive legal code (Brehon) and a common Christian heritage; those were the essential Celtic features enduring over approximately two millennia. This level of continuity in vital areas of life underlines the extent to which the Gaels constituted a recognisable trans-national people, whose clans moved around and settled in different lands of the British Isles, plus the Isle of Man. Its story is reflected rather well in the works of many writers, not the least of which is the accurate and non-complicated short history by Anglo-Scottish Christian Evangelical writer, journalist and missionary, the late Reginald B. Hale.*(7)

Further comment on historic Gaelic origins is the prerogative of the ancient historian and anthropologist, and well beyond this author's level of competence. However, for purposes here, it is enough to say that the validity of the Gaelic peoples is an established fact from history. How effectively Gaelic has permeated language, culture, development and ultimately politics in the modern context, and whether such has been for the betterment of the Gaelic peoples or otherwise, has been a principal topic of this enquiry? It is a subject on which different positions have long been taken; from the likes of Reginald Hindley who in 1990 wrote that Irish Gaeldom was terminally doomed*(8), to Conchuir O'Giollagain (eds) et al (2020) who produced a similarly grim thesis for Scottish Gaeldom's prospects*(9), to the late Kenneth MacKinnon who demonstrated a quiet confidence in the durability of Gaeldom's survival based on lessons learned from the Gaelic history of both nations.*(10)

Of course any such affirmations, not to mention prognostications, are based on subjective criteria of which the greatest is, arguably, uncertainty of Gaeldom's future. That said, the emergence over modern decades of a substantial Gaelic infrastructure in both countries, based around Gaelic-medium schooling, radio and television, designated Gaidhealtachd/Gaeltachtai communities, Gaelic music, arts, drama and publishing, along with the popularity (in Northern Ireland more than Scotland) of Gaelic sports, does bode well for Gaeldom's future, at least in the medium term. Thereafter, the Gaels resilience to not just Anglicising forces, but also those of an increasingly commercialised world, will be determined by the depth and appeal of modern Gaelic infrastructures.

2 *(ii) Is there an Authentic Gaelic Identity?* Culture brings us to questions of identity in contemporary society. To a large degree, that has been the overriding issue for nationalist people in Northern Ireland, and expressed through the medium of the Gaelic language, sports and cultural orientation, along with the all-important political affinity. This enquiry has sought to identify major factors in Chaps 3, 5 & 7. The compelling evidence of diverse writers like

MacPoilin (1997), Staunton (2001), O'Reilly (1999), Phoenix et al (eds) (2005), McCoy & Scott (2000) and even republican radicals like MacIonnrachtaigh (2013) has been documented in corroboration. Most significantly, all those writers point to the inclusion of indigenous Gaelic culture in the nationalist make-up to a level that establishes a clear level of synchronisation between the nationalist and Gaelgeoir outlook.

As has already been established, Gaeil Uladh are essentially driven by political nationalism, but fashioned in the character of Gaelic culture. That its forces have advanced significantly in schooling, media, sports and political acceptance over the past half century, especially since 1985, represents the growing strength and numbers of Ulster Gaels. It also points to a belated and grudging recognition of Gaelic-Irish cultural identity by the UK's Northern Ireland Office, under pressure from nationalist parties, added to the Dublin government and, since 1998, Washington overseers. However reluctant may have been the concession, in essence the concept of a Gaelic Ulster identity is not just recognised, but its interests are now defined and affirmed in international charter. - It will be interesting to see the outcome of a proposed Irish Language Act, to which HMG has already made a direct pledge? On that matter and many others, Brendan O'Leary's learned evaluations of various constitutional options and proposed internal reforms makes for interesting reading.*(11)

With Scottish Gaels, the concept of identity is closely linked to language, and largely regionalised to the Hebrides and West Highlands, plus migrant communities in Glasgow and Edinburgh. Scottish Gaels have also been shown as less politically assertive than their Irish brethren, a factor mourned by Wilson McLeod (2020), but on balance probably a triumph for pragmatism. Accordingly, given the essence of identity in political alignments, the realities of defending a minority and regionalised language with small speaker numbers, as in Scotland, raises questions over its very survival.

For as long as Gaidhlig remains alive, and its cultural projection is maximised, then a combination of political bridge-building – achieved by premier leaders like the late Donald John Mackay of An Comunn Gaidhleach and John Angus McKay of Comunn na Gaidhlig – and gaining support of influential patrons like the late Queen Mother, along with popular cultural events like the National Gaelic Mod, all offer prospects for a viable future.

That was the cold reality of Scottish Gaeldom's beleaguered state in the 1960s and '70s, and that it survived those bleak conditions owed much to a consummate Gaelic lobby, as highlighted by the writings of Thompson (1991) and Pederson (2019). However much this fact may pain Gaelic nationalists, 1960s/70s Scottish Gaelic had little weight to throw around, and depended on Establishment good will for survival.

It was Scottish Gaeldom's blessing to be headed in those critical years by the mercurial and far-sighted Donald John MacKay, about whom it may be fairly concluded had a life's legacy in leading the rescue of his mother tongue. His networking was influential, his strategy effective, his sense of political balance apposite; and from his skilled labours the contemporary world of Gaelic TV, radio, high profile concerts, education, Gaelic signage and publishing throughout Scotland ... all funded by a public purse that in the end proved generous, if not initially willing .... was built upon. Perhaps the latter adds up to a recognition of Gaelic identity by a reluctant British state that went further than any or all of the early 20th century Gaelic activists could ever have dreamt.

Yet it is such a pity that the man from North Uist seems to have been rather forgotten by today's generation of Gaels, and not accorded the distinguished recognition that his life's work merits. While it is not a historian's place to anoint heroes, nevertheless those facts are documented here both for the sake of posterity and also to the hallowed memory of a great Scottish Gael.

2   ***(iii) Do Irish and Scottish Gaels fit the British State?*** This question raises a number of issues about ethnicity, cultural roots, linguistics and such like that go far beyond the realms of this book, and in any case are the province of Gaelic linguists, sociologists and anthropologists, not this humble contemporary historian! Yet even for an historian, there is the basic fact of evolving and troubled relationships between the Anglicised British state and its minority Celtic components. Such has been the reality of Anglo-Scottish, Anglo-Welsh and Anglo-Irish relations down the centuries, with language, cultural, economic and religious strife permeating the discord.

It is self-evident from this book, along with what one assumes to be general public awareness of the course of Anglo-Celtic history, that the British state – headed by the English Crown and its constitutional corollaries – has long viewed Celtic assertiveness with nervous apprehension. MacIonnrachtaigh (2013) and O'Leary (2019) each remind readers that over the centuries in Ireland the Crown suppressed the Gaelic language, culture and clans in order to achieve political control, while MacKinnon (1974) and Pryde (1962) make similar claims for Scotland. Religious suppression was a Crown goal in Ireland, as evidenced by the attempts of Queen Elizabeth I, King James I (& VI), Lord Protector Cromwell and King William III to secure absolute dominance; a view comprehensively documented by Belfast's late and erudite Catholic historian, Dr Ambrose Macaulay (2016 et al).*(12) Therefore, given previous history, is there any basis for an amicable co-existence for Gaelic peoples within the greater British state of the 20th and 21st centuries?

Specifically, do the Gaels of either or both nations have a recognised place, and if so, how has the state accommodated them? Evidence presented here shows that notwithstanding memories of Culloden and de-gaelicising of the Scottish Highlands, post 1746 - the Scottish Gaelic experience has been a positive one over the past 131 years since An Comunn Gaidhealach's founding in 1891. With An Comunn geared to a programme entirely about language protection and its incorporation to the educational system, along with publicising music and culture through the Gaelic Mods, and sponsored by multiple establishment patrons, there was little reason for discord in its relations with the state. In essence, Scottish Gaels being weak and gravely bereft of sizeable speaker numbers, presented no real threat to the British state or Union.

An Comunn's political neutrality, along with large numbers of Highlands and Hebridean volunteers joining the British Army and Royal Navy in both world wars, meant a benign attitude was taken by successive HMGs towards Scottish Gaeldom. Even fundamental Presbyterianism – itself a major part of Highlands and Outer Hebrides life – had a certain redeeming quality when dealing with Protestant administrations at Edinburgh and Whitehall. This contrasted with the predominant Catholicism of Gaels in nationalist Ireland, including Ulster, so disliked by Free Masons and Rangers-supporting apparatchiks concentrated in Edinburgh's Scottish Office. Those realities are portrayed clearly by Tom Devine and Tom Gallagher in their respective studies of Glasgow, Edinburgh and the West of Scotland during much the 20th century.*(13)

Although religious sectarianism was not a big force in Highlands or Hebridean society, the scarcity of liaisons between the two Gaelic worlds throughout the 20th century was a sober reality. Indeed it is hardly fanciful to connect that 'coolness' partly to the Presbyterian-Catholic religious chasm, but also Gaidheal na h-Alba's leaders reluctance to associate with a radical Gaeil Uladh whose political challenge to British rule in Northern Ireland was daunting.

As for Irish Gaels, theirs was a clear dichotomy of confronting the claims and prejudices of a political authority whose rule they despised. It was not so much a cultural battle, as more a struggle for recognition of identity, which in turn would focus on the political rights of the North's Gaelic-leaning population. Put simply, cultural identity defined political alignments, whether or not the British government or its allies took the trouble to understand those complexities.

As has been shown, the fortunes of Gaeil Uladh were prescribed by political limitations imposed on their mainstream constituency by the constitution and power structures of the Northern Irish state. While authors like O'Leary, Cochrane and Phoenix might expostulate on the political mechanics of reform, actually the position of Gaeil Uladh was and remains dependent on the continuing appeal of the Gaelic language, sports, music, culture and arts to its captive audience as defined by the political realities of 20th / 21st century Northern Ireland. There seems little likelihood of that situation changing other than in the modest growth of Gaeldom's constituency, as recently occurred in East Belfast (ref. Chap 7) and also some colleges.*(14)

The other basis by which the British state threw a lifeline to Gaeil Ulaidh was through inter-governmental charters, namely the 1985 Hillsborough Accord (ref. Chap 5) and 1998 Belfast Peace Agreement (ref. Chap. 7). Both treaties explicitly acknowledged the legitimate place of Gaelic-Irish culture, both were underpinned by the UK and Irish governments, and each pledged restorative action to bring Gaeil Uladh inside the civic mainstream of the North.*(15)

3. _**Final Words**_ It seems a pity to park my pen when so much of the "Gaelic Neighbours" story is still evolving, with the final picture far from complete. After all, there is the prospect of

an Irish Language Act and appointment of an Irish Language Commissioner, while the Gaeilscoil movement continues to grow at nursery, primary, secondary and technical levels across the North. There is also the massive inroads made by Gaelic sport, arts and media to Northern Ireland's cultural forum. In Scotland, Gaelic-medium schooling is expanding, albeit at a more modest pace, but the biggest struggle is to halt the declining numbers of Gaelic speakers in the traditional Hebridean Gaidhealtachd. To that extent, the publicist work of An Comunn and its sister groups, along with a generous state fund, can only be positive, but nervous Scottish Gaels anxiously await the results of an impending 2022 Census for progress assessment.*(16)

Ultimately, the Gaelic story in both countries has been one of survival against historic and political odds. Those battles are ongoing, albeit in different forms. Of course, modern Irish and Scottish Gaels boast strong defences and voluntary campaigns, directed at a more beneficent British state than in times past. Whether current constitutional structures remain the same or change in either or both nations may have some bearing on the long terms prospects of the Gaelic language and culture? For now, it can only be assumed that current conditions point to some security of tenure and purpose, but nothing more.

The Gaels of Ulster and Scotland may yet have to resume in some form or other those battles for survival once braved by their fore bears? Time will tell?

FOOTNOTES and REFERENCES

1. Micheal O'Mainnin   'Ag Cor Cuarta: Leabhar DheanLeasa Moir, Clann Diarmada agus Fili Albanacha in <u>Lochtar Chonnact, Leann 5</u> (2018) 105-33 (Scottish poets in North Connacht).

    'Saig in Machal Fathuaid'- On the application and extent of 'The Machra' in North West Armagh. – Eriu_– Journal of the School of Irish Learning, Dublin, 60: 111-129.

    "The same in origin and in blood"; bardic windows on the relationship between Irish and Scottish Gaels in the period c. 1200-1650, Cambrian Medieval Celtic Studies 38 (Winter 1999), 1-51.

2. Wilson McLeod (1) <u>Gaelic in Scotland</u> (2020, EUP, Edinburgh), Chap 1.

    (2) 'The nature of minority languages: Insights from Scotland'. <u>Journal of Cross – Cultural and Inter-Language Communications</u>; 38, 2, pp 141-154 (Feb. 2019).

3. As a priest and Celtic scholar, unsurprisingly, Cardinal Tomas O'Fiaich's dominant interest lay with tracing the missionary trails of the early Gaelic monks. Among the late Cardinal's finest works are:

    <u>Irish Cultural Influence in Europe</u>, 6th to 12th century, Dublin, 1987.

    <u>Columbanus in His Own Words</u> (1974, Veritas, Dublin).

    'The Early Period' in Raymond O'Muiri (Eds) <u>Irish Church History Today</u>, pp 1-12, Armagh, 1997.

4. T.M. Devine <u>To the Ends of the Earth: Scotland's Global Diaspora, 1750-2010</u>; (2012, Penguin, London).

5. Brendan O'Leary (Vol. 1, 2020, Oxford University Press) – 1.3, 1.6 & 1.7.

6. Author's 1996 short publication – <u>Gaelic Nations: Politics of the Gaelic Language in Scotland and Northern Ireland</u> (Bluestack Press, London)

7. Reginald B. Hale <u>The Magnificent Gael</u> (1976, World Media Productions, Manitoba, Canada).

8. Reg Hindley <u>The Death of the Irish Language: A Qualified Obituary</u> (1990, Routledge, London). In particular, see Part 3, pp 161-257.

9. Listed earlier. Conchur O'Giollagain et al (eds), 2020, <u>Crisis of Scottish Gaelic</u> - Chaps 7 & 9.

10. See Ken MacKinnon <u>The Lion's Tongue</u> (1974) and <u>Gaelic: A Past and Future Prospect</u> (1991).

11. O'Leary (2020) – See Volume 3.

12. Although Dr/Monsignor Macaulay's celebrated 2016 publication, The Campaign for Catholic Emancipation in Ireland and England (Four Courts, Dublin), was probably his most erudite, actually this talented Belfast cleric has a series of learned biographies and texts to his distinction, largely focused on Ulster Catholic history.

13. It is worth recalling that the 1923 Church of Scotland General Assembly called on HMG to detain and deport Irish Catholics as politically-disloyal to the Protestant Empire and carriers of infectious disease. A subsequent Church Assembly in 2003 expressed "... shame and remorse ..." for its predecessor's actions, and tendered apologies to Scotland's Catholic population. It is also worthy of note that in May 1982 the Church of Scotland Moderator, Dr MacIntyre, publicly welcomed Pope John Paul 11 to Edinburgh. How times had changed! – See T.M. Devine (eds), <u>Scotland's Shame</u>. Also, Tom Gallagher, <u>Glasgow: The Uneasy Peace</u>.

14. Gaelic sports players – particularly with Gaelic football – from Protestant/Unionist backgrounds though infrequent, were not unknown. This was especially true of macho Rugby players and soccer goalkeepers, whose skills were naturally transferrable. During the mid-1970s, the GAA club at Belfast College of Business Studies (headed by this author!) recruited several key players from non-traditional backgrounds.

15. Paul Rouse, Mike Cronin & Mark Duncan <u>GAA: A Peoples History</u> (Abebooks, ISBN 9781848892255, Belfast/Dublin, 2009).

16. The Scottish Census Survey was delayed from 2021 to 2022 on account of dangers posed to enumerators, plus potential distortions of peoples' residential arrangements, by the Covid 19 Pandemic.

Appendix 1

CUMANN LUTHCHLEAS GAEL / GAELIC ATHLETIC ASSOCIATION

The Gaelic Athletic Association (GAA) is the prime authority managing, preserving and promoting Ireland's ancient Gaelic sports of Hurling (national sport), Camogie (women's Hurling), Gaelic Football and Gaelic Handball. It is organised on a 32-county All-Ireland basis, and has an estimated membership of over 550,000 that extends to most rural and urban parishes, along with schools, colleges and universities, the great majority of whom are participant young men and teenagers. In recent years, with the introduction of ladies football competitions, there has been a corresponding increase in young female membership. Leadership is normally exercised by middle-aged and older figures, with many being ex-players. As Ireland's largest amateur sports organisation, the GAA also has a loyal following among families and communities, with particular strength in rural areas across the island. So too has it developed support and organisations in Britain, USA and Australia.

Very significantly, the GAA asserts its solidarity with Conradh na Gaeilge in promotion of a Gaelic Ireland where the Irish language and Gaelic culture prevail at all levels. That goal has been constant since its formation. Its HQ at Croke Park, Dublin, has been oft-times re-developed to the point of now hosting over 80,000 spectators as the fifth-largest sports stadium in Europe.

Founded in November 1884 in Thurles, Co Tipperary, from the beginning the Association constituted a nationalist vehicle for the Gaelic cultural revival. Gaelic sports were a mechanism for popularising Gaelic culture among the people, which was already under way with the language, arts and literacy revival headed by Conradh na Gaeilge/Gaelic League. Most GAA founders were or had been active Fenians, as well as IRB figures, although Catholic ecclesiastics like Archbishops' Thomas Croke and McHale, along with Charles Parnell and other leaders of the Irish Parliamentary Party, also endorsed the movement.*(1) From 1900 onwards, links between the IRB and GAA were pronounced, and influenced the adoption of certain contentious GAA rules.

Among divisive regulations was the former Rule 27, which prohibited members from either playing or spectating at so-called "foreign sports", meaning Soccer, Rugby, Hockey and Cricket. This was extended in 1920 to include a blanket ban on Gaelic players taking part in all athletics meetings other than those organised by the pro-GAA National Athletics and Cycling Association (NACA). Rule 27 aimed at facilitating the spread of Gaelic sports and strengthening the Irish identity among the nationalist people by eliminating cross-channel popular contenders. However, to its critics, it appeared narrow-minded, xenophobic and an intolerable affront to the liberty of all citizens to choose their own sports. While finally abolished at the 1971 Congress – staged at Queens University, Belfast – until then Rule 27 hung like an albatross around the GAA's neck as a symbol of entrenched bigotry, small-mindedness and a repressive check on Gaelic sport's broader mission to aid the growth of a democratic and inclusive Irish nation.*(2) It also meant that in practice for much of the 20th century the GAA held great sway in rural areas, where recreational facilities were limited and people concentrated into close-knit communities. Additionally, until the growth of telecommunications and large-scale domestic car ownership, along with popular access to competitive secondary and higher education in the 1970s and '80s, those privations all worked in favour of the GAA's culture of restrictive practices.

For one thing, Rule 27 utterly divided society in Northern Ireland, with most Protestants shunning all associations with the GAA and its games.*(3) Secondly, large areas of the North, including nationalist areas like Derry City, North Belfast and even large parts of Newry and Downpatrick remained outside GAA dominance. This was partly out of resentment at the GAA's political prejudices, and partly because soccer was well-established in those areas with long-established leagues and clubs like the former Belfast Celtic, Newry Town, Derry City, Cliftonville, Immaculata and Downpatrick Rec., plus a string of great Catholic players like Pat Jennings, Joe Toner, Jimmy McGrory, Harry McCurry and a youthful Martin O'Neill – all of whom achieved great distinction in the professional game. Indeed as a school boy in North Antrim in 1970, this author (a loyal Hurler) learned to his great discomfort that the glamour of Down's 1968 All-Ireland winners had impacted only marginally on many young fellow students, some of whom had never kicked or hurled a ball under GAA rules. Not for them this author's Sam Maguire Cup-winning Down heroes of 1968, but rather Celtic's 1967 'Lisbon lions', plus successive Arsenal and Manchester Utd teams, laced with Irish players in apparent perpetuity!*(4)

Nor did the GAA achieve a wholly smooth run in Southern society. Although rural recruitment proved successful, both before and after independence in 1922, its insinuations of exclusive patriotism were resented by supporters of Irish rugby (IRFU) and the nascent soccer movement that later blossomed into the League of Ireland.*(5) It is important to remember that while some independence leaders like Michael Collins and Harry Boland were ardent Gaelic sportsmen (along with Collins's fellow Cork native, Sam Maguire, for whom the All-Ireland Senior Football trophy is named!), others were not. De Valera, for example, had been a rugby stalwart all his life, and several top Catholic colleges, e.g. Terenure and Blackrock, Dublin, run by the Holy Ghost Fathers and headed by the mercurial future Archbishop of Dublin, John Charles McQuaid, were rugby-playing establishments, then as now.*(6) The executed medical student, Kevin Barry, had also been a Rugby and Cricket player, and there were many others. As for soccer, 1916 republican activist, later Fianna Fail TD and Defence Minister, Oscar Traynor, had been goalkeeper with Belfast Celtic FC 1910-12, and later President of the Football Association of Ireland (FAI). *(7) He openly challenged the GAA to be rid of its "foreign games" mentality, and accept "...the plurality of all sports in a free Ireland".*(8)

Perhaps the greatest affront to the infant Irish state emanating from Rule 27 occurred with the Douglas Hyde affair in November 1938. An international football game at Dalymount Park, Dublin, between the Irish Free State and Poland, was sponsored by Oscar Traynor and attended by De Valera, then Taoiseach, along with the new Irish President, himself founder of the Gaelic League back in 1891 and a patriotic Gaelic scholar, Dr Douglas Hyde. Of course Dr Hyde's attendance amounted to diplomatic courtesy, as befits the office of head of state, not to mention welcoming Ireland's Polish visitors. Moreover, it is worth recalling that vulnerable and long-scarred Poland had just emerged 18 years earlier as an independent nation, and was destined only 10 months later to be carved up between the barbarous Nazi and Soviet invaders as World War 2 unleashed. Surely there was a case for Catholic Ireland befriending its Slavonic sister nation? Of course those basic considerations were lost on a xenophobic GAA leadership obsessed with its own dubious in-house rules.

President Hyde was rebuked and promptly stripped of his GAA patronage.*(9) This action provoked a near-consensus of outrage from all political parties in Dail Eireann, plus the Catholic Church and Church of Ireland (to which Hyde belonged), Irish media, Conradh na Gaeilge and, most robustly, An Taoiseach, Eamon de Valera.*(10) It would indeed be hard to overstate the immense embarrassment felt by modern generations of GAA figures at their predecessors' actions.*(11) However, de Valera's anger at this affront to the office and person of the Irish Free State's first citizen was vented most poignantly in a meeting with GAA President, Seamus Gardiner, and General Secretary, Padraig O'Caoimh. Indeed all reports of the time point to O'Caoimh and Gardiner beating a very sheepish retreat from the de Valera meeting, desperately unhinged and anxious to rebuild bridges with the Irish state.*(12) It is significant that O'Caoimh, was a long-standing de Valera political supporter from Civil War days, as indeed were so many GAA Southern club and county officials of that time. Hardly surprising that after 1945, when clearly the Free State's War-time neutrality had cost much political good will from Allied powers (with the USSR blocking Irish entry to the United Nations until 1955), De Valera was desperate to rebuild bridges abroad. Only by repairing those strains, could De Valera hope to regain overseas trade and foreign currency, on which the fragile Irish economy – then wreaked by emigration – so depended.

Therefore, marketing Southern Ireland abroad in a positive way was of the essence. The GAA's contrition for the Douglas Hyde debacle was underlined by its swift willingness to assist Mr de Valera's lobbyist efforts by staging the 1947 All-Ireland Gaelic Football final (Cavan v Kerry) at the Polo Grounds, New York, complete with all the accompanying publicity and pioneering radio broadcasts. Yet notwithstanding the latter, the wonder is how after the earlier crass display of ineptitude, still the GAA retained that same discredited Rule 27 for another 33 years? Needless to add, its eventual removal in 1971 was lamented by few on the outside ... and even fewer on the inside!

Another deeply divisive regulation was Rule 21, introduced in 1908 under IRB pressure, so as to ward off risks of military and police spies at a time when many GAA activists doubled as IRB/Sinn Fein volunteers. *(13) This regulation prohibited British soldiers and police officers from joining, and forbade GAA members from having cultural or diplomatic connections, or accepting financial or material inducements from British security forces.*(14) Yet as the research and writings of Dr Donal McAnallen reveal, over the past century the GAA operated Rule 21 inconsistently, most especially during World War 1. Then, so many Gaelic players from all over Ireland enlisted with Irish regiments in the British Army for service in Flanders, France and elsewhere.*(15) Thousands lost their lives, while the number of gallantry medals was impressive.*(16)

Two factors worked towards the long term consolidation of the "military and police ban". First, was the experience of the Irish War of Independence, when atrocities committed by Crown forces over 1919-21, most especially the infamous 'Black and Tans', sullied relations between Britain and Ireland for generations. The Crown forces attack on Croke Park during a Gaelic Football match in November 1920 (in retaliation for a string of IRA assassinations earlier that same day) was a particular low point, and recalled in the GAA's collective memory over the next century.*(17) Significantly, IRA atrocities – of which there were many throughout the same period - were set aside, and indeed many leading 'martyred' figures eulogised in the naming of GAA grounds and clubs, e.g. Kevin Barry, Terence McSweeney and Roger Casement, for whom the Ulster GAA stadium in Belfast was named at its opening in 1956.

Second, was the post-1921 experience of nationalist people in Northern Ireland after partition. The hostility of the Stormont Unionist regime towards the North's nationalist population was consistently reflected in a jaundiced policy by RUC, B Specials/UDR and the British Army towards nationalist representatives and their institutions, including the GAA.*(18) These included Gaelic sports players and clubs, who frequently endured Unionist hostility, as well as police and military suspicions. The military intrusions to Crossmaglen GAA grounds as well as Casement Park, Belfast, were matched by several Loyalist attacks on Gaelic players and premises.*(19) There were also the infamous murders of individual nationalists, like the Miami Showband outside Banbridge, Co Down in July 1975, the slaying of three Gaelic-football-playing Reavey brothers of Whitecross, Co Armagh on 4th January 1976, and shooting-dead of pro-republican Belfast solicitor, John Finucane, in 1989. Additionally, there occurred a murderous assault on a country pub in Loughinisland, County Down (June 1994), resulting in the deaths of 7 customers, including an 87 years old pensioner, Mr Barney Green, none with paramilitary affiliations. While most attacks were accurately attributed to Loyalist paramilitaries, credible evidence emerged of collusion between UVF/UDA assassins and shadowy elements in the UDR and RUC Reserve.*(20) Additionally, the policy of BBC N.I. and Ulster Television in keeping Gaelic games off-air until the 1970s, did nothing to melt the ice with the GAA or its province-wide constituency.

For its part, the GAA somewhat dragged its feet over co-operation with police and civic authorities in basic security matters. Also, there was an insistence on flying the Irish tricolour at all events, even in 'mixed areas' of the North where such displays risked inflaming community tensions. Furthermore, certain GAA county and club authorities were happy to nourish republican support and facilitate collections for republican prisoner funds, while repudiating the few Catholic youths joining the Royal Ulster Constabulary. Another GAA practice of dedicating clubs and premises in memory of IRA 'martyr' figures – many with questionable records – also aroused widespread Protestant angst. Finally, there was the fact that since the Second World War Rule 21 was unofficially ignored by the GAA in Great Britain. A mixture of National Service realities, plus the high numbers of Irish-born and second generation serving as British police officers across England and Scotland, would have made its enforcement barely viable for player recruitment in Catholic communities.*(21) As a result, in places like London and Birmingham several leading club and county players were serving officers of the Metropolitan and West Midlands forces.

In the circumstances, there was little prospect of movement on either side. Most especially, the GAA was ultra-defensive about its Rule 21, and resisted all initiatives aimed at opening up Gaelic games to a wider and non-nationalist following that might have resulted from removal of political hurdles. As has been explained in the mainstream script, political progress that began in 1985 with the Anglo-Irish Agreement and subsequent Belfast Good Friday Accord of April 1998, paved the way for general civic reconciliation and new openings. Then came the 2001 Patten Report on security. As a result, the RUC replacement by a PSNI, and merger of the UDR into a new Royal Irish Regiment, were among the key events that encouraged nationalists and their communal organisations to take a more positive role in civic affairs, including support for the new Police Service of Northern Ireland and justice system.

The GAA's removal of its Rule 21 in November 2001 was widely welcomed as long overdue in most quarters both North and South.*(22) Accordingly, amongst those signing up for positive participation in the new Ireland were the GAA, Gaelic League and sister organisations all composing Gaeil Uladh. As a result of that major change, the GAA found itself rapidly drawn into a positive new sporting partnership alongside the Irish Football Association (Northern Ireland soccer authority) and Ulster Rugby. The latter ensured a raft of public grants and entitlements, plus an active media profile, previously denied to earlier generations of Ulster Gaels.*(23) It also meant the GAA's incorporation to the mainstream of Ulster sporting and cultural life. That story is more fully covered in the major script of Chapters 5 and 7.

FOOTNOTES and REFERENCES

1.

    (i) David Fitzpatrick 'Ireland since 1870'; Chap 7, pp 180-189 – R.F. Foster (Eds.) <u>The Oxford History of Ireland</u> (OUP, Oxford, 1993).

    (ii) R.F. Foster <u>Modern Ireland 1600-1972</u>, Chaps 17 & 18 (Allen-Lane/Penguin, London, 1988).

    (iii) A less academic, impressionistic, but entertaining account was that by Paul Rouse – <u>The Hurlers: The First All-Ireland Championship and Making of Modern Hurling</u> (Penguin, London, 2019).

2. J. Sugden 'Sport, Community Relations and Community Conflict in Northern Ireland'; p. 203, in Seamus Dunn (eds), <u>Facets of the Conflict in Northern Ireland</u> (Macmillan, London, 2001).

3. As is common knowledge, Celtic (Glasgow) and Hibernian (Edinburgh) were each founded by Irish clerics, Bro Walfred and Canon Hannin respectively, while Manchester Utd has always been a kernel for Irish talent from each side of the border. So too has Arsenal long been a favourite among North London's Irish community, and in the 1980 FA Cup final lined out with a total of 8 players from both parts of Ireland.

4. See Terence Brown <u>Ireland: A Social and Cultural History 1922-2002</u> Chaps 2 & 3, pp 35 -91.

5. John Cooney <u>John Charles McQuaid: Ruler of Catholic Ireland</u> (O'Brien Press, Dublin, 1999).

6. R. Holt <u>Sport and the British: A Modern History</u>, p. 240 – Cited in N. Garnham – <u>Association Football and Society in pre-Partition Ireland</u>, p. 135 (Ulster Historical Foundation, Belfast, 2004).

7. See Brian Hanley – 'Oscar Traynor: Unconventional Republican' – <u>History Ireland</u>, Issue 1, Vol 24, Jan/Feb 2016.

8. Ibid.

9. Brian Murphy <u>Forgotten Patriot: Douglas Hyde & the Foundation of the Irish Presidency</u> (Collins Press, Cork, 2016); Chap. 5, pp 151-158.

10. Ibid.

11. Ref. Discussions with Ulster GAA Secretary, Brian McAvoy, who interpreted the affair as "…. reflecting the thinking of a by-gone era".

12. At a meeting held with de Valera on 17th August 1945, O'Caoimh and Gardiner made what amounted to a de-facto apology for their organisation's earlier treatment of President Hyde. Very significantly, the GAA's Central Council acceded immediately to de Valera's demand that as a future patron the President was not bound by the narrow limits of the GAA's "… foreign games mentality …" and would exercise his discretion to attend and honour all games involving the Irish people whether it accorded with GAA thinking or not. Faced with such a fierce excoriation from Taoiseach, Opposition leader, Church and press, the GAA quickly moved compliantly to rebuild its bridges. –See Murphy, pp 151-158.

13. Donal McAnallen (Eds) Reflections on the Revolution in Ulster: Excerpts from Rev. Louis O'Kane's Recordings of Irish Volunteers (Cardinal O'Fiaich Archive, Armagh, 2015).

14. See GAA Official Guide 2000.

15. Donal McAnallen Forgotten Gaelic Volunteers: Ulster GAA Members who fought in World War One (Cardinal O'Fiaich Archive, Armagh, 2019).

16. Ibid.

17. Foster (1988), Chaps 19 & 20. Also, S.J. Connolly Oxford Companion to Irish History (OUP, 2007); pp 222-226.

18. See O'Leary Volume 2, The Second Protestant Ascendancy and the Irish State (OUP, 2019); Chaps 2.2 – to 2.6.

19. Paul Bew and Gordon Gillespie Northern Ireland: A Chronology of the Troubles 1968-1993.

20. A typical example of sectarian Loyalist attacks on GAA clubs was the 1975 burning of the McKenna Gaelic Centre, operated by St Joseph's GAA Hurling Club, Ballycran, near Newtownards, Co Down.

21. National Service in the British armed forces and/or Merchant Navy was compulsory for all young British males for 18-24 months from the end of World War 2 in 1945 until its abolition in 1960. Only Northern Ireland was exempt from National Service.

22. Only hard-line republican irreconcilables centred around the break-away 'Republican Sinn Fein' and the 'Real IRA' opposed the GAA's removal of its political ban on RUC and British Army personnel.

23. Paul Rouse, Mike Cronin & Mark Duncan   GAA: A Peoples History (ISBN-9781848892255; Abebooks, 2009, London/Dublin).

OBITUARY - PROFESSOR KENNETH MACKINNON

Reprinted by kind permission of the Glasgow Herald

Londoner who became leading Gaelic linguist and historian

Professor Kenneth MacKinnon
Born: August 26, 1933
Died: May 21, 2021

It says much for the pull of the Gaelic world that there is a place for everyone. The pages of Irish and Scottish history abound with many 'born-again' Gaels, who have taken to Celtic medium with a vigour defying all prejudice. Ken MacKinnon was a most distinguished convert.

He wasn't quite the full stranger, in that his parents were of Scottish and Northern Irish roots, but his upbringing in London – as evidenced by his life-long Cockney accent – told its own story. Yet this same man forsook a promising career in 1960/1970s Liberal politics to embrace the Gaelic language that he had grown to love.

Given his research achievements over the ensuing 40 years, especially after he moved to Scotland in 1985, Ken's passing has been mourned throughout Gaeldom.

His commitment to the language and culture was inspiring; his advocacy on a par with the ablest contemporaries, his intellectual mind so driven and productive; and yet all governed by the heartfelt principles of his Christian faith. Ken was called to a Lay Preacher ministry in the Methodist Church, a role that he practised vigorously all his life.

In 1939, at the outbreak of war, he was among the many thousands of children who were evacuated from east London to the countryside. He thus spent the war in scenic Cornwall, and this gave him a taste for country living that remained with him all his life.

After peace returned, this talented working-class boy grafted his way through the secondary school system to gain a place at the London School of Economics, where he attained joint honours in Economics and Sociology.

Thereafter, it was National Service with the Royal Artillery, and a two-year posting in Germany. Returning to a teaching career in Essex secondary schools, he was later appointed to head Social Sciences at Barking Technical College.

By now married to Rosalie, and with family on the way, they moved to Southend-on-Sea, where Ken's Liberal affiliations saw him elected to the local council. He eventually became Mayor in 1965.

Notwithstanding a secure teaching career, and a political profile that promised further advance, somehow Ken – as he told me later – felt that his vocation lay in another direction.

Already he had learned Scottish Gaelic at night-school, but was drawn deeper. An M.A. in Sociology and Celtic Linguistics led to a Senior Fellowship with the Social Sciences Research Council, which in turn led to a language research venture on the isle of Harris, in 1972-1974.

From this point, his academic career was re-launched as a Gaelic linguist and historian. He also made the transition to Hatfield Polytechnic (later renamed the University of Hertfordshire), as a sociology and linguistics lecturer, a position that enabled him to pursue research interests more readily.

Over the next three decades, he researched and wrote prodigiously on all aspects of Gaelic in education and the communities. While his principal concern was the survival of Scottish Gaeldom, his scope extended to Scottish migrant Gaels in Nova Scotia, as well as Gaelic-Ulster, Isle of Man, Wales and Brittany.

So also did he pursue the theme of minority languages such as Scots/Lallans, Manx, Welsh, Cornish and Breton, lecturing and writing passionately, wearing his academic cap and others besides. He wrote *The Lion's Tongue* (1974), followed by the acclaimed *Gaelic: A Past & Future Prospect* (1991), which became standard reading for all serious students of Scottish Gaelic.

His Harris study, published as *Language, Education and Social Processes in a Gaelic Community* (1977), marked the first searching analysis of Census data linked to Gaelic usage in recent times. It was eagerly welcomed by the Celtic Studies departments in three Scottish universities, as well as An Comunn Gàidhealach in Inverness.

In 1981 Ken headed a national survey for An Comunn exploring public attitudes towards Gaelic, while in 1994-95 he conducted the first major study into domestic treatment of Gaelic, leading to *Gaelic in Family, Work and Community Domains; Euromosaic Project 1994/95* (1998).

As Professor Robert Dunbar of Edinburgh University commented, Ken's research in the 1990s"... established benchmarks, and standards of excellence, which have underpinned essentially all subsequent work".

Over those three decades Ken published 35 scholarly research papers on assorted aspects of Gaelic education, identity, family and communities, plus his major books.

His writing continued post-millennium, when in collaboration with two Ulster Gaelic academics, Dr Gordon McCoy and Maolcholaim Scott, he produced Neighbours in Persistence: Prospects for Gaelic Maintenance in a Globalising World (2000).

Academic recognition followed, with his appointment to a senior tutorship in the Open University and, later, Honorary Gaelic Fellowships conferred by Aberdeen and Edinburgh Universities.

His mercurial research and writing work was appreciated by the struggling Scottish Gaelic establishment. When Comunn na Gaidhlig was founded in 1984 as an institutional advisory body, he was appointed to it, and played a major role over the years ahead.

He was also a key figure in a Ministerial Advisory Group headed by Professor Donald Meek, which recommended the creation of a statutory Gaelic regulatory authority, Bord na Gaidhlig. It emerged from the 2005 Gaelic Language (Scotland) Act, with Ken appointed and re-appointed to it.

In his last years, though burdened by weakening health, Ken never gave up on his Gaelic interests. He read and wrote with customary passion, while nurturing the extra time spent with his loving wife, Rosalie, and family members: they had two children, Niall and Morag.

Typical of his kindness, he proved to be an encouraging mentor to younger researchers, including this author.

Dr Vincent McKee

SELECT GLOSSARY OF TITLES, NAMES AND ORGANISATIONS

---

1. SCOTLAND/ALBANNAICH

Gaidhlig: - Gaelic in the Scottish dialect.

Gaidheil na h-Alba/'Gaels of Scotland':- A wide-ranging term that embraces the plurality of Gaelic-speakers, districts, learners, cultural activists, poets, teachers, musicians, singers, dramatists, educationalists, writers and political campaigners, both individually and in their various organisations. Term applies not just to the Scottish-based Gaelic community, but also Gaelic speakers and cultural participants located in Scottish diaspora, e.g. Canada and Australasia.

Gaidhealtachd: - A community of Gaelic first-language speakers and pro-active learners; e.g. Isle of Lewis, Isle of Barra, Skye and Oban, etc. Important to note that the term applies equally both in singular and plural tenses.

An Comunn Gaidhealach: - Scotland's oldest national Gaelic lobbyist group; founded in 1891 at Oban. Organiser of the National Gaelic Mod; head office at Inverness. Current Patron: - H.M. The Queen. Past patrons have included His late Majesty, King George V, and H.M. Queen Elizabeth, The Queen Mother (sadly deceased). Distinguished past executives include the late Mr Donald John Mackay (Director 1965-70), from North Uist, Outer Hebrides, to whose life's work and hallowed memory this book is co-dedicated. (See Chaps 2 & 7).

Acair:- Present-day Gaelic publisher, based in Stornoway, Isle of Lewis: / Club Leabhar (Highlands Book Club) - its long running predecessor.

Comhairle nan Leabhraichean:- Gaelic Books Council, based at Glasgow, and currently headed by Miss Alison Lang, Stiuiriche/Director. This body assists with the publication and promotion of Gaelic medium books and books friendly to the interests of Gaelic culture and/or history across Scotland.

BBC Alba: - Scottish Gaelic Television channel.

Radio na Gaidhlig: - National Gaelic Radio – all Scotland.

<u>'Can Seo'</u>: - Gaelic learner series, commenced by BBC Scotland in Autumn 1993.

<u>Comataidh Telebhisean Gaidhlig</u>: - Gaelic Television Authority founded in 1990.

<u>'Machair'</u>:- First ever Gaelic soap opera, broadcast by STV, and ran from 1993-1999. This production starred the distinguished Gaelic actor and singer from the Isle of Harris, Mr Simon Mackenzie – sadly now deceased.

<u>Royal National Mod</u>: - Show-piece festival of Scottish Gaelic music, dancing, choir and individual singing, instrumentalism, recitation, drama, poetry and all manner of Gaelic culture. Staged annually by An Comunn Gaidhealach for over 130 years, this festival is broadcast to the nation and attended by Royalty. The event rotates between various towns and cities around Scotland. Its gold medal winners have in many instances gone on to greater things; e.g. the late Lewis-born Gaelic singer and TV presenter, Calum Kennedy, and 1981 chart-topping performer, Mary Sandeman/'Aneka' – singing 'Japanese Boy'. Another talented Lewis native, Mr Donald John Maciver, was crowned 'Bard of the Mod' in recognition of his many books, poems and educational initiatives in promotion of Gaelic. Indeed the gentleman's outstanding life's work for the Gaelic language, as Bilingual Educational Adviser to Comhairle nan Eilean Siar and Comunn na Gaidhlig, writer, poet and advocate are why this book is co-dedicated to his memory. Sadly, Mr Maciver passed away in 2015.

<u>Gaelic Society of London</u>: - An Comunn's London sister group, established in 1890s, and catering for the cultural, educational and social needs of Scottish Gaelic migrants in the UK capital. Also exerted a subtle influence with lobbying government on behalf of the Gaelic language and its interests. Liaised closely with An Comunn in Inverness. Additional Gaelic lobbyist societies were established in Inverness, Glasgow and Edinburgh, all with similar functions.

<u>Comunn na Gaidhlig</u>: - "Council of the Gaels". This body was created in 1984 by a joint initiative of Gaelic lobbyist groups and the Scottish Office, the latter having endowed it with a suitable annual grant. The aim was to co-ordinate the various Gaelic voluntary organisations, and to act as a unified voice for the cause of Scottish Gaeldom. In the latter respect, the founding goals were fulfilled, not least due to the pioneering work and exceptional lobbyist skills of its early director, Mr John Angus Mackay, OBE, who was positively profiled by his biographer, Mr Roy Pederson, as the 'Gaelic Guerilla'! (See Chap. 4)

<u>Bord na Gaidhlig</u>: - Statutory Gaelic national authority, created under the terms of the Scottish Gaelic Language Act of 2005. Funded by the Scottish devolved government, with a chief executive and Holyrood-appointed members, this body operates from a headquarters in Inverness. Its role is to set and enforce basic rules for the implementation of Gaelic provision by employers, public and private organisations, while evaluating developments elsewhere.(See Chap 6)

<u>Comhairle nan Eileann Siar</u>: - Western Isles Council in Outer Hebrides. Established in 1975 as a purposeful Gaelic, single-tier authority, with a head office in Stornoway, Isle of Lewis. Officially bilingual! Authority's boundaries run co-terminus with those of Western Isles Westminster and Holyrood seats.

<u>Comunn na Camain Albannaich</u>: - A 1980/90s Scottish Gaelic campaigning society, modelled on the Welsh Language Society and Conradh na Gaeilge in Northern Ireland. Not so influential, but acted as a publicist for Gaelic radicals.

<u>Siol Nan Gaidheal/ "Seed of the Gael"</u>: - A radical late 1960s/early70s Scottish Gaelic campaigning group that favoured direct action.

<u>Comhairle Nan Sgoiltean Araich</u>: - 1990s/post-millennium Gaelic Medium Playgroups Council, based at Inverness. Radical in orientation. Founding lead figure – Mr Finlay Macleod.

<u>Comunn an Luchd-Ionnsachaidh</u>: - Scottish Gaelic Learners Association, based at Dingwall.   <u>Cli Gaidhlig</u>:- Gaelic Learners Group.

<u>Feiseann na Gaidheal</u>: - A publicly-sponsored organisation that organises and co-ordinates local Gaelic feiseann (singing, choirs, musical, poetry and drama festivals) in villages, towns and islands among young people across the Highlands and Hebrides. Employs a limited number of full and part-time field officers to organise events and liaise with schools and local councils; amongst them the distinguished Gaelic singer, Mod gold medallist, broadcaster and former Chair of Bord na Gaidhlig, Mr Arthur Cormack, from Isle of Skye. Another talented figure to have emerged from the Feiseann experience is the acclaimed Gaelic instrumentalist, frequently appearing on both Gaelic and mainstream television and radio, Mr Blair Douglas, also from Skye. Feiseann na Gaidheal head office is at Inverness. (See Chaps 4 & 6)

<u>Faclair na Parlamid</u>: - Gaelic dictionary of Scottish Parliamentary business.

<u>Gaidheal Sgoil</u>: - Gaelic medium school.

Proiseacht nan Eilean: - National Gaelic Arts Project, with office in Stornoway, Isle of Lewis, and funded by Scottish Office grant.

Sabhal Mor Ostaig: - Located in Isle of Skye, Inner Hebrides. Founded in 1972 as first-ever Gaelic Further Education institute, the college has since developed as a trainer of Gaelic-medium teachers, as well as educating Gaelic learners and technical students taught through the medium of Gaelic. Since 2009, the college has been an affiliate of the University of Highlands and Islands.

Shinty/Camanachd: - A long-running sport of Scottish Gaels, popular in Skye and parts of the West Highlands, along with migrant Highland communities in Glasgow and Edinburgh. Played with sticks, and similar to the Irish national sport of Hurling. Administered by the Camanachd Association, whose lead figure is Scottish journalist & media commentator, Mr Hugh Dan MacLennan. Over past decades, intermittent games have been held between Irish Hurling and Scottish Shinty selections under compromise rules. Links rather tenuous! Also, though having definite appeal among Highlanders and some Hebrideans, in reality Shinty lacks the broad-based and popular appeal of Hurling in Ireland.

'Runrig' and 'Capercaille': - Two well-known Gaelic 'rock' groups, both from the Outer Hebrides who have each achieved distinction on a nation-wide stage.

Ian Crichton-Smith: - Nationally-renowned bilingual poet and author, native of the Isle of Lewis – sadly deceased.

2. IRELAND/EIREANN – ULSTER/ULADH

<u>Gaeilge</u>: - Gaelic in the Irish dialect.

<u>Gaelgeoir</u>: - Term used to describe a passionate Gaeilge language speaker or learner, and also Gaelic cultural and/or sports activist. – Used in Ireland, but less so Scotland. Because of the circumstances of Northern Ireland, it normally followed that Gaelgeoiri were persons of decidedly-nationalist political views.

<u>Gaeltacht</u>: - A residential community of Irish Gaelic speakers. Plurality of such communities = Gaeltachtai. It is important to note that spellings vary to a minor degree between the different dialects of Connacht, Munster and Ulster, as well as Scotland. Also, the Irish Gaeiltachtai compose two important segments. One is the traditional native-speaking communities, such as remain in Donegal and Connemara, but were more prevalent a century ago. The second is the Nua Gaeltachtai/New Gaeltachts, consisting of Gaelic learners and second language speakers, of which a small community functions in Meath, but the much larger and politically-supported community is that of West Belfast. The latter is now recognised by Belfast City Council, which designated the Gaeltacht Quarter.

<u>Uladh</u>: - Ulster   <u>Beal Feirste</u>: - Belfast   <u>Dhoire</u>: - Derry   <u>Ard Macha</u>: - Armagh

<u>Gaeil Uladh/Gaels of Ulster</u>: - Wide-ranging term that embraces the entirety of Gaelic Ulster. Includes Gaeilge language, Ulster division of Conradh na Gaeilge, other language groups like Gael Linn, Gaeilge medium schools, Gaelic artists, poets, dramatists, literary groups and literary figures, along with musicians, teachers, Gaelic sportsmen and women in Cumann Lutchchleas Gael, plus organisations like Forbairt Feirste, Glor na nGael, Gaelic broadcasters, writers and political advocates. All the main nationalist political parties, such as Sinn Fein and SDLP, are overtly aligned to the vanguard of Gaeil Uladh. Also, fair to say that the Roman Catholic Church in Northern Ireland has been a long term supporter of Gaelic sports, language and culture (See Chaps 3, 6 & 7).

<u>Conradh na Gaeilge/Gaelic League</u>: - Founded in 1893 jointly by Dr Douglas Hyde and Professor Eoin MacNeill, succeeding the older Society for Defence of the Irish Language. Over a relatively short time-span, 1893-1910, Conradh na Gaeilge became the premier Gaelic revivalist body, that co-ordinated some 300 local branches springing up across the island of Ireland. Main activities being the development of community-based Gaeilge teaching,

encouragement of Gaelic feiseann and other festivals in the various communities across the whole of Ireland, including the North; defence of the Gaeltachtai, promotion of the Irish language in schools and universities, and latterly media, arts and drama. Ultimately, Conradh na Gaeilge has had to depend on the sympathy and sponsorship of governments in both jurisdictions of Ireland. Also, CnG has liaised and co-operated with other language revivalist bodies, and, where appropriate, government bodies in Dublin, Belfast and London. Over recent decades, the leadership of C.n.G. has passed into leadership of Ulster radicals like Mr Gearoid O'Caireallain, long-time editor of La (Gaelic newspaper), and latterly Dr Neil Colmer, Gaeilge Studies lecturer at University of Ulster, Derry. During the mid-1970s, former Gaeilge professor at University of Ulster, Dr Diarmuid O'Doibhlin (sadly deceased), was Chairman of Derry County GAA.

Bord na Gaeilge: - Former statutory advisory body for Gaelic affairs in the Republic of Ireland. – Replaced after the ratification of the 1998 Good Friday Agreement by an all-Ireland authority, Foras na Gaeilge.

Comhaltas Uladh: - Recognised since 1926 as Ulster affiliate of the Gaelic League.

Radio Telefis Eireann: - National broadcaster in Republic of Ireland, whose coverage extends to much, but not all of Northern Ireland. Nationalists in N.I. have frequently accused RTE managers and the Southern establishment of being too comfortable with current arrangements, and unwilling to properly embrace events and people in the North. – TG4: - Southern-funded Gaeilge-medium Television Channel. Gives much coverage to Gaelic games and culture.

Ard Scoil, Beal Feirste: - The Gaelic League school in central Belfast, which ran multiple classes, hosted major Gaelic cultural events, and awarded certificates and Gaeltacht scholarships to the residual body of Ulster Gaelgeoiri. Hampered by the refusal of the Northern Ireland Ministry of Education, during pre-1972 days of Stormont Unionist rule, to recognise its certificates and grading system. The Ard Scoil was accidentally destroyed by a fire in 1975.

Feis an Dun: - Feis of Down. Traditionally staged at St Patrick's Park, Newcastle (Co Down), but in more recent years moved between Castlewellan and Newry. Involves Irish language, history, drama, poetry, recitation, dance, choir and individual singing competitions, followed by Hurling, Camogie and Gaelic Football competitions with pipe bands. – First held in 1904, and staged every year thereafter. A de-facto joint enterprise between the Gaelic League and

GAA. In 1950, the Oration (ie. lead speech) at Newcastle was delivered by Eamon de Valera, at that time Oppostion Fianna Fail Leader in Dail Eireann, former/future Taoiseach and eventual President of Ireland.

Feis Na nGleann: - Feis of the Glens - of Antrim. First staged in 1904, and traditionally held at Cushendall and Glenariff/Waterfoot, but also moved around between Loughgiel, Armoy and Dunloy. Held almost every year since the first event. Follows the same cultural and musical agenda as the Feis an Dun, but for sports the emphasis is placed on Hurling. (See Chaps 3 & 5)

Feis an Feirste: - Belfast Feis. – Follows a similar line to other county feiseann.

Glor na nGael: - An independent Six Counties Irish language body, concerned with promoting Gaelic teaching to the wider community. Fought a battle with the Northern Ireland Office to regain funding after the Unionist/Tory Minister, Dr Brian Mawhinney, temporarily stopped funding in 1989, accusing the organisation of being "...a cover for the IRA and Sinn Fein.." in West Belfast. The campaign, which drew major support from abroad, as well as Cardinal Tomas O'Fiaich in Armagh, was eventually successful. (See Chap 6)

Gael Linn: - An Irish language action group, publishing literature and working in North and South.

Cumann Luthchleas Gael/Gaelic Athletic Association (Copiously described and analysed in Chaps 5 & 7, along with Appendix 1). The promotional and governing body for Ireland's two national sports, Hurling and Gaelic Football, along with its sister-body, The Camogie Association, catering for women's Hurling. Founded in 1884, the GAA is Ireland's largest sporting body with some 550,000 members and active organisations in each of the 32 counties. From the beginning, the GAA was an all-Ireland body, dedicated to promoting Gaelic games as part of the popular Gaelicisation of the people, in collaboration with the Gaelic League and other pro-Gaelic cultural organisations.

Pairc an Crocaigh/Croke Park (Dublin): - Headquarters and premier stadium of the GAA, and with All-Ireland Hurling and Gaelic Football finals and semi-finals normally staged there. Other major Gaelic sports stadia include: Casement Park, Belfast; St Tiernach's Park, Clones, Co Monaghan; GAA Athletic Grounds, Armagh City; Fitzgerald Stadium, Killarney, Co Kerry; Parnell Park, Dublin; McHale Park, Castlebar, Co Mayo; Pearse Stadium, Galway; Pairc O'Caoimh, Cork; GAA Sports Grounds, Limerick; & Semple Stadium, Thurles, Co Tipperary. Significantly, Croke Park received a visit by HM The Queen and

HRH Prince Philip (sadly since deceased) on her 2011 state visit to the Irish Republic.

Foras na Gaeilge: - The all-Ireland Gaelic Language executive body, jointly appointed and funded by the governments of Southern Ireland and Northern Ireland respectively. This body was created in 1999, following adoption of the 1998 Belfast Peace Accord, and has offices and full-time staff in Dublin and Belfast. It was charged with two principal tasks: first, as an advisory body to the Dublin and N.I. governments, and, second, as a distributer of public funds to appropriate organisations. Foras has attracted criticism over the years, especially from supporters of La, whose grant it terminated in 2008, thereby hastening its closure. Suspected by radical Ulster Gaelgeoiri of being too close to the Dublin political establishment. (See Chapter 7.)

Comhairle na Gaelscolaiochta: - Gaelic medium schools management authority in Northern Ireland, with a Belfast office and funded by N.I. government.

Naiscoileanna: - Gaelic medium nursery schools.

Bunscoileanna: - Gaelic medium primary schools.

Meanscoileanna: - Gaelic medium secondary schools.

Gaelscoil: - General term used to denote a Gaelic-medium school.

Colaiste Feirste: - Pride and majesty of Gaeil Uladh! Belfast's stand-alone, publicly-funded Gaelic-medium secondary school.

Gaelcholaiste Dhoire: - Gaelic medium secondary school, publicly-funded and stand-alone, operating from Dungiven, Co Derry.

Forbairt Feirste: - Belfast's main Gaelic medium business skills training body. – Publicly funded over recent years.

Gaelchursa: - Vocational Gaelic-medium training programme (publicly-funded) run from West Belfast for young Gaels seeking to enhance basic job skills.

Radio Failte: - Gaelic radio run from a studio in West Belfast.

Culturlann McAdam/O'Fiaich: - Belfast's Gaelic medium cultural, arts, educational and literary centre, based on Falls Road. Without doubt, the heart and soul of Belfast's Gaeltacht Quarter! – Sited in a de-consecrated Presbyterian Church in Falls-Broadway area, the Culturlann was re-developed with public funding, volunteer labour and cross-party nationalist support. Its re-opening was performed by the-then Irish President, Mrs Mary McAleese, herself an Ardoyne native, who returned home to Belfast for the occasion.

Aras na - bhFal: - Gaelic office centre, Broadway, West Belfast.

Cumann Chluain Ard: - The largest and oldest branch of the Gaelic League, situated in a permanent centre in Lower Falls, West Belfast. Has a "No English" rule for members at its educational and social premises.

Gaeltacht Quarter, Belfast: - An area of some 83,000 people in West Belfast, which has long been a hive of Gaelic language, cultural and sporting activity. An estimated 31% of the people are Gaelic speakers. Recognised by Belfast City Council and the Government of Northern Ireland (both at Stormont and Westminster) as an area of unique Irish-Gaelic character. (See Chap 7.)

ACKNOWLEDGEMENTS

There were many obliging persons from Scotland, Northern Ireland and further afield, each of kindly disposition, and without whose help I could never have completed this work. Quite a number are Gaels, but not everyone, and yet it is to those decent souls that I owe so much. Some are already alluded to in the footnotes and references, but herewith is a more comprehensive evaluation.

To the 45 + persons – catalogued in the Bibliography - who so kindly gave of their time and knowledge to respond to my questions in interviews, I am extremely grateful. Many of those people spoke from direct experience of the Gaelic worlds of Scotland and Northern Ireland, while others guided me in clarifying facts and recalling actual situations. Others still pointed me in the direction of literature, reports and further primary evidence, and in so doing aided my practical understanding of matters Gaelic in Alba and Ulaidh alike. Not that I am a stranger to Gaelic culture! Certainly not! However, it was useful to get other perspectives from activists operating in diverse conditions.

In addition, I was aided by Gaelic educational researchers in Belfast and Inverness alike, as well as Mr Jacque Mac Siacais who laid all the resources of Forbairt Feirste (Belfast) at my feet, as did my late friend, Mr Donald John Macivor, during his pivotal leadership of Gaelic schools planning at Comhairle nan Eilean Siar. The sheer kindness of both those people in giving up abundant time so as to ensure I was presented with the most up-to-date material, along with their own perspectives on relevant developments in Scotland and Northern Ireland, speaks volumes of their commitment. Another old friend, Mr Gearoid O'Caireallain, over the course of several years, both during his term as La editor in West Belfast and afterwards throughout a prolonged wheel-chair debilitation, was enormously helpful with information, facts and figures. He further opened doors that introduced me to others. Mr Arthur Cormack of Skye and Mrs Annie MacSween of Lewis also opened their worlds to me, supplying material and so many valuable recalls on Scottish Gaelic affairs. So too did I receive ongoing help from Irish historian, Dr Donal McAnallen, and Mr Roddy Hegarty of the Cardinal O'Fiaich Memorial Library and Archive, Armagh. Two other distinguished Armagh Gaeilgeoiri stand out; namely Monsignor Raymond Murray, priest, writer and confidant of the late

299

Cardinal O'Fiaich, and my old Gaelic Studies teacher, Mr Paul McAvinchey, himself always available by phone and/or email with useful guidance and customary good cheer.

Thank you also to Miss Allison Lang of the Gaelic Books Council, Glasgow, for her valued advice and support over launch and promotions matters. Similar guidance over the Irish launch came from two trusted friends, Mr Sean Og McAteer, Secretary of Down GAA, and Mr Brian McAvoy, Chief Executive of the Ulster Gaelic Athletic Association. Thank you also to Edinburgh Council and its Gaelic Affairs Officer, Mrs Ann McCloskey, for kindly designating the City Library for the Scottish launch, and to Down GAA County Executive, led by Mr McAteer, for facilitating an Irish launch at their Newry HQ, Pairc an Esler.

Several persons kindly commented on drafts of the script, including Dr Ian Henderson, my former under-graduate tutor at Coventry University, himself a native of Aberdeen and patriotic Scot, but long based in the English Midlands. So too did Dr Gordon McCoy, the Gaeilgeoir of East Belfast Methodist Mission, spend endless hours meeting, talking, guiding and assisting me in so many ways, and all this notwithstanding his own grave health troubles. A true and kindly friend indeed! Rev. Monsignor/Dr Ambrose Macauley, long-time Catholic Chaplain to Queens University (Belfast), author, writer and respected Church historian, gave generously of his time and wise counsel right up until his sad death in November 2019. Then there was Mr Nelson McCausland, a Democratic Unionist politician from Belfast, also a Protestant preacher, newspaper columnist and Ulster-Scots cultural activist, who kindly spent much time giving me a Unionist perspective on relevant developments of Ulster Gaeldom, itself most valuable. To Ian, Gordon, Monsignor Ambrose and Nelson, I owe a serious debt of gratitude, not least because their comments enabled me to apply a wider perspective to interpretations of script.

I was further assisted by officials of An Comunn Gaidhealach and Comunn na Gaidhlig, both at Inverness, all of whom I found to be helpful as well as friendly and courteous. Equally, I experienced similar blessings in my dealings with officials at Comhairle nan Eilean Siar, Stornoway, Isle of Lewis, and with Bord na Gaidhlig at Inverness. All persons at the various levels proved a pleasure to deal with. So too did I receive warmth and co-operation from staff at the Culturlann McAdam/O'Fiaich, Belfast, as well as headmasters and stream heads of various Gaelic schools in Belfast, Armagh, Dungiven and Castlewellan.

It would be nice to say that everybody approached gave the desired level of co-operation. However, in all honesty, such was not the case. There were a few instances – regrettably, mostly in my native Northern Ireland – where letters went unanswered, polite emails and phone messages were ignored, and certain people from whom I had expected better, chose not to observe even the basic courtesy of a response to reasonable requests for interviews, reviews and/or relevant materials. Probably best that I avoid mentioning names, as on reading this book those concerned will know exactly to whom I am referring.

One exception I shall make to the anonymity rule, namely the British Society of Authors. This is the London-based writers trade union, to whom I have given full loyalty over three decades as a professional member. During the Covid Pandemic and Lockdown 2020/21, I, like so many authors, was afflicted by grievous worries over finance and sustainment, and thus applied three times, with backing from leading external academics, for assistance from various SOA scholarship funds. What was the response? Answer: Zero on each occasion! - Seems like helping cash-strapped Celtic researchers weighed lightly with that outfit, itself better known for assisting the politically-correct and fashionable novelists of 'Middle England'. Thanks for nothing, Guys and Girls!

Fortunately, the negative was far out-weighed by the positive. As stated elsewhere, I owe so much to my dear late friend, Professor Ken MacKinnon, for his timeless encouragement and monitoring of my scripts. Professor Rob Dunbar, head of Celtic Studies at University of Edinburgh, also proved a most steadfast and kindly friend with reading script, assisting the launch and advising on a multitude of issues arising, all with his calm sense of dignity, tolerance and pleasantness. As a result, we have become good friends. Also, Rob's Edinburgh colleague, Professor Wilson McLeod, was so kind as to take time away from completing his own masterful treatise - published in 2020 - to read and comment at length on initial chapters of my book. Then there was Dr Aonghus Mac Coinneach of Celtic Studies Department, University of Glasgow, who also kindly read and commented on my earlier scripts, and, ditto, Professor Micheal O'Mainnin, at QUB (Belfast). Such fine people, whom it has been my great blessing from Heaven to have encountered!

Other people deserve thanks. Among them are my publisher, Mr Steven Hodder, of Takahe Publishing Ltd, Coventry, who has been professional and yet friendly, always with good advice and workable options. Unfortunately, Steven was himself afflicted by health troubles, but yet made it his business to deliver on all his pledges to me. There was also the talented Scottish design artist, Miss Fiona Rennie, from the Isle of Lewis, to whom credit goes for a most apposite and well-judged front design cover. So also was there Mr Jomal (JB) Baptiste, whose skills as an IT operator saw me through many a crisis.

Another old friend from London, Professor/Lord Peter Hennessy, helped me rehabilitate following a set-back in my business life over a decade ago, and more recently was a consistent and positive encourager, not to mention source of wise counsel. Likewise, the erudite Scottish historian, Professor/Sir Thomas Devine, has in recent times shown me abundant good will, encouragement and assistance as to rank among the new-found friends whom it has been my pleasure to generate from this project. – For those interested, my professional website -www.laganwritingservices.com- will reveal further reasons as to why I hold Peter and Tom in such high regard.

In my private life, my loyal brother, Paul, much-loved lifelong friends, Ann and Siobhan Fitzpatrick - all at home in Co Down- along with my Filipina lady-folk, darling daughter, Patricia, and ever-loving wife, Mary-Jane, have each made such a positive contribution in their own distinctive ways. Thank you all of you!

Sincere thanks too to my personal Confessor and spiritual adviser, Monsignor Patrick Kilgarriff, retired Rector of the English College (RC Seminary), Rome, but these days living in quiet retirement at St George's RC Church & Presbytery, Worcester. Another of my 'old wise owl' friends, Monsignor Pat (himself of Irish descent) extended to me the mature and moral wealth of over 50 years service as a priest to guide my mind and conscience in the direction of God. I could not have carried this project through to completion without the inner peace that comes from answering the call of our Heavenly Creator.

This brings me to the final acknowledgement. As unfashionable as it may appear in these secular times, still, being a committed – however inadequate – Catholic and Christian, it is my considered duty to bear witness to the Lord God in Heaven. Accordingly, for the blessings of health, intellect and capacity, that enabled me to undertake and complete this arduous treatise, I herewith give proper thanks and praise to Almighty God. In the same spirit, may I

Acknowledgements

petition the Lord to grant a merciful judgement to those many kind souls who helped me but did not live to see completion of this work, and thereafter may they enjoy a peaceful eternity. Equally, to those people who helped and are still with us, may each be blessed with all that is good in their lives, now and always.

Again, with grateful thanks to all, and wishing everyone the Lord's peace.

Dr Vincent McKee

BIBLIOGRAPHY

1. Secondary Publications (Books)

Gerry Adams   Before the Dawn: An Autobiography (Mandarin/Heinemann, 1996, London).

A. Alcock, B. Taylor & J. Weldon   The Future of Cultural Minorities (Macmillan, 1979, London).

Olga Balaeva   Ireland as Gaeilge (Orpen Press, 2017, Dublin).

John Bannerman   Studies in the History of Dalriada (Scottish Academic Press, 1974, Edinburgh).

Peter Barberis, John McHugh & Mike Tyldesley   Encyclopedia of British and Irish Political Organisations (Pinter, 2000, London/New York).

Jonathon Bardon   A History of Ulster (Blackstaff, 1992, Belfast).

Geoffrey Beattie   We are the People: Journeys through the Heart of Protestant Ulster (Heinemann, 1992, London).

J.C. Beckett   The Making of Modern Ireland 1603-1923 (Faber & Faber, 1966, London).

Geoffrey Bell   The Protestants of Ulster (Pluto, 1976, London).

Peter Beresford Ellis   The Celtic Revolution: A Study in Anti-Imperialism (Ceridigon, 1985, Wales).

Paul Bew   Churchill & Ireland (OUP, 2016, Oxford).

Paul Bew & Henry Patterson   The British State and the Ulster Crisis: From Wilson to Thatcher (Hodder/Stoughton, 1985, London).

Paul Bew & Gordon Gillespie   Northern Ireland: A Chronology of the Troubles, 1968-1993 (OUP, 1993, Oxford).

Roger Blaney   Presbyterians and the Irish Language (Able, 2012, Belfast)

Andrew Boyd   Brian Faulkner and the Crisis of Ulster Unionism (Anvil Books, 1972, Tralee, Co Kerry).

Jack Brand   The National Movement in Scotland (Routledge & Kegan Paul, 1978, London).

Terence Brown   Ireland: A Social and Cultural History, 1922-2002, 3rd Ed., (Harper-Collins, 2004, London).

Patrick Buckland   James Craig (Gill & Macmillan, 1980, Dublin).

John A. Burnett   The Making of the Modern Scottish Highlands 1939-1965 (Four Courts Press, 2011, Dublin)

H.M. Chadwick   Early Scotland (CUP, Cambridge, 1949).

M. Chapman   The Gaelic Vision in Scottish Culture (Croom Helm, 1978, London).

Patrick J. Clarke   History of a County Down Townland; Drumaroad (QUB, 2004, Belfast).

Feargal Cochrane   Northern Ireland: The Fragile Peace (Yale, 2021, London/New Haven).

Tim Pat Coogan   Michael Collins (Arrow Books, 1991, London).

John Cooney John Charles McQuaid: Ruler of Catholic Ireland (O'Brien Press, 1999, Dublin).

Ciaran Crilly & Michael McCartan et al   History of Kilmegan and Surrounding Area /Uachtar Tire–Castlewellan, Co Down (N.I.)   (Kilmegan & Maghera Historic Society, 2018, Castlewellan, N.I.).

T.M. Devine   The Scottish Nation 1707-2007 (Penguin, London, 2006).

T.M. Devine   To the Ends of the Earth: Scotland's Global Diaspora, 1750-2010 (Penguin, 2012, London).

T.M. Devine   The Scottish Clearances: A History of the Dispossessed, 1600-1900 (Penguin, 2019, London).

T.M. Devine Independence or Union: Scotland's Past and Scotland's Present (Penguin, 2017, London).

T.M. Devine Declarations on Freedom for Writers & Readers (Scotland Street Press, 2020, Edinburgh).

T.M. Devine The Great Highland Famine (John Donald, 1988, Edinburgh).

T.M. Devine (Eds.) Scotland's Shame: Bigotry and Sectarianism in Modern Scotland (Mainstream Publishing, 2000, Edinburgh).

T.M. Devine (Eds.) Scotland in the Twentieth Century (EUP, 1996, Edinburgh).

William Croft Dickinson A New History of Scotland (Nelson, 1960, London).

Chris Dooley Redmond: A Life Undone (Gill & Macmillan, 2015, Dublin).

H.M. Drucker Breakaway: The Scottish Labour Party (EUSPB, 1980, Oxford).

H.M. Drucker (Eds.) Multi-Party Britain (Macmillan, 1979, London).

Owen Dudley Edwards (Eds.) A Claim of Right for Scotland (Polygon, 1988, Edinburgh).

Robert Dunbar The Ratification by the United Kingdom of the European Charter for Regional or Minority Languages: - Mercator- Legislation Working Paper 10, Barcelona/Edinburgh, 2003.

Seamus Dunn (Eds.) Facets of the Conflict in Northern Ireland (Macmillan, 2001, London).

R.F. Foster (Eds.) Oxford History of Ireland (OUP, 1992, Oxford).

R.F. Foster Modern Ireland 1600-1972 (Allen Lane, 1988, London).

Ronan Fanning Eamon De Valera: A Will To Power (Faber & Faber, 2015, London).

Michael Farrell Northern Ireland: The Orange State (Pluto, 1976, London).

D. Figgis The Gaelic State in the Past and Future (1917, Dublin).

Tom Gallagher Scotland Now: A Warning to the World! - Foreword by Alistair Darling (Scotview Publications, 2015, Edinburgh).

Tom Gallagher   Divided Scotland: Ethnic Friction and Christian Crisis (Argyll Publishing, 2013, Argyll).

Tom Gallagher   Glasgow; The Uneasy Peace: Religious Tension in Modern Scotland (Manchester University Press, 1987, Manchester).

Tom Gallagher   Edinburgh Divided (Polygon, 1987, Edinburgh).

N. Garnham   Association Football and Society in pre-Partition Ireland (Ulster Historical Foundation, 2004, Belfast).

E. Gellner   Nations and Nationalism (OUP, 1983, Oxford).

Sile Nic An Ultaigh   O Shiol go Blath The Down Gaelic History (Down GAA, 1990, Newry).

W. Gillies (eds.)   Gaelic and Scotland/Alba agus a' Ghlaidlig (EUP, 1989, Edinburgh).

Risteard Giltrap   An Ghaeilge in Eaglais na hEireann / The Irish Language in the Church of Ireland, 2nd Ed. (Foilseachain Abhair Spioradalta, 2019, Baile Atha Cliath / Dublin).

Dean Godson   David Trimble and the Crisis of Ulster Unionism (Harper-Collins, 2004, London).

Wynn Grant   Pressure Groups, Politics and Democracy in Britain (Harvester/Wheatsheaf, 1995, London).

I.F. Grigor   Mightier than a Lord: The Highland Crofters Struggle for the Land (Acair, 1979, Stornoway).

Reginald B. Hale   The Magnificent Gael (World Media, Manitoba, 1976).

A.H. Halsey   Trends in British Society since 1900 (Macmillan, 1972, London).

Gerry Hassan (Eds.)   The Modern SNP: From Protest to Power (EUP, 2009, Edinburgh).

Peter Hennessy   (Three-Volume series on Post-War Britain) 1. Never Again Britain, 1945-51 (Vintage, 1991, London) – 2. Having it so Good: Britain in the 1950s (Penguin, 2007, London) - 3. Winds of Change: Britain in the Early Sixties (Penguin, 2016, London).

John Hewitt Rhyming Weavers and other country poets of Antrim and Down (1974).

Zig Layton-Henry Politics of Race in Britain (Macmillan, 1984, London).

A.C. Hepburn The Conflict of Nationality in Modern Ireland (Hodder, 1980, London).

Reg. Hindley Death of the Irish Language: A Qualified Obituary (Routledge, 1990, London).

Jack Holland Hope against History: The Ulster Conflict (Hodder & Stoughton, 1999, London).

James Hunter The Making of the Crofting Community (John Donald, Edinburgh, 1976).

Roger Hutchinson A Waxing Moon: The Modern Gaelic Revival in Scotland (Mainstream, 2005, Edinburgh).

Rob Johns & James Mitchell Takeover:-Explaining the Extraordinary Rise of the SNP (Biteback, 2016, Glasgow/London).

Michael Keating & Arthur Midwinter The Government of Scotland (Mainstream Publishing, 1983, Edinburgh).

Charles W. Kegley & Eugene R. Wittkopf World Politics: Trend and Transformation; 8th edition (Macmillan/St Martin's, London/Boston).

James Kellas The Scottish Political System (CUP, 1989, Cambridge).

John Kendle Ireland and the Federal Solution: Debate over the United Kingdom Constitution, 1870-1921 (McGill-Queens Univ. Press, 1989, Quebec).

Ian Kershaw Making Friends with Hitler: Lord Londonderry and Britain's Road to War (Penguin, 1990, London).

Lord Longford/Frank Packenham & Thomas P. O'Neill Eamon De Valera (Hutchinson, 1970, London).

Dorothy Macardle The Irish Republic (Corgi Books, 1968, London).

Ambrose Macaulay The Campaign for Catholic Emancipation in Ireland and England (Four Courts, 2016, Dublin).

Donald Macdonald Lewis: A History of the Island (Gordon Wright Publishing, 1990, Edinburgh).

Eoin Magennis & Cronan O'Doibhlin (Eds.) World War One: Ireland and its Impacts (Cumann Seanchais Ard Macha and Cardinal Tomas O'Fiaich Memorial Library & Archive, 2005, Armagh).

Feargal Mac Ionnrachtaigh Language, Resistance and Revival: Republican Prisoners and the Irish Language in the North of Ireland (Pluto, 2013, London).

J.D. Mackie A History of Scotland (Penguin, 1991, London).

Eamonn Mallie & David McKittrick The Fight For Peace: The Secret Story Behind the Irish Peace Process (Heinemann, 1996, London).

Arthur Marwick Culture in Britain since 1945 (Penguin, 1991, London).

David Mackay We did it Ourselves: Sinn Fhein a rinn e- An Account of the Western Isles Community Education Project/Proisect Muinntir nan Eilean, 1977-92 (Bernard van Leer Foundation, 1996, Glasgow/The Hague).

Donal McAnallen (Eds.) Reflections on the Revolution in Ulster – Excerpts from Rev. Louis O'Kane's Recordings of Irish Volunteers (Cardinal Tomas O'Fiaich Memorial Library & Archive, 2016, Armagh).

Donal McAnallen Forgotten Gaelic Volunteers: Ulster GAA members who fought in World War One (Cardinal Tomas O'Fiaich Archive, 2019, Armagh).

Donal McAnallen The Pursuit of Perfection: The Life, Death and Legacy of Cormac McAnallen (Peguin Books, 2017, London/Belfast).

Gordon McCoy & Maolcholaim Scott (Eds.) Aithne na nGael/Gaelic Identities (Institute of Irish Studies/ULTACH Trust, 2000, Belfast).

Owen McGee Arthur Griffith (Merrion Press, 2015, Dublin).

R.B. McDowell The Irish Administration 1801-1914 (Routledge & Kegan Paul, 1964, London).

Vincent McKee   Gaelic Nations: Politics of the Gaelic Language in Scotland and Northern Ireland in the 20th Century (Bluestack Press, 1997, London).

Vincent McKee   Forty Shades of Blue: Factionalism in the Post-War British Conservative Party from Churchill to Cameron (Takahe, 2017, Coventry).

Kenneth MacKinnon   Gaelic: A Past and Future Prospect (Saltire, 1991, Edinburgh).

Kenneth MacKinnon   Gaelic in Scotland 1971: Sociological and Demographic Considerations of the Census Report for Gaelic (Hertis Pubs., 1978, Hatfield).

Kenneth MacKinnon   Gaelic in Highland Region- the 1981 Census (An Comunn Gaidhealach, 1984, Inverness).

Kenneth MacKinnon   Gaelic Language Regeneration among Young People in Scotland, 1977-1981:- From Census Data (Hertis Pubs, Hatfield, 1984).

Kenneth MacKinnon   Language, Education and Social Processes in a Gaelic Community (Club Leabhar, 1977, Stornoway).

Kenneth MacKinnon   The Lion's Tongue (Routledge, 1974, London).

K. MacKinnon & M. MacDonald   Ethnic Communities: The Transmission of Language and Culture in Harris and Barra – Report to the UK Social Science Research Council (Hertis Pubs, Hatfield, 1980).

Hugh Dan MacLennan   Shinty in Scotland:- Not an Orchid (Kessock Communications, 1995, Inverness).

Hugh Dan MacLennan   Shinty: 100 Years of the Camanachd Association (Balnain Books, 1993, Nairn, Scotland).

MacLeod M. & Smith-Christmas C.   Gaelic in Contemporary Scotland: The Revitalisation of an Endangered Language (EUP, 2018, Edinburgh).

Domhnall Iain MacLeoid   Dualchas an aghaidh:-The Gaelic Revival in Scotland 1890-2020 (Clo-beag, 2011, Inverness).

John Macleod   When I heard the Bell: The Loss of the Iolaire (Birlinn, 2010, Edinburgh).

Aodan MacPoilin (Eds.) The Irish Language in Northern Ireland (ULTACH Trust, 1997, Belfast).

Marcas Mac Ruairi In the Heat of the Hurry: A History of Republicanism in Co. Down (Foilseachain Bhoirche, 1997, Castlewellan, Co. Down).

Iain MacWhirter Road to Referendum (Cargo Publishing, 2013, Glasgow).

Wilson McLeod Gaelic in Scotland:- Policies, Movements, Ideologies (EUP, 2020, Edinburgh).

Wilson McLeod Revitalising Gaelic in Scotland: Policy, Planning and Public Discourse (Dunedin Academic Press, 2006, Edinburgh).

Wilson McLeod Divided Gaels: Gaelic Cultural Identities in Scotland and Ireland, 1200-1650 (OUP, 2004, Oxford).

Seamus Mallon – with Andy Pollak Seamus Mallon Memoirs: A Shared Home Place (Lilliput Press, 2019, Dublin).

Gabrielle Maguire Our Own Language: An Irish Initiative (Clevedon, 1991, Belfast).

Kate Martin (Eds) Feis: The first twenty-five years of the Feis Movement (Feisean nan Gaidheal Alba, 2006, Portree, Isle of Skye).

Donald E. Meek The Scottish Highlands: The Churches and Gaelic Culture (World Council of Churches, 1996, Geneva/Edinburgh).

James Mitchell & Gerry Hassan Scottish National Party Leaders (Biteback, 2016, London).

Ed Moloney & Andy Pollak Paisley (Poolbeg, 1986, Dublin).

Brian Murphy Forgotten Patriot: Douglas Hyde and the Foundation of the Irish Presidency (Collins Press, 2016, Cork).

John A. Murphy Ireland in the Twentieth Century (Gill & Macmillan, 1973, Dublin).

Gerard Murray & Jonathan Tonge Sinn Fein and the SDLP: From Alienation to Participation (O'Brien Press/Hurst & Co Publishers, 2005, Dublin/London).

John Murray & Catherine Morrison   Bilingual Primary Education in the Western Isles of Scotland:- Introduction by Dr Finlay Macleod. (Acair, 1984, Stornoway, Isle of Lewis).

Raymond Murray (Very Rev. Monsignor) Archdiocese of Armagh: A History (Archdiocese of Armagh, 2000, Armagh).

Tom Nairn The Break-up of Britain: Crisis and Neo-Nationalism (NLB, 1977, London/Glasgow).

K. Nicholls Gaelic and Gaelicised Ireland in the Middle Ages (Macmillan, 1972, Dublin).

Conor Cruise O'Brien Parnell and his Party 1880-1890 (Clarendon, 1957, Oxford).

Conor Cruise O'Brien States of Ireland (Panther Books, 1974, St Alban's).

Seamas O'Casaide The Irish Language in Belfast and County Down (1930, Dublin).

Eamonn O'Ciossan Buried Alive: A Reply to Reg Hindley (Dail Ui Chadian Pamphlets, 1991, Dublin)

Brian O'Cuiv (Eds.) A View of the Irish Language (Irish Government Stationary Office, 1969, Dublin).

Conchur O'Giollagain et al (Eds.) The Gaelic Crisis in the Vernacular Community: A comprehensive sociolinguistic survey of Scottish Gaelic (Aberdeen University Press, 2020, Aberdeen).

Fiona O'Hanlon, Wilson McLeod & Lindsay Patterson Gaelic Medium Education in Scotland: Choice and Attainment at the primary and early secondary stages (Bord na Gaidhlig, 2010, Inverness).

Cornelius O'Leary & Ian Budge Belfast; Approach to Crisis: A Study of Belfast Politics, 1613-1970 (Macmillan, 1973, London).

Brendan O'Leary A Treatise on Northern Ireland, Vol. 1, Colonialism (2019, Oxford University Press/OUP, Oxford). Vol. 2, Control (2019, OUP). Vol. 3, Consociation and Confederation (2019, OUP)

Brendan O'Leary & John McGarry (Eds.) The Future of Northern Ireland (OUP, 1991, Oxford).

Terence O'Neill The Autobiography of Terence O'Neill; Prime Minister of Northern Ireland, 1963-1969 (Rupert Hart-Davis, 1972, London).

Camille C. O'Reilly The Irish Language in Northern Ireland: Politics of Culture and Identity (Macmillan/St Martin's Press, 1999, London/New York).

Neil Oliver A History of Scotland (Phoenix/Orion Books, 2010, London).

Torkel Opsahl The Opsahl Report on Northern Ireland: - Eds. by Andy Pollak (Lilliput Initiative, 1992/93, Dublin).

P. O'Snodaigh Hidden Ulster (Clodhanna Teo, 1973, Belfast).

Alan F. Parkinson & Eamon Phoenix (Eds.) Conflicts in the North of Ireland 1900-2000: Flashpoints and Fracture Zones (Amazon, 2010, Belfast/London).

Lindsay Paterson The Autonomy of Modern Scotland (EUP, 1994, Edinburgh).

Roy Pedersen Gaelic Guerrilla: John Angus Mackay, Gael Extraordinaire (Luath Press, 2019, Edinburgh).

Eamon Phoenix Northern Nationalism (Ulster Historical Foundation, 1994, Belfast).

Eamon Phoenix Nationalist Politics, Partition and the Catholic Minority in Northern Ireland 1890-1940 (Blackwater, 1973, Belfast).

Eamonn Phoenix, Padraic O'Cleireachain, Eileen MacAuley & Nuala McSparran et al (Eds.) Feis na nGleann: A Century of Gaelic Culture in the Antrim Glens (Stair Uladh/UlsterHistorical Foundation, 2005, Belfast).

John Prebble The Lion in the North: One thousand Years of Scotland's History (Book Club Associates, 1974, London/Glasgow).

Richard Parry Scottish Political Facts (Clark, 1988, Edinburgh).

Murray Pittock The Road to Independence? Scotland since the Sixties (Reaktion Books, 2008, London).

George Pryde Scotland from 1603 to the Present Day: A New History (Nelson, 1962, Edinburgh).

Jerome Quinn Ulster Football & Hurling: The Path of Champions (Wolfhound Press, 1993, Dublin).

Merlyn Rees Northern Ireland: A Personal Perspective (Hard Cover, 1985, London).

Oliver Rafferty, S.J. The Catholic Church and the Protestant State: Nineteenth Century Irish Realities (2008, Jesuit Press, Dublin).

Albert Reynolds My Autobiography (Transworld Ireland, 2009, London).

Mairi Robinson The Concise Scots Dictionary (University of Aberdeen, 1985).

Paul Rouse The Hurlers: The First All-Ireland Championship and Making of Modern Hurling (Penguin, 2019, London).

Paul Rouse, Mike Cronin & Mark Duncan GAA: A Peoples History (ISBN – 9781848892255; Abebooks, 2009, London/Dublin).

Paul Routledge John Hume: A Biography (Harper/Collins, 1997, London).

David Ross Scotland: History of a Nation (Lomond Books, 2017, Glasgow).

S.S. Rokkan & D.W. Urwin The Politics of Territorial Identity: Studies in European Regionalism (Sage, 1982, London).

Alex Salmond The Dream Shall Never Die: 100 Days that changed Scotland Forever (William Collins, 2015, London).

Roger Sawyer (Eds.) Roger Casement's Diaries: 1910: The Black & the White (Pimlico, 1997, London).

Enda Staunton The Nationalists of Northern Ireland, 1918-1973 (Columba Press, 2001, Dublin).

Meic Stephens Linguistic Minorities in Western Europe (Gomer Press, 1976, Llandysul).

A.T.Q. Stewart The Narrow Ground: Aspects of Ulster, 1609-1969 (Faber, 1977, London).

Rev. Alexander Stewart   Elements of Scottish Gaelic Grammar (Peter Hill, 1801, Edinburgh).

A.T.Q. Stewart   Edward Carson (Gill & Macmillan, 1981, Dublin).

Donald Stewart   A Scot at Westminster (Catlone Press, Nova Scotia, 1994).

Frank Thompson   History of An Comunn Gaidhealach: The First Hundred Years (ACG, 1991, Inverness).

Derek S. Thompson (eds.)   The Companion to Gaelic Scotland (Basil Blackwell, 1983, Oxford).

P. Trudgill   Language in the British Isles (CUP, 1984, Oxford).

R. Wardaugh   Languages in Competition (Blackwell, 1987, Oxford).

Moray Watson & Michelle Macleod (Eds.)   The Edinburgh Companion to the Gaelic Language (EUP, 2010, Edinburgh).

Colin H. Williams (Eds)   Legislative Devolution and Language Regulation in the United Kingdom (Geolinguistics.org/geo 32 articles/GEO-32-Williams-art.pdf), Cardiff University.

Gordon Wilson   SNP:- The Turbulent Years, 1960-90 (Scots Independent Newspapers Ltd, 2009, Edinburgh).

C.W.J. Withers   Gaelic in Scotland, 1698-1981: The Geographical History of a Language (John Donald, 1984, Edinburgh).

C.W.J. Withers   Gaelic Scotland: The Transformation of a Culture Region (Routledge, 1988, London).

J.H. Whyte   Church and State in Modern Ireland, 1923-1979 (Gill & Macmillan, 1984, Dublin).

J.N. Wolfe Government and Nationalism in Scotland (EUP, 1969, Edinburgh).

Carlton Younger   A State of Disunion (Frederick Muller, 1972, London).

Olaf Zenker Irish/ness is all Around Us: Language Revivalism and the Culture of Ethnic Identity in Northern Ireland (Berghan Books, 2013, Berne, Switz).

2. Journals/On-line Articles/Chapters/Pamphlets/Speeches/Websites

BBC Northern Ireland & Radio Ulster (Belfast):- News websites; www.bbc.co.uk/news/uk-northern-ireland-50099598.

BBC-NI:- *'Hearts and Minds'*, 26th April, 2001; Televised debate on GAA's Rule 21, Mr Francie Brolly, then Sinn Fein (sadly deceased) v Dr Vincent McKee.

Oliver Brown *'Gaelic and Politics in Scotland'*; Scots Independent, 8, 201, 1934.

Conradh na Gaeilge:- *'Irish Language Act: Discussion Document'* – March 2017.

Conradh na Gaeilge:- *'Public Opinion on the Irish Language – Annual Analysis'*; 2016, Belfast.

Gael Linn   Aspects of a Shared Heritage: Essays on Linguistic and Cultural Crossover in Ulster (Gael Linn, 2015, Dublin/Armagh).

Joni Buchanan   *'The Gaelic Communities'*, in Autonomy of the New Scotland; Eds. by Gerry Hassan & Chris Warhurst, Mainstream Press, 2002, Edinburgh.

Sian Carden   *'Post-Conflict Belfast Sliced and Diced: The case of the Gaeltacht Quarter'*; 20, School of History & Anthropology, QUB, Belfast, 2011.

J. Crehan S.J., *'Freedom and Catholic Power'*, Studies, 40, pp 158-166, 1951.

Robert Dunbar   *'A unilingual minority language college in a multilingual university: Sabhal Mor Ostaig'*; pp 197-214, European Journal of Language Policy, 3, Edinburgh, 2011.

BBC News Online:- *'EU Green Light for Scottish Gaelic'* (7th October, 2009).

Wynn Grant   *'Pressure Groups in Britain'*, Social Studies Review, October 1987.

Henry MacDonald *'Enigma of Gaelic Funding'*; Guardian, 5th February, 2010.

Compton Mackenzie *'Catholic Barra'*, in The Book of Barra; Eds by John Lorne Campbell, pp 1-25, (1936)/ Acair, 1998, Stornoway).

Kenneth MacKinnon   *'Gaelic Language-Use in the Western Isles'*; in Studies in Scots and Gaelic: Proceedings of Third International Conference on the

Languages of Scotland; Eds. by A. Fenton & D.A. MacDonald – Edinburgh, 1994.

Kenneth MacKinnon *'Gaelic in the Census – a Tenacious Survival'*; in Gaelic:- Looking to the Future; - Andrew Fletcher Society, pp 11-20, Dundee, 1985.

Kenneth MacKinnon *'The Dynamics of Scottish Gaelic'*; in Watching One's Tongue – Aspects of Romance and Celtic Languages; pp 177-200, Eds. by P.S. Ureland & I. Clarkson, Liverpool University Press, 1996.

John P. Mackintosh *'The new appeal of Nationalism in Scotland'*; New Statesman, pp 408 – 412, 27th September, 1974.

Malcolm Maclean *'The Place of Gaelic in Today's Scotland'*; in Scotland the Brave: Twenty Years of Change and the Future of the Nation, pp 252-259, Eds by Gerry Hassan & Simon Barrow (Luath Press, 2019, Edinburgh).

Diane MacLean *'Gaelic Television: Building Bricks without Straw'*; International Journal of Scottish Theatre and Screen, 11, Edinburgh, 2018.

R. MacLennan *'The National Question and Scotland'*; pp 505-510, Communist Review, 4, Glasgow/London, 1932.

Malcolm MacLeod *'An Comunn Gaidhleach'*; Scottish Review, 37, pp 365-375, Edinburgh, 1914.

Malcolm C.J. MacLeod *'Foreword:- The Gaelic Movement'*; The Celtic Annual 1918-19: Year Book of Dundee Highland Society; 6, pp 2-3, Dundee, 1919.

Rev. Malcolm Macleod *'The Highland Pulpit and the Preservation of the Gaelic Language'*; An Comunn Gaidhealach, pp 12-14, 26, Inverness, 1930.

Eoin MacNeill *'Appeal to the Clergy of Ireland'* - in Kevin B. Nowlan (Eds.) The Making of 1916: Studies in the History of the Rising (1969, I.G.S.O., Dublin).

Daithi Mac Sithigh *'Official Status of Languages in the UK and Ireland'*; - Common Law World Review, 47 (i), pp 77-102, 2018.

John Campbell MacMaster *'The Highlands and the Revival of Gaelic'*; - An Comunn Gaidhealach, pp 50-53, 25, Inverness, 1930.

Bibliography

Donal McAnallen, David Hassan & Roddy Hegarty (Eds.) *'The Evolution of the GAA: Ulaidh, Eire agus Eile'*; - Comhairle Uladh CLG, Cardinal Tomas O'Fiaich Memorial Library & Archive, Armagh, 2004.

Gordon McCoy *'Irish in Northern Ireland' – An on-line short history of notes, data and guidance material*; - CNG, Belfast, 2015.

Vincent McKee *'Contemporary Gaelic Language Policies in Western Scotland and Northern Ireland since 1950: Comparative Assessments'*; <u>Contemporary Politics</u>, Volume 1, No. 1, Spring 1995, London.

Vincent McKee *'Politics of the Gaelic Language: Northern Ireland and the Scottish Hebrides'*; <u>Occasional Paper, South Bank University</u>, London, 1994.

Vincent McKee *'Where Language Refuses to Die: The Gaelic/English Bilingual Policies and Partnership of Newry & Mourne and Western Isles councils'*; <u>Municipal Journal</u>, 15-21 March, 1991, London.

Vincent McKee *'The Gaelic Language in Scotland and Ireland'*; <u>Talking Politics</u>, Vol. 11, No 1, Autumn 1998, Manchester.

Vincent McKee *'Rule 21 Needs to Go: Gaels must contribute towards building the New Ireland'*; <u>Opinion Piece</u>, <u>Irish News</u> (Belfast), 19th April, 2001.

Vincent McKee *'GAA has moral duty to offer friendship to old foes'*, <u>Irish Post</u> (London), 28th May 2001.

Vincent McKee *'Time is ripe for GAA to embrace the Spirit of Good Friday'*; <u>Irish Sunday Life</u>, Belfast, 21st October, 2001.

Wilson McLeod *'The nature of minority languages: Insights from Scotland'*; <u>Journal of Cross-Cultural and Inter-Language Communications</u>; 38, 2, pp 141-154, February, 2019.

Kevin McMahon (Eds.) *'Creggan – Journal of the Creggan Local History Society, Co Armagh – Cardinal Tomas O'Fiaich Memorial Issue'*, Co. Armagh, 1991.

Michael Montgomery *'The Language in Seventeenth Century Ulster Scots'*; <u>Ulster Folklife</u>, 1989, Belfast

Cera Murtagh *'Balancing Act'*; <u>Holyrood Magazine</u>, pp 42-43, 31st Jan, 2011, Edinburgh.

Northern Ireland Department of Education (Belfast):- Data supplied, 2021.

Tomas O'Fiaich *'The Language and Political History'*, in <u>A View of the Irish Language</u>; Eds. by Brian O'Cuiv (Irish Govt Stationary Office, 1969, Dublin).

Tomas O'Fiaich *'Irish Missionaries: - The Early Period'*; in <u>Irish Church History Today</u>, Eds. by Raymond O'Muiri, pp 1-12, Armagh, 1997.

Tomas O'Fiaich (Posthumous) – Edited by Kevin McMahon <u>Letters from Louvain 1950-52</u> (Cullyhanna Community Enterprises, 1994, Co Armagh).

Pol O'Muiri *'The Irish Review'* – An Ghaeilge (1993, Belfast).

David Pollock *'John Macleod, Champion of Gaelic'* – Obituary, <u>Glasgow Herald</u> (24th March, 2018).

P.S. Robinson *'The Anglicisation of Scots in Seventeenth Century Ulster'*; pp 50-64, <u>Studies in Scottish Literature</u>, 1991, Belfast/Glasgow.

Paul Rouse *'Off the Ball: 50 Years after the Ban was lifted by the GAA'*:- <u>U-TUBE</u>, 30th March, 2021.

Alex Salmond *'Sabhal Mor Ostaig Lecture:-Government Plans for Gaelic'; delivered at St Cecilia's Hall, Edinburgh, 19th December, 2007.-Ref. BBC Scotland, News Reports.*

Maolcholaim Scott *'When Planter was the Gael'*; <u>Fortnight Supp.</u>,1993, Belfast.

<u>Seanchas Ard Mhacha/Journal of Armagh RC Diocesan Historical Society</u> – Eds. Rev. Fr Patrick J. Campbell & Very Rev. Monsignor Raymond Murray – Vol. 9, No. 1, 1978; Saint Patrick's Cathedral, Armagh, Northern Ireland.

Jennifer Todd *'Nationalist Political Culture in Northern Ireland'*- Paper presented to UK Political Studies Association Annual Conference, Plymouth Polytechnic, 12th - 14th April, 1988.

Jennifer Todd *'Northern Irish Nationalist Political Culture'*; pp 31-44, <u>Irish Political Studies</u>, 5, 1990, Dublin.

Liam Mac An Tsagairt *'Father Larry Murray'* (Eigse Oirialla, 1983, Dundalk).

Liam Turbitt *'GAA should value Rule 21'*; <u>Irish Sunday Life</u>, 21/10/2001.

3. Unpublished Academic Dissertations/Theses

Bernard Conlon   The Northern Ireland Civil Rights Association: Comparative Perspectives; M.A. Dissertation, University of Ulster, Coleraine, 1984.

Michael Mac Giolla Ghunna   The Gaelic League in Belfast 1895-189; M.A. Dissertation, Queens University, Belfast, 1998.

Mary K. MacLeod The interaction of Scottish educational developments and socio-economic factors on Gaelic education in Gaelic-speaking areas, with particular reference to the period 1872-1918; Ph.D. Thesis, University of Edinburgh, 1981.

Marsaili Macleod   The Meaning of Work in the Gaelic Labour Market in the Highlands and Islands of Scotland; Ph.D. Thesis, Univ. of Aberdeen, 2008.

J.B. McAleenan/Seamas MacGiolla Fhinnein   Criostai Ui Ghripin; M.A. Thesis, Dept. of Irish Studies, University of Ulster, Coleraine, 1990.

Martin O'Brien Margaret Thatcher and Northern Ireland: -Special Focus on the 1985 Hillsborough Accord; - Dissertation for Master of Social Sciences, Queens University, Belfast, 1993.

4. Reports, Records, Briefings, Official Records and Group Constitutions

An Comunn Gaidhleach:- Annual reports, 1981-2012, Inverness.

Assessments of the 1981 Scottish Gaelic Miscellaneous Provisions Bill, 1981 – ACG Directorate, Inverness.

Anglo-Irish Accord (Nov. 1985):- Co-signed at Hillsborough Castle, Co. Down, between governments of the UK and Irish Republic (HMSO, Belfast/London).

Bord na Gaidhlig (Glasgow/Inverness): Annual reports 2008-2012 & 2019/2020.

Bord na Gaidhlig (Glasgow/Inverness):- Figures & Data on the extent, numbers and locations of Gaelic Medium schooling across Scotland – kindly supplied by Mrs Joanne McHale, Education Research Officer, BNG, May 2020.

Bord na Gaidhlig (Glasgow/Inverness):- 'The National Gaelic Language Plan, 2012-2017: Growth and Improvement'; 2012.

Belfast Agreement (April, 1998):- Co-Signed at Belfast between the principal political parties of Northern Ireland, and endorsed by the governments of UK and Irish Republic (HMSO Belfast/London).

Comhairle na Gaelscolaiochta (Belfast):- Irish Gaelic Medium Education, Data and Figures for Gaelic schools and Streams across Northern Ireland; kindly supplied by Acting Chief Executive, Mrs Maria Thomasson, and Senior Researcher, Mr Tarlach Mac Giolla Bhride – April/May 2021.

Cumann Luthchleas Gael/Gaelic Athletic Association, Official Guide (2002, Updated version) – Croke Park, Dublin. Also, reports for Annual Congress, 1971-205, plus Down and Antrim County GAA conventions, 1971-2004.

Comhairle nan Eilean Siar (Stornoway, Isle of Lewis), Bilingual Policy Document (1978) and Update (1986).

Comunn na Gaidhlig:- 'Campaign for Secure Status for Gaelic', Inverness, 1997; *'Framework for Growth: A National Policy for Gaelic Education'* (1997).

Camilla Kidner *'Spice Briefing'*, Education (Scotland) Bill, 2015, Edinburgh.

Election Manifestos 1983-2019:- Scottish National Party, Scottish Conservative & Unionist Party, Scottish Labour Party, Scottish Liberals & Liberal Democrats, Scottish Social Democratic Party (1983-1997), Scottish Green Party. - Northern Ireland Social Democratic & Labour Party, Sinn Fein, Ulster Unionist Party, Ulster Democratic Unionist Party, Northern Ireland Alliance Party. - Fianna Fail, Fine Gael, Irish Labour Party, Irish Progressive Democrats. -British Labour Party, British Conservative Party and British Liberal Democrats, Green Party.

Foras na Gaeilge (Belfast/Dublin) Website 2018 – 2021.

Foras na Gaeilge (Belfast/Dublin): Briefing paper on proposed new budgetary planning, 17th January, 2014.

Neil Fraser *'A Review of Aspects of Gaelic Broadcasting'* - Report to Scottish Office, London/Edinburgh, 1998.

Gaelic Language Act – passed by devolved Scottish Parliament, 2005: (HMSO, 2006, Edinburgh/London).

John M.K. Galloway *'Estimation of Numbers and Distribution of Adult Learners of Gaelic in Scotland – Final Report'*; <u>Comunn na Gaidhlig</u>, Inverness, 1995.

<u>Highlands Council (Inverness)</u>:- Report of Gaelic Education Group, headed by Dr Donald John Macleod (1997).

Dan Hull *'A Summary of Proposed Funding Changes for the Irish Language Voluntary Sector: Recent Developments'*; pp 2-4; <u>Northern Ireland Assembly</u>, Research and Library Service Briefing Paper, 67/11, 2nd June, 2011.

Richard Johnstone et al *'The Attainments of Pupils receiving Gaelic Medium Primary Education in Scotland'*; 1999, University of Sterling, Scottish CILT.

Cathail O'Donnaighle – Data & reports on Gaeilge Medium education in nursery and primary schools across Northern Ireland, 1991-97, Belfast.

Fiona O'Hanlon, Wilson McLeod & Lindsay Paterson (Report) *'Gaelic Medium Education in Scotland: Choice and Attainment at primary and early secondary stages'*; 2010, Bord na Gaidhlig, Inverness.

Micheal O'Mainnin *'Ag Cor Cuarta: Leabhar Dheann Leasa Moir, Clann Diarmada agus Fili Albanacha'*; in <u>Lochtar Chonnact, Leann 5</u> (2018), pp 105 – 33 (Scottish poets in North Connacht).

'Saig in Machal Fathuaid' on the application and extent of *'The Machra'* in North West Armagh. – <u>Eriu – Journal of the School of Irish Learning</u>, Dublin, 60: pp 111-129.

'The same in origin and in blood'; Bardic windows on the relationship between Irish and Scottish Gaels in the period c. 1200-1650, <u>Cambrian Medieval Celtic Studies</u>, 38 (Winter 1999), pp 1-51.

<u>Edinburgh Festival Reports</u>, 1997-2018.

<u>UK Population</u> – Census Results for GB, inclusive of Scotland & Northern Ireland – 1901, 1911, 1921, 1931, 1951, 1961, 1971, 1981, 1991, 2001, 2011 (HMSO, London, Edinburgh & Belfast).

<u>ULTACH Trust</u> (Belfast) Reports 1996-2012.

M.B. O'Mainnin & J. Carruthers *'Empowering Multilingualism? Provisions for Place-names in Northern Ireland and the Political and Legislative Context'*; in

Robert Blackwood & Deirdre Dunlevy:- <u>Multilingualism in Public Places</u> (Bloomsbury Academic Press, 2021, London).

Newspapers and Journals consulted for general and specific reports:-
(i) <u>Scotland</u>:-*'Glasgow Herald', 'Scotsman', 'West Highland Free Press', 'Aberdeen Press and Journal', 'Daily Record', 'Stornoway Gazette' and 'Scotland on Sunday'. 'Radical Scotland', Student magazines of Universities of Edinburgh, Glasgow and Aberdeen, and successive journals from An Comunn Gaidhealach, Comunn na Gaidhlig and independent off-spring groups.*

(ii) <u>Ireland</u>:- *'Irish News'(Belfast), 'Belfast Newsletter', 'Belfast Telegraph', 'Northern Whig'(Belfast), 'Mourne Observer' (Co Down), 'Down Recorder' (Downpatrick), 'Newry Reporter', 'Andersonstown News' (Belfast), 'La' (Belfast), 'Irish Times' (Dublin), 'Irish Independent' (do) and former 'Irish Press' (do). Also, journals of QUB Students Union, 'Fortnight', Conrad na Gaeilge, Gael Linn, 'Foinse' (Galway) and specialist GAA publications across Ulster & Ireland.*

(iii) <u>UK</u>:- *'Times', 'Guardian', 'Daily Telegraph', 'Independent', 'New Statesman', 'Spectator', 'Municipal Journal' and 'Tablet'.*

5. <u>Interviews/Personal Discussions/Correspondence with Author</u>

I am sincerely grateful to the following persons from Scotland and Northern Ireland who over a thirty-year period so kindly gave of their time, specialist knowledge and empirical experiences to share in such ways as enhanced this study. Sadly, many of the individuals named are no longer alive, but their contributions ensure that with this author they are held in fondest memory.

<u>Mr Trevor Abbot; Academic Registrar - St Mary's University College, Belfast</u>:- Correspondence with author, 29th November, 2021.

<u>Mr Michael Bartlett; Teacher, Isle of Lewis</u>:- Multiple discussions held throughout August 1992 at his residence, Barabhas, Isle of Lewis.

<u>Mrs Catriona de Beine; Head of Gaelic Medium Stream, St Catherine's College, Armagh</u>:- 11th November, 2021, Armagh.

Bibliography

Mr Arthur Cormack; Native speaker from Isle of Skye, Gaelic singer, Feisean organiser and past Chair of Bord na Gaidhlig:- Multiple discussions in London, Lewis, Inverness and by telephone and Skype, 1993-2022. Friend of author.

Mr Noel Eadie; Lewis native speaker, Gaelic musician and choral organiser:- Discussions 14th August, 1991, Stornoway.

Mr Roddy Hegarty; Director of Cardinal Tomas O'Fiaich Memorial Library and Archive, Armagh; Multiple discussions and correspondence, 2016-2022.

Dr Donal McAnallen; Historian and Writer:- Multiple conversations and correspondence throughout October – December, 2019 and Summer of 2020, Belfast & Dungannon.

Mr Paul McAvinchey; Retired Head of Irish and English Studies, St Patrick's College, Armagh:- Numerous telephone conversations, personal meetings, correspondence and emails from 2016 until 2022, Armagh.

Dr Aonghus MacConneach; Gaelic Academic and Historian, University of Glasgow:- Discussions and correspondence, August 2018, Glasgow.

Mr Jake MacSiacais; Head of Forbairt Feirste and political activist, Belfast:- 5th August & 10th August, 2020, Belfast.

Mrs Colma McKee: - 23rd November, 2021, Gaelchursai/ Forbairt Feirste, Belfast.- No relation of author!

Mr Murdo Macdonald; Teacher/Gaelic linguist/ Lewis native (deceased):- Multiple discussions with this gentleman, a longstanding dear friend, at his Aberdeen home 1992 – until his passing in October 2014.

Dr Calum Macdonald:- Former MP for Western Isles, 1987-2005, and Junior Minister, Scottish Office.- Interview, 7th August 1992, Stornoway.

Mr Michael MacGiolla Ghunna; Gaeilgeoir Headmaster Colaiste Feirste, and Gaelic researcher:- 12th November, 2021, Belfast.

Rev. Donald Michael Macinnes; Native Gaelic speaker from Isle of Lewis, community activist, and now Church of Scotland/Presbyterian minister, Glasgow. Discussions 8th 14th & 20th May, 1992, Stornoway.

Mr Donald John Maciver; Gaelic educationalist, administrator and poet/writer (deceased):- 15th August, 1991, Stornoway; 20th August, 1992, Stornoway;

18th August, 1993, Stornoway; 8th April, 1994; 30th June, 1997 & 24th August, 1997 (all Stornoway); 15th October and 16th October 1997 (both Inverness). – Mixture of telephone and personal meetings.- Personal friend of author!

Mr Donald (deceased) & Mrs Seonaig Maciver; native Gaelic speakers:- Discussions at their home, Callinish, Isle of Lewis, throughout August 1993.

Mr Simon Mackenzie; Gaelic actor, singer and cultural activist, native of Isle of Harris (deceased):- Discussions 8th August 1991 and 16th August 1992, Stornoway, Isle of Lewis.

Professor Kenneth MacKinnon (deceased);– Each time by telephone from his home at Ross-shire, Scotland – 20/28th July, 2009; 15th August 2015; 20th November 2016; 18th October 2017; 20th January, 16th February, 20th / 29th March, 18th May, 23rd July 5th August 16th & 18th September, 20th October, 21/22nd November, 18th December 2018; 11th March & 3rd May, 2019; 8th August, 2019; 30th September, 2019; 20th December, 2019; 5th March, 2020; 18th August, 2020; 30th August, 2020; 19th November 2020; 4th & 10th February and 18th April 2021. –See Obituary, Appendix 2.

Mr Iain-Harry Maclennan; Gaelic native speaker (deceased):- Discussions held 16th 17th and 20th August, 1993 at his residence, Callinish, Isle of Lewis.

Mrs Peggy Maclennan; native Gaelic speaker, local community choir organiser/ singer (deceased):- Discussions at Back, Isle of Lewis, 18th August, 1993.

Mr Hugh Dan MacLennan; Gaelic speaker, lead figure in Scottish Camanachd (Shinty) Association and Shinty broadcaster/writer:- Discussions by telephone and correspondence, August-November 2019, Inverness.

Mr Calum Macleod; (Lewis migrant, deceased):- Discussions held 12th April 1993 and 27th February, 1994, at events staged by Gaelic Society of London in the Capital.

Mrs Dolina Macleod; Gaelic Language Bilingual Development Officer:- Several discussions held at her Lewis home, 1991 & '93, and offices of Comhairle nan Eilean Siar, Stornoway, Isle of Lewis.

Mr Finlay Macleod; Gaelic medium educational activist:- Discussions on 19th August, 1993, Stornoway, and 14th October, 1997, Inverness.

Mr Aodan Mac Seafraidh; Tutor, researcher and Gaeilgeoir activist:-
Discussions by telephone, 19th October, 2021, Belfast.

Mrs Annie MacSween; Gaelic local historian and bilingual educationalist:-
Each time, from her Barabhas, Isle of Lewis, home by telephone, and
subsequently by email and personal correspondence: - 18th November, 2018;
20th January, 19th March, 3rd May, 6th July & 21st September 2019; 14th March,
12th April; 10th June, 18th August, 9th November & 21st December, 2020; 24th
February, 20th May & 18th July 2021. – Friend of author!

Very Rev. Monsignor/Dr Ambrose Macaulay (sadly deceased): Respected
Church historian, Catholic priest and scholarly writer. Various meetings and
discussions in Belfast, 2018 & 2019. Friend of author.

Mrs Mary McAleenan; Gaelic community activist in Down Gaelic Athletic
Association, former Hon. Secretary – Liatroim GAA Club (oldest in Down), and
widely-respected matriarch of acclaimed Gaeilgeoir McAleenan family,
Liatroim, Co Down. Multiple discussions, personal/telephone, 1997-2022.

Mr Brian McAvoy; General Secretary & Chief Executive, Ulster Council, Gaelic
Athletic Association:- Various dinners, meetings, telephone discussions at
Newry, Armagh and throughout N. Ireland, 2018-2022.

Mr Nelson McCausland; Ulster Protestant/Democratic Unionist Assembly
Member for North Belfast, and former Minister in Northern Ireland Executive:-
Generally, a reliable 'bell-weather' of Ulster Unionist opinion! Various
extended telephone discussions throughout 2018 & 2019, Belfast.

Dr Gordon McCoy, Gaeilgeoir Author, Researcher and Tutor:- 15th July & 2nd
November, 2021, plus several times throughout Jan. & February, 2022. Belfast.

Professor Wilson McLeod; Gaelic academic, author and historian, University
of Edinburgh:- Correspondence - August 2018 and 2020/21, Edinburgh.

Very Rev. Monsignor Raymond Murray; Catholic priest, Gaeilgeoir, journal
editor and justice campaigner. Discussions Aug. 2017- Sep. 2018, Armagh.

Murray family, Back, Isle of Lewis - namely Mrs Catherine Rose, her late
husband, Mr Donald Murray, and late mother, Mrs Joanne Searle, along with
daughters, Seonaig and Catriona:- at their residence, August 1993, and at
various Gaelic events across Lewis & Inverness, 1991-97.

Mr Tarlac O'Branagain; Gaeilgeoir policy researcher, Forbairt Feirste:- 23rd & 24th November, 2021, Belfast.

Mr Diarmuid O'Bruadair; Gaelic educationalist and Headmaster, Meanscoil Doire:- Discussions, 11th November 2021, Dungiven, Co Derry.

Mr Gearoid O'Caireallain; Life-long Gaeilgeoir writer, journalist and dramatist; founder and long-stay editor of 'La', Irish language newspaper published from Belfast Gaeltacht Quarter:- Multiple meetings, discussions, telephone calls and sharing of correspondence and information, 1994-2021, Belfast.

Professor Micheal O'Mainnin; Head of Celtic Studies, QUB, and leading Gaeilgeoir academic: - Correspondence 24th November, 2021; Interviews 12th October, 2019 and 27th January, 2020; QUB, Belfast.

Mr Gearoid O'Machail; Gaeilgeoir campaigner, writer and organiser of Gaelic Cultural Centre, Armagh:- 11th November, 2021, Armagh.

Mr Roy Pedersen; Biographer, Writer and Scottish Nationalist politician on Highlands Council:- Discussions over May & July 2020, Inverness.

Mrs Ciara Pickering; Head of Gaelic Medium Stream, St Malachy's High School, Castlewellan:- 9th November, 2021, Castlewellan, Co. Down.

Mr Maolcholaim Scott; Gaeilgeoir writer & former Gaelic Language Officer, Newry & Mourne Council:- Interviews/discussions 1991-1997 and July 2021, Newry and Belfast.

Mrs Chrissie Stewart; - Native Gaelic speaker, widow of late elected Member for Western Isles, 1970-87, Right Hon. Donald Stewart MP, but herself now sadly deceased:- Discussion at her late residence, Stornoway, 19/08/1993.

Rev. Hugh Stewart; Native Hebridean Gaelic speaker, former finance officer with Comhairle nan Eilean Siar, now Church of Scotland/Presbyterian minister, Uig, Isle of Lewis. Discussions 18th August, 1993, Stornoway.

SELECT INDEX

BIOGRAPHY

Dr Vincent McKee is an accomplished contemporary historian with established interests in British, Irish, Scottish and Philippines political and church affairs. He has researched, broadcast and published scholarly papers on all four areas in journals like 'Parliamentary Affairs', 'Contemporary Record', 'Social Studies Review' and many others, plus newspapers like the 'Guardian' and 'London Independent', and journals like the 'Catholic Herald', 'Tablet' and 'Church Times' (Anglican) etc. Additionally, in recent years, Dr McKee, a committed ecumenical Catholic/Christian, has developed serious interests in Church history and current affairs, and has begun to write relevant papers and articles, with a long term project in mind. His Doctorate (Ph.D.) was awarded in 1996 by London Guildhall/Metropolitan University for an academic treatise on British Social Democracy, and from which several published papers followed. From 1996 until 2009, Dr McKee was Visiting Professor of Comparative Politics at the Graduate School, Catholic University of Santo Tomas, Manila. Author of a short book in 1997, Gaelic Nations, in fact Gaelic Neighbours marks a major re-write, development, revision and substantial upgrade of that same broad theme, and was done at the suggestion of his late Scottish mentor and friend, Professor Ken MacKinnon. This work took five years in the writing, and was boosted by the author's lifelong associations with Gaelic games in his native Co Down (N.I.), where he played Hurling for the county minor team, and the Gaelic League both in Ireland and Scotland. In 2017, his acclaimed history of factions and divisions in the post-1945 British Conservative Party, 'Forty Shades of Blue'

was published and launched at Westminster Cathedral, London, by the prize-winning British historian and peer, Lord/Professor Peter Hennessy. Dr McKee is currently working on a biography of the late Irish Primate, Cardinal Tomas O'Fiaich, while tentatively planning a history of Catholicism in British political life since 1900.

Away from writing, Dr McKee is a native of Castlewellan, Co Down, domiciled for 45 years in Coventry; still an ardent follower of Down's Senior Hurling team, and long-standing supporter of Hibernian F.C., Edinburgh. He is happily married to his beautiful Filipina wife, Mary-Jane; has one adult daughter, Patricia (32), one son, 'Little John' (aged 13), four grandchildren, namely Vicente (12), Mary-Colette (6) and two infant twins, Lorenzo and Pedro – all Filipinos, and each one the apple of his eye!

ALSO BY THIS AUTHOR:

1. Gaelic Nations (Bluestack Press, 1997) – Available on Amazon.

2. Forty Shades of Blue: Factionalism and Divisions in the Post-War British Conservative Party from Churchill to Cameron (Takahe, 2017). – Available from Amazon and all good bookstores.